D0278033

An Introduction to Industrial Relations

Industrial relations are as old as industry, yet the emphasis within the subject is constantly shifting to keep pace with changing realities in the workplace. Michael Jackson's well-known student text, *Industrial Relations*, has now been rewritten and thoroughly updated to give a comprehensive overview of industrial relations today.

Beginning with an analysis of various theoretical approaches to industrial relations, the author summarizes the origins and development of the subject. His new text looks at the impact of recent legislative changes, technological developments and the growing currency of 'human resource management' theories.

The book offers a comparative approach, making extensive use of material from outside the UK, notably from America, Europe and the Pacific Rim, and examines the implications of recent EEC legislation for industrial relations in the 1990s.

An Introduction to Industrial Relations will be of special value to students on industrial relations courses and to those studying industrial relations as part of a more general social science course. Above all, its careful analysis of developments in the 1980s will enable students to understand the climate of industrial relations in the future.

Michael P. Jackson is Head of the School of Management at the University of Stirling, and Professor of Industrial Relations. He has written extensively on industrial relations and his previous books include *Trade Unions*, *Youth Employment*, and *Policy Making in Trade Unions*.

An Introduction to Industrial Relations

Michael P. Jackson

London and New York

First published 1991 by Routledge
11 New Fetter Lane, London EC4P 4EE

Simultaneously published in the USA and Canada
by Routledge
a division of Routledge, Chapman and Hall, Inc.
29 West 35th Street, New York, NY 10001

© 1991 Michael P. Jackson

Typeset by Selectmove Ltd, London
Printed and bound in Great Britain by
Mackays of Chatham PLC, Chatham, Kent

British Library Cataloguing in Publication Data
Jackson, Michael P. (Michael Peart) 1947–
  An Introduction to Industrial Relations
  1 Great Britain. Industrial relations
  I Title II Jackson, Michael P. (Michael Peart) 1947–
  Industrial relations
  331.0941

ISBN 0–415–05686–1

Library of Congress Cataloging-in-Publication Data
Jackson, Michael P., 1947–
  An Introduction to Industrial Relations/Michael P. Jackson
  p. cm.
  Includes bibliographical references and index
  ISBN 0–415–05686–1
  1 Industrial relations.   I Title.
  HD6971.J25 1991
  331--dc20   90–25308
                                                        CIP

Contents

Tables

Preface

My textbook *Industrial Relations* was written in the mid-1970s and first published in 1977. Subsequently two further editions were published. Developments in industrial relations have been so substantial since the mid-1970s that it is clear that a fourth edition is no longer appropriate. This text has similar aims to the book first published in 1977, but it is substantially different. The differences are not simply in terms of the detail of, say, trade union membership or legislation on industrial relations: the differences also reflect changes that have taken place to the balance of interest within the subject and apply to the structure of the book.

I have learnt a great deal from staff and students at the University of Stirling where I have taught industrial relations for the past twenty years. I am grateful to John Leopold who read and commented on parts of the text. I have been fortunate to be assisted by secretarial staff who typed and re-typed the manuscript with good humour, and I am particularly grateful to Jennifer Cooper and Moira Taylor.

Abbreviations

ACAS	Advisory, Conciliation, and Arbitration Service
ADST	Approved Deferred Shares Trust
AEU	Amalgamated Engineering Union
AFL	American Federation of Labor
AFL–CIO	American Federation of Labor – Congress of Industrial Organization
APEX	Association of Professional, Executive, Clerical, and Computer Staff
ASLEF	Associated Society of Locomotive Engineers and Firemen
AUEW	Amalgamated Union of Engineering Workers
CBI	Confederation of British Industry
CIO	Congress of Industrial Organisation
CNPF	Conseil National de Patronat Français
DAF	Danish Trade Union Confederation
DEC	Danish Employers' Confederation
DGB	Deutscher Gewerkschafts Bund
EEC	European Economic Community
EETPU	Electrical, Electronic, Telecommunications, and Plumbing Trade Union
ESOP	Employee Share Ownership Plan
GCHQ	Government Communications Headquarters
GMBTU	General Municipal and Boilermakers Trade Union
HRM	Human Resources Management
ITU	International Typographical Union
LO	Landsorganisationen Sverige (Swedish Trade Union Confederation)
MNE	Multinational Enterprise
MSF	Manufacturing, Science, Finance

NATSOPA	National Society of Operative Printers, Graphical and Media Personnel
NICE	Nationally Integrated Caring Employees
NLRB	National Labor Relations Board
NTUC	National Trades Union Congress (Singapore)
NUPE	National Union of Public Employees
OECD	Organisation for Economic Co-operation and Development
SACO SR	Confederation of professional unions representing employees with academic training
SAF	Swedish Employers' Confederation
SOGAT	Society of Graphical and Allied Trades
TASS	Technical Administrative and Supervisory Section
TCO	Central Organisation of Salaried Employees
TGWU	Transport and General Workers' Union
TUC	Trades Union Congress

1 Industrial relations as a field of study

'Industrial relations are as old as industry, and, being inherent in industry, will always remain as a feature of industrial life.'[1] However, industrial relations as a field of study, as distinct from an area of activity, has a much shorter history both in Britain and most other countries. In Britain, although many earlier writers[2] commented on aspects of industrial relations, it was the Webbs who made the first major and comprehensive contribution to the subject, and that was not until the end of the nineteenth century. They published two books of particular importance, *A History of Trade Unionism*[3] and *Industrial Democracy*.[4] The former examined the development of trade unionism in Britain (Allen says, 'There was in a sense, no trade union history until they [the Webbs] wrote it'[5]), while the latter, in many ways a more significant work (Bain and Clegg refer to it as industrial relations' 'major and perhaps only classic'[6]), looked at the functions of trade unions. In most other countries, also, many economists and political scientists only commented on aspects of industrial relations as this subject was not their main concern. In many cases specialist interest in the subject began later than in Britain.

EARLY DEVELOPMENT OF AN ACADEMIC SUBJECT

Much of the early writing on industrial relations tended to place considerable emphasis on an 'institutional' and 'factual' approach. Authors concentrated their efforts on describing the situation as they saw it; in the main they produced 'guide books' to current practice rather than theories and explanations. This was true, for example, of the studies of union structure that appeared in the 1950s. They described the structures of unions, the election of officials, the collections of dues; questions were asked, but as Bain and Clegg ·

comment,[7] they were questions like, 'Why do some unions elect their officers and others appoint?' rather than those which might have led to the formulation of general theories. The main aim of such works was to describe and classify what was available or what came to light with a little searching or digging.

The institutional approach was best exemplified in Britain by the work of the 'Oxford Group'. This is the name that was given to a number of academics who at one time or another were linked to research or teaching of industrial relations at Oxford University. The group had its origins in the appointments of Flanders to a senior lecturership and Clegg to a fellowship at Oxford in 1949. It later expanded to include people like Fox, Marsh, Hughes and McCarthy.

The group had a tremendous impact on British industrial relations. They dominated the Donovan Commission[8] – Clegg was a member of the Commission and McCarthy its research director – and provided members for a host of other investigations and government advisory bodies, and produced a vast amount of published material.

Turner described the work of the group in the following way:

> The 'Oxford Line' might be described as combining an industrious extension of established avenues of inquiry and particularly a meticulous pursuit of institutional detail, a preference for the short-term rule of thumb over the broader generalisation, a rather low awareness of those disciplines – in ascending order, of sociology, statistics and economics – which may illuminate the field with normative observations, and a variety of propagandist mini-reformism which insists partly in leading people boldly in the direction they appear to be going anyway.[9]

Another commentator described the Oxford Group as 'fact grub-bers'.[10] Such descriptions are a little unfair, for a number of members of the Oxford Group made important contributions to industrial relations theory. For example, Clegg produced work on industrial democracy of major importance[11] and Flanders was one of the main exponents of the application of systems theory to British industrial relations.[12] Further, the Industrial Relations Research Unit at Warwick University, originally centred on a number of members of the Oxford Group, from its earliest days campaigned for greater weight to be given to theory in the study of industrial relations.[13] Nevertheless, the group as a whole gave the impression that it placed considerable emphasis on an institutional approach if only because of the weight of its work in that area.

However, the institutional approach was by no means characteristic only of British industrial relations. It also dominated, for example, the US scene. Dunlop argued that 'far too much of the writing concerned with industrial relations, particularly in the United States, which has the largest output measured in bulk, has lacked intellectual rigour and discipline'.[14] Industrial relations research, he said, essentially was concerned with 'fact gathering'.

Fatchett and Whittingham[15] pointed to a number of reasons why there was such an emphasis in industrial relations writing. One of the most important reasons, they suggested, was 'the involvement of industrial relations academics as consultants or government advisers': this meant that they had 'an interest in making existing institutions work'[16] and in examining their detailed operation. Others centred their explanation on a different line of reasoning; writers like Slichter, Healy and Livernash[17] argued that it would be impossible to formulate valuable theories of industrial relations. This clearly leads into a more general debate about explanations of human behaviour and the nature of the social sciences.

DEVELOPMENT OF THEORY

Systems approach

In recent years, though, the dominance of the institutional approach to industrial relations has been challenged. The first, and probably the most influential, major challenge has been linked to the work of Dunlop.[18] Dunlop, an economist, modified the work of sociologists, in particular that of Parsons and Smelser[19] to enable him to discuss the industrial relations system. His major work, *Industrial Relations Systems*, was first published in 1958 and since then has been taken as a basis for analysis by other authors and commentators.

The importance of Dunlop's work is such that it is worth spending a little time looking at his theory. Essentially Dunlop's theoretical framework viewed the industrial relations system as a subsystem of the wider society or the 'total social system'. Thus, the wider society was seen as providing certain external influences and constraints but not as completely dominating industrial relations. Therefore, the industrial relations system had a similar status to, for example, the economic and political systems, with which it can overlap.

An industrial relations system, according to Dunlop, 'at any one time in its development is regarded as comprised of certain actors, certain contexts, an ideology which binds the industrial relations system together, and a body of rules created to govern the actors at the place of work and work community'.[20] The creation of rules was seen to be the central aim of the industrial relations system, and Dunlop isolated three main groups of 'actors' who took part in the rule making process:

1 a hierarchy of managers and their representatives in supervision;
2 a hierarchy of workers (non-managerial) and their spokesmen;
3 specialised government agencies (and specialised private agencies created by the first two actors) concerned with workers, enterprises and their relationships.

However, the actors were not completely free agents; they were confronted by the environment and were influenced and limited by it. The important features of the environment, though, 'are determined by the larger society and its other subsystems and are not explained within an industrial relations system'.[21]

The significant aspects of the environment were:

1 the technological characteristics of the workplace and work community;
2 the market or budgetary constraints which impinge on the actors;
3 the *locus* and distribution of power in the larger society.

These aspects of the environment could influence the industrial relations system in a variety of ways. For example, the technology could influence the form of management and employee organisation and the problems it could pose for supervision; market and budgetary constraints could influence the ease with which products could be sold (and as a result wage increases) and the availability of labour; and the distribution of power within the industrial relations system would be greatly affected by and responsive to the *locus* and distribution of power in the wider society.

The industrial relations system according to Dunlop was held together by an ideology or a common set of ideas and beliefs. The ideology defined 'the role and place of each actor' in the system 'and that defines the ideas which each actor holds towards the place and function of others in the system'.[22] It was recognised that each of the actors in the industrial relations system may have their own ideology. However, an 'industrial relations system requires that these ideologies may be sufficiently compatible and consistent so as to permit a common set of ideas which recognise an acceptable role for each actor'.[23]

The rules that govern behaviour in the workplace and work community could be expressed in a variety of forms. For example, they could be the regulations produced by the management hierarchy, the rules laid down by any worker hierarchy, the orders of governmental agencies, collective agreements and the customs and traditions of the work community.

The industrial relations systems approach, as developed by Dunlop, found many supporters. In Britain, it greatly influenced the work of Flanders.[24] He used the notion of an industrial relations system to argue that the core of the subject involved the study of certain regulated or institutional relationships in industry.[25] It is clear, he said, that 'not all the relationships associated with the organisation of industry are relevant'; only those associated with the employment function need to be considered and not, for example, trade relationships between one enterprise and another or an enterprise and its customers. This led Flanders to define industrial relations as 'a study of the institutions of job regulation'.[26]

However, a number of people argued that although there was considerable merit in Dunlop's work it was deficient in certain respects and modifications were essential.

For example, Bain and Clegg argued that there were two central defects in the systems approach, as used by Dunlop and Flanders. First, there were certain ambiguities in the way the concept of a 'system' was used. Dunlop's work, in particular, was closely linked to the Parsonian analysis of social systems

and his argument that it is 'an ideology or a set of ideas and beliefs commonly held by the actors that helps to bind or integrate the system together as an entity' might be taken to imply that an industrial relations system was 'naturally' stable and integrative and 'necessarily' strove to perpetuate itself.[27]

Such a notion, Bain and Clegg recognised, had 'conservative implications' and was unacceptable; they sympathetically quoted Eldridge who argued that 'in sociology, the sources of conflict and cooperation, order and instability must have an equally valid claim to problem status'.[28]

Second, the systems concept does not point to all of the important explanatory variables. Dunlop's formulation of an industrial relations system largely omits such behavioural variables as human motivations, perceptions and attitudes, while Flanders argued that 'personal, or in the language of sociology "unstructured", relationships have their importance for management and workers, but they lie outside the scope of a system of industrial relations'.[29] Bain and Clegg argued that if Dunlop and Flanders were attempting a full explanation of industrial relations behaviour and its determinants, as Dunlop suggested, then behavioural variables could not be completely dismissed. The extent to which behavioural variables will be important will differ but clearly they will be important in certain circumstances. To ignore the aims and interpretations of the actors would seem to hinder significantly an understanding of the processes of job regulation.

Bain and Clegg, therefore, suggested modifications that might be made to the approach of Dunlop and Flanders. First, they suggested that if the problems connected with the conservative overtones of the approach were to be avoided, the notion of a system needed to be used as a 'heuristic device' rather than as a 'theory of social action'. Thus, an industrial relations system should 'be regarded as a model within which facts may be organised and must be misunderstood as having predictive value in itself'.[30] Second, the concept of a system needed to be broadened to include behavioural and unstructured variables. In short, 'the subject of industrial relations may be defined as all aspects of job regulation – the making and administering of the rules which regulate employment relationships – regardless of whether these are seen as being formal or informal, structured or unstructured'.[31]

These kinds of criticisms have been echoed by many other writers.[32] Nevertheless, this has not necessarily led to the abandonment of systems theory altogether. Thus, although Wood recognises the criticisms of systems theory, he argues that 'for all its inadequacies' it can be used as a 'valuable point of departure'.[33] Bain and Clegg probably came the closest to rejecting it outright, but argued that providing modifications were made, the systems approach (in which all aspects of the environment and human behaviour are to be taken into account in explaining industrial relations) could be used. A few other writers have gone further and rejected the notion of the systems approach. For example, Margerison[34] feels that the conservative implications of the approach are too fundamental and cannot be altered without major changes to the theory. However, such views are not widespread and have been roundly condemned by the majority of the writers.[35]

This kind of strategy is interesting for it raises the question of why systems theory, despite the defects noted by commentators, has remained so influential. The answer seems to be that it held out the prospect of academic respectability. It could provide industrial relations with a central body of theory, to a certain extent both with its own language and with an air of scientific precision. This has been the goal of industrial relations writers for many years, and Dunlop explicitly recognised the contribution that he believed systems theory could make to its achievement.

Social action approach

An alternative to systems theory which has had some influence in industrial relations, also comes from sociology in the form of the social action approach. The social action approach has its origins in Weberian sociology (although some of its manifestations move away from a strict adherence to the Weberian tradition). The social action approach is one in which actors' own definitions of the situation in which they are engaged are taken as an initial basis for the explanation of their social behaviour and relationships. In contrast to approaches which begin with some general and normative psychology of individual needs in work, or with some conception of the needs of an efficiently operating industrial enterprise, an action frame of reference directs 'attention systematically to the *variety of meanings* which work may come to have for industrial employees'.[36]

The social action approach can be clearly contrasted with the systems approach; while the systems approach 'tends to regard behaviour as a reflection of the characteristics of a social system containing a series of impersonal processes which are external to the actors and constrain them',[37] the action approach stresses the way in which the individual influences the social structure and 'makes society'.[38] As described the social action approach can be viewed as the opposite side of the coin to the systems approach, and it clearly deals with one of the major criticsms of the systems approach (that is, that it does not pay sufficient attention to behavioural influences).

A number of studies have claimed that they have used a social action approach in their analysis; one of the best known of such studies is that of Goldthorpe *et al.*[39] They argued that they found an instrumental orientation to employment amongst their sample of 'affluent workers' and that although their 'affluent workers' need not be typical of workers in general (in fact, because the central aim of the study was to test the embourgeoisement thesis they were chosen because they were atypical), there were trends in modern industrial life which suggested that an instrumental orientation to work was likely to be adopted by many other workers. The trends in modern industrial life to which they pointed centred on changes in family life and structure; for example, the growing importance of the conjugal family might strengthen the tendency for the workers to seek expressive and effective satisfactions through family relationships, rather than through the workplace, with the result that work increasingly may be seen as a way of providing the means to obtain satisfaction elsewhere. However, the details of their argument are relatively unimportant, for as they state, their discussion of, for example, the changes in family relationships, was intended as an outline of 'some probable consequences for working class economic life of already observable trends within British society at large' rather than as an 'unconditional prediction about the future course of events'.[40] What is more important is their method. They sought to explain the orientations to work of individuals not by reference to, say, the technology used by the industry in which they worked, but by reference to their non-work experience. The individuals themselves thus became the centre of attention, not the social structure. In this way they were able to argue that they adopted an action approach and commended it to others.

The Goldthorpe *et al.* thesis has had a major impact on British sociology and, therefore, has been the subject of careful scrutiny.[41] A number of writers have challenged their conclusions on the 'orientations to work' theme but the study has been widely accepted as pathbreaking and an early example of the social action approach in industrial sociology.

It is clear that while the social action approach has many adherents it is also open to a variety of interpretations and emphases. For example, at one extreme the emphasis placed on individual meaning can be such that the relevance of discussing elements of social structure at all is drawn into question and the approach moves very close to ethnomethodology and phenomenology. Silverman's work can be seen in this light.[42] He stressed the importance of examining 'taken for granted assumptions'. To discuss reality without doing this, he suggested, would be erroneous, for what is reality to one person may be different from what is reality to another. Such an argument clearly raises many questions, most of which are outside the scope of this discussion. However, it is clear that Silverman's work could lead one to disregard social structure as an influence on behaviour almost completely.

Others would reject this stance and argue that a social action approach cannot merely be based on an analysis of the meaning or reality for individuals but needs to make some kind of assumption about the nature of social structure as a starting point. Thus, Eldridge argues that social action 'cannot be understood in a totally free floating way',[43] but needs to be grounded on some appreciation of the likely influence of social structure on behaviour.

The challenge, then, would be to find some way of showing the reciprocal nature of the relationship between social structure and behaviour. This might be done by adopting a 'step-by-step'[44] or an 'incremental' approach. From this point of view the social structure, at any one point in time, limits social action. Thus, a worker's ability to take strike action or an entrepreneur's ability to invest in machinery may be limited by their personal and by more general economic conditions. Of course, different workers and different entrepreneurs might view the same economic conditions in different ways; but the ways in which they perceive and understand current economic conditions may themselves be strongly influenced by their previous experience which in turn may, at least in part, be a function of their own position in the social structure.

However, this only provides a starting point. The choice made by the actor, in part, will determine a new social structure. To continue with the example, when the worker makes a decision on strike action and the entrepreneur makes a decision on investment, they will be helping to determine the environment for future similar decisions. If the worker decides to take strike action, he or she may gain extra income as well as experience in industrial conflict. This will affect their ability to take strike action and their perception of possibilities in the future. They will also change, however marginally, the established pattern of strike action in general. Similarly, if the entrepreneur decides to invest, he or she may increase the product base and gain experience in a different market. This may affect the long-term financial stability and increase knowledge of investment possibilities. In turn, this will also affect the position of competitors, and to some extent, the market and the willingness of financiers to invest in certain products.

In this way the actor can be seen as creating the social structure and step-by-step may help to change it. Thus, the relationship between social structure and the actor is not one way: there is a complex interrelationship.

FRAMES OF REFERENCE

In the case of the study of industrial relations in Britain, it is arguable that sociology has had its greatest influence not through system theory or the social action approach, but through the discussion of 'frames of reference'. This discussion was initiated by Alan Fox in a research paper for the Donovan Commission.[45] In this paper, Fox did not attempt to provide an all-embracing theory, nor even to provide a particular methodolody; rather he attempted to demystify industrial relations. He argued that

> sociology as a discipline confers its greatest strength when it helps us, at least to some limited degree, to reduce our dependence on the blinkers of our own social reconditioning and thereby to escape from the self-fulfilling prophecies of what is, must be.[46]

Initially, his attempt at demystification was based on the discussion of two frames of reference. In defining what is meant by a frame of reference, he referred to the work of Thelen and Whithall.

> Each person 'perceives and interprets events by means of a conceptual structure of generalisations or contexts (which consists of) postulates about what is essential, assumptions as to what is valuable, attitudes about what is possible and ideas about what will work effectively. This conceptual structure constitutes the frame of reference of that person.'[47]

Thus, the frame of reference embodies 'the main selective influences at work as the perceiver supplements, omits and structures what he notices'.[48]

The two frames of reference outlined in his initial research papers were the unitary and the pluralistic. The unitary frame of reference, he argued, stressed the importance of a common goal for the enterprise; there is no room, given this frame of reference, for divisions within the enterprise, for all participants have the same basic aim (the efficient functioning of the enterprise) and all will share in the rewards which will accrue from the attainment of this aim. According to people accepting a unitary frame of reference, the closest analogy to the industrial enterprise is that of the team.

> What pattern of behaviour do we expect from the members of a successful and healthily functioning team? We expect them to strive jointly toward a common objective, each pulling his weight to the best of his ability. Each accepts his place and his function gladly, following the leadership of the one so appointed. There are no oppositionary groups or factions, and therefore no rival leaders within the team. Nor are there any outside it; the team stands alone, its members giving allegiance to their own leaders but to no others.[49]

Those who subscribe to the unitary ideology will, therefore, tend to define transgressors as aberrants. The manager who firmly believes in the unitary ideology will find it difficult because of his or her conviction of the rightness of management rule, not only to acknowledge the legitimacy of challenges to it, but also to grasp 'that such challenges may at least be grounded in legitimacy for those who mount them'.[50] To them the transgressors must know in their own hearts that they are doing wrong and hurting others needlessly. Explanations for their actions will stress the failure of those concerned to understand the true position because of poor communications and the work of agitators.

The unitary ideology has a great deal of support in industry and in governments. Many managers accept the unitary ideology: it is, as Fox points out, a useful instrument of persuasion and can serve to confer legitimacy on their actions. Poole *et al.*, in reporting a national survey, suggest that

> the bulk of British managers maintain a preference for a 'unitary' system of decision making control within the enterprise. This was apparent in a pronounced hostility to the power of trade unions, antipathy to forms of participation that circumscribed managerial powers within the organisation and a limited amount of personal commitment to collective representation.[51]

The unitary ideology is also implicit in many government statements which discuss issues in terms of 'the national interest'. Many government inquiries and reports have shown an acceptance of the unitary ideology in aspects of their work: for example, the Devlin report on labour relations in the port transport industry argued that one of the causes of industrial conflict was the work of unofficial shop stewards' committees. It recognised that many of the unofficial leaders were genuine in their desire to improve conditions on the docks and operated with the best of intentions. However, it argued that others 'find industrial agitation a satisfactory way of life . . . whose concern it is to make sure that there is always something to agitate about'.[52]

Fox argued that the unitary ideology played an important part in the provisions of the 1971 Industrial Relations Act. One of the central aims of the Act was to reduce the incidence of what was termed 'disruptive' and 'disorderly' behaviour by the use of external legal controls. Similar, comments can be made about the legislation introduced by the Conservative governments in the 1980s.

The unitary ideology also has considerable support in the academic sphere. A great deal of the work of the human relations school[53] falls into this category. The human relations school emphasises the importance of social relations in industry. It argues that a great deal

of conflict is the result of poor social (or human) relations. In order
to avoid or overcome conflict they suggest methods of improving
human relations: for example, better communications.[54] However,
they largely ignore differences in interest as a source of conflict; a
common interest is merely assumed.

The pluralistic frame of reference, on the other hand, adopts a
different approach Fox argues. The pluralistic ideology accepts that
an enterprise contains people with a variety of different interests,
aims and aspirations; it is, therefore, a coalition of different interests
rather than the embodiment of one common goal. Ross, for example,
argues that we should view an organisation as a 'plural society,
containing many related but separate interests and objectives which
must be maintained in some kind of equilibrium'.[55] This clearly has
implications for the government of an industrial enterprise.

> The problem of government of a plural society is not to unify,
> integrate or liquidate sectional groups and their special interests
> in the name of some overriding corporate existence, but to control
> and balance the activities of constituent groups so as to provide
> for the maximum degree of freedom of association and action for
> sectional and group purposes consistent with the general interest
> of the society as conceived with the support of public opinion, by
> those responsible for government.[56]

Given such views, conflict is not abnormal, but is to be expected.
Management and governments should not expect blind obedience,
nor try to suppress any ideas or aims which conflict with their own;
their aim, rather, should be to try to reconcile conflicting opinions and
keep the conflict within accepted bounds so that it does not destroy the
enterprise altogether.

The pluralist ideology, like the unitary ideology, has a large number
of adherents; it, too, has found considerable support in the academic
sphere. It has links with the works of Schumpeter, Durkheim,
Kornhauser, and Kerr, and its use in industrial relations recently has
been defended by Clegg.[57] Its influence can also be seen in a number
of Government reports; the most striking example is that of the report
of the Donovan Commission. In one of its early passages the Donovan
Commission described the nature of the business enterprise:

> The running of large businesses is in the hands of professional
> managers . . . while in the long term shareholders, employers and
> customers all stand to benefit if a concern flourishes, the immediate
> interests of these groups often conflict. Directors and managers

have to balance these conflicting interests, and in practice they generally seek to strike whatever balance will best promote the welfare of the enterprise as such.[58]

The pluralist ideology also has found support in certain management circles. For example, Kelly, in an article entitled 'Make Conflict Work For You', argued that the old human relations theories which assumed that conflict was harmful, should be avoided because they did not square with the facts. He said that if it was handled properly, conflict 'can lead to more effective and appropriate arrangements . . . The way conflict is managed – rather than suppressed, ignored or avoided – contributes significantly to a company's effectiveness'.[59]

However, the pluralist ideology itself has been attacked consistently, not only from the unitary, but also from a more radical perspective. One of the major sources of criticism has been that the pluralist ideology, while it recognises the inevitability of conflict, also implies a degree of equality between the conflicting parties. Many have argued that such an equality does not exist. Eldridge, for example, quotes the following passage from Miliband:

> What is wrong with pluralist-democratic theory is not its insistence on the factor of competition but its claim (very often its implicit assumption) that the major organised 'interests' in these societies, and notably capital and labour, compete on more or less equal terms, and that none of them is therefore able to achieve a decisive and permanent advantage in the process of competition. This is where ideology enters and turns observation into myth.[60]

Eldridge argues that pluralism must accept that there are important inequalities in society and that what might be defined as 'disorderly and undesirable industrial conflict from one pluralistic perspective might from another pluralist perspective be regarded as promoting a new and more desirable form of integration'.[61] Similar criticisms of the pluralist perspective can be seen in the work of a number of other writers including Gouldner[62], Rex[63] and Wright Mills.[64]

From such a perspective pluralism can be just as important a method of mystification as the unitary ideology. The implication that there is some kind of balance of power between the different parties in the organisation, combined with the insistence on the importance of compromise, creates a climate in which it will be suggested that each side in the conflict should be allowed to express and maintain 'its own point of view'. Such a climate is an ideal mechanism for resisting fundamental change and, according to the radical criticism, for ensuring the maintenance of existing inequalities.

Such criticisms have now been accepted by Fox. In a number of pieces of work he seems to have moved away from his early adherence to the pluralist stance. In an essay published in 1973, he concluded that 'pluralism may operate as an ignoble myth by offering a misleading picture of the realities of social power, thereby serving those who, by the test of *cui bono?*, have an interest in the propagation of a comforting and reassuring message'.[65] In that particular essay, Fox did not dismiss pluralism completely: he argued that although it may not have intellectual validity, it might be valuable as a way of achieving a more acceptable society within the *status quo* (more civilised ways of conducting business, and a reduction in social inequalities). However, in a later publication,[66] Fox appeared to go further and challenge pluralism even on the pragmatic level. He suggested that if managers tried to operate on the basis of the pluralist ideology, they would find it very difficult to meet shop-floor leaders and workplace groups who did not accept the validity of the pluralist image, and saw their interests as being very different to those of management.

Whether Fox really moved away from pluralism and accepted a more radical perspective, though, has been the source of debate; Wood and Elliott argued that, even in the later work quoted above, Fox did not abandon pluralism: rather this work 'is best viewed as an attempt to develop and modify pluralism in response to changing conditions'.[67] They claimed that Fox's approach, based on more rank-and-file participation in management and the development of a shared purpose of social justice, implied that Fox still accepted evolutionary social change rather than a revolutionary socialist perspective.

Clegg also questioned whether Fox moved away from pluralism by arguing that the definition of pluralism used by Fox in those works was wrong. According to Clegg, pluralism does not imply (as he says Fox seemed to suggest) that there is a balance of power and that compromise will be the inevitable result of industrial conflict. There is, Clegg argued, reason to believe that normally conflict will be resolved by compromise because there are 'few associations – or governments – which do not prefer to make a further concession rather than take the chance of destroying the social order'.[68] Nevertheless, pluralism, he said, accepts the possibility that because of the strength of other moral values, a compromise need not necessarily be reached. He pointed to two examples to back up his statement – the dispute between the mine owners and mine workers in 1926 and the dispute between the government and the miners in 1974. There were, he said, many skilled and patient hands at work on both occasions but none of their products served to forestall the starvation of the miners into submission in 1926, or the electoral defeat of the Conservative government in 1974. It seems reasonable to conclude that no acceptable compromise was available.[69]

Clearly, these examples could be extended by a third from the same industry, the miners' strike of the mid-1980s which was concluded not with a compromise, but with what many saw as a defeat for the miners. Clegg suggested then, that the criticisms made by Fox of the pluralist position were misdirected, and the points he made could be accepted by the pluralist. Not everyone accepts this view: Hyman, in a review of the origins of pluralism (in which he shows the different assumptions of the American and British pluralist tradition)[70] questions Clegg's interpretation of the pluralist position.

A RADICAL CRITIQUE

Whatever the precise nature of the stance adopted by Fox, it is clear that the criticisms of the pluralist perspective that he and others outlined, could be linked to an alternative, more radical, approach. Such an approach is presented most clearly through the Marxist thesis. This emphasises the central importance of the division between those who own the means of production and those who merely have their labour to sell.

Capitalists and wage-workers stand at each side of the labour market as buyers and sellers respectively of the commodity 'labour'. Wage-workers, as the owners of this commodity, present themselves on the labour market in order to sell their labour in exchange for the financial means to sustain their existence. This labour is completely valueless to them until it is combined with the means of production. However, since these are owned by the capitalists, wage-workers can capitalise on their labour only by selling it. Capitalists, for their part, present themselves on the labour market in order to purchase the labour required for the profitable deployment of their means of production.[71]

From this point of view, then, the interests of capitalists and workers directly conflict. The advance of one set of interests must be at the expense of the other, 'An unceasing "power struggle" is therefore a central feature of industrial relations.'[72]

However, unlike some pluralists, Marxists do not assume a rough equality of power between these different interests. To the contrary, they explicitly assume an imbalance of power, with the owners of the means of production using their superior power to influence events. This is not to suggest that workers can do nothing to combat the power of the capitalist. The development of trade unions is an important advance, strengthening individual workers by reducing the competition between them. Nevertheless, although trade unions may provide some protection and some advancement, the owners of the means of production remain the strongest side; 'Marx believed, moreover, that industrial development would increase the balance; mechanisation would create a growing pool of unemployment, under-mining trade union strength.'[73]

In the long term the Marxist theory is not pessimistic, for it predicts the overthrow of the capitalist system. Nevertheless, until that happens, industrial relations are crucially affected by the conflict between capital and labour, and by the superior power of capital. This superiority does not simply affect the price to be paid for labour but also affects working arrangements and conditions

> Because capitalist enterprise is concerned only with the pursuit of profit and labour is bought and sold as a commodity, and treated impersonally as a factor of production, the economic and human interests of employees are sacrificed under the coercive power of the capitalist. It is this inherent exploitation that builds conflict into the social relations in production.[74]

As far as the academic study of industrial relations is concerned, the radical critique of pluralism gained ground in the 1970s. In part, this was a reflection of developments in the practice of industrial relations. The challenge to managerial authority on the shop-floor seemed to set a new agenda and to pose new questions. In part, also, it was a reflection of a change in emphasis within other parts of the social sciences. In sociology, the attractions of functionalism had started to wane. After a period in which Bell's *The End of Ideology*[75] and Kerr *et al.*'s[75] *Industrialism and Industrial Man*[76] had epitomised the centre of the debate, others who challenged the pluralist assumptions gained the attention. Such a challenge in itself was not new, of course, but the recognition gained by this work, and the way in which it started to set the agenda, marked a major shift.

In the case of industrial relations, more attention was starting to be paid to conflict, not just to the resolution, but also to the causes of conflict. The centre of the Marxist argument, the inevitability of conflict within a capitalist society, started to dominate. In Britain a new cohort of writers entered the arena, basing their analysis explicitly on a Marxist perspective. Hyman's textbook *Industrial Relations: A Marxist Introduction*[77] was published in 1975, but this is just one of a number of publications by this and other writers adopting such a perspective.

One of the most interesting debates during this period centred on the 'degradation of work' thesis. This will be looked at in more detail in Chapter 9, but for now it is probably sufficient to record that the argument advanced by Braverman[78] was that scientific management allied to the use of new technology had led to greater managerial control over the work process. Braverman explicitly claimed that his work was based on Marxist theory. The Braverman thesis was extensively discussed, particularly in the UK. Interest in it by students of industrial relations indicates how attention was shifting from the institutions of industrial relations to the sociology of work.

HUMAN RESOURCES MANAGEMENT

If the radical critique of pluralism was notable for having caught the imagination and set the agenda in the 1970s, Human Resources Management must be seen to have fulfilled much the same role in the 1980s. As with developments in the 1970s, there are links with changes taking place in the practice of industrial relations. The changed economic conditions, and also in many countries changed political conditions, weakened the position of labour. This was most noticeable in the USA where arguably the position of labour was already most vulnerable. Trade union membership fell and many employers took an openly anti-union stance. The de-recognition movement gained ground as employers sought to persuade workers that trade unions were irrelevant to their needs. Elsewhere in the West, similar moves have taken place. In many countries union membership has fallen and attention has been focused on a new range of issues. The issues at the centre of debate have been single union agreements, compulsory and pendulum arbitration and no-strike deals. Other moves have served to marginalise the position of unions. The debate over the 'flexible firm' relates to a range of issues, many of which lead to the role of unions being called into question. Management interest in appraisal and performance-related pay have emphasised the individual rather than the collective interests of workers.

In the USA the anti-union movement has been firmly associated with Human Resources Management and this association has led to concern about the use of the term in the UK. Fowler has suggested that Human Resources Management seeks to ensure the complete identification of employees with the aims and values of the company.[79] A great deal of emphasis is given to the desirability of developing a corporate culture and this can be seen as a way of integrating the employees into the central aims of the organisation and denying different interests. In particular the role of unions in providing a degree of balance in the exercise of economic authority is denied.

> American literature openly accepts that HRM works best in non unionised companies. At the heart of the concept is the complete identification of employees with the aims and values of the business – employee involvement but on the companies terms. Power, in an HRM system, remains very firmly in the hands of the employer. Is it really possible to claim full mutuality when at the end of the day the employer can decide unilaterally to close the company or sell it to someone else? The absence of any discussion of power in HRM literature indicates a blindness to the role of trade unions in providing a degree of balance in the exercise of economic authority.[80]

One of the difficulties in this matter is that at one level Human Resources Management need not have such an association. An emphasis on the importance of people to the success of any organisation and on the value in treating employees as a resource, could be seen in quite a different light. Armstrong has suggested that a view of Human Resources Management can be developed which is not as crude as that sometimes portrayed. He bases this view on four principles:

1 Human resources are the most important assets an organisation has, and their effective management is the key to its success.
2 This success is most likely to be achieved if the personnel policies and procedures of the enterprise are closely linked with and make a major contribution to the achievement of corporate objectives and strategic plans.
3 The corporate culture and the values, organisational climate and managerial behaviour that emanate from that culture will exert a major influence on the achievement of excellence. This culture must therefore be managed, which means that organisational values may need to be changed or reinforced, and continuous effort, starting from the top, may be required to get them accepted and acted upon.

4 Integration, in the sense of getting the members of the organisation working together with a sense of common purpose, is an
important aim of HRM, but this must take account of the fact
that all organisations are pluralist societies in which people have
differing interests and concerns which they may well feel need to
be defended collectively.[81]

The fourth of these principles must be seen as an important extension
of some of the views expressed from within Human Resources
Management. The extent to which it is compatible with the third
would need more discussion.

It is also arguable that Human Resources Management, as expressed
above, is not a great deal different than personnel management. The
importance of recognising the effective management of people as
critical to the success of an organisation, and the value of seeing
employees as a major resource to be harnessed for the benefit of
the organisation, are not new. Personnel managers have had an
attachment to such ideals for many years even if they have not
found it easy to get their senior managerial colleagues to share
their enthusiasm. In practice, if this view is taken, then one of the
justifications for using the new term (which Armstrong accepts) is
that it might be a way of persuading senior managerial colleagues to
pay more attention to the importance of the effective management
of people. However, there is some evidence that where the ideals of
Human Resources Management are taken seriously the result (and
really the intention) is to show that managing people is not simply
a personnel function but the key element in managing a business
and therefore the concern of everyone with a line management
responsibility. In this way short-term functions may still be given
to the personnel specialist but the concern with longer-term strategic
matters may pass out of their hands.

The intention here, though, is not to conclude a debate about the
nature and values of Human Resources Management. The aim, rather,
is to indicate that the agenda has changed. At one level the agenda
has changed sufficiently to allow some from within Human Resources
Management to challenge the relevance of industrial relations as a
subject for study. It is claimed that the interests expressed by that
subject are outdated. At another level the agenda has at least changed
so much that discussions of industrial relations have to take account
of the possibility of a long-term decline in union membership in some
countries, of a challenge to the notion that most workers will have their
pay and conditions determined as the result of collective bargaining,

and of the development of a range of policies by major firms which seem to be predicated on a reduced if not negligible influence of trade unions over their affairs. Human Resources Management can be seen to be advocating, not simply reflecting, this changed agenda.

The growing influence of Human Resources Management can be seen in the academic study of industrial relations. Students of industrial relations have always been widely dispersed across a variety of different disciplines. The growth of interest in business education generally has given an opportunity for those interested in industrial relations to press the claims of their area. Where this strategy has succeeded it has meant industrial relations frequently being located under the umbrella of Human Resources Management. This has not been without some discomfort. Over the previous decades, industrial relations struggled to develop its interest in theory, some seeking a theoretical core. Frequently, as has been illustrated, this meant taking in ideas from disciplines such as sociology where students of industrial relations were located. However, with increasing concentration in business studies and human resources management, the pressure is towards skills. Of course, the teaching of skills should lean on theory but the emphasis on practice as opposed to theory is noticeable nevertheless. There has also been a shift in the disciplines leant on: psychology has gained while sociology and politics have declined.

It would, of course, be wrong to portray such moves too starkly. Academic fashions are important, but not everyone follows them. The dominance of Human Resources Management should not be overstated today any more than the dominance of the radical critique should be overstated for the 1970s. The importance of each is that at times they have helped to change the agenda. It is impossible at this stage to say how long Human Resources Management will dictate the agenda. While the ideals it embodies are widely discussed today their dominance is dependent on a variety of factors, not the least of which is the political climate.

SUMMARY

Industrial relations, as a subject of study, started being dominated by a concern with description. Such 'fact gathering' has given way to a greater attention to theory. Initially systems theory was seen to be attractive, because although it was based on debates within sociology, it seemed to offer the opportunity to develop something distinctive which would allow industrial relations to be seen as a discipline rather than a field of study.

The criticisms of systems theory drew attention to alternatives for the development of theory that could be applied to industrial relations. The social action approach drew attention to the way that actors can be seen to have a degree of freedom of manoeuvre, not simply constrained by their position in the social structure. The discussion of frames of reference started to direct attention to conflict though the early discussion by Alan Fox was criticised for limiting itself to the pluralist critique.

The last two decades have seen major shifts in the agenda. Initially the radical critique of pluralism, principally though not exclusively expressed through Marxism, took the initiative, though more recently the challenge of Human Resources Management has been felt. The changes in academic fashion have brought new dimensions to the subject which make it very different to that that the Webbs wrote about in their 'classics' at the turn of the century.

2 The origins, growth, and development of trade unions

The discussion of trade unions is divided between three chapters. In this chapter, the growth and development of unions is looked at, essentially until the end of the 1970s. In Chapter 3, the problems faced by unions in the 1980s, and into the 1990s, are examined. In Chapter 4, the aims of unions, their internal organisation and government are considered.

BRITISH TRADE UNIONS

The account of the Webbs

Discussion of the origins and early development of British trade unions has been dominated by the work of the Webbs. In the first edition of their book, *The History of Trade Unionism*,[1] they outlined the major stages in the development of trade unions up to the end of the nineteenth century; in the second edition they covered the period to 1920.[2]

'A trade union,' the Webbs said, 'as we understand the term, is a continuous association of wage-earners for the purpose of maintaining or improving the conditions of their working lives.'[3] They failed, they said, to find any evidence in their research of the existence of such organisations prior to the latter part of the seventeenth century. However, they were able to discover 'traces of sporadic combinations and associations'[4] by the end of the seventeenth century and isolated complaints about the activity of combinations of skilled workers in certain trades by the beginning of the eighteenth century. As the century progressed the complaints about the activities of combinations gradually increased until by the middle of the century 'the Journals of the House of Commons abound in petitions and counter-petitions revealing the existence of journeymen's associations in most of the skilled trades'.[5] Finally, they inferred that the movement had been widely extended by the end of the eighteenth century because of 'the steady multiplication of the Acts against combinations in particular industries, and their culmination in the comprehensive statute of 1799 forbidding all combinations whatsoever.'[6]

In the Webbs's view the Combination Acts of 1799 and 1800 were a landmark in the history of trade unionism. There had been numerous attempts to outlaw combinations prior to 1800, but there were significant differences between such attempts and the Combination Acts. In the earlier statutes prohibition was incidental to the regulation of industry. Many associations were allowed to function quite openly and even those that were declared unlawful were only spasmodically interfered with. However, the Combination Acts were different; they were not merely a 'codification of existing law' or an 'extension from particular trades to the whole field of industry' but represented 'a new and momentous departure'. They made a direct attack on combinations and covered all combinations, whatever their nature.

The Combination Acts were eventually repealed in 1824 following the success of Hume and Plaice in securing the appointment of a select committee of the House of Commons to enquire into their operation. The statute of 1824 repealed all existing legislation and stated that in future the mere act of combination should not be grounds for prosecution under common law. Although the 1824 Repeal Act was modified a year later, the break with the old laws had been made and this effectively concluded what the Webbs termed the trade unions' 'struggle for existence'.

The years 1829 to 1842 were called the 'revolutionary period' by the Webbs. It was the time when workers turned their attention towards political action and mass movements; centrally it was the time of the formation of Robert Owen's Grand National Consolidated Trade Union. The union, of which Owen eventually became president, was established in 1834 ostensibly to support workers involved in a dispute at Derby, but it quickly expanded its aims; it proposed to rationalise the existing structure of trade unions and to provide assistance for all workers on strike. The union was an immediate success; the Webbs suggested (although this assessment has since been challenged) that its membership quickly reached the 500,000 mark. However, its success was short-lived. The Government, concerned about the growth in support for the union, determined to take action (in 1834, for example, six labourers from the village of Tolpuddle,

Dorset, were prosecuted for taking unlawful oaths and sentenced to transportation to Australia for seven years – they became know as the 'Tolpuddle Martyrs') and the union itself failed to provide the expected protection for its members. Support for the union faded, and it finally collapsed when the treasurer absconded with its funds.

The significance of the period 1829 to 1842 for the Webbs was that it was a time when workers turned to mass political action. They believed that the Grand National Consolidated Trade Union was inspired by 'Owenite socialism' – an ideological movement – and the later success of Chartism merely served to confirm their assessment.

The period 1829–42 ended, said the Webbs, in 'bitter disillusionment'; however, the trade unionists of the next generation were

> largely successful in reaching their more limited aims . . . Laying aside all projects of social revolution, they set themselves resolutely to resist the worst of the legal and industrial oppressions from which they suffered, and slowly built up for this purpose organisations which have become integral parts of the structure of a modern industrial state.[7]

In 1851, the Amalgamated Society of Engineers, Machinists, Smiths, Millwrights and Pattern Makers was founded (later to become known as the Amalgamated Society of Engineers) and this union formed the 'new model' for the future development of trade unions in Britain up to the last quarter of the nineteenth century.

The new union had few links with the Owenite Socialist societies of the early nineteenth century; it was a conservative body which restricted entry to skilled men, demanded high subscriptions and pursued an extremely cautious path. The key to its success was its stability; it had an 'admirably thought-out financial and administrative system which enabled [it] to combine the functions of a trade protection society with those of a permanent insurance company, and thus [obtain] financial stability undreamt of'.[8] It was this strength and stability which enabled it not only to survive a defeat in a strike a year after its foundation but also in the late 1850s to make three generous donations to support workers on strike in the building industry. Further, it was this strength and stability which persuaded others to follow its lead and model their organisations on it (for example, the Amalgamated Society of Carpenters and Joiners, formed in 1860).

The new model stood the unions in good stead when they were examined by the Royal Commission on Trade Unions in 1867. There had been a great deal of apprehension about union activities, and this reached a climax in 1866, the year before the Commission was established, with the 'Sheffield Outrages'.[9] However, the Commission's report was far less hostile to trade unionism than had been feared. Both the majority and minority reports recognised that measures needed to be taken to legalise trade unions. As a result, two pieces of legislation, the Trade Union Act and the Conspiracy and Protection of Property Act, were introduced in 1871 and 1875 respectively, which effectively legalised union activity. The favourable outcome, the Webbs argued, was the result of the case presented to the Commission by five leading trade unionists, representatives of the 'new model', who they referred to as 'the Junta'. They were able to assuage fears about militancy and concentrate on detailed aspects of the unions' work (such as friendly society benefits).

The final period dealt with in the first edition of the Webbs's book, covered the years 1875 to 1890. It was during this period that trade unionism was extended to the manual and unskilled occupations; this extension was termed 'new unionism' by the Webbs.

'New unionism' was effectively born in the late 1880s in the London area. In 1888 a group of women matchmakers at the Bryant and May factory came out on strike and although they had little organisation or funds, they managed, with the help of Socialist supporters, to achieve many of their aims. The following year Will Thorne led a largely successful strike at the South Metropolitan Gas Company and later that year London dock workers, led by Tillet, Mann and Burns came out on strike. With the help of financial support from trade unionists in Australia, they achieved what became known as the 'dockers' tanner'.

These successes led, in many cases directly, to the setting up of unskilled workers' unions. The Dock, Wharf, Riverside and General Labourers Union was set up in Scotland and the North of England; the General Railway Workers Union was started to cater for the unskilled workers who could not afford, or were not allowed, to join the Amalgamated Society of Railway Servants; the Agricultural Labourers Union was revived; in fact, unions were established to cover almost all unskilled workers.

New unionism differed from the 'model unions' in two important ways. First, it appealed to a different group of workers. Whereas the 'model unions' concentrated on skilled workers, new unionism concentrated on the unskilled; this meant that subscriptions had to be lower (the unskilled workers could not have afforded the high subscriptions of the 'model unions'), and they had to be more open in their recruitment policy. Second, the strategy of the new unions was different from that of the 'model unions'; whereas the latter were more conservative, cautious bodies, the former were more aggressive, encouraging the use of direct action, and gaining their strength from numbers rather than careful organisation.

In the second edition of their book the Webbs extended their coverage from 1890 to 1920. They termed this period 'thirty years' growth'. They noted that in 1892, after two centuries of development, there were only 1.5 million trade unionists out of a population of around 40 million; by 1920 there were more than 6 million trade unionists out of a population of about 48 million. Thus, trade union membership had increased from 4 per cent of the population or 20 per cent of male manual workers in 1892, to 12 per cent of the population or 60 per cent of male manual workers in 1920. With the exception of slight pauses (1893–5, 1902–4 and 1908–9) the growth in membership had been continuous for the whole 30 years. 'No less significant,' they argued, was 'the fact that the increase [was] not confined to particular industries, particular localities, or a particular sex, but [took] place, more or less, over the whole field.'[10]

Trade unionism did not grow during this period without opposition; it was attacked from a variety of stances and with a variety of weapons. Undoubtedly the most spectacular attack was through the law. The unions' ability to organise strikes was attacked in two particular cases in 1900 and 1901, *Quinn* v. *Leatham*[11] and *The Taff Vale Railway Company* v. *The Amalgamated Society of Railway Servants*.[12] They both introduced the notion of 'civil conspiracy'. Prior to these cases it was imagined that trade unions were protected against action for conspiracy by the provisions of the 1875 Conspiracy and Protection of Property Act, but this only dealt with the question of criminal not civil conspiracy. These judgements threatened the operations if not the very existence of British trade unions, for they brought about the possibility of a trade union having to pay damages for the effects of a strike. 'The immediate result was very largely to paralyse the Executive Committees and responsible officials of all Trade Unions.'[13]

Another law case in 1911 challenged the right of unions to make contributions to political parties. By the beginning of the twentieth century the unions had recognised the importance of a political arm and most of them had embraced the recently formed Labour Party. The Osborne judgement of 1911[14] called the link between the political and industrial sections of the labour movement into question. Osborne, a member of the Amalgamated Society of Railway Servants, challenged the right of the union to introduce a compulsory levy to support the Labour Party. The Law Lords decided that the union was going beyond its powers as stated in its objects, and therefore that its actions were *ultra vires*.

The civil conspiracy and the political contribution issues served to emphasise to the unions the importance of securing an effective political voice; the decisions of the courts could only be overturned in Parliament. Yet the speed with which the decisions were overturned (through the Trade Disputes Act of 1906 and the Trade Unions Act of 1913) also served to show that by the beginning of the twentieth century trade unions and trade unionists were already an important political force which could not be ignored. They proved in the 1906 general election, when fifty-four sympathetic 'Lib–Lab' candidates were returned, how important trade union support and the trade union vote could be.

The importance of trade unions was again emphasised during the First World War. The trade union leaders were instrumental in persuading workers to accept compromise and make sacrifices for the war effort. This is not to say that all workers accepted the lead (the success of the shop stewards' movement is sufficient evidence that many workers were dissatisfied with official union policy); nevertheless, in the event union leaders obtained sufficient backing to enable them to give the Government vital support. By the end of the war the trade unions were, as the Webbs assert, 'tacitly accepted as a part of the administrative machinery of the state'.[15]

Criticisms of the Webbs's account

Although the Webbs's account of the origins and development of British trade unions has been influential, it has not escaped criticism. The criticism has dealt both with the detail of their account and their general approach.

A number of writers have challenged the Webbs's view of the origins of trade unionism in Britain. The best-known exponent of this point of view is Tannenbaum.[16] He argues that British trade unions have their origins, not in the combinations of the late seventeenth century as asserted by the Webbs, but in the craft guilds of the Middle Ages. The craft guild was, and the trade union is, an association of people with a similarity of interest and a sense of community. This community of interest has been, and is, fostered by the division of labour. In the case of the guilds the division of labour led to the separation of different trades, and in the case of unions the division of labour led to the separation of workers from employers.

The movement from guilds to unions, Tannenbaum argues, was merely a reflection of changes in technology; in the earlier period the technology led to stress being placed on the kind of trade, in the latter period the technology led to stress being placed on the position within the enterprise.

Although the Webbs examined the craft guilds they argued that the guilds could not be seen as the origins of British trade unions. They wrote, 'we assert, indeed, with some confidence, that in no case did any Trade Union in the United Kingdom arise, either directly or indirectly from a Craft Guild'.[17] There were, as far as they were concerned, major differences between the craft guild and the trade union; the crucial figure in the former was the master craftsman who owned the instruments of production and sold the produce, while the crucial figure in the latter was the employee who owned neither the means nor the fruits of production.

Banks argues that the differences between the approaches of writers like Tannenbaum (and Brentano[18] and Howell[19] in the nineteenth century) and writers like the Webbs must 'not be regarded as a simple matter of truth versus error'.[20] The differences, he says, are a consequence 'of contrasting emphases on the dissimilar as opposed to the similar ways in which men have gone about the business of working together to produce things'.[21] As such they are clearly a product of different views about the nature of industrial society.

Two aspects of the Webbs's account have been criticised in detail by Pelling and Musson. Pelling[22] questions the Webbs's assertion about the importance of the Combination Acts of 1799 and 1800. He argues that they did not have such a dramatic impact as is often assumed for they were relatively mild when compared to previous legislation inhibiting the development of unions (the 1797 Act against unlawful oaths provided for penalties of up to seven years' transportation while the Combination Acts provided for maximum penalties of three months' imprisonment or two months' hard labour) and anyway they were not strictly enforced (they were virtually a dead letter in Scotland because they were not adapted to the needs of Scottish legal procedure). Musson[23] argues that it is wrong to view the movement towards the establishment of one national union as being linked too closely to a particular political philosophy (the Webbs stressed its links with Owenite Socialism). He suggests that the movement was much broader, a mainly endogenous trade union movement encouraged psychologically if not legally by the repeal of the Combination laws. Clearly the Grand National was not, as the Webbs recognised, the only attempt to form a national union; earlier attempts had been made in 1818 to establish the 'Philanthropic Society' or the 'Philanthropic Hercules' and in the late 1820s by John Docherty to establish the 'Grand General Union of Operative Spinners of Great Britain and Ireland'.

Allen[24] criticised the Webbs's account both from the point of view of its detail and its overall approach. For example, he criticised the way the Webbs emphasised the importance of the administrative structure of the Amalgamated Society of Engineers. Allen suggested that the engineers' administrative structure was by no means unique, 'The main characteristics of the constitution of the Amalgamated Society of Engineers had appeared in a number of unions since the early 1830s. They had been forced on them by economic and industrial pressures.'[25] He also criticised the importance the Webbs gave to the role of individual trade union leaders during the 1860s and 1870s (the Webbs placed considerable emphasis on the work of 'the Junta') and on their failure to see any link between the extension of trade unionism to unskilled workers in the late 1880s and early 1890s and the earlier expansion, then contraction, of unionism amongst the same section of the labour force in the 1870s.

Allen's most important criticisms, however, centred not on detail but on the Webbs's general approach. He argued that the Webbs 'made formal union organisations central and dominant in their work and mentioned other factors only in so far as they impinged directly on trade union affairs'. They largely ignored factors like economic and social conditions, factors which he said should be regarded as causative. Trade unions, he argues, ought to be examined in the contexts of their whole environments with the primary and secondary social and political forces isolated and assessed. Allen accepted that the behaviour of personalities may also be examined but asserted that they must always be seen in their contexts, 'Persons respond to situations rather than create them; they may influence timing and intensity but rarely direction.'[26] By adopting such an approach Allen is himself the source of a controversy which will be examined later in more detail (see pp. 51–2).

Developments since 1920

The Webbs's account finished at 1920 but, of course, there have been important developments since then. One of the best known has been the growth of trade union membership. The Webbs estimated that there were about 6 million trade union members in 1920; by the end of the 1970s the total was approaching 14 million. However, the growth in membership has not been as steady or as consistent as that recorded by the Webbs. For a while, in the 1920s and early 1930s, trade union membership fell and the 6 million total was not reached again until the beginning of the Second World War.

In fact, British trade unions faced major difficulties in the inter-war years. They suffered a number of important defeats in the industrial arena, probably the most significant of which were those involving the miners.[27] The unions were also badly affected in the early 1930s by the depression; many employers refused to engage union members while others sponsored rival 'company' unions (of which the best known are probably the Spencer unions[28]). In addition the trade unions were adversely affected by changes in the law. The Trade Disputes Act of 1927 made sympathetic action in furtherance of a trade dispute illegal unless it was taken by workers from within the same industry as the original dispute. Further, the Act prohibited certain other forms of industrial action by classifying them as 'intimidation' and weakened the ability of the unions to support the Labour Party by reversing the procedure established for raising the political levy in the 1913 Act; it required workers to 'contract in' to pay the political levy rather than assuming that they wanted to pay unless they 'contracted out'.

Other important developments which took place after 1920 can be narrowed down to three main areas: amalgamations, changes in the industrial structure, and the growth of white collar unionism.

A number of important amalgamations took place after the First World War and in the 1920s. These were encouraged by a change in the law (the Trade Union (Amalgamation) Act of 1917 made it easier to arrange amalgamations by reducing the size of the poll and the majority necessary to approve them); however, they were also encouraged by a recognition of the benefits of amalgamation. National negotiations became much more common during the First World War (partly as a result of the Munitions of War Act 1915 and the reports of the Whitley Committee[29]) and in such circumstances it seemed advantageous for local unions to amalgamate to form national organisations. There was also a belief that the larger unions created as the result of amalgamations would give workers greater strength and bargaining power (this was a belief which also led to many interunion alliances such as the Triple Alliance of the early 1920s,[30] through which unions agreed to cooperate on a certain range of issues).

A number of Britain's major trade unions were formed as a result of amalgamations during this period. For example, the British Iron, Steel and Kindred Trades Association was formed in 1917, the Amalgamated Engineering Union was formed in 1921, the Transport and General Workers' Union was formed in 1922 and the National Union of General and Municipal Workers was formed in 1924.

The major changes in industrial structure took place after the main amalgamations. Two important strands can be discovered. The first is the growth of new industries, using new technology and often sited in previously non-industrialised parts of the country (the chemical industry is a good example). The second is the decline in a number of traditional industries, such as coal mining and textiles. The changes had important implications for the trade union movement. The first meant that new areas were opened up for unionisation; in certain cases new unions emerged (for example, the Chemical Workers Union) while in other cases existing unions expanded (particularly the general unions, such as the Transport and General Workers' Union, and some of the old craft unions who agreed to open up their membership to less skilled workers, such as the Amalgamated Engineering Union and the Electrical Trades Union). The second meant that a number of established industrial unions lost membership even though they retained their proportion of the workforce. The best example is probably that of the Miners Federation of Great Britain whose membership fell by over 200,000 between 1929 and 1939; the fall was almost exactly in line with the decline in the size of the workforce over that period.

The major growth in white collar unionism has occurred since the Second World War. Between 1948 and 1979, the number of white collar workers in trade unions increased from less than two million to over five million. Initially, the increase was simply a reflection of the growth in white collar occupations (in fact, the increase in white collar unionisation was slower than the growth of white collar occupations between 1948 and 1964, with the result that union density amongst white collar workers declined), though since the mid-1960s the increase in white collar union membership has also been a reflection of the greater tendency of white collar workers to join trade unions (thus the increase in white collar union density as well as membership between 1964 and 1979).

Interpretation of such figures needs to be approached with caution. Definitions cause some difficulty; both definitions of white collar workers[31] and definitions of white collar unions. In this latter context, it might be noted that a number of authors have pointed out that the associations representing white collar workers vary in their adherence to traditional trade union principles and in the extent to which they reasonably might be classified as trade unions. For example, Lumley[32] has pointed out that not all associations organising white collar workers centrally try to influence the occupational and employment interests of their members, while Blackburn[33] argues that some associations do not embrace the broad social and political movement of which trade unions are a part.

White collar union membership varies considerably from industry to industry. For example, in Britain, about 87 per cent of all employees and about 80 per cent of white collar employees in the public sector are union members, but the proportions are far lower in some sectors of private industry, especially the distributive trades (where membership is around 13 per cent). Nevertheless, there was a significant increase in certain parts of the private sector in the 1970s; union density amongst white collar workers in manufacturing rose from 12.1 per cent in 1964 to 44 per cent in 1979.

The growth in the proportion of the working population engaged in white collar occupations clearly presents a major challenge to the trade union movement. Traditionally, highly unionised industries like mining and dock work, where relatively few white collar workers are engaged, are offering employment to fewer people, whereas traditionally lowly unionised industries, like professional services, insurance and banking, where large numbers of white collar workers are engaged, have grown dramatically. Estimates suggest that white collar workers soon will outnumber manual workers and if the trade union movement is to maintain its total membership and its general influence then it has to be able to increase its penetration of this sector. However, success in this matter will also have important consequences for the nature of the union movement. The attitudes and orientations of the new white collar members are unlikely to be the same as those they are replacing from the more traditional

Table 2.1 White collar and manual worker trade union membership in Britain, 1948–79

	White collar membership (000s)	Density (%)	Manual worker membership (000s)	Density (%)
1948	1,964	30.2	7,398	50.7
1964	2,684	29.6	7,534	52.9
1970	3,592	35.2	7,587	56.0
1974	4,263	39.4	7,491	57.9
1979	5,125	44.0	7,578	63.0

Sources: R. Price, G. S. Bain, 'Union Growth Revisited: 1948–1974 in Perspective', *British Journal of Industrial Relations*, vol. XIV, no. 3 (1976), pp. 339–55; also their 'Union Growth in Britain: Retrospect and Prospect', *British Journal of Industrial Relations*, vol. XXI (1983), pp. 46–8

manual sectors. The precise implications are impossible to forecast but clearly one area in which changes may occur is that of industrial and political priorities.

The end product of these developments was that by the 1970s the UK had a strong union movement (see Table 2.1). It was, of course, very different than it had been at the beginning of the century, not just because it covered about half of the workforce compared to little more than ten per cent at the beginning of the century, but also because it was a movement which had seen major structural change. A small number of large unions dominated the scene; the eleven largest unions accounted for almost two-thirds of all trade union membership, and a number of individual unions such as the Transport and General Workers' Union and the Amalgamated Union of Engineering Workers claimed over a million members each. The dominance of the manual worker unions was also starting to be challenged and, possibly symbolically most important, the National Union of Mineworkers was shortly to lose its seat on the General Council of the Trades Union Congress.

The end of the 1970s, however, in many ways represented a high point for trade unions in the UK. Their membership and their influence subsequently fell back. Although if one looked at the year-on-year figures, one could not argue that the period since the Second World War had been one of consistent growth, for there were individual years when membership fell back, nevertheless, it was clearly a time when the union movement looked for major advances and saw setbacks as temporary. In the next chapter the changes that took place in the 1980s will be looked at.

Trade union structure

Many commentators[34] have noted how the history of the development of British trade unions has had an important impact on structure. British unions have not been planned or organised by any central agency; rather they have evolved in a complex overlapping fashion. As a result the structure is not neat and tidy; instead of being arranged in easily definable categories British trade unions are distributed bewilderingly in a number of often competing patterns.

Of course, this has not prevented authors from trying to categorise British unions to enable them to present an overall picture of union structure.[35] For example, many have tried to isolate three, or sometimes four, different types of union. These are, first, the craft union, historically the oldest, being traced back to the 'model

Table 2.2 Growth of trade unions in Britain, 1901–78

Year	Number of trade unions	Number of members	Union density
1901	1,322	2,025,000	12.4
1911	1,290	3,139,000	17.1
1921	1,275	6,633,000	34.3
1923	1,192	5,429,000	32.9
1924	1,194	5,544,000	33.1
1925	1,176	5,506,000	32.4
1926	1,164	5,219,000	30.4
1927	1,159	4,919,000	28.4
1928	1,142	4,806,000	27.5
1929	1,133	4,858,000	27.2
1930	1,121	4,842,000	26.5
1931	1,108	4,624,000	25.0
1932	1,081	4,444,000	23.9
1933	1,081	4,392,000	23.5
1934	1,063	4,590,000	24.4
1935	1,049	4,867,000	25.0
1936	1,036	5,295,000	27.2
1937	1,032	5,842,000	29.3
1938	1,024	6,053,000	29.8
1939	1,019	6,298,000	31.6
1940	1,004	6,613,000	33.9
1941	996	7,165,000	36.3
1942	991	7,867,000	39.3
1943	987	8,174,000	43.1
1944	963	8,087,000	44.2
1945	781	7,875,000	41.5
1946	757	8,803,000	43.5
1947	734	9,145,000	44.4
1948	735	9,319,000	45.1
1949	726	9,274,000	44.5
1950	732	9,289,000	44.0
1951	735	9,535,000	44.9
1952	719	9,583,000	45.0
1953	717	9,523,000	44.3
1954	703	9,556,000	43.9
1955	704	9,741,000	44.2
1956	685	9,778,000	43.9
1957	685	9,829,000	44.1
1958	675	9,639,000	43.1
1959	668	9,623,000	42.6

Table 2.2 continued

1960	664	9,835,000	42.8
1961	655	9,916,000	42.5
1962	649	10,014,000	42.1
1963	643	10,067,000	42.0
1964	635	10,216,000	42.3
1965	623	10,323,000	42.2
1966	615	10,260,000	42.6
1967	596	10,188,000	42.8
1968	576	10,189,000	43.1
1969	555	10,468,000	44.4
1970	532	11,174,000	47.7
1971	511	11,120,000	47.9
1972	487	11,391,000	48.7
1973	495	11,507,000	48.5
1974	507	11,755,000	49.6
1975	501	12,193,000	51.7
1976*	473	12,386,000	51.8
1977	481	12,846,000	53.3
1978	462	13,112,000	54.3

Sources: H. Pelling, *A History of British Trade Unionism* (Pelican, Harmondsworth, 1971), pp. 280–3; Department of Employment, *British Labour Statistics: Historical Abstract, 1886–1968* (HMSO, London, 1968); Department of Employment, *Gazette*

Note: *Figures for the number of unions in 1976 and after are not directly comparable with earlier years because of changes in definition.

unionism' of the nineteenth century. Second, the industrial union, of which two variants might be described: one is the 'monopoly industrial union' which organises all workers in one industry, while the other is the 'single industry union' which does not organise all of the workers in an industry, but restricts its recruitment to that industry. Third, the general union: ideally open to all workers irrespective of industry, grade or geographical region. Fourth, the occupational union which is distinguished from the craft union on the ground that entry to the occupation is more clearly based on 'academic' qualifications.

While such attempts at categorisation may be useful when attempting to present a quick overall picture, they clearly are an oversimplification. In particular, few British unions fit any of the categories exactly. For example, there are very few examples of purely craft unions; most of the old craft unions, like the AUEW, have now opened up their ranks to non-craft members. Similarly, there are no monopoly industrial unions (the closest example was probably the National Union of Mineworkers until the advent of the Union of Democratic Mineworkers) and most general unions concentrate their attentions on certain sections of industry (the Transport and General Workers' Union has a particularly strong hold on the transport industries while the General Municipal and Boilermakers Trade Union traditionally held greatest influence amongst gas workers and employees of local authorities). Further, Turner[36] has argued that this kind of classification presents a static view of trade unions and does not help one to analyse their growth and development (he argued that a distinction between 'open' and 'closed' unions would be more valuable for this purpose).

Turner also noted that the complex structure of British trade unions has been the source of much concern. He has argued that the 'question of trade union structure is central to all the major problems of British industrial relations'.[37] For example, it influences the effectiveness of incomes policy, the extent to which accelerating technological change can be absorbed, the settlement of disputes, the number of unofficial strikes and the degree to which trade unions can widen collective bargaining to cover non-wage issues.

Clearly, if this view is accepted, then 'multi-unionism' is a major problem in Britain. It has been estimated that 4 out of every 5 trade unionists in Britain work in a multi-union establishment and about 1 in 6 belong to a grade of worker in which two or more unions are competing for members. And many would claim that multi-unionism is the breeding ground for interunion conflict.

In these terms, interunion conflict can take a number of different forms. For example, it can take the form of a 'recognition' dispute; that is, a dispute over which of one or more unions should have the right to represent a group of workers (such disputes frequently occur in newly unionised areas, such as industries built on the basis of new developments in technology). Alternatively, it can take the form of a 'poaching' dispute; that is, a dispute which arises when a union attempts to recruit workers who are already members of another union. Again, it can take the form of a 'demarcation' dispute; that is, a dispute over which group of workers should be permitted to undertake a particular task. Frequently the workers will be members of different unions though this is not always the case; sometimes they have been members of different sections of the same union.

Interunion conflict of this kind clearly creates a number of problems for employers. For example, demarcation disputes (or agreements) may mean that management has to accept a form of work organisation which differs from their ideal. Further, interunion conflict may lead to difficulties in collective bargaining; the attitudes may be determined almost as much by their wish to 'score points' off a rival union as their wish to pursue a particular claim. Again, if interunion conflict is the 'cause' of strikes then it may be thought to lead to a loss of production.

However, it is not only employers who see the British trade union structure as the cause of the problems. In the past governments have frequently commented critically on union structure and campaigned for changes. For example, they have argued that a 'simpler' union structure would result in 'better' industrial relations; as Turner noted, they have also felt that it would make the operation of an 'incomes policy' easier. It is also clear that many trade union leaders have believed that there might be benefits from a restructuring of the movement.

Initially there was considerable support within British trade unions for restructuring on the basis of industrial unionism. In particular, during the First World War the leaders of the shop stewards' movement felt that industrial unionism, by uniting workers in one industry, would give greater revolutionary potential. Since that time industrial unionism has lost some of its appeal; the TUC examined the idea in some detail at Congress in 1927, 1946 and 1963 but stopped short of suggesting adoption. Although industrial unionism still has supporters in other circles (a comparison is often made between the 'tidy' industrial union structure in Germany and the 'complex' structure of unions in Britain), the difficulties and disadvantages associated with it are now more widely recognised. For example, the Donovan Commission argued that it had theoretical as well as practical disadvantages; not only would it be difficult to introduce in Britain because of the impracticability of 'unscrambling' the existing structure, but if it ever were adopted it might also discourage labour mobility.

Although support for industrial unionism has faded within the British trade union movement, interest in less radical restructuring has by no means disappeared. The spur to such attempts is no longer 'revolutionary potential' but more efficient organisation. Many union leaders feel that they may be dissipating too much of their energy on interunion conflict, energy which could be better utilised in recruitment and bargaining. Thus, although a TUC report argued that a wholesale restructuring of the trade union movement was impractical, it said that consideration should be given to ways of stimulating the 'process of piecemeal and ad hoc developments by which changes have come about in the past'.[38]

Central to this strategy is the encouragement of amalgamations between unions operating in the same or related areas. A number of amalgamations took place in the 1960s and 1970s, partly encouraged by the relaxation of statutory conditions controlling amalgamation (through the Trade Union (Amalgamation etc.) Act 1964). In the four years following the passing of the 1964 Act more than 50 amalgamations were effected; and between 1969 and 1971 there were 60 mergers affecting 429,000 union members. The pace slowed somewhat in the late 1970s, only 28 taking place between 1975 and 1979.[39]

Other less spectacular piecemeal and *ad hoc* developments have been the growth in fairly loose forms of association, such as federations and working arrangements (though, as Hughes comments,[40] relatively little is know about working arrangements; they are as yet largely 'uncharted water'). The TUC has also established machinery to deal with any problems of interunion conflict that may arise. This machinery dates back to 1921 when the TUC set up its disputes committee to hear complaints from one union against another. Over the years the committee built up a body of 'case law' which was codified in the Bridlington rules (laid down at the 1939 annual conference of the TUC).

However, Hyman[41] has argued that concern with the problems of the structure of British trade unions is one-sided and misplaced. It is one-sided because it is 'frankly managerial in orientation'.[42] The presupposition he says is that trade unionism should be a source of orderly industrial relations, a means of control over the labour force:

> The fact that multi-unionism may cause certain problems for managerial control should not be accepted as a valid basis for criticism of union structure; for if this were an appropriate criterion, it might be argued that managerial control could best be increased by abolishing trade unionism altogether.[43]

As an aside, it might also be noted that interunion conflict is recorded as the cause of relatively few strikes in Britain. It is misplaced partly because it reflects a 'tendency to exaggerate the importance of formal union structure'.[44] According to Hyman, the existence of sectional organisation is a consequence rather than a cause of sectionalism within the working class (though he recognises that at times it can reinforce sectional consciousness). It is also misplaced partly because the British union structure is only confusing if it is examined in a static fashion (that is, if it is looked at solely in terms of current membership patterns). It should be looked at rather in a historical perspective: 'union structure is not a fixed phenomenon but a process, the historical outcome of the interdependent but not purposefully integrated strategies of a variety of fragmented employee groups'.[45]

The Trades Union Congress

One of the most interesting aspects of the British trade union movement is the existence of a central coordinating body, the Trades Union Congress. The TUC has its origins in the 1860s; the first meeting was held in Manchester in 1868. However, it was a while before it developed into the kind of body it is today. Initially many of the major unions refused to send delegates (the Manchester Conference was ignored by the Conference of Amalgamated Trades and both the London and Glasgow Trade Councils) and for a number of years it had a provincial image. In its early years it also lacked a clear political ideology or commitment; Allen comments that by the early 1880s, although 'the value of interunion unity had been empirically illustrated', it still 'did not have any continuing political significance. There was no coherent ideological basis for unity; no reasoned case for heightening workingmen's consciousness in their class solidarity'.[46] It was not, in fact, until the 1890s, after the emergence of 'new unionism' that the TUC began to take a stand committed to 'socialist' rather than 'liberal' principles, and even in the 1890s the old order and beliefs were not overturned without a bitter struggle.

Nevertheless, the TUC eventually embraced a socialist philosophy and played an important role in the formation of the Labour Party. Subsequently there was and still is a strong link between the TUC and its affiliated unions and the Labour Party. Not only do the trade unions contribute a large sum to Labour Party funds through affiliation fees and special donations, but they also sponsor Labour Party Members of Parliament and have important direct and indirect representation on Labour Party committees, both at the local and national level.

In terms of the number of unions, only a minority are members of the TUC; nevertheless in terms of membership the vast proportion of trade unionists are members of unions that are affiliated to the TUC (TUC affiliated unions accounted for about 90 per cent of total union membership in the 1970s and although the figure is now lower as the result of changes in the 1980s the TUC still represents most union members), and there has been a slow but noticeable movement on the part of many unions representing professional workers towards membership of the TUC in recent years.

The TUC never has had control over the detailed day to day operations of British trade unions; it is merely an organisation where matters of common interest can be discussed and which represents member unions in negotiations with outside bodies. Nevertheless, at times this coordinating role has proved to be extremely important. The TUC took the lead, after the election of a Labour government in 1974, in negotiating and drawing up the 'social contract'. Although the influence of the TUC in national affairs waned after the election of the Conservative government in 1979 it did not disappear altogether. Over the years it has developed as a specialist organisation able to give advice and guidance to member unions and despite inevitable internal disagreements it is still recognised as the authoritative voice of the British union movement, representing it on numerous official committees.

GROWTH AND DEVELOPMENT OF TRADE UNIONS OUTSIDE BRITAIN

Superficially there are a number of similarities between the growth and development of trade unions in the USA and Britain. For example, in both countries the first stable trade union organisation developed amongst skilled workers. In Britain, the first stable developments are represented by the 'model unions' of the mid-nineteenth century; in the USA, the first stable developments are represented by the American Federation of Labor, an alliance of craft unions established in 1886. Neither of these early attempts at union organisation was inspired by any particular political philosophy; both were cautious, essentially economic movements. Similarly, both trade union movements faced fierce opposition from employers in the inter-war years; in both Britain and the USA this took the form of, for example, the refusal to employ unionists and the establishment of company unions. Further, today in both countries the trade union movement is represented by a single central organisation; in Britain the TUC, in the USA the AFL-CIO.

However, these similarities are only superficial; there are, in fact, many important differences. For example, although trade unionism first developed amongst skilled workers in both countries, it subsequently expanded its coverage far faster in Britain than in the USA. In Britain trade unionism had spread to unskilled workers by the turn of the century whereas in the USA it remained a craft-dominated movement well into the twentieth century. In fact, it was not until the 1930s that trade unionism in the USA made significant inroads into manual work and mass production industries (the major extension came after the New Deal Legislation when the industrial unions developed and mass production workers in industries like steel, textiles and automobiles were unionised).

Similarly, although the trade union movement in both countries suffered in the inter-war years, in the USA the employers' attack on the unions was much more comprehensive and in many senses more effective. Under the banner of the 'American Plan' the National Association of Manufacturers led the fight for the open shop 'as the natural habitat for the free and independent American workingmen'.[47] Trade unions were castigated as 'un-American', workers were subjected to 'yellow-dog' contracts (under which employees agreed not to join a trade union), and management launched the 'welfare capitalism' movement (which introduced devices like profit sharing schemes and company pensions intended to persuade the worker that gains could be made without unions) and sponsored company unions. Some indication of the success of these moves can be gained from the fact that by 1926 company unions had about half as many members as the American Federation of Labor (at that time the main union organisation) and that unions in the USA lost almost a third of their membership between 1920 and 1929.

Again, although both the British and US unions are represented by one single central organisation, there are considerable differences in the history and coverage of the organisations. In Britain the TUC became the major central trade union organisation well before the end of the nineteenth century and its position was not seriously challenged, certainly until the 1980s. The history of the central union organisation in the USA has been rather different. The position of the American Federation of Labor as the main central union organisation was challenged on a number of occasions in the nineteenth and early twentieth centuries. For example, in the early twentieth century, it was challenged by the Industrial Workers of the World, a militant organisation founded in 1905 by union leaders impatient with the AFL's cautious line. Further, in the 1930s, a dispute occurred within the AFL which led to a major split in the organisation. The split was precipitated again by the conservatism of the AFL leadership. A number of younger labour leaders had for many years felt unhappy about the direction of the AFL's policy and their discontent came to a head at the convention of 1934. Dissatisfied delegates decided to set up a body known as the Committee for Industrial Organisation; although they saw the Committee operating as a pressure group within the AFL, the AFL leadership expelled the unions which had joined and forced them to set up a separate organisation. The Committee for Industrial Organisation unions had considerable success in the years immediately after their expulsion, initially in the automobile industry, though later also in a number of other mass production industries, including steel. In 1938, the Committee for Industrial Organisation changed its name to the Congress of Industrial Organisation and began to rival the AFL in terms of size and influence; by the end of the Second World War the total membership of the two organisations was roughly equal. The two organisations clashed on numerous issues, initially most crucially over the political role of trade unions; the AFL remained a much more conservative body than the CIO for many years, less interested in explicitly political issues. These differences proved important enough to keep the two organisations separate for 20 years and it was not until 1955 that they finally reunited. Even by the end of the 1970s the united organisation (the AFL-CIO) could not claim to represent all USA unions, for a number of major ones were not members (the two largest unions in the USA, the International Brotherhood of Teamsters and the United Auto Workers, which had a combined membership of three million were not members).

The result was that by the end of the 1970s trade unions in Britain and the USA differed markedly. Whereas in Britain almost 50 per cent of the labour force were members of a trade union, in the USA the percentage was only about 25. Union organisation was particularly weak amongst white collar and public employees in the USA, which was of some importance given the higher proportion of the labour force in white collar occupations in the USA than in Britain.

The differences between trade unions in Britain and Europe are as great, if not greater, than the differences between unions in Britain and the USA. For instance, few European unions have historical roots as long as either their British or US counterparts. The most dramatic example is provided by the German trade unions. They were devastated by Nazism before, and rebuilt afresh by the allies after, the Second World War (it has been argued that the weakness of German trade unions during the 1930s was one of the reasons for the growth of Nazism and that the allies encouraged the development of unions after the war as a bulwark against any such repetition). The Italian trade unions had a similar, although not directly parallel, history. They also were greatly influenced by the political developments of the 1930s when they came under strong authoritarian control and modern Italian unions have little in common with those earlier bodies.

Although unions in other European countries have not been subjected to such dramatic change as those in Italy and Germany, few have a long history. For instance, although French trade unions can be traced back to the nineteenth century, their major development did not occur until the 1930s when the Matignon agreement of 1936, which followed a period of industrial strife that culminated in a major national strike, recognised the freedom to organise and belong to a trade union and to conclude collective labour contracts.

Campbell Balfour[48] argues that the growth of European unions was affected far more by political decisions than was the case with British unions. The Matignon agreement is a classic example. In this sense European unions have more in common with their US than their British counterparts, for when British unions have received assistance from the law it has usually been of a negative kind (for example, the Trade Disputes Act relieved them of certain legal liabilities) whereas trade unions in the USA have benefited from positive legislation (the Wagner Act of 1935 gave the unions bargaining rights).

One of the other major comparisons made between British and European unions is in terms of overall structure. It has been argued that European unions (again like those in the USA) have a much simpler structure than their British counterparts. The example often referred to is that of the German unions. Since the Second World War German unions have been structured on the basis of industrial unionism. There are seventeen major industrial unions, each covering a defined sector of the economy (for example, one union covers engineering, another chemicals, another building, and so on). The seventeen unions are brought together in a central organisation, the Deutscher Gewerkschafts Bund, a far stronger coordinating body than the British TUC. The DGB receives 12½ per cent of the dues of the seventeen member unions, and the leader of each of the unions sits on its executive (this gives it far more authority than the British TUC to speak for the whole of the trade union movement).

Unions in Sweden also have a relatively simple structure. The main confederation, the LO, organises more than 90 per cent of blue collar workers through twenty-one industrial unions. There are, however, two other trade union confederations: the TCO and the SACO SR. The TCO represents white collar workers, and although the four largest unions are organised on an industrial basis others are organised on an occupational basis. The other confederation, SACO SR, represents professionals and the unions are organised on the basis of academic background.

No other European country has a trade union movement with a structure as simple as that of Germany or Sweden. Netherlands probably comes closest, for since 1945 there has been a move in the Netherlands towards a rationalisation of union structure on the basis of industrial unionism. It is probably fair to argue, though, that no other European country has a trade union movement with a structure as complex as that of Britain. No doubt one of the reasons for this is the relatively late growth and development of European unions.

It is worthwhile noting one factor which complicates union structure in most European countries that is unimportant in Britain. Most European trade union movements are bedevilled by major political and religious divisions. For example, in France and Italy there are divisions between Communist and Socialist as well as between Christian and secular unions; in most other European countries, although the split between Communist and Socialist is no longer of importance, the religious divisions are crucial.

Finally, it should be mentioned that many European unions have covered smaller proportions of the workforce than their British counterparts (probably partly, though not entirely, as a result of their internal divisions). French trade unions provide the best example, but in many other countries the trade union movement is in a similar position. In West Germany, for instance, trade union membership at the end of the 1970s was only about 37 per cent of the working population. Exceptions to this rule are Belgium and Denmark where unions claim a membership density figure of around 65 per cent. Outside the EC the Swedish membership has been well in excess of 80 per cent.

Table 2.3 Trade union density by country, selected years, 1895–1975

	1895	1900	1910	1920	1930	1940	1950	1960	1970	1975
Australia	5.4[a]	9.0[b]	21.0[c]	42.2	43.5	40.4	56.0	54.5	50.5	54.3
Canada			15.0[d]	13.5[e]	18.3[f]	32.8	34.5	34.7	34.6	
Denmark			15.3[g]	35.1[d]	32.0	42.4	51.9	59.6	62.5	66.6
Germany	2.5	5.7	18.1	52.6	33.7	n/a	33.1	37.1	36.3	37.2
Great Britain	10.1	13.1	16.0	48.2	25.7	33.4	43.8	43.5	47.2	49.2[h]
Norway	n/a	3.4	7.6	20.4	18.3	n/a	n/a	61.5	61.8	60.5
Sweden	1.2	4.8	8.3	27.7	36.0	54.0	67.7	73.0	80.4	87.2
United States	3.0[i]	5.5	9.0	16.7	8.9	16.4	28.0	26.3	27.1	25.1
Japan				7.5			46.2	32.2	35.4	34.4

Sources: G. S. Bain, R. Price, *Profiles of Union Growth* (Blackwell, Oxford, 1980); Honansoa, *Encyclopedia of Japan*

Notes: [a]1896, potential union membership figure obtained by interpolating between 1891 and 1901; [b]1901; [c]Potential union membership figure obtained by interpolating between 1901 and 1911; [d]1921; [e]1931; [f]1941; [g]1911; [h]1974; [i]1897.

Trade unions in Japan have some links with their counterparts in North America and Western Europe, though there are distinctive features which have been seen as increasingly important over the years. As in many other countries the first important union organisations developed amongst skilled workers, such as printers and iron workers. These late nineteenth-century bodies were directly influenced by developments in the USA. A number of leaders that had direct personal experience of the American Federation of Labor tried to establish a similar body in Japan (the Rodo Kumiai Kiseikai, or the Society for the Formation of Labour Unions). The American model was also followed in a later attempt to establish a national union federation when the Yuaikai was set up in 1912. Initially a conservative body, the Yuaikai achieved considerable success during the boom conditions around the First World War and changed both its stance and its name, to Sodomei (Japan Federation of Labor) in 1919.

Trade unions in Japan, like those in many other countries, faced major problems during the depression, problems which were exacerbated by internal divisions. The more radical elements were driven underground and the unions found it increasingly difficult to organise. The union movement in Japan was effectively destroyed in the late 1930s. The parallels for this period between Japan and Western European countries, like Germany and Italy, were close.

The militarists gained direct state control over labor with the establishment of Sampo (Sangyo Hokoku Kai or Industrial Patriotic Association) in the late 1930s. With the formation of Sampo, an independent labor movement, however moderate, could not be tolerated for long. By 1941, the unions had dissolved or gone underground like similar 'labor fronts' in Nazi Germany and Fascist Italy. Sampo's functions included allocating workers on a priority basis to industries deemed most essential for military purposes. In organising the Sampo movement, not only were all labor unions abolished, but each company set up its own internal councils from top to bottom devoted to improving productivity and expending production for the war effort under supervision of the government.[49]

After the war, industrial relations in Japan were developed under the influence of the allied powers. Once again, industrial relations in Japan were subject to American influence. Trade unions were given official encouragement, and legislation similar to that of the Wagner Act was introduced. Union membership grew rapidly and by

1949 there were over 6.5 million union members, giving a density of 56 per cent.

There were setbacks nevertheless. In 1947 a planned general strike was prohibited by General MacArthur and in subsequent years labour legislation was modified, particularly in respect of public sector employees. Trade unionism in Japan also developed in a very distinctive fashion, being dominated by enterprise unions. Essentially an enterprise union consists of all employees up to management level in a firm, irrespective of occupational status. In some large enterprises a number of individual unions will join together, effectively to form a federation. There are also some links between enterprise unions within the same industry and a number of national confederations of which the most important are Sohyo and Domei. However, the individual enterprise unions retain a great deal of effective power.

Considerable attention has been paid to the phenomenon of enterprise unions in Japan. Amongst the explanations suggested[50] are that they are an outgrowth of the wartime patriotic labour organisations at each enterprise (the Sampo), that they were encouraged by American influence after the Second World War because they seemed to form an almost non-existent base and that they were the only kind of unions that employers would tolerate. It is also clear that enterprise unions have particular relevance in a system where employees expect lifetime engagement with one employer. Although the system of 'permanent employment', where employees see their career within the enterprise and gain extensively through seniority, is far from universal in Japan, its traditional importance in large firms is of some consequence for the structure of trade unions. In practice, trade unions in Japan have had much more success in large enterprises and the public sector (in the mid-1970s unionisation rates in private sector enterprises employing 500 or more people were over 63 per cent, but in private sector enterprises with between 499 and 100 employees they were less than 32 per cent with steeply declining percentages for smaller firms, while unionisation in the public sector was over 75 per cent[51]).

One of the implications of enterprise unionism and the 'permanent' employment system is that workers identify strongly with the company. Bargaining takes much more account of the economic position of the company than it does in other circumstances. It is one of the reasons for cooperative attitudes frequently noted as a feature of Japanese industrial relations. Enterprise unionism also frequently means that union officials come from within the company, and they may see service with the union as a way of gaining promotion within the firm. This has led some observers to argue as a result that 'Japanese union leaders are not highly professional'.[52] As with all such stereotypes there needs to be an element of caution for fear of overgeneralisation and, as will be discussed later, the economic difficulties of the 1970s have put some strains on the system.

Unionisation in Japan continued to grow throughout the 1950s, 1960s and 1970s. Success in some areas are worth special mention, particularly in some branches of financial services. However, although union membership increased fairly steadily in the years following the Second World War, from over 6.5 million in 1949 to over 7.2 million in 1959, and to over 12 million in the 1970s, unionisation did not keep pace with the growth in the number of employees. The figure for 1949 represented about 56 per cent of the workforce; the figure for the 1970s represented only about 34 per cent.

Australian trade unions probably exhibit as much similarity with their British counterparts as those of any other country. The first unions in Australia had clear direct links with Britain for they were formed in the 1830s and 1840s by migrant Britons. Subsequent development was not always as firmly linked, but it closely followed the British model. For example, the first important stable trade union organisation developed amongst skilled craftsmen in the 1850s and these unions, like their British counterparts, were essentially conservative bodies emphasising the importance of strong organisation rather than a Socialist philosophy. The first group of manual workers to be unionised to any extent were again, as in Britain, the miners, and when trade unionism spread more generally to manual workers during the latter part of the nineteenth century it was through a different style of union, termed 'new unionism'.[53] Further, Australian trade unions were instrumental in the formation and growth of the Labour Party at the end of the nineteenth and beginning of the twentieth century.

However, the twentieth-century development of trade unions in Australia has been rather different. Gollan[54] notes that in the early twentieth century there was considerable support for national (which has a different connotation in Australia than in Britain given the Federal system of government) and international trade unionism in Australia. For example, soon after the turn of the century many union leaders supported an American-founded organisation, the Industrial Workers of the World: the move towards national unionism came later and is best represented by the Workers Industrial Union of Australia which achieved its peak in terms of popularity in the 1920s. Whilst there are some parallels between this latter movement and attempts at greater cooperation between British unions (through devices like the Triple Alliance) the comparison cannot be taken too far and there is certainly no evidence of any direct link.

Superficially, there are still many similarities between the British and Australian trade union movements; Australian, like British unions, are still organised around a number of bases, such as craft, general and industrial unionism. However, if one looks closer then one sees considerable differences between the two union movements. Probably the most crucial is the way in which Australian unions have developed within a framework of compulsory arbitration. Although some Australian trade unionists have always opposed such legal controls the bulk of influential leaders have welcomed them.

It is also worth noting, that in the years following the Second World War there was a decline in the density of trade union membership in Australia; for example, from 56 per cent in 1950 to 54 per cent in 1975. However, these figures need to be treated with caution for over the same period there was an increase in the crude total trade union membership figures by about 300,000. The reason for these contradictory trends is the substantial increase in the labour force, part of which occurred through immigration.

Few African unions have a long history and most are small and poorly organised. Early unionisation was opposed by colonial governments who saw a link between unions and opposition to their rule. Later this policy changed and unions were seen as a way of bringing some order and control to labour relations. The unions that were encouraged, though, were often European in character and ill-suited to their task. Allen[55] has referred directly to the European influence on unionism in Eastern Africa suggesting that the ability to speak English fluently was a crucial qualification for trade union office which served to widen the gulf between union leaders and members.

After independence, governments took a close interest in the role of trade unions. The demands of industrialisation led them to adopt a much more interventionist role and in doing so, to restrict the activities of unions. It also led to government intervention to restructure trade unions. In Ghana the government replaced 85 small unions with 24 and then 10 industrial-based unions. A similar move towards industrial unionism was made in Zambia. In both of those countries, the state also intervened to establish a new central union organisation.

In South-East Asia, the pre-independence period also saw a link between trade unionism and anti-colonialisation. However, as in Africa, there was a change in the attitude of colonial administrations as unions came to be seen as a way of bringing greater order into labour relations. In countries like Malaya and Ceylon, a tightrope had to be walked to encourage unions that would help to maintain industrial peace but not become involved in political activities.

After independence, trade unionism in many of those countries – as in Africa – was influenced by factors like the demands of economic development and the desire of the state to tightly control political as well as industrial events. In Malaysia, this led to government attempts to neutralise communist influence in trade unions. One move in this direction was the Trade Union Ordinance of 1959 which limited trade union organisation to similar occupations or trades and therefore limited the size of trade unions.

In Malaysia, trade unions failed to extend their influence to any significant degree. In the 1980s only about 12–13 per cent of the workforce were in a union and unions were particularly weak in the private sector (in the public sector about half of the workforce was unionised). On the other hand, in Singapore, the state and the unions formed a much closer relationship. The strong links between the ruling People's Action Party and the National Trades Union Congress allowed the latter to organise around a quarter of the workforce by the end of the 1970s. Following a difficult period at the end of the 1960s the party and the union congress reached an agreement on 'modernisation' and this allowed the NTUC to increase its total membership by an average of 15,000 a year between 1971 and 1979.[56]

In Hong Kong, trade unionism has been affected by a number of different factors. In their review of trade unionism in the colony, England and Rear[57] point to the importance of political developments in mainland China, such as the impact of the cultural revolution in 1967, and the impact of the state of the labour market. In this latter case, the existence of a labour surplus for many years made recruitment difficult and although the labour market conditions changed in the 1960s, this was not entirely beneficial, for many employees were persuaded that they could improve their position without the help of trade unions. In practice, it was not until the late 1960s and early 1970s that union membership began to increase significantly; even so, the rapidly rising size of the workforce meant that the percentage in union membership only rose from 12.8 per cent in 1961 to 13.1 per cent in 1971. In Hong Kong, the strength of unions lies in public utilities and communications; the weakness lies in manufacturing.

GROWTH AND DEVELOPMENT OF TRADE UNIONS: GENERAL EXPLANATIONS

A number of writers have concentrated on the similarities in the growth and development of trade unions in different countries. This has led them to argue that trade unions are the inevitable result of certain structural changes in society, usually structural changes associated with industrialisation.

One of the best known of such authors is Tannenbaum.[58] His writing was mentioned earlier in connection with the origins of British unions. The argument advanced on that issue was that trade unions were linked to craft guilds because they were both associations based on a community of interest; they were different simply because of the different contexts in which they developed. This argument is extended to show how one can account for the growth and development of trade unions. He asserts that the industrial revolution destroyed the traditional community in work which the medieval guild provided,

> Hence the trade union emerged as the 'spontaneous grouping of individual workers thrown together functionally. It reflects the moral identity and psychological unity men always discover when they work together'. In brief, 'the organisation of workers is essential in a modern industrial society, and if unionism did not exist it would have to be invented'.[59]

This line of thought is given support, if on rather a different level, by the systems approach. From this point of view all aspects of society are interrelated and changes that occur in one part will necessarily have consequences for the rest of the system. In this way, the development of trade unions can be seen as a response to other events, rather than as a movement in its own right. For example, Smelser,[60] in his study of the Lancashire cotton industry in the late eighteenth and early nineteenth centuries, isolated a number of structural changes involving industry (the decline in the 'putting out' and the growth of the 'factory' system) and the family (the separation of home from work). He argued that it was in direct response to the changes in the structure of industry and the family that unions in the cotton industry developed into organisations much more like their present-day equivalents.

One of the consequences of industrialisation has been an increase in the scale of operation in industry. A number of writers have suggested that this has had an effect on the growth and development of trade unions. The argument essentially is that the larger the unit the more likely it is that workers will recognise a common interest and the more likely it is that they will see themselves as separate and distinct from management (it is also argued that unions find it easier to organise and service workers in larger units). Such a view can be seen in Lockwood's explanation for the unionisation of clerks.[61] At a more general level, Price and Bain were able to show that in manufacturing industry, the larger the establishment the more likely it is that workers will be unionised[62] and this has been confirmed by the Workplace Industrial Relations Survey for the whole of the private sector (in organisations with less than 100 employees union density averaged 20 per cent but in organisations with 50,000 or more employees it averaged 60 per cent).

Of course, in Western nations, industrialisation has been linked to the development of capitalism. From the Marxist point of view the development of capitalism is seen as the crucial factor underlying the growth of trade unions. For example, Allen argues[63] that trade unions are a direct result of a society which has, as one of its main precepts, the sale of labour and a division between sellers on the one hand, and buyers (and thereby controllers) on the other. Trade unions are essential in such a society for the defence of those who sell their labour, but would be unnecessary, certainly in their present form, in a different kind of society.

Stated in this form it is difficult, using this approach, to account for the different rates of unionisation in different industries, areas, and the like, unless one could argue that in some way these differences were related to the differential development of capitalism. In practice, this point, at least in part, is met by Allen when he recognises that consideration needs to be given to the importance of individual values and consciousness. Thus, although he states that the existence of a free labour market is a necessary condition for the growth of trade unions, he argues that the actual emergence of trade unions is determined by social values,

> All members of a free labour market are in the same basic economic position but whether or not they realise this will depend on their social images which are in turn a product either of traditional values or social class position.[64]

Allen is not suggesting that the development of class consciousness is totally independent of the social structure, but at least he is recognising the possibility of differing levels of consciousness between workers and the importance of these differing levels of consciousness for the growth of unions.

Essentially, then, Allen is suggesting that workers will join trade unions if they recognise where their real interests lie. Other explanations for the growth of unions stress the importance of the evaluation made by workers but suggest that different factors will influence the conclusion reached. For example, a number of writers have stressed that union membership has both costs and benefits for an industrial worker. The costs include subscriptions, employers' displeasure, diminution of employment prospects and the like, while the benefits might include higher wages and greater job security. Of course, costs and benefits are not static over time, nor are they the same in different industries or for different grades of worker. One suggestion has been that costs and benefits vary according to general economic prosperity. Thus, Wolman has put forward a 'prosperity theory' of union growth: union membership can offer the greatest benefit for the lowest cost during economically buoyant times, so that 'union growth is positively correlated with prosperity, rising when business is good and falling when business is bad'.[65] Others have questioned the detail of this theory; Davis[66] has compared the movement of union membership with a condition of 'prosperity' in 61 cases (covering 4 major countries) and found that although in two-thirds of the cases in which the year was classified as one of prosperity there were marked rises in union membership, in 25 per cent of such cases union membership declined. This led Davis to argue that other factors, as well as prosperity, such as the quality of union leadership and the attitude of the state, need to be taken into account, although he did not reject the importance of prosperity entirely. A mix of factors, some of which are concerned with economic conditions, also has been put forward by Bain and Elsheikh[67] as an explanation for union growth. They produced an equation taking the rate of change in prices, the rate of change in money wages, the rate of unemployment, and government action into account, which they argued could explain much of the variation in union density in a number of Western nations.

A number of authors have pointed out that the costs and benefits of union membership might change not just on a national basis in relation to changes in the general economic position, but also on a more restricted basis, affecting individual groups and trades. Thus, it might be argued that if a lowly unionised group found that its economic position was worsening, such a group might be tempted to turn to union action to recover its position, or might believe that union action potentially offered benefits that in the past it had been able to achieve in other ways. Such a view has been influential in attempts to explain the increasing unionisation amongst many groups of white collar workers. Lockwood[68] was able to show that many clerks had suffered a decline in their relative earnings position and that this might have been one of the reasons for their increasing interest in joining trade unions. Others have widened this discussion, beyond simply changes in earnings, and noted that the position of white collar workers, relatively, has worsened in other ways: for example, they no longer enjoy the same superiority over manual workers in terms of fringe benefits that they used to. However, Loveridge[69] has argued that while a decline in the relative position of white collar workers will be important in persuading them of the benefits of joining trade unions, on its own this will not be sufficient: another important ingredient will be realisation of this decline.

The explanations reviewed to date, at one level, all have had one thing in common. They have stressed the importance of one or other aspect of social structure in determining the level of union membership. Few of them have been crude theories, merely suggesting that changes in one variable will automatically result in a change in unionisation. Nevertheless, to differing degrees, many of them can be attacked for seeing individual attitudes simply or largely as the result of an element or elements of the social structure, and for limiting the degree of influence and freedom they afford to the individual union leader. Of course, some of the above theories can be, and have been, modified to take these kinds of factors into account. For example, the discussion of consciousness by some Marxists allows a wider discussion of industrial attitudes and variations than has been suggested so far; it has already been noted that Davis recognised the importance of the quality of union leadership as well as the importance of economic conditions; and more account could be taken of individual assessments (and their sources) of the costs and benefits of union membership.

It would be possible to devise theories which went further than this in rejecting elements of the social structure as an explanation for union growth. However, it may be that to do so would be just as unwise as it would be to rely entirely on structural factors. Banks has argued that the aim of the sociologist should be to provide an explanation which avoids the extremes of either school of thought, 'The problem, in brief, is to devise a theory which will indicate just how much of history is determined by processes beyond human control and how much is consciously willed.'[70]

The answer proposed by Banks is to use what he terms the 'step-by-step' approach, through which the trial and error progression which men use in their efforts to create something new from whatever features of their circumstances they find amenable to manipulation can be analysed. He says

> From this point of view a trade union movement is a 'socially constructive' grouping of organisations whose activities may be defined in terms of objectives, shared by their members, provided it is understood that sometimes these objectives are achieved, but also that others are given up when they are seen as no longer relevant or no longer desirable in the new circumstances which have arisen.[71]

This view enables one to examine and see not only why certain developments are successful but also why others are unsuccessful.

The example which Banks presents to illustrate the way that his approach might be used compares the attempts to develop general unionism and the emergence of 'new model' unions in Britain. The failure of general unionism, he says, may 'be symptomatic of the fact that desire alone will not result in a revolutionary new order' while the success of the 'new model' unions 'indicates how innovation in the social, as in the material world, takes its point of departure from the nature of the circumstances with which men have to cope'.[72]

SUMMARY

In this chapter considerable attention has been focused on the growth and development of the trade union movement in Britain. Discussion of early history has centred on the writing of the Webbs, although criticisms of their approach have been noted. Modern trade unionism in Britain is often said to have started in the mid-nineteenth century with the establishment of unions for skilled craftsmen. However, the extension of unionism to unskilled workers did not take place until nearly fifty years later and the major increase in union membership did not occur until the beginning of the twentieth century. The period from the end of the First World War onwards, initially, was one of conflict and decline, but much of this lost ground was later regained and the union membership total at the end of the 1970s (around 13 million) covered substantial proportions of white collar as well as manual workers and was an all-time high.

Interesting comparisons can be made between the growth and development of the trade union movement in Britain and other countries. For example, although there are similarities between the British and USA union movements these are largely superficial.

Unionism is much less extensive and was firmly established later in the USA than in Britain. Similarly, few European trade unions have historical roots as long as their British counterparts and in many instances their growth and developments have been much more directly influenced by political decisions than was true in the British case. It is also worth noting that in most European countries trade union movements are divided on both political and religious grounds. Initially, the Australian unions showed the greatest similarity to British trade unions, though later development has been rather different, in particular because of the way Australian trade unions have worked within a framework of compulsory arbitration.

Explanations for the growth of trade unionism and subsequent development have varied greatly. Some have centred on what has been referred to as a structuralist approach; this suggests that trade unionism is an inevitable result of certain features of, or changes in, society. Others have placed greater emphasis on the way that trade unions can be seen as a response to the motives and actions of individuals. Writers like Banks have tried to bridge such extreme viewpoints with what he terms the 'step-by-step' approach.

3 Trade unions: an uncertain outlook

BRITISH TRADE UNIONS

In the last chapter it was noted that the period from the end of the Second World War to the end of the 1970s was one of almost continuous growth for trade unions. The challenge facing students of industrial relations was to explain this growth and to pay attention to the variations in unionisation rates between industries, different workplaces, and different categories of employees. The position changed dramatically at the end of the 1970s and the future of trade unions in the UK looked less certain.

Table 3.1 shows the number of trade union members in the UK between 1979 and 1988. Over that period membership dropped substantially from 13,289,000 to 10,238,000. At the same time the proportion of the working population in membership declined from 49.9 per cent to 36.3 per cent. In part, this decline in membership and the unionisation rate can be linked to the decline in the number of people in work. When people lose their jobs they frequently resign their union membership. This does not always happen, for in some cases there are important benefits to be gained from retaining membership, especially where the union might play a key role in finding new employment (this helps to explain why some skilled workers unions, particularly in the printing industry, have a high proportion of unemployed members). Some unions also offer benefits to their members when they are unemployed and others make special arrangements for unemployed workers. However, the majority of people leave union membership when they lose their job. As a result, if union membership is shown as a percentage of those in employment rather than as a proportion of the total working population (which includes the unemployed), the decline in unionisation does not seem so dramatic; as can be seen from Table 3.1 the unionisation rate

Table 3.1 Union membership in the UK, 1979–88

Year	Number of unions	Number of members (000s)	Working population (000s)	Employees in employment (000s)	Unionisation using working population (%)	Unionisation using employees in employment (%)
1979	453	13,289	26,627	23,173	49.9	57.3
1980	438	12,947	26,839	22,991	48.2	56.3
1981	414	12,106	26,741	21,892	45.3	55.3
1982	408	11,593	26,677	21,414	43.5	54.1
1983	394	11,236	26,610	21,067	42.2	53.3
1984	375	10,994	27,265	21,238	40.3	51.8
1985	370	10,821	27,714	21,423	39.0	50.5
1986	335	10,539	27,791	21,387	37.9	49.3
1987	330	10,475	27,979	21,584	37.4	48.5
1988	314	10,238	28,211	22,226	36.3	46.1

Source: Annual Abstract of Statistics, 1990

per cent in 1987. Nevertheless, the decline in unionisation, even on this basis, is still of some importance.

The impact of the reduction in union membership can be taken a stage further by looking at figures for individual unions. Table 3.2 shows the comparable membership totals for some of the largest unions in 1979 and 1987. Only one of the unions, the Royal College of Nursing, saw an increase in membership over that period. Some unions saw a massive decline: membership of the Transport and General Workers Union declined by about 35 per cent and that of the National Union of Mineworkers by almost 44 per cent. Unions, like the Transport and General Workers, which had seen membership rising steadily over the previous decades, saw a collapse to a level marginally lower than that achieved in 1961.

More detailed evidence of the changes that took place in union membership can be seen from the Workplace Industrial Relations Survey.[1] At the time of writing data was only available for the first half of the 1980s. One of the issues which the data from this survey allowed to be addressed was the proportion of workplaces where employees were members of a trade union. Overall, there was no change between 1980 and 1984 (in each case 73 per cent of establishments reported trade union membership). However, within this overall figure there were significant variations. In particular, there was an important decline in trade union presence in private manufacturing industry

Table 3.2   Membership of selected UK trade unions, 1979–87

	Membership (000s)	
	1979	1987
Transport and General Workers Union	2,086	1,349
Amalgamated Engineering Union	1,299[1]	815
General Municipal, Boilermakers and Allied Trade Union	1,132[1]	803
Nation and Local Government Officers Association	753	750[2]
Nation Union of Public Employees	692	651
Association of Scientific, Technical and Managerial Staffs	491	390[2]
Union of Shop, Distributive and Allied Workers	470	387
Electric, Electronic, Telecommunication and Plumbing Union	444	369
National Union of Mineworkers	372	211[2]
National Union of Teachers	291	225
Confederation of Health Service Employees	213	208
Royal College of Nursing	162	258
Civil and Public Services Association	224	149[3]
National Union of Railwaymen	170	118
Iron and Steel Trades Confederation	110	44

Source: *Social Trends*, no. 19, HMSO, London, 1989, p. 179

Notes: [1]Comparable data not available owing to changes in structure/amalgamation; 1979 figures based on estimates from TUC reports.
[2]Figures relate to 1986.
[3]Membership fell by 43,000 in 1985 with the transfer of a block of members to the National Communications Union.

(in 1980, 77 per cent of establishments reported that some of their employees were members of a trade union whereas in 1984 the figure had fallen to 67 per cent) compensated for by an increase in the presence of unions in private services and a filling in of the few remaining gaps in the public sector (virtually every workplace in the public sector had trade union members in 1980 but there were some that did not and these were unionised by 1984).

Of course, stability in the proportion of establishments reporting the presence of union members does not necessarily conflict with the evidence reported earlier about the decline in the overall proportion of the workforce and employees in trade unions because reports about the presence of trade union members could conceal changes in the density of union membership within the establishment. An analysis of this matter is hampered because the data on union density from the Workplace Industrial Relations Survey is not compatible between 1980 and 1984.

The position with regard to trade union recognition is somewhat similar to that reported for the proportion of establishments where employees were members of trade unions. Overall, there was very little change in the proportion of establishments recognising trade unions between 1980 and 1984 (in fact, there was a marginal increase). However, there were significant differences within this overall trend, with a notable decrease in private manufacturing (the proportion of establishments where one or more unions were recognised dropped from 65 per cent in 1980 to 56 per cent in 1984). The decline in recognition was even greater in engineering and vehicles. The explanation for this decline, put forward by Millward and Stevens, related to the falling proportion of workplaces in manufacturing (and in engineering and vehicles in particular) with trade union members: when there were trade union members managements were no less likely to recognise unions in 1984 than they had been in 1980. Again the decline in union recognition in manufacturing establishments was compensated for by an increase in recognition in the public sector and private services.

This kind of argument could be repeated for other areas looked at by the Workplace Industrial Relations Survey relating to trade union membership. For example, in the case of the closed shop (where the survey, unlike some others,[2] showed a significant decline in the use of the closed shop) there were important differences between different sectors of industry with the most marked decline in private manufacturing industry.

The problems that trade unions in the UK have faced since the end of the 1970s have to be put in the context of the economic conditions of the time. This goes beyond the argument outlined above that with high unemployment we should expect a decline in the number of union members because most people leave their union when they lose their job. As noted, the decline in unionisation rates was marked even if only those in employment were considered. There is little doubt that harsher economic conditions have made recruitment and retention of members more difficult for unions, even when those members or potential members have been in work. In the last chapter, the 'prosperity theory' was examined and although it was not accepted as a full explanation for union growth and development, it was recognised that it pointed to issues of importance. The prosperity theory could suggest that the economic conditions of the 1980s made it more difficult for unions to persuade members and potential members that they could gain direct benefits from membership of a union. In particular, the perception that unions 'lost' a number of well publicised strikes drew into question their ability to gain higher wages and defend their members' interests.

Trade unions in the UK also faced government hostility at the same time. Government hostility towards trade unions in Britain, or towards what they would portray as the abuse of union power, has been a notable feature of the industrial relations scene since 1979. The general political stance of Conservative governments has been that the operation of free-market forces, largely unfettered by government intervention, is the best way of determining priorities and allocating resources. Trade unions, so this view would contend, often hinder the operation of free-market forces, introducing rigidities, for example into the pay structure. Trade unions have stopped wages falling and high wage levels are an important cause of unemployment. The emphasis on individual freedom within this ideology also leads to suspicion of trade unions. Individual freedom is threatened by the activities of trade unions: included in this would be the belief that the freedom of individual employees not to join a trade union is threatened by the closed shop.

The belief of the post-1979 Conservative government in Britain that trade unions, certainly trade unions in their present form, are not only a threat to individual liberty but also a threat to economic stability, led to a range of legislation which has curbed union activity. The 1980 and 1982 Employment Acts inhibited the closed shop and placed obstacles in the way of trade unions seeking to take industrial action. The 1984 Trade Union Act introduced the idea of regular secret ballots for the election of union leaders before strike action and over political funds. The 1988 Employment Act extended the provisions on ballots, established a commissioner for the rights of trade union members and stopped unions taking action against members who refused to obey a strike call or who crossed a picket line.

The post-1979 legislation is an important example of government hostility towards trade unionism as it exists in Britain today. However, government is not simply important in the way in which it can introduce legislation to curb the activities of trade unions – it is also important in the way in which it can set the 'tone' for other employers. Government can encourage employers to recognise unions, and in certain circumstances such encouragement can be important; by the same token apparent government discouragement can also be important. The attempt of the British government to withdraw the right of employees to join trade unions at GCHQ and the restriction on the bargaining rights of teachers' unions have clearly confirmed for anyone with residual doubts that the government was not convinced of the benefits of unionisation.

Alongside government hostility has been a noticeable change of attitude on the part of employers. The general acceptance of trade unions after the Second World War meant that the bitter struggles for recognition in which unions had engaged in earlier years faded from memory. At times they reappeared: the dispute at Grunwick's is the best illustration. In the 1980s not only did the number of public confrontations increase (the example of News International has already been referred to), but also, and more importantly, a number of employers developed policies which assumed the irrelevance of unions. These employers were not on the fringes of the labour market and they were not the hirers of 'cheap labour': rather, the whole emphasis was to provide a more attractive reward package and a more attractive employment setting than employees might expect elsewhere. The aim was to develop an image of a 'good employer' where employees were treated and rewarded well.

This has been accompanied by the movement towards a more flexible work organisation. In such an arrangement the barriers between different skills may be broken down, and a distinction may be drawn between 'core' and 'peripheral' staff with the former being offered higher status and greater security in return for functional flexibility. One commentator has argued that the 'Donovan-inspired priorities of the 1960s and 1970s seem less central nowadays',[3] and the focus instead is firmly on flexibility. There is some debate about how far the moves towards greater flexibility have been, and can be, taken. There have been a number of well reported moves towards the breakdown of barriers between skilled manual workers, but it would be wrong to see this as a uniform picture; such moves have been concentrated in certain sectors and little has happened that has crossed the manual/non-manual divide. It should also be recalled that in many instances moves towards greater flexibility have occurred within unionised workforces. Nevertheless, where moves occur, they pose some problems for unions. The idea of 'single status', the blurring of the distinction between worker and manager in terms of facilities and benefits, and the development of new reward packages, all sit uneasily with the traditional view of unionism. There is a degree of similarity between the kind of situation in which core workers are likely to find themselves in 'flexible work organisations' and the kind of ideology being promoted by the 'good employer' that seeks to persuade employees that unions are irrelevant.

Industries using 'new technology' provide a particularly interesting extension of this discussion. New technology (usually microelectronics is being referred to) may be seen as offering management opportunities to negotiate greater flexibility on the part of the workforce. In some cases it may be argued that increased flexibility is essential if the best use is to be made of the opportunities that the technology affords. Many of the examples of flexible working come from this sector and in many instances unionisation rates are low. However, some writers have suggested caution in over-emphasising the importance of technology in this regard. Thus, it has been argued that the 'effects of technical change upon job content are to a large extent determined by factors other than the technology itself'.[4] These other factors include the nature of the product (or service), the state of the product and labour markets, and the power and strategies of workers and management. In some cases management, rather than seizing the opportunity of maximise the changes in work organisation, may seek to minimise them. Sometimes this is to gain the cooperation of the workforce, in other instances there are technical and commercial reasons.

It is difficult at the moment to discern how strong a challenge the moves reviewed above pose. The firms being referred to are not in the majority and there may be limits to the extent to which other employers can or want to adopt the model being presented. One of the important issues then is the extent to which the employers referred to might be seen as setting a target for others. Thus:

> One possibility . . . is that the household name, nonunion firms in the UK (e.g., IBM and Marks and Spencer), have become, as a result of their reputations as 'companies of excellence', increasingly the pattern setters in terms of employment practices and arrangements: they have tended, in other words, to replace the unionised 'pace setters' of the 1970s (e.g., ICI), in terms of providing the best practice model to emulate.[5]

Reviewing a number of studies in this area Beaumont was able to suggest that a relatively high proportion of recently established firms are non-union. These were not, though, he said, the USA-owned, high technology companies frequently talked about, but British-owned, single, independent establishments of relatively small size. In such establishments employee relations were seen by the founders as involving good informal communications and flexible working practices with little need for technical advice or the emulation of practices in larger establishments.

Specifically we found relatively little evidence of an overlap between the working practices of US and British-owned nonunion establishments. Accordingly, if the former, as well as the household name nonunion firms in the UK, are acting as opinion leaders it is not among these particular establishments that they are exerting an influence at least not at this initial start-up stage.[6]

At the same time as unions in the UK were facing adverse economic conditions and hostility from government and employers they were having to deal with changes in the structure of employment which served to reinforce their difficulties. There have always been variations in unionisation between industries. The decline in manual work and the expansion of white collar work posed problems long before the 1980s, as did the decline in employment opportunities in some of the traditional heavily unionised industries. These trends continued in the 1980s, in some instances with added impetus because of the downturn in economic conditions. Between 1976 and 1986 employment in metal goods and metal engineering declined by 493,000, in vehicle and transport equipment by 322,000, in metal and mineral products by 299,000, in transport by 123,000, and in energy and water by 61,000. All of these industries were relatively highly unionised: in the order in which they have been listed, the unionisation rates were 55 per cent, 81 per cent, 68 per cent, 85 per cent and 88 per cent. The contrast is with industries like banking, insurance and finance, where employment increased by 709,000; in business services where it increased by 383,000; in hotels and catering, where it increased by 211,000; and in wholesale distribution where it increased by 162,000. Unionisation rates in those industries (again in the order in which they have been listed) were 43 per cent, 21 per cent, 21 per cent and 32 per cent.

The analysis from the Workplace Industrial Relations Survey takes this discussion a stage further. It puts together the impact of changes in the structure of employment with the size of the establishment. Thus, when looking at the proportion of workplaces reporting that employees were members of a union, Millward and Stevens suggested that the main reason for the decline in the presence of unions in private manufacturing was the closure of a number of large plants that had strong union traditions. When looking at union density they noted that the firms in the private sector that contracted substantially between 1980 and 1984 were the ones with the highest union densities. This led Millward and Stevens to conclude that 'the greater loss of employment by large, highly unionised workplaces is a major factor behind the contraction of trade union membership since the end of the 1970s'.[7]

Other changes were taking place to the structure of employment. These include, an increase in the proportion of the workforce in part-time employment (from 17 per cent in 1981 to 23 per cent in 1986), an increase in the female labour force (in 1979 the civilian labour force was composed of 15.6 million males and 10.4 million females but by 1986 the figures had changed to 15.5 million males and 11.2 million females) and an increase in the number of people who were self-employed (from 1.9 million in 1979 to 2.6 million in 1986).

Many of these changes in the structure of employment overlap and are linked. For example, women are heavily represented amongst part-time workers and are heavily represented in the service sector. At the same time, a large proportion of the self-employed are engaged in activity in the service sector. In all of these instances unions traditionally have had difficulty in recruiting (the difficulty in recruiting has been particularly marked amongst part-time female employees), and, taken together with the attitudes of employers and government and the adverse economic circumstances, they give an indication of some of the difficulties that unions face.

In the last chapter, the discussion of explanations for the growth and development of trade unions drew attention to a number of the factors that have been listed. Of course, because the time period being discussed was different, the details were not the same. Nevertheless, consideration of issues like economic conditions, government policy and the attitude of employers all featured in the earlier discussion. The review of the impact of industrialisation has links with the consideration of changes in the structure of employment. The argument was put forward, however, that the consideration of such structural factors, the environment in which unions have to operate, was important but not sufficient. Consideration also needed to be given to the way that unions and their leaders reacted to such conditions. The same is true when looking at the problems facing unions in the 1980s. Unions and their leaders have had some freedom for manoeuvre on this matter. In practice, the debates over how they should react are worth reviewing in a little detail, precisely because they illustrate that unions and their leaders had choices to make.

THE UNION RESPONSE

Some unions took the developments of the 1980s as an indication that if they were to survive and prosper, they had to change. For example, they had to be willing to meet the demands of employers for single union agreements, for no-strike agreements, and the like. They also had to be more relevant to employees who were as concerned about profit-sharing deals and employee participation as they were about basic wage rates. In Britain the EETPU is the union most associated with this approach though others, like the AEU and the GMBTU, have also made moves in the same direction in some instances. The most newsworthy agreements have been reached on 'greenfield sites'. A recent report on such agreements listed the EETPU's agreement with Toshiba over its Plymouth site; the same union's agreement with Inmos at Newport, Sanyo at Lowestoft and BICC Coming Glass at Deeside; and the AEU and GMBTU's agreements with Findus for its Newcastle plant. It also referred to the TGWU's agreement with Continental Can at Wrexham which:

> gives it sole recognition and gives all staff salaried status the same pension, sickness and holiday schemes, and a common dining room and car park, in return for complete flexibility in working practices which are aimed at ruling out 'who-does-what' disputes.[8]

Probably the most widely discussed of such agreements, though, is that negotiated by the AUEW at the Nissan plant in the North East. The main provisions of this agreement were:

> recognition of a single union, the AUEW, for all staff up to and including the level of senior engineer; a complex procedure agreement involving ACAS and pendulum arbitration as its final stages; complete flexibility and mobility of labour, with provision for necessary training; an expanded role for supervisors, and for only two job descriptions for manual staff-technician and manufacturing staff; and common conditions for all staff, including monthly payment, common hours of work and shift and overtime premia, and no clocking on.[9]

In a speech to the 1984 Trades Union Congress an EEPTU delegate outlined the basis of the strategy being followed in these kinds of agreements:

> In my view – and some may disagree – industrial relations is not about waging some ideological battle but about improving the quality of the working life of the members whom we represent. These agreements, first of all, provide for the egalitarian factory, with everyone from the managing director to the janitor enjoying the same conditions of employment. They provide for an elected forum that gives the workers a real and genuine say in how the

company is run. They provide, in exchange for the flexibility the worker has to give, the right of every worker to be trained for additional skills and the company are obliged to train them. Of course, they also provide for a new form of arbitration, which is widely used in America and Canada, to settle differences that cannot be resolved by negotiation. This is a mechanism, unlike a strike, that inflicts no damage on either party, yet it guarantees the workers that if they have a sound and meritorious case they are going to win that disagreement, irrespective of the bargaining power the economy might impose upon them.[10]

The same speaker rejected the description of 'no strike agreements' for such deals. He argued that such a description was misleading because no voluntary agreement can deprive a worker of the right to strike and because such a label implies that workers were being denied the right to combat the authority of the employer. The central aim behind these deals, it was suggested, was to enhance the individual and collective rights of the workers concerned. It was management, not workers, from this point of view, who were really making the concessions, and that was why many managements have rejected such deals when they have been offered:

> People may jeer but it is rather strange, you know: I offered this agreement to GEC and to Thorn EMI in two plants where we have sole bargaining rights and these two companies have emphatically turned it down. They are typical of the vast majority of British employers. The reason they have turned it down is that they have not been prepared to dilute, let alone surrender, the control that they have over these two companies, which is what this agreement would require of them.[11]

The point being made here, that single-union, flexible-working, no-strike agreements demand changes on the part of management, is worth emphasising. Atkinson, in his description of the 'flexible firm',[12] argues that firms have to accept the costs of flexiblity. These costs include direct economic ones, such as the cost of re-training, and less direct, but still important ones, like the breaking down of status barriers.

The approach of unions, like the EEPTU in Britain, though, has resulted in enormous controversy. At one level there is dispute over the balance of advantage in such agreements. The debate here in some ways mirrors that over productivity deals in the 1960s, when some union leaders, and commentators, argued that unions who entered such agreements were giving up basic rights in return for short-term financial gain. There is also a dispute over how many workers can really benefit from the kind of agreements that the EEPTU has negotiated. The 'flexible firm' may offer its 'core groups' greater security but it can also mean less security for 'peripheral' groups. The increasing use of short-term contracts, casual employment and subcontracting are examples of such moves. In this context it is interesting to note Atkinson's comment that the implication of what he terms 'the flexible firm', is that 'an individual's pay, security and career opportunities will increasingly be secure at the expense of the employment conditions of others, often women, more of whom will find themselves permanently in dead-end, insecure and low paid jobs'. At a more fundamental level, the charge has been laid that by reaching no-strike, flexible working agreements, unions are changing the nature of trade unionism. It is, the critics argue, moving more towards 'slick professional, non-party political trade unionism'. It is unionism in which the employers have a dominant role. Under this system it is not 'who the workers want to represent them but who the employers want to represent the workers.'[13]

An example of this latter kind of criticism was given in the debate which has already been referred to at the 1984 Trades Union Congress. Rodney Bickerstaffe, speaking for the National Union of Public Employees, argued that:

those unionists at Hitachi and other companies in the country who are signing away the right to strike are undermining my members and essential workers throughout the country.

He went on to suggest that the government saw the activities of unions like the EEPTU as a way of undermining 'real' trade unions and 'real' trade unionism.

If the government cannot ban unions, you know what they will do? They will initiate and encourage sweetheart unions and sweetheart deals. We have already got them. We have them in education, we have them on the railways, we have them in the health service. We have a union called 'NICE' in the health service. It does not take industrial action. It is a 'good' union.[14]

The other strategy that unions can adopt to try to meet the challenge they face (it must be noted that the two strategies are not necessarily mutually exclusive, though at their extremes they represent different views about the nature of the union movement and its future), is to examine ways of improving the performance and attractiveness of unions without a fundamental change in their role or objectives. The strategy document drawn up by the TUC Finance and General Purpose Committee, and eventually presented to the 1984 Annual Congress was a recognition of the problems facing trade unions in Britain (the defeat of the Labour Party in the 1983 General Election was also a major blow to the unions and a spur to action), and a series of proposals about how progress might be made. The resolution presented to Congress highlighted the need for unions to cooperate more closely together. The mover of the resolution spoke of the 'self-inflicted wounds' which were the result of 'competitive trade unionism' and argued for more centrally provided services, particularly in the area of new technology. The resolution itself said:

> Congress additionally expresses its concern that there is a considerable duplication of essential, expensive membership services, when a pooling of resources and expertise would be to the advantage of trade union membership.[15]

One of the most important issues highlighted, though, was the need for improved communications between union leaders and members:

> Above all, there is one specific area where we must all be greatly concerned to improve our performance and that is in communications, communications from ourselves to our members and from our members to the leadership of the movement at all levels.[16]

The report to the 1985 Annual Congress highlighted the moves that were subsequently made under a number of headings: union communications; union membership and organisation; union finance and administration; and new technology and union services. In examining how the strategy might be furthered in the future, however, the report emphasised the limitations of the TUC's role:

> while the TUC will accept its responsibility for helping to ensure that steady progress is made, it will be for each union to determine its own strategy for the 1990s. The TUC's key role must continue to be that of providing opportunities for unions to share their experiences in the difficult task of meeting the organisational, administrative and financial requirements for unions to flourish in the future.[17]

The initiative taken by the TUC through the strategy document led to debate within unions about the approach being adopted. The claim was made that too much ground was being given away and that it was a threat to the traditional role of trade unions. Some saw the approach as focusing on the wrong problems. In its confidential response to the TUC, the TGWU argued that the main problem lay not with the unions, but with the environment in which they had to operate:

> The introduction of the document presupposes that there is a crisis (or at least serious problems) in the union movement because of declining membership, reduced bargaining power, a poor public image and status, the widening gap between union and individual members, and a poor relationship with the Government. Some of this is true, some is exaggerated, but whatever the case, it should be made crystal clear that the cause of these problems is not the internal structure of trade unions. It is the result of the economic slump and the hostility of the Government.[18]

Others were concerned that too little was said about the commitments to and acceptance of the link with the Labour Party. Media discussions of the 'new realism' within the trade union movement did not help. However, Bassett argued that even unions which rejected the 'new realism' took up some of the issues highlighted in the TUC strategy document. Thus, he said that though NUPE leadership were 'vociferous opponents of new realism', which was seen as 'collaboration with a hated Government', they picked up its principal strands of thoughts, particularly on the need for greater membership involvement.

This debate within the trade union movement over how to react to the challenges faced, while a critical illustration of the fact that there are choices, not simply constraints, also has particular relevance, for it led to a decision by the Trades Union Congress to expel one of its members, the EEPTU. Unions have been expelled from the TUC before, and this has not had any long-lasting impact on the unity of the movement. However, this expulsion raises more problems. It opens the door to recruitment battles, and, with the Union of Democratic Mineworkers also outside the TUC, raises the prospect of a focus being developed for an alternative central organisation. At the time of writing it is unclear whether or not this possibility will be realised but if it were, then it could be of major importance for the trade union movement in the UK.

One of the other reactions on the part of unions for the challenges they face, has been to look once again towards amalgamation. Major changes have taken place in the white collar sector with the formation of the Manufacturing Science and Finance union from TASS and APEX (TASS itself amalgamated earlier with a number of smaller unions like the Tobacco Workers Union and the Pattern Makers and Sheet Metal Workers). In the printing industry, SOGAT 82 was formed through amalgamation and further rationalisation is currently proposed for unions in that industry. A number of general unions gained from amalgamation with smaller specialist unions. Discussions are also being held about an amalgamation between the Transport and General Workers Union and the National Union of Mineworkers and between the National Union of Seamen and the National Union of Railwaymen.

TRADE UNIONS IN OTHER COUNTRIES

The problems facing the British trade union movement are by no means unique. The most acute problems in another Western nation are probably being felt in the USA. The union movement in that country has never been able to extend membership to the same proportion achieved in other Western countries, and so it was particularly vulnerable to challenge in the 1980s. Union membership in the USA declined from 28.9 per cent in 1975 to 16.8 per cent in 1988. In some industries trade unions retained strength; for example, in transport and public utilities membership stood at 33.1 per cent of wage and salary earners in 1988, and the comparable figure for government service was 36.7 per cent. However, the corollary is that they became very weak in others: in 1985 unionisation rates were 2.6 per cent in finance, insurance and real estate, 6.7 per cent in wholesale and retail trades and only 18.7 per cent in mining.

The environment in which USA unions had to operate in the 1980s had many parallels with that facing unions in the UK. Economic conditions were difficult, particularly in the early 1980s: for example, the unemployment rate rose from 5.8 per cent in 1979 to 9.7 per cent in 1982. It should be noted, though that this rise was less dramatic than occurred in the UK and the subsequent recovery of unemployment rates occurred faster. Parallels can also be drawn in the political environment. The Reagan administration clearly signalled its suspicion of trade unions. The confrontation between the government and the air-traffic controllers where the government was willing to dismiss strikers *en masse* was seen as a clear indication of its attitude. In Chapter 1 it was noted that employers in the USA used the Human Resources Management movement to challenge trade unions, and de-recognition ballots increased as employers used the legal provisions that had earlier been a mechanism for unions to gain rights to enforce ballots against them. More generally, the changes in the structure of industry that caused problems for unions in the UK were well advanced in the USA at the same time. The proportion of white collar employees and the percentage engaged in service sector industries were all higher in the USA than in the UK.

Similar difficulties can be noted in Japan. Although unemployment rates did not rise as fast in Japan in the late 1970s and early 1980s as they did in most other Western nations (the unemployment rate reached 2 per cent by 1977 and rose to 2.8 per cent in 1986, but such totals are small by comparison with those in other countries, even allowing for some hidden unemployment), Japan was not immune from the economic effects of the recession that followed the oil crisis. Growth rates declined from the double figures of the late 1960s and early 1970s to 4 or 5 per cent in the mid-1970s and this led to some major changes. Between 1973 and 1978, about 1 million, or 10 per cent, of the labour force in manufacturing was lost. More generally, pressure was put on the permanent system of employment. Traditionally, about a third of the Japanese workforce has been employed under this system, and it has been particularly important for males and those working in large firms. In the 1970s, some employers were forced to reduce their 'permanent' workforce through inter-firm transfers, delayed recruitment and early retirement. Cole records that to 'keep the discharges from becoming a major social problem, the government took the new step of providing subsidies to encourage them to hold on to excess labor'. As a result, the permanent system of employment has not been destroyed, even though it has been shaken a little.

> In short, a variety of mechanisms developed, all of which served to preserve the core of permanent employees. There was some whittling down of this core in severely hit industries, but for the most part large-scale employers did manage to save the jobs of regular male employees.[19]

The future is more difficult to predict, especially whether the permanent system of employment could survive another economic crisis.

At the same time as Japan has been dealing with these economic problems, changes have been continuing to the structure of employment. The decline in manufacturing industry has already been noted. Over the same period, the service sector expanded. Whereas in 1963 it accounted for 42 per cent of civilian employment, and 49 per cent by 1973, by 1983 it had risen to 56 per cent. This change in the structure of employment had a direct effect on unionisation. The manufacturing sector is the most highly unionised and, although some parts of the service sector have higher unionisation rates than in some other countries, much of the service sector is composed of relatively small firms where unions find it difficult to organise.

The combination of difficult economic circumstances and further changes in the structure of employment meant a difficult environment for trade unions. Kuwahara has claimed that against this background 'many companies have adopted a tougher stance towards unions, claiming public support for such policies'.[20] Employees also seem to have become more concerned with the competitive positions of their companies, and in some cases this appears to have weakened their support for trade unions. Overall, unionisation rates have declined. In 1987, there were 12,272,000 union members, representing 27.6 per cent of the workforce. In 1970 over 35 per cent of the workforce were in trade unions.

Of course, the economic difficulties facing Japan in the 1970s and 1980s need to be put into context. As has been noted, the unemployment rate in Japan has been low compared to that of most other Western nations, and Japan has been popularly viewed as one of the most successful economies. Again, popularly, part of its success has often been put down to its cooperative industrial relations system and attempts have been made to replicate aspects of that system elsewhere. In Britain, replication has been encouraged in part as the result of investment by Japanese multinationals. In other parts of South-East Asia government direction has encouraged moves towards aspects of the Japanese system, particularly enterprise unions. In Singapore a report of a committee on productivity by the National Productivity Board in 1981 recommended the promotion of 'house unions'. Leggett draws direct links between 'house' and 'enterprise' unions. 'House unions', he said, 'had been rationalised from Japanese experience was more conducive to harmony at work and fostered company loyalty, and, thereby, increased productivity, profits and wages more than did craft, occupational or industrial unions'.[21] Thirteen new house or enterprise unions were promoted by the main national trade union confederation, the NTUC, between 1981 and 1984. Leggett noted that figures for mid-1984 from the Ministry of Labour, showed that 28 enterprise unions organised 20 per cent of NTUC affiliates. Blum and Patarapanich argue that there is 'little evidence that house unionism has resulted in any generally marked enthusiasm among workers', or that it 'is helping Singapore's economy or improving workers' wellbeing',[22] though they were writing in the mid-1980s when the experience with house/enterprise unions was limited.

In Malaysia, similar moves have been made towards house/enterprise unions. O'Brien notes[23] how from the early 1980s, the Malaysian government started to look East to the Japanese model of industrial relations. The encouragement of house/enterprise unions was part of this movement and a substantial emphasis on such unions was quickly established with over a quarter of all registered union members being members of house/enterprise unions.

The pattern of decline found in the UK, USA and Japan in recent years is repeated in a number of other countries. However, it is by no means typical of all industrialised capitalist countries. Table 3.3 shows unionisation rates in 17 advanced capitalist countries, noting changes between 1979 and 1985. Whilst there was a decline in 7 countries, there was an increase in 8 and no movement in another 2.

The position of Canada is particularly interesting, not simply because union membership in absolute terms, and as a proportion of employees in employment, increased, but also because it provides a fascinating contrast with the position in the USA. Traditionally, the economies of Canada and the USA have been strongly linked and such links have extended to the union movements. In the 1970s about half of all union members in Canada were in 'international'

Table 3.3 Trade union density in advanced capitalist countries

Country	Density 1979 (%)	Density 1985 (%)	Change 1979–85 (% points)
Denmark	86	98	+12
Belgium	77	84	+7
Sweden	89	95	+6
Ireland	49	51	+2
Austria	59	61	+2
Norway	60	61	+1
Canada	36	37	+1
Finland	84	85	+1
West Germany	42	42	0
France	28	28	0
Switzerland	36	35	−1
Australia	58	57	−1
Japan	32	29	−3
Italy	51	45	−6
Netherlands	43	37	−6
United Kingdom	58	52	−6
USA	25	18	−7

Source: J. Kelly, *Trade Unions and Socialist Politics* (Verso, London, 1988), p. 269

unions, which meant that the unions operated in both Canada and the USA. In some cases, then, unions with headquarters in the USA were operating in two different environments. In one, the USA, union membership was declining, but in the other, Canada, union membership was increasing.

A number of factors help to explain the growth of unions in Canada. The first is that although 'international' unions traditionally have played a dominant role in Canada, this role has been declining. The 'Canadianisation' of unions has been a significant development and has proved an advantage for recruitment. The proportion of Canadian trade unionists in international unions fell from 53.2 per cent in 1975, to 39.4 per cent in 1985. Interestingly the reason for this change has not been a decline in the membership of international unions, but an increase of about 1 million in the membership of Canadian unions. The second factor that needs to be taken into account is the increasing penetration of unions in the public sector. Unionisation in the private sector has been broadly maintained, although it has been subject to challenge, particularly in the construction industry. The third factor is that the Canadian union movement has benefited from changes in legislation and a greater willingness on the part of authorities to enforce pro-union legislation. Gunderson and Meltz have drawn particular attention to the importance of provincial legislation in this context.

> In the case of Canada, the responsibility for labor relations rests with the provinces. Fewer than ten per cent of workers are covered by Federal legislation. Prior to the period of time under consideration (1975–1985), three jurisdictions granted their public employees the right to organise and strike: Saskatchewan in 1944; Quebec in 1964; and the Federal government in 1967. In 1973, four more provinces passed similar legislation. In 1975, schoolteachers in Ontario were given the right to strike, in fact, full-time teachers were required to belong to one of the various teachers' associations.[24]

Other legislation gave some protection for unions, like the anti-strikebreaking laws in Quebec and Ontario, and the check-off arrangements for collecting union subscriptions in British Columbia, Saskatchewan, Manitoba, Ontario and Quebec. Two important court cases showed how labour legislation could be used to favour unions when 'unfair practices' by companies resulted in substantial monetary settlements.[25]

THE DISORGANISATION OF CAPITALISM

The experience of unions in the late 1970s and 1980s has excited considerable interest and debate. One of the most valuable contributions to this debate has been conducted under the heading of the disorganisation of capitalism. It has been particularly valuable because it has sought to indentify changes in industrial society which might be common and at the same time identify different responses to them.

Lash and Urry[26] identified three different phases of capitalist development: liberal, organised and disorganised. For these purposes the critical distinction is between organised and disorganised capitalism. Organised capitalism can be taken to have begun in most Western nations in the late nineteenth century. According to Kocka it consisted of a number of interrelated features, including the concentration of capital, the separation of ownership from control, an increasing role for the state, and the 'growth of collective organizations in the labour market, particularly of regionally and then nationally organized trade unions and of employers' associations, nationally organized professions etc.'.[27] Disorganised capitalism is a characteristic of Western societies from the 1960s onwards. Again there are a number of key features which include the growth of world markets, a continued expansion of white collar workers, a decline in the importance of manufacturing and extractive industries, a decline in the average size of plants, a decline in the salience and class character of political parties, the growth of new social movements (such as students', anti-nuclear, ecological and women's movements) which draw energy away from class politics, and a decline 'in the importance and effectiveness of national level collective bargaining procedures in industrial relations'.[28]

An understanding of the problems facing trade unions in the 1980s, so the argument would proceed, has to take account of the range of factors listed above as distinguishing disorganised capitalism. Particular emphasis might be placed on the decline in the importance of 'class politics'. Lash and Urry saw a decline in the collective identity of the working class arguing that there is 'virtually no unified working class' able to bargain with capital and the state. This arose from a number of developments but emphasis might be placed on the split between workers in the private export-oriented sector and those in the public sector, with the former displaying increased hostility to public expenditure.

Lash and Urry's study led them to look at experience of labour in five different Western nations. They argued that the 'politics of British industrial relations has disorganized sooner, more abruptly and more profoundly than in other European nations'.[29] This was in part because the 'second shop stewards' movement' of the 1960s led to a breakdown of the old arrangements for collective bargaining and partly because of the failure of the attempt of the Labour government in the 1970s to introduce closer relationships between the state and the unions (neo-corporatism) – a failure which itself can be partly explained by the fact that it was introduced at a time 'when its preconditions (especially the existence of an importantly "national" economy and of centralised trade unions) were clearly being undermined'.[30] When the Conservative government gained power in the late 1970s it was able to take advantage of, and widen, the splits in the labour movement. It attacked the national unions and its legislation made national industrial action much more difficult.

> Central to post-1979 Conservative strategy have been the Employment acts of 1980, 1982 and 1984. These were rather unusual in comparison with industrial relations legislation in the other countries being discussed here in that they did *not* attempt to control the shopfloor through the extension of national union power with respect to the workplace. Instead national unions and the labour movement in general were the object of attack. The legislation was characteristically disorganized capitalist. The provisions on secondary picketing in the 1980 Act would tend to decentralize conflicts to the plant level, although this legislation was used in a rather different (and devious) way by Rupert Murdoch against the print unions in January 1987. The balloting provisions of 1984 were intended to have a similar atomizing function.[31]

The position of labour in some of the other countries looked at by Lash and Urry has echoes of that in Britain. The USA and France were said, like Britain, to have union densities that seemed to have entered into secular decline. Other countries, in particular West Germany and Sweden, seemed to show a different position. In West Germany union density was on the increase and in Sweden the figures had held constant. In both of those countries apparently successful attempts had been made to maintain unity in the trade union movement.

One of the explanations for the differences observed was that if labour is an important actor in organised capitalism it is able to shape the development of disorganised capitalism and therefore remain an important actor. This would seem to have some appeal if one compares, say, Sweden to the USA. However, the case of Britain is more difficult to fit into this model. Labour was an important actor in organised capitalism but seemed to lose its place in disorganised capitalism.

Thus Britain's working class as a collective actor ought to bear more similarities with the German and Swedish cases than with the American and Japanese cases – that is, it ought to wield considerable resources in the era of a disorganizing capitalism. Yet if we look in 1987 at membership levels, results of industrial conflicts, a number of indices of shop floor power and the content of flexibility agreements, British labour seems only to have taken a beating, and capital (with of course enormous doses of aid from the state – consider the miners' strike of 1984–5 and Wapping, for example) has almost solely determined the course of the new reconstruction.[32]

According to Lash and Urry it is not sufficient simply to look at the strength of labour in the organised phase and transpose this to the disorganised phase. The strategies that labour adopts can also be important. In the case of the British labour movement three factors are highlighted. First, it is suggested that British unions have adopted a blanket rejection of moves to introduce labour flexibility and therefore left employers to take the initiative, whereas in Germany and Sweden trade unions have taken a role in the initiation of flexibility in the workplace with the result that they have been able to exercise some control over it. Second, British unions, unlike their German and Swedish counterparts, have ignored moves to increase participation in the workplace, with the result that only employers are making use of them. Third, labour market dualism (splits between the private export-oriented and the public sectors) does not have to lead to labour movement dualism, but in Britain seems to be doing so.

The account of Lash and Urry has echoes of the work of Muller-Jentsch[33] and Touraine[34]. However, some of its assumptions are open to challenge. Kelly[35] notes a number of criticisms. For example, he points out that many of the factors that were supposed to herald the decline of class politics today were also present in the 1930s.

In the 1930s Depression, the traditional heartlands of the industrial working class in steel, coal, textiles and shipbuilding, went into major decline; new industries sprang up in the Midlands and the South, many on greenfield sites with unorganised labour forces; craft or batch production was giving way to the mass production of consumer durables; population was moving from the depressed periphery of Britain into the boom towns of the Midlands and the South; workers were increasingly moving into new suburban estates; some employers were attempting to consolidate new patterns of industrial relations through national bargaining; and trade unions faced the daunting task of organising new groups of semiskilled production workers in towns and cities where the labour movement had traditionally been weak.[36]

In practice, the negative effects of the 1930s did not herald a long-term decline but were followed by a period of growth for the union movement. This would suggest, so Kelly argues, that the problems of the 1980s might also be overcome.

Greenfield sites and green labour forces do not remain green for ever, and unless it can be shown that there is something qualitatively different about the new manufacturing plants of the 1970s and 1980s (and Lash and Urry have not shown this), there is every reason to believe that in time these new facilities too will be organised by trade unions.[37]

Further, Kelly argues that service sector workers can be organised. Increasingly, service sector employment is being concentrated in large firms where unions traditionally have found recruitment easier.

Kelly's criticisms have some force but may be based on too harsh an interpretation of Lash and Urry's work. In their book Lash and Urry were attempting to explain what had happened and clearly pointed to some of the dangers they saw for the British union movement. They saw choices for the union movement and they saw strategy as important. They did not, therefore, adopt a deterministic stance. Their examples from Sweden and Germany illustrated that union movements did not inevitably face decline. They emphasised that they distanced themselves from the 'farwell to the proletariat' line of argument. One of the differences, however, may be that Lash and Urry see the need for the unions to adopt strategies which Kelly sees as both unnecessary and undesirable.

SUMMARY

The decline in union membership in the UK in the 1980s occurred against a background of changed economic conditions, a changed industrial structure, and a less positive attitude towards trade unions on the part of government and employers. In other countries a similar decline in union membership can be noted but there are examples where this has not been the case. The disorganisation of capitalism thesis is an attempt to explain different trends in union membership and to put the discussion into the context of broader developments in advanced industrial societies.

4 Trade unions: aims, objectives, and government

AIMS AND OBJECTIVES OF BRITISH TRADE UNIONS

The 1913 Trade Union Act defined a trade union in the UK in the following way:

> The expression 'trade union' . . . means any combination whether temporary or permanent, the principal objects of which under its constitution are . . . the regulation of the relations between workmen and masters, or between workmen and workmen or between masters and masters, or the imposing of restrictive conditions on the conduct of any trade or business and also the provision of benefits to members.[1]

Such a definition, however, is not entirely satisfactory. Under its terms many employers' associations could and did register as 'trade unions'. While the legal desirability of such a situation may be debated, it is clearly important for students of industrial relations to be able to distinguish between trade unions and employers' associations.

An alternative definition of a trade union is that provided by the Webbs:

> A Trade Union, as we understand the term, is a continuous association of wage-earners for the purpose of maintaining or improving the conditions of their working lives.[2]

This definition enables one to distinguish a trade union from an employers' association. It also expresses what many people feel is the central purpose of a trade union. It does not, however, cover all of the objectives of British trade unions.

The majority of British trade unions, for example, also have political objectives. They have sought to change society as a whole and have found it impossible to separate the industrial from the political. On occasions they have tried to pursue their political aims directly. In the early part of the twentieth century the views of the syndicalists gained sway, a view that syndicates, workplace based trade unions, could themselves initiate and form the basis for revolutionary social change. In 1910 Tom Mann, a leading trade unionist, started a monthly journal, *The Industrial Syndicalist*, and the Industrial Syndicalist Education League. Later the ideas of guild socialism, a 'milder' version of syndicalism that placed less emphasis on the role of direct action by workers and placed more constraints on the freedom of workers when controlling their own industries, gained in popularity. The appeal of such ideas started to wane in the 1920s, and although they have re-emerged at times, particularly in the 1960s, the view that trade unions should pursue their political aims directly, the view that they themselves should be directly the main vehicle for political change, has not gained majority support.

In the main, British trade unions, rather than trying to pursue political objectives directly, have sought to pursue them through an associated political party, the Labour Party. Table 4.1 shows the number of Labour Party Members of Parliament sponsored by trade unions between 1970 and 1987. From this table it can be seen that in 1987, 139 of the successful Labour Party candidates were trade union sponsored. The unions also affiliate members to the Labour Party, contribute to finances and, at the time of writing, controlled a large proportion of the vote at annual conferences through the block vote system.

Virtually all trade unions, as well as aiming to bargain on behalf of members and having political objectives, also aim to provide a variety of friendly society benefits for their members (about 20 per cent of all the expenditure of trade unions is on friendly society benefits). Again, many of the larger trade unions aim to provide educational facilities for their members, though, as Smith notes, 'there is a danger that union education will become a casualty of the financial pressures affecting unions as it did in the 1920s'.[3] Most unions, individually, and collectively through the TUC, also aim to represent their members in discussions with government (both central and local) and present their members' case to inquiries, commissions and the like.

Another indication of the breadth of the objectives of British trade unions can be gained by looking at the aims expressed in their rule books and constitutions. For example, the National Union of Mineworkers includes amongst its objectives the presentation of:

evidence and information to Government, Parliament, Municipal, Local Government, Official and other Commissions, Committees and bodies of Enquiry or Investigation or authorities [and the] establishment of Public ownership and Control of the mining industry.[4]

Table 4.1 Trade union sponsored Labour Party Members of Parliament

	1970	1974 February	1974 October	1979	1983	1987
Amalgamated Union of Engineering Workers'	17	22	21	21	17	17[†]
Transport and General Workers' Union	19	23	22	20	25	33
National Union of Mineworkers	20	18	18	16	14	13
Association of Scientific, Technical and Managerial Staffs	7	9	12	8	10	8
General Municipal Boilermakers and Allied Trades Union	12	13	13	14	11	11
National Union of Railwaymen	5	6	6	12	10	8
National Union of Public Employees	6	6	6	7	4	9
Union of Shop, Distributive and Allied Workers	7	6	5	5	2	8
Association of Professional, Executive, Clerical and Computer Staff	3	6	6	5	3	3
Transport Salaried Staffs Association	4	3	3	3	*	2
Union of Post Office Workers	1	2	2	2	*	1[‡]
Electrical, Electronic and Telecommunications, and Plumbing Trades Union	3	3	3	4	3	2
Union of Construction Allied Trades and Technicians	2	2	3	2	1	1
Post Office Engineering Union	1	2	2	2	3	2[§]
Iron and Steel Trades Confederation	2	2	2	2	1	1
Other Unions	5	4	5	10	11	20
Total	114	127	129	133	115	139

Sources: D. Butler, D. Kavanagh, *The British General Election of February 1974* (Macmillan, London, 1974); *The British General Election of October 1974* (Macmillan, London, 1975); *The British General Election of 1979* (Macmillan, London, 1980); *The British General Election of 1983* (Macmillan, London, 1984); *The British General Election of 1987* (Macmillan, London, 1988)

Notes: *Not separately identified in 1983; [†]In 1987, AEU 12, TASS 5; [‡]Union of Construction Workers in 1987; [§]In 1987, National Communications Unions.

Other unions stress the importance of the provision of benefits for their members. The Transport and General Workers' Union, for example, aims to assist members by providing cash benefits 'in times of dispute, victimisation, sickness and accident',[5] and legal aid. Others have put forward broader political aims, like extending old age pensions, and free state education, primary, secondary and further.[6]

Some commentators in looking at this range of objectives have suggested that a distinction between what they have called 'welfare' and 'business' unionism might be helpful. The former term implies that while trade unions are interested in industrial matters relating directly to their membership, this is not their sole concern: they are also a pressure group and a 'cause movement' with wider aims and aspirations. Emphasis should be placed on 'wider' in this phrase, because reference is being made to general political aspirations, for higher old age pensions, free education and the like referred to earlier, rather than a more proximate objective such as the nationalisation of coal mines, as in the case of the National Union of Mineworkers. Business unionism, on the other hand, implies that the objectives of unions are much more restricted: they concentrate on industrial matters and show an interest in political matters only when they are of direct relevance to their members.

If this distinction is accepted for the moment, then British trade unions would be classified as 'welfare unions'. It is not only, of course, because of the aspirations of individual unions that one would make this claim, but also because of the broad range of interests of the trade union movement in general in Britain.

However, a note of caution needs to be drawn before accepting this distinction. How should one determine the aims and objectives of trade unions: should we refer as we have to rule books and to the action of unions (in supporting a political party), or should we refer to the aims and aspirations as described by union leaders and members? In this context, it is important to recognise that many officials and members of British unions stress the importance of 'welfare objectives' far less than the rule books. For example, in their survey of union officials, Clegg, Killick and Adams[7] noted that officers gave a low priority to political objectives, even though such objectives were given high priority by most of the rule books concerned. Similarly, Goldthorpe *et al.* argued that the majority of the affluent workers they interviewed adopted an instrumental orientation towards trade unionism. Thus, they said: 'the significance which unionism has for these workers is largely confined to issues arising in their employment which are economic in nature and local in their scope and origins'.[8]

The only exceptions they noted were the craftsmen and they argued that even though craftsmen seemed to approve of the wider aims of the trade union movement the 'immediate questions of wages and conditions of service'[9] were of prime concern. Nevertheless, the distinction between welfare and business unionism does have some value, if only because it enables one to stress the variety of approaches taken by trade unions towards political matters, and in the case of British unions, that political objectives are on the agenda, even if they are not given the same value by all participants.[10]

AIMS AND OBJECTIVES OF TRADE UNIONS IN OTHER COUNTRIES

Poole[11] has attempted to classify trade unions in different countries according to what he terms their 'strategic objectives'. Any such classification is bound to face problems, but Poole's at least allows one to start looking at this matter in a systematic fashion. Three categories are put forward: trade unionism under collective bargaining; disjunctive-type unions with political, religious or nationalistic objectives; and trade unionism under socialism.

Trade unions seek to achieve their principle objectives through collective bargaining when they emphasise industrial purposes. They seek to improve the terms and conditions of their members primarily (though not exclusively) through negotiating with employers rather than, say, through political action. Such an approach is typical amongst most Western industrialised nations from Scandinavia, to most of Western Europe (including the UK), to North America, to Australia and Japan. Poole excludes France and Italy from this list and the reason for their exclusion will be referred to later.

The argument that there is a degree of common purpose and method amongst this first category of countries is persuasive. The emphasis on improving terms and conditions of employment and on using collective bargaining to do so is important. However, as Poole recognises, and as Clegg recognised in his book, *Trade Unionism Under Collective Bargaining*,[12] there are still major differences within the category. For example, while trade unions in all of these countries appreciate the value of political action, as well as collective bargaining, to achieve benefits for their members, the extent of their pursuit of broader political objectives of benefit to society at large rather than just their members, varies. If one uses here the distinction between welfare and business unionism, most of the countries have trade unions that embrace welfare unionism but some do not. The classic example is the USA. Unions in the USA have no formal links with a political party (they frequently suggest support for the Democratic party, though they do not always do so, and on occasions have supported a 'split ticket', that is, support for different parties for different posts), and they have no open aspirations to change the political system. A study from the International Labour Organisation following a visit to the USA said that they were:

> struck in [their] discussion with union leaders by the almost total absence of any questioning of the bases of the American economic and social system. Unlike many labour movements in Europe and elsewhere, the trade unions in the United States [did] not appear even to consider, still less to advocate, any major change in the system in which they [operated], in spite of the many bitter battles that have occurred between unions and capital.[13]

Although, as has already been argued, one should be careful about accepting the distinction between welfare and business unionism, US unions clearly are different in important respects from most of their Western counterparts. In most other Western nations there are links between trade unions and political parties. In Australia the links between the unions and the Labour Party are, if anything, stronger than in the UK. For much of the 1980s the Labour Party had as its leader, and Australia as its prime minister, an ex-leader of the central trade union confederation. The links between political parties and the trade unions differ in other countries: in Sweden, unions affiliate to local branches of the Social Democratic Party; in West Germany, although there is no direct affiliation, there are strong links, and typically many members of the Social Democratic Party elected to the Bundestag are trade union members (some, though relatively few, are former trade union officials); while in Japan, two of the main national union centres are linked to different parties (Sohyo for the Japan Socialist Party and Domei to the more middle of the road Democratic Socialist Party). However, in all cases, the links are stronger than in the USA and are important evidence that even trade unions that see their main focus as operating through collective bargaining, frequently have broad political objectives that they pursue through an associated political party.

Other differences exist between the trade union movements that primarily seek to achieve their objectives through collective bargaining. The levels of unionisation, for example, vary from the very high levels of Sweden to the much lower levels of the USA. Poole also pointed to significant variations in internal government, a topic that will be referred to again later in this chapter.

Disjunctive-type trade unions with political, religious or nationalistic objectives form the second category highlighted by Poole. Many trade union movements that now centre on collective bargaining at one time would have come within this category. Currently the bulk of trade unions in the Third World would be so categorised. There is an emphasis in this case on political or legislative means of achieving objectives. In developing countries the emphasis is linked to an 'omnipresent role of the state itself'.

> Indeed, the association between political purposes in trade unions and an extensive role for the state has been observed in many developing countries. In his authoritative review of labour relations in southern Asia, Schregle thus demonstrated this relationship in all the principal countries covered (Pakistan, India, Nepal, Bangladesh, Sri Lanka, Thailand, Malaysia, Singapore, Indonesia and the Philippines) and observed, generally, that in nations where economic, social, political and cultural developments are subject to deliberate government planning, the state is never passive in the sphere of labour relations . . . The situation in much of Latin America is similar; for instance, in Venezuela, the backbone of the labour movement is the Confederation de Trabajodores de Venezuela (CTV), with affiliates comprising 90 per cent of organised labour. But, as with other 'unions, federations and confederations', this organisation has retained its political character and functions as much as an extension of a political party as a collective bargaining agent.[14]

It would be easy to see this second category as little more than a stage along the road to 'mature' unionism with the dominance of collective bargaining. However, there are dangers in this view, and in this context it is important to recognise that Poole puts France and Italy into this second category. In both of these countries, unions place much more emphasis on political objectives and political means of achieving objectives. There are also strong religious associations and together the strengthening of political links these suggest union movements different from those in the rest of Western Europe. In practice, Poole, rather than linking this category of trade unions just to the stage of industrialisation, suggests that other factors need to be taken into account as well; the cultural and ideological backgroup (particularly important in France and Italy) and the dominant role of the state.

The third category is trade unionism under socialism. In this case, trade unions are closely linked to the state. The argument put forward is that the protective functions performed by trade unions in capitalist societies are unnecessary in a society where the means of production are owned by the state. The classic example is provided by the USSR. According to Porket,[15] Soviet trade unions are 'subordinate to the Party and have to ensure the execution of assigned tasks'. As a result, they have limited autonomy, instead playing a major role in ensuring production targets and the economic plan are met. Trade unions have not had the right to strike (though this has not prevented expressions of industrial unrest on occasions), and are seen to have a role in labour discipline. Nevertheless, they do retain something of the protective function, particularly at the local level where they defend their members against management and bureaucratic abuses. This has led Ruble[16] to talk about 'dual functioning' organisations.

The USSR system has provided an important model for other Eastern bloc countries. Nevertheless, there are important differences between countries. In China, the trade unions came under attack during the cultural revolution and, although membership levels increased subsequently, they were only about 50 per cent a decade later. The Chinese trade union movement now has protective as well as productive functions. In Yugoslavia, the decentralisation that occurred after the end of the Second World War under the influence of Tito extended to trade unions. The links with workers' councils are of particular and distinctive importance.

The most important deviation from the USSR model though, undoubtedly occurred in Poland, with the establishment of Solidarity in 1980. The importance of Solidarity was that it went beyond simply seeking to defend workers against excesses to become a focus of opposition to the state. The aim of 'free' trade unionism was a claim for a fundamental break from the Soviet model, rather than a modification of it. At one time, Solidarity claimed around 10 million members, the vast majority of non-agricultural workers. The action taken against Solidarity is an indication of the extent of the threat it posed. It was a union with immense political as well as industrial significance. It sought to bargain like trade unions in the West, to conclude collective agreements, and to be autonomous. Such a development was a threat to the central state. Although its first phase did not last long, being suppressed by martial law in December 1981, it was not destroyed completely as an organisation or an idea, and re-emerged in 1989 to sign an agreement with the government which compromised some of its more radical ideals, but nevertheless heralded a major potential change in Polish society with the possibility of an officially sanctioned opposition to the dominant Communist party.

The emergence of Solidarity in 1980 has to be put in the context not simply of the economic problems faced in Poland at that time, but also the strength of the Polish cultural identity and the importance of the Roman Catholic Church as a source of alternative values within a socialist state. The re-emergence of Solidarity towards the end of the 1980s had much to do with the reforms introduced by Gorbachev in the USSR, but of importance throughout the Eastern bloc. The political changes that took place at the end of the 1980s and during 1990 had considerable significance for trade unions.

INTERNAL ORGANISATION OF UNIONS IN THE UK

The basic level of union organisation in the UK is the branch. Every union member will be attached to a branch or its equivalent and through this attachment gain much of their influence on policies adopted by the union. The branch will normally appoint its own officers and have a degree of autonomy, the details of which vary from union to union, but for many matters the branch will have to work within a policy framework determined by higher level, ultimately national, bodies.

Three basic types of branch organisation can be highlighted: the workplace based branch where all members are employed at the same factory, plant, or other workplace; the single-employer branch, where all members work for the same employer but do so at different locations; and the multi-employer branch, where membership will usually be drawn from a geographical area, but with members being engaged by a number of different employers. Of these three basic types, the multi-employer branch is the most common (currently about 40 per cent of union members are in such branches) though the number seems to be falling (the Workplace Industrial Relations Survey[17] reported that in 1984, 42 per cent of manual and 19 per cent of non-manual members were in multi-employer branches, compared to 54 per cent and 26 per cent in 1980). Both of the other types of branch organisation seem to be growing, particularly the single-employer branch (the Workplace Industrial Relations Survey suggested that membership of such branches had grown from 24 per cent for manual members and 49 per cent for non-manual members in 1980, to 32 per cent and 64 per cent in 1984). Workplace based branches seem to have increased their importance amongst manual workers (24 per cent of manual members were in workplace based branches in 1984 according to the Workplace Industrial Relations Survey, compared to 21 per cent in 1980), but seem to have decreased in importance amongst non-manual workers (from 18 per cent to 15 per cent over the same period).

There are significant differences in the use of the types of branch organisation between unions. For example, in the Amalgamated Engineering Union multi-employer branches are the most important form of organisation (though there is some evidence that their importance is declining even in that union). In the National Union of Public Employees, on the other hand, the single employer branch is dominant, a reflection of the concentration of that union on the public sector. In the largest union in the UK, the Transport and General Workers' Union, all three types of branch organisation are used, but it is in that union that workplace branches have had the greatest impact, though such branches are nevertheless of less importance overall to that union than multi-employer branches. Single employer branches are particularly important amongst non-manual unions. They are dominant in, as one might expect, public sector unions, like the National and Local Government Officers' Association and the National Union of Teachers, but are also the principal form of branch organisation in many other white collar unions.

The different types of union branch operate rather differently. For example, the workplace-based branch is likely to be relatively small, to meet less frequently than other types of branch organisation, but to attract a higher proportion of members to meetings. At the other extreme, geographically based, multi-employer branches, tend to be much larger, to have more frequent meetings, but to attract a lower proportion of their membership to such meetings. A comparison might be given to illustrate the range of difference in terms of size: the Workplace Industrial Relations Survey found that the median size of workplace-based branches of manual workers was 38, whereas the median size of multi-employer branches of manual workers was 908 (the median size of single employer branches, to complete the comparison, was 354). These differences in structure and operation are not difficult to understand. The difference in terms of proportion of members attending meetings, for instance, clearly is linked to ease of attendance.

Alongside the issue of union branch organisation the question of union recognition at the workplace needs to be considered. Unions normally have some representation when they are recognised by the employer, though the nature of that representation varies. Manual workers are frequently represented by a shop steward, though in some industries that term is not used as such (probably the best known variation is in the printing industry where the father of the chapel fulfils the steward's role). Again, normally the shop steward will be an employee at the place of work, though in some instances, particularly in the public sector, a steward might service members in another workforce, especially where the number of members is small. An alternative model is for workplace representation to be provided by a full-time union official. This model is used sometimes in the manufacturing industry though overall it is nothing like so important as representation through a shop steward. A similar pattern of workplace representation can be found amongst non-manual workers, though the use of the term 'shop steward' as such is less common.

In many instances, there is a hierarchy of stewards or workplace representatives. The appointment of a 'senior steward' is most common, as one might expect, in workplaces with a large number of members, and is particularly noticeable in the manufacturing industry. In some cases a senior steward might, in practice, be spending all of his or her time on union affairs. The Workplace Industrial Relations Survey reported that full-time stewards or conveners were a particular feature of large-scale manufacturing industry, occurring in 70 per cent of workplaces they surveyed with 1,000 or more manual workers (for comparison, it might be noted that they were present in only 3 per cent of establishments of all sizes recognising manual unions). Similar positions are established in some non-manual workplaces (the equivalent often being the chair or secretary of large workplace branches in the public sector), but overall they are only present in a very small proportion of cases.

Although, overall, senior stewards and conveners are only present in a minority of workplaces where unions have recognition, where they are present they often play a key role. They 'act as advisers to ordinary stewards in the initial stages of processing claims and grievances, and may take over their presentation at higher initial stages of procedure'. Frequently they have worked for some time in the plant and have considerable experience of negotiations. This enables them to hold valuable knowledge of precedents and the like. In many cases management seems to have accepted this development. In some instances offices are provided by management to facilitate the work of senior stewards and conveners. Goodman notes that although

> the development of shop stewards' committees and hierarchies exposes management policies to deeper scrutiny, they can also prove useful to managements. If a works' convener or a small committee of shop stewards has the confidence of other stewards then they will enable management to discuss and reach agreement on plant wide issues . . . Moreover, many managers find it much easier to develop a working understanding and good personal relationships with senior stewards and conveners which are not as easy to achieve with outside officials with whom they have much less frequent contact.[18]

In many firms, because of the range of people employed, workshop and shop steward committees have not been restricted to one union. Multi-union committees are important in a number of industries, in particular in engineering and motor vehicles. Such committees are often organised on a similar basis to single union committees, with a convener or chairman, but in many cases they have considerably more freedom of action. Formal trade union organisation, to date, has only managed to deal with the problems arising from multi-union establishments in a limited number of instances. When the informal shop steward combine has filled the gap left by formal organisation, then it has proved extremely difficult to control. In a sense, it has been responsible to no one body and therefore has had no clear master.

In some industries, informal committees also have been established to coordinate the action of shop stewards in different plants of multi-plant enterprises. They normally consist of the conveners or senior stewards from each factory and hold meetings at regular intervals, both to facilitate communication and to coordinate action, 'Again the stewards appear to be attempting to fill a gap left by the geographical or industry focus of internal trade union organisation.'[19]

A number of studies have tried to develop typologies of shop stewards. Miller and Form[20] identified three different types of steward: the job or management orientated steward; the union orientated steward; and the employee orientated steward. Dufty,[21] in a study of Australian shop stewards, found the Miller and Form typology useful, though in the case of two of the three types distinct sub-types were identified. A study of shop stewards in Britain by Batstone *et al.*,[22] drew up a different typology based on two cross-cutting dimensions: the extent to which emphasis is placed on a delegate or a representative role and the extent to which union principles are pursued. These two dimensions yielded four categories, two of which were said to be empirically significant: the 'leader' (adopts a representative role and tries to implement union policy) and the 'populist' (lacks commitment to union principles and acts as a delegate rather than as a representative). This typology was broadly supported by Marchington and Armstrong,[23] though they changed the definitions of some of the dimensions and categories: in particular, the 'union principles' dimension was redefined as 'orientation to unionism'.

Recent research in Britain suggests a possible change in the role of the shop steward. Schuller and Robertson[24] in their study found that shop stewards spend more of their time communicating with each other than with their members, possibly a function of increasing formal and informal shop steward organisation. This is important when it is linked to Brown's[25] findings about the increasing use of the check-off to collect membership fees. In the past the collection of fees by stewards had been an important contact with members.

The above description indicates that much of the work of unions is carried out by lay officials. They will sometimes be given time off for union affairs and in some cases may find that they are spending almost all of their time on union business. However, such officials are not employees of the unions. All unions of any size, though, have full-time employees. They may range from individuals who provide particular services, like education and research officers, to those whose job it is to administer the affairs of the union and negotiate on its behalf. This latter group of people clearly have a critical role to play and, although much comment is made about them, particularly in the media, surprisingly little is known about them as a result of academic research. The size of this group is difficult to define but estimates suggest that there were about 3,000 in the 1960s, falling to, say, 2,500 in the 1980s.

One of the few substantial pieces of research on full-time union officers undertaken in recent years is the study by Watson (she excluded national officials from her study and instead concentrated on regional secretaries, regional officials, area organisers, district organisers and district secretaries). She looked at the role currently played by such officers, noting that this seemed not to have changed much, at least in its broad outline, over the years.

All officers spend considerable time in meetings of one kind or another, and, as a consequence, time was taken up in travelling to and from such meetings . . . Meetings were with a wide range of groups and individuals. The most frequently mentioned across the range of unions were meetings with shop stewards; branch secretaries and members; departmental and line managers; officials of other unions; national research and educational officers of the union TUC, ACAS and employers' federations (especially at regional level); campaign organisers; educational institutions; elected local government representatives; members of industrial tribunals, equal opportunities and MSC boards; members of training boards, skill centres and Constituency Labour Party representatives.[26]

Watson also used the distinction developed by Brown and Lawson[27] between organisers and negotiators to look at differences in emphasis in the work of officers by unions. In unions like the National Union of Hosiery and Knitwear Workers and the Union of Construction, Allied Trades, and Technicians, the organising part of the work seemed to be emphasised: one of the reasons quoted was the problems facing the knitting industry, the hostile environment of construction work and the need for officers to pay particular attention to recruiting and retaining members. In the National Union of Public Employees organising was also given high priority, with emphasis placed on the need to develop lay members' skills and abilities so that they could deal with their own negotiations.

To these NUPE officers, 'organising' is an important concept related to educating and developing members and lay representatives to stand on their own feet and take on the major responsibility of negotiation and recruitment at the local level.[28]

Negotiation was seen as being much more on a par with organising in the British Association of Colliery Management, while in the National Union of Mineworkers negotiation was emphasised, though the role of officers always has to be placed in the context of the wider set of conditions negotiated at higher level. Watson also noted that many union officers saw dealing with individual grievances as an important part of their work, and pointed out that this cannot be entirely separated from organising and negotiating.

One of the most interesting aspects of Watson's study, though, was the comparison between the role of union officers and that of industrial relations managers. A number of similarities were noted:

both groups occupied a similar indirect, advisory and intermediary position with regard to their organisations and constituencies. Both groups had to deal with conflicting pressures: 'members of both occupations acknowledge that they are placed in a position where one of the primary tasks is to manage, control and manipulate those conflicts of interest which they regard as inherent or endemic to the employment relationship'.[29] The actions of both groups can also be crucial in terms of how smoothly the 'system' is kept running. They are not, of course, free agents but they occupy critical positions and the actions they take can make a significant difference to the way events develop. The scope for trade union officers and industrial relations managers to take independent action was stressed by Watson:

> And whilst it must be acknowledged that the social structure imposes major constraints on the possibilities for human action, the potential always exists for human beings to modify the social order.[30]

The major difference between industrial relations managers and trade union officers comes from the loyalties they offer: industrial relations managers have loyalty to only 'one boss' whereas trade union officials are answerable to thousands of members. This difference places most stress on the trade union official and significantly changes the detail of the job undertaken.

INTERNAL ORGANISATION OF UNIONS IN OTHER COUNTRIES

There are, as one might expect, major differences in the internal organisation of unions in Western nations. The position in much of Western Europe is confused by the presence of works councils which can fulfil some of the representative functions at the local level that otherwise might be left to trade unions. The complexity might be illustrated by referring to the position in France.

The structure of local representation of workers' interests in France has evolved over a lengthy period and the complexity is in part a reflection of the pressure felt at particular points in time. Three kinds of representation might be mentioned: the employee delegate, the works committee and the union organisation. The employee delegate in France dates back to the 1930s. The delegate is elected by the workforce and is not a union representative though successful candidates often have been nominated by the union. Essentially the role of the employee delegate is to deal with a range of issues that might be classified under the heading of 'industrial grievances'. The works committee is also an elected body, but one which has a mainly consultative role, although on certain issues, like profit sharing, its agreement may be essential. The works committee, like the employee delegate, is not part of the union though the majority of members are nominated for election by the union. Union organisation at the workplace is a relatively recent phenomenon, really occurring since 1968. Such organisation works alongside the other bodies, and the union, as well as appointing committees, may appoint its own stewards. Such a range of representative bodies makes for a less than tidy picture and at times there is confusion over functions and responsibilities.

> The representative bodies do not form a coherent system but have grown in an 'ad hoc' way. Moreover, with the complex and sometimes imprecise legal framework, there is some confusion of functions among the various bodies, not least because individual representatives frequently fulfill several functions. Often there is a lack of candidates to be appointed as stewards to fill the various elected positions. In the large firms the stewards often coordinate the activities of the works committee and the employee delegates. Although this may be accepted by managers in big firms, in smaller firms managers may resent what they see as union interference.[31]

In other Western European countries the position is not always as complex, but the challenge to the representative function of unions in the workplace posed by works councils introduces an important complicating dimension. In some instances unions have made moves to try to remedy their relatively low profile in the workplace. In the Netherlands, for example, traditionally unions were organised on a geographical basis at the local level. In the post Second World War years, some moves were made by unions to try to build up workplace based organisation, but without a great deal of success. Renewed interest in the development of such an organisational base occurred in the 1960s, and many unions succeeded in establishing a dual workplace and geographical structure:

> For example, the Industrieband NVV introduced a 'A line' based on geographical groups, and a 'B line' based on plant groupings. These two lines together elect the members of 'district councils' (giving each member two forms of representation). The 14 district councils elect the union council (78 members).[32]

Albeda, commenting on these developments agreed that this new structure reflected 'the shifting focus of trade union activity – from the local, regional and national interest to the plant'.[33] At the same time moves were made by Dutch unions to establish a system of workplace representatives.

Outside Western Europe the strongest workplace based organisation by trade unions can be seen in Japan and in other countries in South-East Asia, like Malaysia and Singapore, that have tried to mirror some elements of the Japanese system of industrial relations. Enterprise unions, while not necessarily just workplace based, clearly imply a concentration of power away from national union federations. While such federations exist in Japan, their relative lack of importance has been noted.

In North America and in Scandinavia, by contrast, power in unions appears fairly highly centralised in national union centres and federations. The American 'union boss' is frequently portrayed as having enormous power, and to some extent that is true, but the local union still has a wide range of responsibilities. In Sweden, the image of a high degree of centralisation is again largely correct, but the importance of the local union organisation, the clubs, and the extension of the role of the union safety steward, should not be overlooked. Korpi,[34] argues that the works club has always enjoyed considerable independence and local union activity has been no more under the control of the union hierarchy than it has been in Britain.

In Australia, the union branch has traditionally covered a wide geographical area and inevitably this has hampered its effectiveness at the workplace compared to some other movements. However, in recent years, Australian unions have made moves to strengthen their workplace based organisation. Organisation at that level has tended to be informal, though in the 1970s a number of unions made moves to establish shop stewards and workplace committees.

It is impossible in a brief summary not to over-generalise the position. While all unions have some local organisation the extent to which it is based on, is effective in, or faces challenges in, the workplace, varies enormously and the current position is the culmination of years of development. The same is true if one tries to characterise union full-time officials and the variety between countries. There is no doubt that such variety exists. The position in Japan where an official may see his or her job as a way of getting promotion within the enterprise, and where such involvement in union affairs may be encouraged by the employer with this in mind, is one which is built upon the particular kind of unionism, enterprise unionism, adopted in Japan, and is not replicated where enterprise unionism does not flourish. This does not mean, of course, that on occasions full-time officials (or even lay officials) may not use their union experience as one qualification for certain management positions, but this is still rather different than the link engendered by enterprise unionism in Japan. The characterisation of the 'union boss' in the USA has already been mentioned and clearly it would be wrong to overlook the distinctive character and role of union officials in that country. In other countries the very strong links with political parties have an impact on the appointment of union full-time officials. This is particularly the case in Italy, for instance, where the associated political party has been able to directly influence the appointment of some union full-time officers.

One general factor, however, might be mentioned in making a comparison between Britain and other countries. One of the traditional differences between Britain and other countries has been the relatively low resort to the law in Britain as far as industrial relations are concerned. Of course, this is changing, but the traditional position is still of some importance. The importance of the law for industrial relations has been one factor in pushing unions in other countries, maybe often faster than in Britain, to appoint specialists and professionals as union officials. Robertson and Sams have suggested that in Britain unions will be forced to move in this direction if they are to remain effective organisations and to respond to the changing climate. However, by no means everyone agrees:

> Robertson and Sams suggest that unions may have to be prepared to look towards a highly skilled class of professional and administrator to accommodate to changed circumstances . . . Yet it seems from my interviews that direct recruiting and moves towards 'professionalism' are not desirable and do not offer a solution. The stress on 'vocation', 'dedication', 'non-economic motivation' and an intense and personal commitment suggest that these are highly valued attributes central to the characteristics of a good full-time officer. Consequently, the answer appears to be in more resources to fund an increase on the numbers of full-time officers and the development of specialist backup services, perhaps even jointly funded and shared between a number of trade unions.[35]

One of the questions raised by a discussion of full-time officials is the extent to which they play a crucial role, not simply in the administration and organisation of the union but also in determining policy; that is, to what extent do the ideas and character of the full-time officials determine the policy of the union, and to what extent is that policy determined by the aims and aspirations of the members? The issue of how important full-time officials are in policy making is central to the extensive debate on union internal democracy.

UNION GOVERNMENT AND DEMOCRACY

It has long been recognised by commentators that few trade unions are organised on the basis of primitive democracy. Thus there are few unions in which all major decisions are taken directly by all members. Most unions have adopted the principle of 'representative democracy'; there is some method by which members elect, appoint, or approve of leaders who take decisions on their behalf.

The question of democracy is clearly important for trade unions. Stein comments that the 'trade union is philosophically and traditionally a democratic institution which differs from other types of association, notably the business corporation, in the degree to which it emphasises internal democracy'.[36]

However, a number of researchers have argued that trade unions organised on the basis of 'representative democracy' betray their democratic philosophy and ideals. The starting point for much of this discussion is the work of Michels.[37] He put forward what he termed the 'iron law of oligarchy'. This suggested that oligarchy (rule by the few) is an inevitable result of large-scale organisation: in other words, democracy and large-scale organisation are incompatible. His theory is probably best summed up by the statement 'who says organisation says oligarchy'.

Michels's theory was developed after a study of a number of different 'democratic organisations', including trade unions. These organisations, he argued, needed to develop a bureaucratic structure in order to attain their ends: the 'sheer problem of administration necessitates bureaucracy'.[38] However, the price of bureaucracy is the concentration of power at the top of the organisational hierarchy and the lessening of the influence of rank and file members.

> The leaders possess many resources which give them an almost insurmountable advantage over members who try to change policies. Among their assets can be counted (a) superior knowledge, e.g., they are privy to much information which can be used to secure assent for their programme; (b) control over the formal means of communication with the membership . . . and (c) skill in the art of politics.[39]

The domination of the bureaucratic leaders is also facilitated according to Michels by what he termed 'the incompetence of the masses'. Few members attend meetings of the organisation; the 'pulls of work, family, personal leisure activities, and the like, severely limit the amount of actual time and psychic energy which the average person may invest in membership groups'.[40] Further, few members have the level of education and 'general sophistication' necessary to participate fully in the affairs of the organisation.

Michels went on to argue that not only will the organisation be dominated by an exclusive oligarchy but also that such leaders will pursue ends which may be personal and differ from those held by the membership in general. The rank and file member views the organisation as a means to another end, but to the leader the organisation has become the 'end' itself for job, status and power are dependent upon it. As a result, leaders often adopt a conservative stance merely designed to protect their own position.

Michels's theory has been re-examined in a variety of different contexts. One of the most important, using a trade union setting, is the work of Lipset, Trow and Coleman,[41] who examined, as a case study, the government of the International Typographical Union. They argued that the ITU was not dominated by an oligarchy because there was an organised opposition within the union and this prevented any one group gaining unfettered control. However, this organised opposition was only able to operate effectively because of a number of unusual circumstances. First, members of the ITU were more interested and involved in the work of the unions than one might have expected. This was partly because of the nature of the craft of printing; the high status of printers and their irregular hours of work had led to the creation of a strong occupational community, which in turn had fostered the desire of printers to participate in the affairs of their union. Second, the borderline or marginal status of printing between the middle and the working class meant that there were different groups with different values within the union. Third, a fairly high proportion of the printing trades were organised before the union was formed and, as a result, the various sections of the union had a long history of autonomy which led them to strongly resist efforts to create a centralised structure. Fourth, as a result of earlier problems, the union had developed a number of devices designed to enable the whole of the membership to participate in major aspects of decision making; these included the election of officers by the whole of the membership and provisions for referenda of the membership.

Fifth, the results of elections were accepted; ruling groups had not tried to preserve their position by 'illegal means' after an election defeat.

As a result, Lipset, Trow and Coleman argued that the ITU was really a deviant case study. The organised opposition was only able to exist because of 'favourable dice throws'. In normal circumstances such a favourable environment would not exist and the internal organisation of trade unions would permit control by an oligarchy.

This line of reasoning has some similarities with the work of Martin.[42] Although Martin argues that Lipset *et al.* were wrong to discuss democracy on the basis of a definition which used a parliamentary analogy, and that instead it should be discussed on the basis of the survival of faction (which limits the ability of the executive to ignore rank and file opinion), his list of factors likely to encourage the survival of faction has some similarity with the list Lipset *et al.* suggested would encourage the institutionalisation of opposition. For example, Martin's list included the political culture of the union, the strength of workshop organisation and the type of technology.

There is a considerable body of evidence which lends support to the Michels/Lipset argument. For example, a number of studies of British unions have pointed to the low level of membership participation in union affairs. Goldstein, in his study of the Transport and General Workers' Union,[43] found that attendance at branch meetings was very low (he only classified 4 per cent of semiskilled and unskilled members as 'active') and Goldthorpe *et al.*[44] found low attendance rates for branch meetings in their study of affluent workers (only 7 per cent of their car workers attended branch meetings regularly). The Workplace Industrial Relations Survey suggested that attendance at branch meetings averages about 7 per cent of total membership.[45] Voting in elections for national officials is also notoriously low, though in some unions much higher votes have been obtained (this has been the case in recent elections for the presidency of the National Union of Mineworkers).

Further, a number of studies, again in British unions, have shown how union leaders often go beyond their formal role of merely administering conference decisions. In some cases this has been because conference decisions have not been specific enough, while in other cases trade union officials have merely ignored decisions with which they have disagreed. Discussing the actions of Lord Carron during the latter part of his presidency of the Engineers'

Union, Clegg used the phrase 'Carron's Law' to describe the way in which Carron

> cast the block vote of his union at meetings of the Labour Party Conference and the Trade Union Congress as he thought was right, rather than with close regard for the decisions of his own conference or the preference of the majority of his union's delegates at the meeting.[46]

In many cases chief officers were able to do this because of election procedures. In some instances they did not have to submit themselves for periodic re-election (for example, in the National Union of Mineworkers and the National Union of Railwaymen, though recent legislation is leading to changes in such matters), and even when they have done so, it has been unusual for incumbent officers to be defeated, partly because they have been seen by the union members as 'the union representative' and few challengers are likely to be well known by the bulk of the membership.

Of course, evidence on the problems of the democratic control of trade unions can be gained from outside the British context. For example, Matthews argues that in Australia 'the working trade union member has little opportunity for playing a significant role in the making of the national policies of his union.'[47] Policy making is the prerogative of 'professional' full-time officials or small executive committees which are subject to very little general control. Similar comments can be made about European trade unions. Thus, Blanpain[48] has discussed the gap between the aims and aspirations of trade union leaders and rank and file members in Belgium, while Guigni,[49] has referred to the problems of the democratic control of decisions in Italian unions; other commentators on Italian industrial relations[50] have noted the rank and file 'backlash' (in the form of unofficial strikes) against official leaders.

Hyman[51] has argued that US unions are, if anything, less democratic than their British counterparts. In Britain, he suggests, the local union organisation can provide some kind of buffer against the influence of national leaders. In the USA this is less likely to happen, because the branches are not managed (as is often the case in Britain) by lay officials but by full-time officials who are appointed and controlled by the national leadership. Further, in the USA, the extensive patronage which is at the disposal of the national leadership 'as well as the collaborative relationships often enjoyed with employers . . . is a source of considerable power over the rank and file'.[52]

However, a number of writers have counselled caution in the

interpretation of this evidence. While few argue that unions, like other 'democratic organisations', have not on occasions been the subject of oligarchical control, they suggest that the problems of democratic control may have been exaggerated. This line of reasoning is evident in the work of Turner.[53]

Turner, in his study of the growth and development of British trade unions, suggested that there were three different styles of union government. The first was what he termed the 'executive democracy'; this type came closest to the concept of primitive democracy, for the unions were characterised by high membership participation, few full-time officials, and little distinction in status or interest between membership and leaders. Such a style of government is typical, Turner argued, of 'closed' occupational unions which have rigid membership controls. The second category was termed the 'aristocracies'. In these unions, the officials are still subject to close scrutiny but by one section rather than the whole of the membership. This situation is typical, for example, of closed craft unions who have expanded their membership recently; the craft section may retain the right and ability to control the leadership but this privilege may not extend to all sections of the union. The third category is that of 'popular bossdoms'; they are characterised by a low level of membership participation and by the greatest difference between the members and the professional officials on which they depend. In such cases senior officials will operate more or less free from control by the bulk of the membership and, in effect, will be able to appoint their own successors. This style of government is typical of open unions covering a wide range of occupations (normally termed 'general' unions).

As Hughes argues, 'Turner's three types of union government involve an element of arbitrariness; the reality of union government and its relation to participation is more complex than his classification allows for'. Further, it is clear 'that this approach is no more than a beginning for causal analysis of factors governing levels of membership participation'.[54] Nevertheless, Turner has made a useful start to such an exercise and illustrates the variety of experience. Although some unions are run by oligarchies, others manage to maintain at least elements of democratic control; only the third of Turner's categories fits in with the Michels model.

This line of reasoning is taken a stage further by Banks. He argues that an analysis of representative democracy shows 'that the theory of oligarchic tendencies in trade unions is unsubstantiated by the facts'. He suggests that this is because the union leadership at all levels 'is regularly challenged by the members'.[55] Thus, he says that what Lipset, Trow and Coleman

> failed to appreciate is that representative democracy works on the principle that between the rank and file member and the top men there are very many aspiring leaders whose challenge must be met and whose political skills are not negligible. A proper study of the mechanisms of representative democracy must include an investigation of the part played by district, regional and national assemblies in the development of such skills amongst the erstwhile rank and file.[56]

Support for this view can be gained from Clegg's analysis[57] of the government of British trade unions. He suggests that there are a number of checks on the power of national union leaders. For example, in many unions there are a number of elected representatives who, although they are not an organised party, oppose the established union leadership certainly more frequently than was suggested by Lipset, Trow and Coleman. Similarly, the decentralised structure of many unions means that the regions and areas have considerable power (for example, in the General, Municipal and Boilermakers' Union and the National Union of Mineworkers) and the national leadership cannot impose any general policy without their cooperation.

It is also clear that the workplace itself (as Martin recognised) can be a base for a further alternative source of power. There is a great deal of evidence that workshop groups can, and often do, work independently from the central union organisation. Shop stewards are frequently important in this context. McCarthy and Parker, in a survey conducted for the Donovan Commission, noted the crucial role of the shop stewards in workplace communications.

> 40 per cent of union members get their information about what is happening in the union from their steward. Slightly more members get such information from their union journal, but when it is borne in mind that 54 per cent of the members who see a union journal get it from their steward, the steward is clearly the main source of keeping members informed.[58]

Other studies have noted the way in which shop stewards have been able to use their position to build a power base to rival the official union structure. Cyriax and Oakshott[59] have referred to the position at Briggs Motor Bodies factory at Dagenham where the shop stewards ran their own fund raising activity and published their own independent journal and newsletters.

As a result, Banks[60] puts forward a theory which argues that unions are really 'polyarchies'; this is a situation in which there are a series of checks and balances between the leaders and a minority of active union members. Reviewing this theory, Hyman[61] asks whether if unions are to be described as polyarchies they can also be described as democracies. He clearly feels that they cannot. The crucial factor, he suggests, is that despite the checks and balances the majority of union members still do not influence policy.

Banks adopts a different attitude. He argues that studies of union democracy and the participation of union members in decision making cannot be based entirely on structural factors 'The study of participation . . . can ill afford to ignore the effect of personality and other differences in people and their circumstances which influence the likelihood of their filling participatory roles'.[62] A democratic system of union government is one in which institutional barriers that might prevent members from participating or expressing their opinion have been eliminated. It is not one which 'results in all the members in the system having the same or equal motives for so behaving'.[63]

A more radical approach has been adopted by Allen.[64] He does not centre his analysis on the 'number of exceptions to the rule' or on checks and balances, as do most of the other writers looked at so far; rather he argues that much of the work on union democracy, and in particular that of Lipset, Trow and Coleman, used an incorrect definition and measure of democracy. Trade union democracy is not, as they suggested, analogous to state democracy; while it is reasonable to examine internal procedures when looking at state democracy, it is not reasonable to do so when looking at trade union democracy. Trade unions, he says, are voluntary organisations which members can leave, and which members will leave, if they disagree with the way their affairs are being conducted or their policies are being determined. Clearly the same is not true of a state. As a result, when examining trade union democracy, it is important to look at their objectives and achievements rather than their internal procedures; in other words, one should look at the extent to which they are fulfilling the ambitions and needs of their members.

Allen's thesis has been the subject of considerable criticism. Such criticism can be narrowed down to four main points. First, trade unions, it is argued, are not voluntary organisations, to the extent that in some industries workers cannot leave a union without also losing their job (for example, where a closed shop exists, though it should be noted that Allen opposed the closed shop because he saw it was a way of restricting a worker's ability to move out of a trade union when dissatisfied). Second, it is suggested that members often are in no position to be able to evaluate the actions of trade union leaders because information and alternative views are rarely presented. Third, it has been pointed out[65] that union membership figures are not necessarily a good guide to membership satisfaction: members may leave a union for many reasons (like a change of job) not just because they are dissatisfied with its policy. Fourth, a union's aims are not normally well defined: the difference in aims between leaders and rank and file members was referred to earlier.

Nevertheless, despite these criticisms, there is some support for an element of Allen's thesis. Many writers accept that if a union leader is seriously challenged by his members, especially if that challenge takes the form of members leaving and setting up a rival union, then the union leader has to respond. Even Lipset,[66] who generally was critical of Allen's thesis, accepted this point. He recalled how John L. Lewis, President of the United Mineworkers of America, changed his policy dramatically in the 1930s after he had lost a substantial proportion of his members. However, it is important to stress that such writers would still argue that it is unusual for members to challenge leaders and, therefore, such a mechanism is far from being an adequate check on a leader's power. It is also important to recognise that the manner of any response from a trade union leader to a challenge from his members may vary. A union leader may (as according to Lipset *et al.*, Lewis did) change union policy to fit in more with members' aspirations. On the other hand, a union leader may feel that to change policy would be wrong, either because they disagreed fundamentally with the change being demanded, or because they believed that the change would harm the overall position of the union even if it would suit the group who were issuing the challenge. As a result their response may not be to change policy in the way demanded, but to make organisational changes to try to strengthen their position and weaken the challenge to it.

SUMMARY

Trade unions are frequently viewed principally as bodies which seek to further the industrial objectives of their members, but while this is undoubtedly an important function it is not the only one. There are important differences in the extent to which such other functions, especially political aims, are pursued, and these differences can be followed through into a categorisation of trade unions.

The internal organisation and management of unions, has understandably received considerable attention. The role of lay and full-time officials has been studied and variations between unions noted. There has also been great interest in the extent to which the internal affairs of unions can be seen to be governed on a 'democratic' basis.

5 The industrial enterprise, management and employers' associations

INDUSTRIAL CONCENTRATION

A starting point for a discussion of the industrial enterprise has to be a consideration of changes in the extent of concentration of activity (reflected in the size of the firm and the establishment) and the effect of such changes on industrial relations. Until recently most attention had centred on increasing concentration. Although Clegg's assertion[1] that such concentration of activity was fairly continuous from the industrial revolution to the 1970s had been challenged (Child[2] noted that in the USA there appeared to be little increase in overall concentration between the First World War and the late 1940s, and in Britain there was little change between the mid-1930s and early 1950s) few denied the more general point he made. The position seems to have changed somewhat since the end of the 1970s and this needs to be examined in some detail. However, first the trend towards industrial concentration that was noted until the 1980s and is by no means irrelevant after that, will be looked at and the industrial relations implications considered.

A number of different measures can be used when examining industrial concentration and while they may represent a different emphasis they all show the same trend. Thus in Britain whereas firms employing more than 10,000 workers only accounted for 14 per cent of employment in manufacturing industries in 1935, by 1979 the corresponding figure had risen to 35 per cent. A similar picture emerges if one examines the size of the plant rather than the size of the firm. Thus, whereas in 1935 plants employing 1,000 workers or more only accounted for 22 per cent of employment in manufacturing industries, by 1979 the corresponding figure had risen to 41 per cent.[3]

Boyle[4] has referred to a similar trend in the USA. Table 5.1 shows the increase in the share of manufacturing assets held by the 100 and 200 largest corporations between 1925 and 1984. From this table it can

Table 5.1 Share of US manufacturing assets held by the 100 and 200 largest corporations: 1925–84

Year	Share of assets	
	100 largest	*200 largest*
1925	34.5	–
1927	34.4	–
1929	38.2	45.8
1931	41.7	49.0
1933	42.5	49.5
1935	40.8	47.7
1937	42.1	49.1
1939	41.9	48.7
1941	38.2	45.1
1948	38.6	46.3
1950	38.4	46.1
1952	39.3	47.7
1954	41.9	50.4
1956	43.9	52.8
1958	46.0	55.2
1960	45.5	55.2
1962	45.5	55.1
1964	45.8	55.8
1966	45.8	56.1
1968	48.8	60.4
1970	48.5	60.4
1972	47.6	60.0
1974	44.4	56.7
1976	45.4	58.0
1978	45.5	58.3
1979	46.1	59.0
1980	46.7	59.7
1981	46.8	60.0
1982	47.7	60.8
1983	48.3	60.8
1984	48.9	60.7

Sources: S. E. Boyle, *Industrial Organisation* (Holt, Rinehart & Winston, New York 1972), and Statistical Abstract of United States

Note: Figures after 1970 and 1974 not directly comparable with earlier ones.

be seen that not only did these firms increase their share significantly over the period (in both cases by more than 14 per cent), but also that by 1984 the largest 100 firms held a larger proportion of assets than the largest 200 firms had held in 1929.

This trend towards industrial concentration, of course, was not confined to Britain and the USA. Child[5] noted the marked trend towards industrial concentration in West Germany and France over the same period and the rapid development of the giant enterprise in Italy and Japan[6] since the 1950s. Norgrens commented that in 'the judgement of some, the degree of [industrial] concentration is greater in Sweden than in West Germany or the USA'.[7] Moves towards greater concentration were particularly rapid in Sweden in the early 1960s and by 1963 the 100 largest private industrial undertakings accounted for 46 per cent of industry's total value added and 43 per cent of total industrial employment.

Singh[8] tried to explain this tendency towards concentration as a response to the liberalisation of world trade and increased international capital movements since the late 1960s. 'There is considerable evidence', he claimed, 'that in both Western Europe and Japan large firms, as well as Governments, favoured bigger economic units in the belief that this would help them to face competition from larger United States firms'. Consequently governments 'permitted mergers to occur without much legal interference, if not with outright encouragement'. In turn US companies 'tried to become larger still so as to face growing European competition'.[9]

There are a variety of alternative explanations. For example, Aaronovitch and Sawyer[10] argued that the trend towards concentration could best be explained by reference to the 'costs of rivalry'. These included factors like advertising and the need to maintain stocks in order to preserve a reputation for reliability. Pryor[11] argued that the degree of concentration was inversely related to a country's size. Industry in a small country was unlikely to be able to rely on the domestic market and size was an advantage in international markets.

The increase in the size of the business enterprise has been seen to be of considerable importance for industrial relations. A number of writers have attempted to show a direct link between the size of the enterprise and certain aspects of industrial relations. For example, Revans[12] argued that there was a relationship between organisational size and industrial conflict, studies by the Action Society Trust[13] suggested a link between size and absenteeism, while Talacchi[14] saw a relationship between job satisfaction and size. However, many authors claimed that the effect of size on such items was not direct; they normally argued that it operated through 'structural intermediaries'. For example, an increase in organisational size may lead to an increase in impersonal rules, which in turn may lead to increased conflict, or a decrease in job satisfaction. A number of writers pointed out, though, that 'structural intermediaries' can be affected by factors other than size with the result that attempts to isolate and measure a size effect may not always be accurate, and Ingham[15] argued that a number of the studies on the effect of size were too restrictive (they did not look at all of the different measures of morale). There is also a view, though, that the size effect need not necessarily operate through structural intermediaries like bureaucratisation. Prais,[16] Edwards[17] and Marginson[18] all have taken this view. Marginson also has argued that company rather than plant size may be particularly important.

It has been suggested that the growth in the size of the firm and the plant also has had an important impact on industrial relations in other ways. For example, it has been one of the factors responsible for the growth in the size of trade unions and the transfer of power in trade unions and collective bargaining to the national level. At the same time there is evidence that because of this trend towards large-scale units and national organisation, local organisation was neglected by both employers and trade unions. One of the consequences was the establishment of informal arrangements both within and between local management and employee groups.

For instance, many writers noticed the growth in the number of shop stewards in British industry in the 1960s and 1970s: estimates varied but tended to centre around a figure of 175,000 to 200,000. Some also noted that there was a positive relationship between the size of the establishment and the appointment of shop stewards. Thus, Marsh, Evans and Garcia, in their study of industrial relations in the engineering industry[19] estimated that whereas less than 50 per cent of establishments with less than 100 employees had shop stewards, the comparable figure for establishments with 250 employees or more was about 90 per cent. In large firms there seemed to be even more incentive than in smaller ones for shop stewards to take an independent line and develop informal communications, both between themselves and with management. Brown *et al.*[20] noted a strong positive correlation between the size of the workplace and the appointment of full-time stewards and the specialisation of the shop stewards' role.

The increase in the size of the establishment also meant that it was more likely than before that more than one union would be organising the workforce. This, in turn, increased the potential for interunion conflict: however, it also increased the benefits of local level interunion cooperation through shop stewards' combines. Such combines were essentially *ad hoc* bodies and as a result were able to pursue an independent course.

The complexity of modern industry, in one sense at least, also seemed to increase the power of certain workgroups. For example, in the motor vehicle industry the level of interdependency of work units is such that if one of the units ceases production for any length of time, production soon has to halt elsewhere. This, undoubtedly, increased the bargaining power of 'strategic workgroups' It meant that, for instance, the cost of a dispute in terms of lost production was high – in many cases far higher than the immediate cost of a settlement.

The above discussion has been based on the trends identified in the 1960s and 1970s towards greater industrial concentration. There are signs, however, that a change has taken place in recent years. Table 5.2 gives information on industrial concentration in manufacturing industries in the UK. It shows that there has been a significant decline in the proportion of workers employed by firms with 10,000 or more workers and in establishments with 1,000 or more workers. The Workplace Industrial Relations Survey[21] also showed that 19 per cent of establishments in manufacturing saw a decline in their workforce of between 5 and 20 per cent between 1980 and 1984, while a further 29 per cent saw a decline in their workforce of more than 20 per cent. While some establishments in manufacturing increased their workforces, the number doing so was far fewer. The Workplace Industrial Relations Survey also provided information beyond the bounds of manufacturing industry. The picture was broadly the same in the public sector (both nationalised industries and public services), though the size of the decline was concentrated in the 5–20 per

Table 5.2   Industrial concentration in manufacturing in the UK, 1979–85

Year	Workers employed by firms employing 10,000 workers or more (%)	Workers employed in establishments employing 1,000 workers (%)
1979	34.9	40.9
1980	33.9	38.5
1981	31.3	36.8
1982	30.5	34.9
1983	29.3	33.5
1984	24.9	31.8
1985	25.4	30.9

Source: Report on Census of Production, Summary Tables.

cent rather than the over 20 per cent band. In private services there were also a number of establishments where the size of the workforce declined, though in this sector more showed an increase.

The picture is rather complex with different trends identifiable in different parts of the economy. It is not made easier to disentangle by the decline in the relative importance of both private manufacturing and the public sector. Despite such difficulties it is still important to record that the earlier trends on industrial concentration have not been sustained, and in certain important areas have been reversed. It is also important to record that, with government encouragement, small firms have become more important. Whereas in the mid-1970s they provided work for about 5 million people, estimates suggest that by the mid-1980s that total had risen to around 6 million.

One also needs to add in to this picture changes which have been taking place within firms. Many firms in both the manufacturing and service sectors have disaggregated their businesses into separate divisions and profit centres, and in so doing have decentralised responsibility for decision making across a wide range of areas. Similar moves have also been made in parts of the public sector – like British Rail – while devolution of responsibility to heads for school budgets can be seen as a move in the same direction.

None of this is to suggest that the large, multi-establishment firm is no longer important: to the contrary it is still of enormous significance and comments made about the relationship between size and aspects of industrial relations still have force. What it means, though, is that some attention needs also to be paid to other matters. In a later chapter there will be discussion about the devolution of responsibilities for collective bargaining within firms. Others have looked at industrial relations in small firms. Despite Rainnie's[22] caution that small firms are not part of an identifiable homogeneous group he points to some of the attitudes adopted in small firms to matters like union membership.

> Many small firm owner/managers view trade unions as an unwarranted and unnecessary intrusion into their 'right' to manage their firm as they see fit. Research has shown that managers will actively recruit groups of workers they feel to be disadvantaged in the labour market, more flexible, and less likely to join trade unions.
>
> 'Trouble makers' who still insist on joining and trying to organise trade unions are harassed or at best eased out. The rest are left with the option of like it, lump it or leave.
>
> Workers are left alone and isolated. This process is exacerbated by

the operation of work systems that atomise the workforce turning worker against worker. Response is necessarily individualistic, either through labour turnover, or knuckling under to bonus schemes that serve even further to divide workers from each other.[23]

Rainnie also says that workers in small firms often find it difficult to get recognition for the union they join because of indifference on the part of the union themselves who see workers in small firms as difficult and expensive to organise.

Similar comments have been made from the experience of other countries. In Japan, although the large enterprise has gained much attention, over 80 per cent of all employees work for small and medium-sized enterprises (in this context small enterprises are seen as firms with less than 20 workers and medium-sized enterprises as firms with less than 300 workers) and this proportion has been growing in recent years.

Chalmers[24] has noted that wages tend to be lower in small firms and unionisation less frequent. As the size of the firm declines, she suggests, so the imbalance of power increases.

> Arbitary arrangements are the order of the day in the majority of firms in Japan's private sector – its small firms. If a worker does not accept the terms, he can quit. If he is fired, his capacity to seek reversal in the courts is severely limited. The minor unions that exist are ill-equipped to give support or initiate industrial action around the issue. Moreover, the circumstances under which people work in the peripheral sector virtually preclude unionization.[25]

THE MULTINATIONAL ENTERPRISE

One of the features of recent industrial development has been the increasing importance of the multinational enterprise. Bone says

> A multinational enterprise is one which undertakes direct foreign investment. It will own or control income-earning assets in more than one country, and in doing so will produce goods or services outside its country of origin. It is nearly always engaged in international production.[26]

Some writers have pointed out that most multinationals are based in one country simply with branches in others (there are exceptions, like Royal Dutch Shell and Unilever which are based in two countries). As a result some have argued for the use of the term 'transnational corporation' rather than multinational. Wilson describes transnational corporations as bodies which 'derive a substantial part of their revenues by operating in more than one country'.[27] However, he argues that the term multinational is now in such common use that it would be difficult to replace it with the transnational corporation.

Before the Second World War British multinationals were of major importance. Dunning[28] has estimated that the stock of accumulated British foreign investments was $6,500 millions in 1914 and had risen to $10,500 millions in 1938. These figures represented 45.5 per cent and 39.8 per cent of the world totals. Many other Western European countries also had significant foreign investments at the same time: Hertner[29] has described the development of German multinationals.

The major expansion in the activities of the multinational enterprise, however, occurred after the end of the Second World War. Companies based in the USA, in particular, were encouraged to undertake foreign investment by a number of developments. On the one hand there were restrictions on expansion inside the USA; there were constraints on mergers and the 'steam had gone out of the domestic economy'. On the other hand, there were considerable inducements to invest and produce abroad. Many Western European countries were desperately short of capital and foreign currency and had little option but to accept US investment. Further, countries like Canada and Australia had a wealth of natural resources attractive to developers which they were unable to exploit themselves. Hymer[30] notes that Canada, for example, 'allowed an almost unrestricted flow of capital'.

Although the USA still houses the majority of multinational firms (see Table 5.3) they by no means have a monopoly. Firms based in the UK and Europe began another round of expansion in the 1950s and after. More recently there has been a considerable expansion in the amount of foreign investment by Japanese, Brazilian and South Korean firms.

Multinationals based in different parts of the world seem to have grown and developed differently. Currently there are identifiable areas of predominant interest. Wilson[31] has suggested that USA multinationals are particularly dominant in Latin America, accounting for about three-quarters of all foreign investment, while UK-based multinationals are much more likely to operate in Africa.

Multinational firms have expanded most spectacularly in industries using advanced technology; their size clearly gives them a major advantage when it comes to providing the large sums necessary for development in this sector. Firms like ICI, Shell and IBM probably epitomise this kind of multinational. However, although multinational

Table 5.3 World's fifty largest industrial firms

Rank	Company	Headquarters	1983 sales ($000)	1983 net income ($000)
1	Exxon	New York	88,561,134	4,977,957
2	Royal Dutch/Shell group	The Hague/London	80,550,885	4,174,736
3	General Motors	Detroit	74,581,600	3,730,200
4	Mobil	New York	54,607,000	1,505,000
5	British Petroleum	London	49,194,886	1,562,873
6	Ford Motor	Dearborn, Mich.	44,454,600	1,866,900
7	International Business Machines	Armonk, NY	40,180,000	5,485,000
8	Texaco	Harrison, NY	40,068,000	1,233,000
9	El du Pont de Nemours	Wilmington, Del.	35,378,000	1,127,000
10	Standard Oil (Ind)	Chicago	27,635,000	1,868,000
11	Standard Oil of California	San Francisco	27,342,000	1,590,000
12	General Electric	Fairfield, Conn.	26,797,000	2,024,000
13	Gulf Oil	Pittsburgh	26,581,000	978,000
14	Atlantic Richfield	Los Angeles	25,147,036	1,547,875
15	ENI	Rome	25,022,358	(928,925)

Table 5.3 continued

Rank	Company	Headquarters	1983 sales ($000)	1983 net income ($000)
16	IRI	Rome	24,518,447	NA
17	Unilever	London/Rotterdam	20,291,583	583,614
18	Toyota Motor	Toyota City (Japan)	19,741,094	918,421
19	Shell Oil	Houston	19,678,000	1,633,000
20	Occidental Petroleum	Los Angeles	19,115,700	566,700
21	Française des Petroles	Paris	18,350,186	101,548
22	Elf-Aquitaine	Paris	18,188,156	488,451
23	US Steel	Pittsburgh	16,869,000	(1,161,000)
24	Matsushita Electric Industrial	Osaka (Japan)	16,719,440	766,060
25	Petrobras (Petroleo Brasileiro)	Rio de Janeiro	16,258,011	485,888
26	Philips Gloeilampenfabrieken	Eindhoven, Netherlands	16,176,941	226,631
27	Pemex (Petroleos Mexicanos)	Mexico City	16,140,013	(5,238)
28	Hitachi	Tokyo	15,804,301	603,287
29	Siemens	Munich	15,724,273	296,074
30	Nissan Motor	Yokohama (Japan)	15,697,733	416,337
31	Volkswagenwerk	Wolfsburg (Germany)	15,693,352	(51,083)
32	Daimler-Benz	Stuttgart	15,660,437	404,580

33	Philipps Petroleum	Bartlesville, Okla.	15,249,000	721,000
34	Sun	Radnor, Pa.	14,730,000	453,000
35	United Technologies	Hartford	14,669,265	509,173
36	Bayer	Leverkusen (Germany)	14,615,594	295,889
37	Hoechst	Frankfurt	14,558,235	128,987
38	Renault	Paris	14,467,765	(206,769)
39	Fiat	Turin (Italy)	14,446,548	NA
40	Tenneco	Houston	14,353,000	716,000
41	ITT	New York	14,155,408	674,510
42	Nestlé	Vevey (Switzerland)	13,303,618	600,360
43	BASF	Ludwigshaften on Rhine	13,250,424	202,464
44	Chrysler	Highland Park, Mich.	13,240,399	700,900
45	Volvo	Goteberg (Sweden)	12,963,008	26,588
46	Imperial Chemical Industries	London	12,750,075	573,003
47	Proctor & Gamble	Cincinnati, Ohio	12,452,000	866,000
48	BAT Industries	London	12,083,087	475,987
49	R. J. Reynolds Industries	Winston-Salem, NC	11,957,000	881,000
50	Mitsubishi Heavy Industries	Tokyo	11,916,259	98,396
	Totals		1,211,907,851	46,729,374

Source: Fortune, 20 August 1984, p. 177
Note: Figures in parenthesis are provisional.

firms have an advantage in the advanced technology sector, they are not restricted to it. Multinationals have made important inroads into areas like food products, motor vehicles and cosmetics. Firms like Ford, General Motors and Unilever are obvious examples from this sector.

Recently a number of writers have discussed the activities of multinationals, and in particular their expansion, not in terms of market power,[32] or maximising efficiency by internalising trade within firms, but in terms of the 'New International Division of Labour'. This is an idea which seeks to highlight the way in which the distribution of functions within the world economy is changing. It is suggested that the developed countries retain the high skilled areas of production but that low skilled, standardized production is given to the developing, low wage, economies. The multinational has an important, though not the only, role to play in this matter. Its decisions about where to locate production, and its use of cheap labour in developing countries, clearly fit into the model. The problem with this model is not that the factors it draws attention to are unimportant or that multinationals do not act in the way described. The problem is that it is not a complete explanation either of the international division of labour or of the behaviour of multinationals. Schoenberger has looked specifically at the investment decisions of multinations and argues that there has not been a major shift away from the developed to the lower labour cost developing countries. 'Clearly, the bulk of foreign manufacturing investment remains oriented to relatively high-cost, major foreign markets despite the theoretical possibility of de-linking production and locating it separately in order to produce costs.'[33]

Dunning has described multinationals as 'amongst the most power-ful economic institutions' in capitalist society.[34] Wilson records that it has been calculated that 'the turnover of the ten largest multinationals is greater than the active gross national product of 80 nations',[35] while Bean[36] notes that in the mid-1970s multinationals were responsible for one-fifth of the world's output (excluding centrally-planned economies). He goes on to recall that at that time the production of multinationals was growing at 10–12 per cent a year, nearly twice that of the growth of world output, and while he accepts, that 'the relative rate of expansion of new MNE activities may now be slowing in comparison to that achieved over the last two decades', he argues that it 'still remains impressive'.[37]

The impact of multinational activities in individual countries is also important to note. In developing countries the importance of multinational investment may be indicated not simply by its size but also by the key role it can play in an economic development strategy. In developed countries as well, though, multinational investment can be of major importance. For example, in Canada about 35 per cent of the assets of all firms are foreign owned, chiefly by USA multinationals. In Belgium about one-third of all industrial turnover is accounted for by foreign-owned companies. Also in the USA, the home of many multinationals, foreign investment is important. Foreign investment in manufacturing industry in the USA rose from $8.2 billion in 1973 to $50.7 billion in 1984. Servan-Schreiber's comment,[38] that in both developing and developed countries the economic power of multinationals will be greater than indicated by the bare figures because it is likely to be concentrated in technologically advanced sectors of the economy and involve equity capital (that is, ownership of the enterprise), is worthwhile noting.

A number of commentators have argued that governments and unions have been slow to realise the importance of such developments. McMillan has said that although 'from a political and legal perspective it seems difficult to avoid the conclusion that both saints and sinners occupy the multinational arena' an even more striking conclusion is that 'governments, labour unions and consumer movements seem singularly hesitant to catch up with current economic realities and the need to provide countervailing power to check the multinational'.[39]

However, greater interest has been shown in the activities of the multinational enterprise of late. The report of a UN study group highlighted some of the costs to a country of allowing or encouraging investment by multinational corporations. One of the most important was the dominant position gained by some multinational enterprises in both domestic economics and the world scene. This can result in a reduction of 'the ability of Governments to control the behaviour of foreign firms' and must therefore raise questions concerning 'economic sovereignty'.[40] Similarly, Roberts has noted that 'a growing number of politicians and other groups which influence public opinion' have argued that the 'multinational corporation represents a threat of some kind to national economic and social interests'.[41] This has led to the belief that control over foreign investment may be important if a government is to remain 'master in its own house'. This point was emphasised by Hymer, writing specifically about Canada, when he argued that as a result of the flow of foreign investment Canada had 'surrendered a great deal of national independence'.[42]

Trade unions have recognised the importance of the growth of the multinational enterprise in three main areas. First, they have seen how investment by a multinational enterprise can easily be withdrawn. This in itself can lead to the threat of major redundancies and disruption which may in turn be used as an important bargaining counter by employers in negotiations. Such tactics are not restricted to multinationals but they are particularly effective when they are used by them. Second, they have seen how multinationals can have an important advantage in other ways at the bargaining table; for instance, they have enormous economic strength which could be put to use during a dispute. Third, they have recognised that multinationals might introduce a different approach to industrial relations which is based on the tradition of the multinationals' home country. This approach is what Perlmutter described[43] as 'ethnocentric' (he argued, in fact, that not all multinationals operated in such a fashion: some were 'polycentric' and based their industrial relations policy on that adopted in the host country, while others were 'geocentric' adopting a global strategy which allowed for differences between their operation, within different countries). There is some evidence that USA multinationals are particularly likely to try to impose their own approach to industrial relations as workers in the host country. In the UK they have led the move towards single-union deals and in some cases non-unionism. A number of studies[44] have shown how USA multinationals have concentrated more formal authority at corporate headquarters and kept tighter control over the policies adopted by subsidiaries. Japanese multinationals have also tended to base their industrial relations policies for their subsidiaries to some extent on the system they have used at home. They have also had a more general influence on the countries where they have established subsidiaries. For example, in the UK Japanese-style management has been adopted by some UK-based companies, although Oliver and Wilkinson argue[45] not as successfully because they have taken elements out of the Japanese model rather than the package as a whole. European multinationals have been less likely to try to export their home-based approach to industrial relations and they have tended to give more freedom to their subsidiaries, though there are a number of examples which show that this is not an invariable rule.

Trade unions have tried to take action to counter all of these dangers. Action to deal with the first problem has taken the form of canvassing governments to make moves to exert greater control over the ability of multinationals to 'run away' overseas. Action to deal with the second problem has centred on the development of links between unions in different countries and the growth of international trade union federations. Few of these attempts have been particularly successful. The most successful have been in the motor vehicle and chemicals industry. There have also been two examples of international collective bargaining, one from the shipping and the other from the entertainment industry. Miscimarra[46] has documented this latter example but also noted that it has been the exception rather than the rule. Any move towards international collective bargaining is likely to be fiercely resisted by employers who would see it as a way of raising terms and conditions to the highest current level and therefore increasing costs. As far as the third problem is concerned unions have often tried to resist the introduction of 'foreign' industrial relations practices, though this has sometimes been difficult because of the way in which governments have negotiated special terms with multinationals to attract them to 'greenfield' sites where they can more easily introduce industrial relations procedures. There is some, though far from clear, evidence that multinationals generate more strike activity when they try to introduce foreign practices[47] in the UK: this has been most noticeable with USA-based multinationals.

Such recognition of the problems that can be caused by multi-nationals also led, in 1976, to the Organisation for Economic Co-operation and Development drawing up guidelines designed to control the situation. The guidelines included tougher 'anti-bribery' provisions (a number of multinationals had been involved in 'bribery allegations' and 'scandals' earlier in 1976), rules specifying the extent to which governments can demand that multinationals disclose information about their business, and taxation agreements which are designed to make it easier to control 'transfer pricing' (there is a need for fiscal authorities to fix the 'true' prices of goods and services transferred between parts of a multinational company so as to ensure that they are not deprived of revenue). These guidelines were revised in 1979 and again in 1984. However, they remain voluntary and as Rajot has argued[48] although many multinationals in practice act in accordance with them, few have explicitly affirmed their support.

OWNERSHIP AND CONTROL

Berle and Means[49] argued, in the early 1930s, that the increase in the size of the business enterprise had led to the separation of ownership from control. This argument was based on the belief that large organisations were forced to employ specialist managers who had little or no personal stake in the enterprise. Such managers were likely to enjoy considerable freedom of action because 'ownership is so widely distributed that no one individual or small group (of shareholders) has even a minority interest large enough to dominate the affairs of the company'.[50]

The tendency for large-scale organisation to lead to the separation of ownership from control was by no means a new idea; it had been noted many years before by a number of other writers (for example, Adam Smith, Marx). However, Berle and Means in their revision of the thesis suggested that it had implications far beyond those noted by earlier writers. They argued that the separation of ownership from control had led to such fundamental changes in the nature of classical capitalism that it no longer existed.

The Berle and Means thesis gained widespread support in subsequent years in political, industrial and academic circles. For example, in 1956 Crosland argued that in Britain top management was 'independent not only of the firm's own shareholders, but increasingly of the capitalist or property owning class as a whole'.[51] This, he said, was causing fundamental changes to the nature of capitalism; management by capitalism was being replaced by managerial capitalism.

Burnham also lent support to the Berle and Means thesis when he argued that the increasing power of managers was leading to what he termed a 'managerial revolution'.[52] He suggested that changes were taking place in society which would create 'a quite different set of major economic, social and political institutions' and that managers, because of their ability to perform indispensable bureaucratic functions, would emerge 'as the dominant or ruling class'. Burnham's vision of future social and political changes went beyond the Berle and Means thesis, but his insistence on the importance of managerial power clearly lent support to it.

Many other writers have supported the Berle and Means thesis (for example, Cyert and March[53]) by emphasising the fundamental difference between the aims and aspirations of managerial personnel and owners. Managers, it is suggested, unlike owners, will not necessarily aim for profit maximisation (they have little or no direct interest in doing so); rather they will aim for a 'satisfactory' level of profits. Managers are likely to pursue other goals, such as the long-term growth of the enterprise (see Marris[54]).

While such views are widely held they have not gone unchallenged; Child[55] has summarised the criticisms made by what he terms the Marxist school (although he recognises that some of its adherents, such as C. Wright Mills, have not been Marxists). This school, Child says, argues that the differences between ownership and control merely amount to a functional differentiation which has no real effect on the underlying structure of class relationships in society. It states that, first, because in many firms there are such a large number of shareholders control can be gained without the ownership of anything like 50 per cent of the shares. Further, ownership is now becoming concentrated in the hands of major institutions (insurance companies and pension funds). Second, the power of large shareholders is increased by the system of interlocking directorships which means that individuals may be able to extend their influence from one organisation to another (if, for example, the second organisation relies on the first for commercial success). Third, although top managers may not always be major shareholders they may have a great deal of their personal wealth tied up in an enterprise and therefore are unlikely to pursue policy detrimental to business ownership. Fourth, many senior managers have a similar social background to shareholders and accept the respect for property which that induces. Fifth, the policies which an enterprise may pursue are limited by market forces. For example, if an enterprise did not pay sufficient attention to profits then it would leave itself open to a takeover.

Although these criticisms cannot be accepted uncritically there is now a body of evidence to support some of their major points. For example, in Britain institutional shareholders have increased their holdings dramatically in recent years. In 1963 individuals owned 54 per cent of all shares while insurance and pension funds owned 16.4 per cent. In 1988 individuals owned 18 per cent and insurance and pension funds 62 per cent. Moves have been made to try to reverse this trend. The programme of privatisation has increased the spread of shareholding so that by 1988 27 per cent of the adult population held shares compared to 7 per cent in 1979 but it has not been able to halt decline in the proportion of the market held by private investors. Similarly, recent investigations in the United States have found that managers are still frequently owners of considerable property in absolute terms (often encouraged by stock option schemes). In Britain, share option schemes are also important and have been encouraged particularly since 1979, while research by Francis[56] suggests that in many cases individual families still exert control over major companies. Other research in both Britain and the USA[57] has concluded that propertied and non-propertied managers are likely to share the same general value orientation and to enjoy common social relationships. The work of Scott and Hughes[58] on business in Scotland provides evidence on another of the criticisms. They point to the importance of interlocking directorships and identify some of the main links in this complex pattern.

Other evidence suggests that at least the most successful business enterprises pursue the goal of profit maximisation and that the distribution of profits may not have changed significantly in recent years. As a result Child's earlier conclusion seems to be supported by the most recent evidence:

> the popular managerialist thesis that the separation of business ownership and control is one of the most momentous developments in modern capitalist society fails to remain convincing when placed alongside the available evidence. This evidence suggests instead that in such society there are wider economic, social and technological constraints operating on the business enterprise which tend to minimise the behavioural differences between owner-managers and non-propertied managers.[59]

THE MANAGERIAL FUNCTION

One of the other important results of the growth in the size of the enterprise is the division and specialisation of the management function. There is now a considerable body of evidence which shows that increasingly management is being seen as a profession for which formal educational qualifications are essential. This has been referred to in a number of studies of managers in different countries: for example, Dalton[60] (USA), Clark[61] (UK), and Hall *et al.*[62] (Europe).

However, a number of writers have noted that British managers are often less well qualified than their American and European counterparts. For example, while Dubin recognises that a 'high percentage of candidates for managerial, professional and executive positions in American industry have some sort of technical preparation for their future careers through college and university education', he argues that 'until recently the situation has been quite different in British industry. Most managerial recruits to industry had little or no training or education directly linked to their business employment';[63] although Deeks[64] found a significant difference between the under- and over-forty age groups. A study of European managers[65] found that British executives were the least highly educated (the proportions with a university education varied from 40 per cent in Britain to 89 per cent in France). Crockett and Elias[66] argued that despite the expansion of business schools in recent years the higher level of qualifications of young managers in Britain is no more than a reflection of the general increase in the level of education, while the Constable and McCormick[67] and the Handy[68] reports drew attention to the lack of formal education and training of British managers and made a series of proposals for management education which found expression in the 'Charter Initiative'.

Parker *et al.*[69] note that the selective entrance requirements for management are one of the main reasons for the 'differentiation of management from other levels of employment'. This in itself has added to the problems facing one group, the foreman, whose status in industrial organisations has been ambiguous for many years. A great deal has been written[70] in the past twenty years or so about the problems of the foreman, in particular about the way in which his status has been reduced and his role confused. The ambiguity of the foreman's position has also meant that in many cases promotion prospects have been curtailed; although in one survey[71] 50 per cent of the foremen interviewed said that they had a reasonable hope of promotion it is clear that promotion will not be to the level of senior management.

The growing professionalisation of management is closely linked to the increasing specialisation in the management function. One of the consequences of this specialisation of particular importance for industrial relations is the designation of personnel managers. Although personnel management in the UK can be traced back to before the First World War, in its early days it was little more than an industrial branch of social work (it was often referred to as welfare work) and it was not until after the Second World War that it began to be seen as relevant to industrial relations. During the past thirty years the specialism has made great strides. The preoccupation with the need for a professional identity which emerged after the Second World War has endured. The Institute of Personnel Management has played a key role in establishing widely-recognised qualifications developing professional education and codes of conduct. The Institute also plays an important role in providing specialist information for members, running courses and publishing two journals. The Institute has clearly made important advances though it still remains the case that not only do many large companies not demand that their personnel managers have the Institute's qualification but many senior personnel managers are not members of the Institute. The British Workplace Industrial Relations Survey[72] suggested that only about half of all personnel managers have the Institute's qualification while only about a quarter are members.

Personnel managers began to take on more industrial relations functions in the 1960s and 1970s. This was particularly true in manufacturing industry although this also applied more generally, in part being the result of the growth in workplace bargaining. The Donovan Commission, though, reporting during this period, was critical of many firms that did not have a clear personnel policy or, it said, even a clear view of what one should be. In this context British firms suffered by comparison with comparators in other countries, particularly those in the USA.

One of the most important developments affecting the current role of personnel managers, though, has been the emergence of Human Resources Management. This appears to have had two rather difficult implications. One has been that more attention has been paid to the issues that personnel managers see as important and in particular recognition of employees as a key resource. The second has been to take some of the responsibility for 'managing people' out of the hands of personnel managers and to give it to line management.

> Common to many organisations, whether they are simply reacting to the economic situation or undertaking more wide-ranging change, is the assumption or re-assumption by first line managers of responsibility for such matters as absence, appraisal, discipline, grievances, which had gravitated to the personnel department. At workplace level it means that line managers . . . take overall responsibility and in some cases the lead in negotiations with shop stewards. At the company level in those organisations which are inclining towards the 'human resource management approach', it can mean senior line management and even the chief executive take the initiative in chairing personnel policy committees, and are identified with programmes of major change such as 'customer care' and 'working with pride' campaigns.[73]

The position varies enormously from one organisation to the next. Not all firms have embraced the 'Human Resources Management Approach' and even those that have done so have varied the way it has been implemented. Tyson and Fell[74] have developed a typology of the roles that personnel managers can play. The roles are characterised as the 'clerk of works', the 'contracts manager' and the 'architect'. The first of these roles is very much a routine one covering record keeping, interviewing applicants and preparing documents; the second role is geared towards policy, but relatively short-term policy, particularly over agreements with trade unions and dealing with day-to-day industrial relations problems; the third role concerns the holder being involved in policy making as a member of a senior management team with a seat on the board of directors. The 'architect' role is one which sees personnel management given equal status with other aspects of the organisation's work. The role of personnel management may vary between organisations, though as Sisson[75] argues different roles may also be seen at different levels in multi-establishment organisations, and those fulfilling the role of the architect may well have considerable experience as a line manager as well as a personnel manager at some time in their career.

EMPLOYERS' ASSOCIATIONS

It is not easy to isolate the precise origins of employers' associations in any particular country, for most grew out of early combinations which involved little more than a tacit understanding on a restricted range of issues. This is not to underestimate the importance of such combinations nor to ignore the crucial role they played in fixing and maintaining wage levels. Rather, it is to emphasise that few combinations had a formal structure and therefore few were easily visible.

In most countries employers' associations can only be directly traced back to the late nineteenth and early twentieth centuries. The growth of such organisations has been closely linked, by many writers,[76] to the extension of unionism to unskilled workers. For example, it has been claimed that in Britain modern employers' federations were inspired by the growth of 'new unionism'. Thus, Clegg[77] argues that the Shipping Federation was established in 1890 with the purpose of defeating the closed-shop policy of the Sailors' and Firemen's Union, and the Manufacturers Federation for the boot and shoe industry was formed in 1891 in response to the growth of the National Union of Boot and Shoe Operatives. Similarly in Germany the Crimmitschau strike in Saxony is thought to have led to the formation of two multi-industry organisations which later became the Confederation of German Employers' Associations. Again, in France, Oechslin[78] argues that the real development of employers' associations occurred at the beginning of the twentieth century (the union of Metal and Mining Industries and the Federation of Textile Manufacturers' Associations were formed in 1901, the National Federation of Building and Public Works was formed in 1904 and the Federation of Electricity Associations was formed in 1907) as a direct response to the growth of trade unionism.

Some of the leaders of the early associations argued that they had no direct interest in industrial relations; they were merely 'business organisations'. For example, the London Master Builders, on forming their association, resolved that their object was 'to promote a friendly feeling and an interchange of useful information'.[79] In their evidence to the 1867 Royal Commission they claimed that they had never dealt directly with strikes (although they had supported other bodies which had dealt with such matters).

However, Clegg argues that in reality British employers' associations played a much more important role in industrial relations prior to the First World War. In some industries they were instrumental in introducing methods of collective pay regulation (before stable unions were formed); in others they took the initiative in developing collective bargaining; in still others they set up central disputes procedures (the engineering industry is a classic case documented by Wigham[80]).

A similar comment was made by the Donovan Commission. Again, talking about employers' associations in Britain, they said that up to 1914 'they were innovators' in collective bargaining.

> In industries such as coal and iron they instituted collective regulation of pay on the employers' side of industry before stable unions were formed; in iron, in hosiery and in other industries it was the employers who took the initiative in developing collective bargaining with unions on a district basis; in several of our most important industries, including engineering and building, the employers' association forced the unions, in some instances through prolonged lock-outs, to accept the first principle of industry wide bargaining – that local disputes should be submitted to a central conference before a strike or lock-out is begun.[81]

The link between early employers' associations and industrial relations in other countries has been referred to by a number of writers. Chamberlain and Kuhn[82] have referred to the link in the USA, while Isaac and Ford[83] have argued that by the late nineteenth century Australian employers' associations were playing a major role in industrial disputes.

The importance of the role of employer's associations in Britain in industrial relations was pointed to by a Donovan Commission research team.[84] A later survey by the Commission on Industrial Relations in the early 1970s confirmed this.[85] However, more recent evidence has suggested that subsequently a change may have taken place. In some industries employers' associations continue to play a major role at a national level negotiating terms and conditions of employment on behalf of their members. A survey from Warwick University reported by Brown,[86] and the British Workplace Industrial Relations Survey,[87] both suggested that multi-employer bargaining remained important in construction, printing and clothing. They also reported, though, that employers' associations played a much less important role in some other industries. This issue has been taken up by Sisson, in a number of publications,[88] who has suggested that the importance of national bargaining through employers' associations has declined, certainly when compared to the position in other European countries.

Of course, the role of employers' associations as far as industrial relations is concerned is not restricted to pay bargaining. They also operate disputes procedures, provide advice on a range of industrial relations matters, and represent members, for example, on government bodies. The available evidence suggests that in some of these areas the role of employers' associations has been increasing in recent years. For example, the survey conducted from Warwick University suggested that employers had made more use of association disputes procedures in the last few years.

However, while it is important to stress the role played by employers' associations in industrial relations it is also important not to suggest it is the only one (most associations are also trade organisations and in some instances this is a major reason for the membership of associations) or to confuse it. Dunlop[89] refers to employers' associations as the 'bosses' unions. This is confusing because they are not a trade union for managers (they represent owners not managers) and because it implies that employers had to band together to protect their interests in the same way as employees. There is no doubt that employers gained strength from banding together; however, there is also no doubt that on their own they were much stronger than individual employees.

There is some evidence that the role of employers' associations outside the area of industrial relations has become increasingly important. Earlier it was mentioned that employers' associations are usually trade organisations: they are also important pressure groups. Jackson and Sissons[90] have echoed this latter point, noting the enduring importance of employers' associations as political pressure groups. Possibly the most successful pressure group has been the National Farmers' Union which has maintained an effective Parliamentary lobby in both the UK and Europe. Other employees have lobbied over a variety of matters from the cost of power to policy on import controls and levies. Employers' associations have also regularly provided representatives for a range of official committees, commissions and bodies like industrial tribunals and wages councils.

Employers' confederations can also fulfil a lobbying role. Sisson[91] has noted the important role of the CBI in opposing the proposals of the Bullock Committee. In Britain employers' confederations have rarely tried to go beyond such a role.

> There was a short period in the early 1970s when it looked as if the CBI might develop a more important role. For example, in 1971–72 the CBI was able to persuade its members to hold down prices voluntarily in the hope of creating a better climate for pay restraint. The CBI was also involved in tripartite discussions with the TUC which Edward Heath's Conservative Government initiated before introducing a statutory prices and incomes policy in late 1972. Later under the same government, it was involved in informal discussion with the TUC in an attempt to resolve the miners' dispute of 1973–74. Thereafter, it drew back from so called 'tripartitism'.[92]

In other countries, though, employers' confederations have taken a much broader role including negotiating on behalf of members. The contrast can probably best be seen by pointing to the position in Sweden where the employers' confederation has had a key role to play on collective bargaining since its formation in 1902. It negotiates a framework with the national trade union organisations which provides a basis for wage negotiations in individual industries. In other countries the position has not been as clear as in Sweden but employers' confederations have still played a wider role than in Britain. For example, in Italy the employers' confederation bargained with the main union organisation prior to the Second World War and although its role in this regard has been reduced in recent years it still continued to act as a bargaining agent in some areas. In West Germany employers' confederations are not bargaining agents in their own right but are intimately involved in coordinating the bargaining of branch organisation.[93]

The role of employers' associations and confederations, then, varies greatly between countries (and also in some aspects within countries). A number of factors might be isolated as helping to explain why they have taken on the roles they have. For example, an attempt to understand why there are variations in the extent to which associations/confederations are involved in collective bargaining might look at the structure of bargaining.

As a generalisation it might be argued that the greater tendency towards workplace and local bargaining the less likelihood there is that the employers' association will have an impact on bargaining.

Looking internationally it is certainly possible to find evidence to support the argument. For example, in Sweden where there is strong central collective bargaining machinery, it has been noted that the employers' main organisation, the Swedish Employers' Confederation (the SAF) plays a major role. Johnston argues that because of the centralisation 'the Swedish labour market has reached the stage where a handful of key figures could provide the employer members'[94] for negotiations with the trade unions. A similar situation exists in Denmark. The centralised collective bargaining arrangements enable the main employers' body, the Danish Employers' Confederation (DEC) to conduct all negotiations on behalf of its members; further, the Confederation rules prohibit members from shortening working hours, granting a general wage increase, introducing a new minimum wage, changing holiday entitlement or entering into procedural agreements with unions, without first referring the matter to its central council. On the other hand, in the USA where plant bargaining is far more widespread, trade unions normally bargain with individual employers, although, of course, employers often still consult together over industrial relations issues and reach informal arrangements. Beal and Wickersham[95] note the example of the agreement between the New York City publishers that if any one of their papers is hit by a strike, all the others will suspend publication. However, they stress that although this is an illustration of a strong pledge of support from competitors, the bargaining is undertaken by the firm alone. In addition, there are examples of employers' associations bargaining on behalf of their members; this happens in the construction and the garment industries. Nevertheless, there is still a clear difference between the extent to which employers' associations bargain on behalf of their members in Sweden and Denmark, and the USA. The theory stated in this form, though, is too unsophisticated. It might be noted, for example, that to a certain extent the employers' association will be able to determine the structure of collective bargaining. In France, for instance, employers are far better organised than the trade unions. Their strength is concentrated through their national federation, The Conseil National de Patronat Francais (CNPF). Selekman *et al.* have argued that 'by means of its strength, power and discipline' the CNPF has been able 'to take a strong line in bargaining and . . . to dictate the level at which bargaining is carried out'.[96]

Further the extent to which employers' associations will be involved in collective bargaining will be determined not only by the level of collective bargaining but also by the extent to which their organisation matches the bargaining structure. Thus, it has been noted[97] that bargaining in Britain has increasingly been concentrated at the local level, and local employers' associations or associations with local affiliates are much more likely than national associations to play a major role in industrial relations. For instance, when the Donovan Commission research team asked representatives of employers' associations to indicate important areas of their work, those who worked for national associations gave high priority to the representation of members' interests with the government, whereas representatives of local associations often placed more emphasis on relations with trade unions and industrial relations. Similarly, it was recorded that all federations with local affiliates reported that they had disputes machinery but only 58 per cent of associations that did not have any local affiliates reported disputes machinery.

Sisson has taken this a stage further by arguing that the continued reliance on multi-employer bargaining through employers' associations in Western Europe, compared to the reduction in the importance of such bargaining in many parts of British industry, can be explained by the failure of multi-employer bargaining in Britain to neutralise trade union activity in the workplace.

> Whereas previous studies have suggested that multi-employer bargaining in Britain declined because it failed to settle actual pay and conditions in the workplace, the present study has argued that it did so because of its failure to neutralize the workplace from trade union activity. In contrast with the other countries, multi-employer bargaining in Britain developed on the basis of procedural as opposed to substantive rules and those rules took the form of "gentleman's agreements" rather than legally-enforceable contracts. The relatively sparse coverage of substantive issues gave the employer in Britain few points of legitimate defence in the event to his unilateral action being challenged. The voluntary nature of the rules also meant that the employer found it difficult to enforce the peace obligation that was the key feature of disputes procedures.[98]

Another factor which will influence the extent to which employers' associations play a major role in industrial relations will be the nature of their membership. In some instances major employers have stayed outside associations. This has often weakened the ability, if not the desire, of the associations to attempt to bargain on behalf of the industry; the large employers are able not only to disregard the bargain themselves, but also because of their size are able crucially to influence, say wage rates, generally. In some cases, large companies have refused to join associations because they have not felt able to influence decisions sufficiently or to abide by association policy: in Britain this has been particularly felt in the engineering industry, in newspaper publishing and in the clothing industry (each of the associations suffered from the withdrawal of large firms in the 1970s). In an effort to overcome this problem, a number of employers' organisations have amended their rules in the past few years. Gill *et al.*[99] note that in the Chemical Industries Association this has meant introducing the category of the 'non-conforming member'; such members retain autonomy in industrial relations. In the case of the CBI (formed in 1965 from the British Employers' Confederation and the Federation of British Industries) this has meant admitting individual firms, who are not members of constituent associations, to membership.

From some points of view, therefore, employers' associations are more complicated bodies than trade unions and on occasions it is more difficult to generalise about them. In the past few people have examined their operations in any detail; they have been the 'forgotten area' of industrial relations. This led Clegg to note that 'the history of British employers' associations has not been written'[100] and Isaac and Ford to comment that 'in Australia, as in other industrialized countries, the study of employers' associations has lagged considerably behind the study of unions and industrial tribunals'.[101] However, an appreciation of their method of operation is an essential part of any study of industrial relations. Although they are not only interested in industrial relations they clearly can have an important impact on it.

SUMMARY

One of the most visible developments in industrial nations this century has been the growth in the size of the firm and the plant even though in recent years this growth has been halted. The size of the firm and plant has an impact not only on the commercial but also on the industrial relations side of operations. However, the growth in the size of the firm has not been constrained by national boundaries: one of the results has been the increasing proportion of production concentrated in the hands of the multinational enterprise. Again, this has had important consequences for industrial relations.

Berle and Means argued that as the firm grew in size so there was a growth in division between ownership and control. Ownership continues to reside in the hands of shareholders but control has passed to specialist managers, many of whom will have different aims and different orientations. This thesis has been extremely influential in both academic and political circles; however, it is not without its critics. A group of writers, whom Child refers to as the Marxist School, argues that the division noted by Berle and Means is merely a functional differentiation which has no real effect on the underlying class relationships in society.

Whatever the outcome of this argument there is little doubt that in recent years major changes have taken place within the ranks of management themselves. For example, there is evidence of growing specialisation of the management function and increasing specialist training for managers. This has created major problems for one group of employees, the foreman, but has also led to the emergence of personnel management as a specialism.

Employers' associations have received relatively little attention from students of industrial relations. Yet they are bodies with a history often almost as long as the trade unions operating in the same area and are bodies which can have a major influence on the direction of industrial relations. It is important to note, however, that employers' associations differ considerably in the roles they perform. Some place great emphasis on trade and commercial functions but relatively little on industrial relations, whereas others adopt the opposite stance. One of the factors that seems to be related to the kind of function undertaken is the structure of the organisation (in particular, whether or not it has a strong local organisation) though there are other factors to be taken into account, which make a straightforward explanation difficult.

6 Collective bargaining: an introduction

NATURE OF COLLECTIVE BARGAINING

The term collective bargaining was coined by the Webbs[1] and was used to refer to negotiations concerning pay and conditions of employment between trade unions on the one hand and either an employer or an employers' association on the other. Flanders[2] argued that the Webbs's view of the nature of collective bargaining, if not their definition, was erroneous. He suggested that the Webbs saw collective bargaining as being exactly what the words imply, a collective equivalent to individual bargaining; he called this the classical view:

> Where workmen were willing and able to combine, they preferred it to bargaining as individuals with their employer because it enabled them to secure better terms of employment by controlling competition among themselves. And the greater the scale of the bargaining unit – so it appeared – the greater their advantage.[3]

However, Flanders said that the Webbs were not 'comparing like with like'. Collective bargaining is a 'rule making' activity which regulates but does not replace individual bargaining. It is best seen as a method of job regulation which should be compared to unilateral regulation (by employers, employees or the state) rather than to individual bargaining. Flanders highlighted a number of differences between collective and individual bargaining.

First, Flanders argued, an individual bargain is about the buying or selling of a particular commodity whereas collective bargaining does not involve the buying or selling of anything; it is merely an agreement on the conditions under which buying or selling will take place. Second, an individual bargain usually stipulates in detail the terms and conditions of trade, whereas in collective bargaining only the minimum terms and conditions are specified. Third, individual bargaining is essentially a market activity (it is about buying and selling) whereas collective bargaining is essentially a political activity (a strike or lockout is really a diplomatic use of power; neither side intends to break the relationship completely as they both realise that eventually they will have to reach an agreement). Fourth, because collective bargaining is a political rather than an economic activity, different factors have to be taken into account; collective bargaining, for example, is frequently undertaken by professional negotiators who recognise the need to maintain relationships with the other side and therefore will not necessarily press their advantage to the full. Fifth, collective bargaining, unlike individual, is not restricted to a discussion of economic matters, but is concerned with other issues; it is concerned for example, with workers' rights, the control of industry and so on.

Flanders's views on the nature of collective bargaining overlap with those of a number of other writers; he discussed the work of Chamberlain and Kuhn.[4] They argued that three theories are held about the nature of collective bargaining. The first is really the same as that which Flanders called the classical view of collective bargaining: it sees collective bargaining essentially as a means of contracting for the sale of labour. The second views collective bargaining as a form of industrial government: its principal function is to lay down the rules and set up the machinery for the government of industry. The third views collective bargaining as a method of management it stresses the functional relationship between unions and companies and suggests that they combine through collective bargaining to make decisions from which they can both benefit.

These three theories are not mutually exclusive or incompatible. To a certain extent they can be seen as reflecting different stages in the historical development of collective bargaining. Flanders wrote:

> Early negotiations were mainly a matter of fixing terms for the sale of labour; the agreements might consist of no more than standard piecework price lists. Later came the need for procedures for settling disputes on these and other issues between the parties, which sometimes took the form of setting up joint bodies possibly with an independent chairman; this provided a foundation for the government theory. Only when eventually agreements were made on subjects that entered into the internal decision-taking process of a business enterprise, was there a basis for the managerial theory of collective bargaining.[5]

Flanders believed that the managerial theory of collective bargaining had a great deal to offer. It stressed that labour is interested not only in the price gained through wages but also in the management of the enterprise. The only danger Flanders saw was that it might be imagined (as initially suggested, though later rejected, by Chamberlain) that through collective bargaining trade unions are taking over or becoming part of the management function. Such a view would be erroneous, for what unions are doing through collective bargaining is merely setting limits on management action. Management is confronted by demands from a variety of different groups wanting to fulfil their aspirations through the medium of the enterprise: 'work groups on the shop floor and functional groups within the managerial hierarchy, but also external groups – the suppliers of materials and of capital, shareholders and customers'. Management's task is to reach one decision which will 'bind all participants into the company's operations'.[6]

However, Flanders's thesis has been criticised by Fox.[7] He argues that Flanders's criticism of the Webbs's notion of collective bargaining is erroneous. Fox suggests that Flanders made a number of errors in his comparison of individual and collective bargaining. First, Flanders used MacIver and Page's definition of an individual bargain: 'the process by which the antithetical interests of supply and demand, of buyer and seller, are finally adjusted (so as to end) in the act in exchange'.[8] The pitfall in this explanation, according to Fox, is that it is assumed that bargaining always ends 'in the act of exchange'. In many instances this is not the case: instead the negotiations are broken off and no exchange is concluded. As an alternative explanation Fox argues that individual bargaining should be viewed as having three distinct though normally sequential elements: first, a bargaining process during which the parties deploy argument, present evidence and issue threats; second, this element may or may not end in an agreement which adjusts the antithetical interests of buyer and seller; third, this element may or may not result in a contract into which both parties decide to enter. Fox recognises that in practice these elements may appear to be fused into a single process, but suggests that it is important to distinguish them for analytical purposes so as to emphasise that a contract may not be the end result of the bargaining process. Thus Fox argues that it is erroneous to suggest that individual and collective bargaining are different because one ends in a contract whereas the other ends in rule making; neither bargain necessarily ends in agreement (in both cases this is a possibility, but no more).

Second, Fox attacks Flanders for arguing that there is a difference between the individual and the collective bargain in that the latter, but not the former, is a political process involving 'the diplomatic use of power'. Fox does not deny that collective bargaining involves the 'diplomatic use of power'; his argument is that so does individual bargaining. Thus he suggests that in an individual bargain the employer

> may or may not consider it in his interests to bring his full superiority of bargaining power to bear upon the employee – the possibility of his not doing so is explicitly recognised and explained by the Webbs – and the occasional employee who finds himself in a strong position may or may not choose to take maximum short-term advantage of it – probably not if he has in mind the desirability of a long-term relationship with his employer.[9]

The difference between the individual and the collective bargain is not that the 'diplomatic use of power' is seen in one and not in the other; the difference 'is precisely what the Webbs said it was – a difference in the disparity of power'.[10]

Third, Fox challenges Flanders's assertion that the individual and the collective bargain differ in that a refusal to conclude a contract is taken at face value in the former case, whereas in the latter case it is seen to be a bargaining ploy; the assumption behind a strike is not that the employees will seek a job elsewhere if the employer refuses to meet their demands but that sooner or later their present employer will be compelled to reinstate them. However, Fox argues that the differences between the collective and the individual refusal are more convincingly seen as ones of contingency rather than principle.

> The reason why the individual refusal is associated with the notion of moving on if the employer declines to improve his offer is because the disparity of power is so great that the individual hardly expects any other course to be practicable. The collective refusal, on the other hand, embodies the hope that sufficient power can be deployed to bring the employer to terms. Neither expectation is necessarily realised.[11]

Perhaps the most important criticism of Flanders's work made by Fox, though, centres not on the detail of the differences between individual and collective bargaining but on the implications of Flanders's general approach. A major conclusion of Flanders's line of reasoning is that the main function of collective bargaining and trade unionism is political rather than economic. The argument is that workers are concerned now just as much, if not more, with issues of management as they are with economic questions such as wage rates. Thus, Flanders gave support to Chamberlain and Kuhn's notion of 'managerial bargaining', through which workers try to influence decision making in the enterprise, and to the view that workers join unions and unions gain their *raison d'être* from their non-economic activity (they represent an interest group and enhance the status of workers). Fox recognises that the evidence on the motives of unions in undertaking bargaining, and of workers in joining unions, is at times contradictory and inconclusive. However, he argues

> that the intensity of conviction, effort, and feeling which many trade unionists appear to invest in pay claims hardly seems to be given sufficient recognition and weight in the Flanders analysis, and that with respect to theoretical formulations we should declare that the issue is still open rather than accept Flanders' suggestion to foreclose it by downgrading the economic motivations and achievements of collective bargaining.[12]

It is also important to remember that while Flanders viewed managerial issues as the major cause of concern of collective bargaining, he only accorded unions restricted scope in this area. The function of collective bargaining and unions was to lay down guidelines and conditions; unions should not attempt to take over managerial functions through collective bargaining.

BARGAINING STRUCTURE

Any definition of collective bargaining has to take into account the enormous variety of different types of machinery involved. A number of examples might serve to illustrate this. There are differences, for instance, in terms of the level at which bargaining takes place. National bargaining between unions, sometimes groups of unions, and employers' associations can be compared to bargaining at an individual workplace. In between there are examples of company-level bargaining and bargaining within an individual cost centre, which may cover a number of workplaces. The different levels of bargaining are likely to involve different people. National negotiations are likely to involve national union officials, sometimes officers of an employers' association, and senior national staff from firms in the industry. Local bargaining may involve full time and/or lay officials on the union side and personnel representatives and/or a factory manager on the employer's side. It also needs to be recognised that, say, pay may be determined in an establishment as the result of bargaining at a number of different levels: for example, certain aspects of pay may be nationally determined while others may be determined at the establishment. Sometimes, also, national bargaining may only determine minimum levels of pay which can be enhanced by local bargaining.

Other differences include the coverage of bargaining: that is, whether the bargaining machinery covers, say, a section of the workforce in an industry or all workers. In most instances, there will be a division between manual and non-manual workers, but there may also be divisions within these categories, such as by skill. The structure of trade unions may influence these matters. One union representing all workers in an industry may encourage broader bargaining units while a number of different unions operating in an industry may encourage narrower units. However, one cannot make this into a rule, for individual unions may bargain on behalf of different groups within an industry through different bargaining units, while a number of different unions may come together to represent a range of categories of worker through one bargaining unit.

Variations might also be noted in the form that bargaining takes and the scope of agreements. The first of these issues really refers to the way in which an agreement is recorded. Many agreements, though by no means all, are written. As a generalisation, the higher the bargaining level the more likely it is that the bargain will be formally recorded in a document, whereas the lower the bargaining level the less likely any agreement will be formally recorded. Workplace agreements may simply pass into custom and practice. Even national, formally recorded agreements, will often not be legally enforceable between the two parties who reached the agreement. In the UK, enforcement is more likely to be through the incorporation of any such agreement into the individual contract of employment. The second issue, the scope of the agreement, indicates the range of matters covered by any bargain, and this can vary enormously. As was indicated in the Webbs's definition of collective bargaining, pay is seen as a critical element, but most collective agreements go beyond pay, to other conditions of employment, and sometimes to matters like work organisations.

Negotiations will also take place on both procedural and substantive matters. The latter will determine the conditions that should apply to the groups of workers covered, the rates of pay, the hours of work, holidays, sick pay, and so on. The former will determine how discussions on these matters will take place and what will happen if they break down. Some will specify that in the event of the parties concerned being unable to reach agreement the matter should be referred, say, initially to a higher level of bargaining (differences at the local level might be referred to the regional or national level), and if there is no agreement at that stage some kind of third party intervention may be specified. A number of different kinds of intervention are possible. Conciliation is an attempt by a third party to bring the parties together and act as 'honest broker', but no more. Mediation suggests that the third party might go a little further and try to see if specific alternatives would be acceptable. Arbitration is the most direct form of intervention, when the third party 'rules' on the matter in dispute. There are many variations in these devices, some of which will be discussed in the next chapter when looking at recent developments in bargaining and others which will be discussed when looking at the role of the state. Reference to the role of the state means that it is important to stress that where third party intervention is allowed for in 'procedure' agreements, that intervention might be specially designed by the parties concerned simply for use in that industry or might be provided by the state.

The emphasis above, then, has been on the enormous variation in bargaining structures. Some of the complexity of bargaining arrangements should also be emphasised and this might be done most effectively by reference to the bargaining machinery in one industry. The textile industry in the UK is in practice an amalgamation of a number of different activities and each of them has separate bargaining arrangements even though in many cases an individual company may span many, if not all, activities and an individual union may represent workers in a number of different types of activity.

In one sector, knitting and hosiery, negotiations are conducted through a National Joint Industrial Council with the executive committees of the employers (the Knitting Industries Federation) and the union (the National Union of Hosiery and Knitwear Workers) meeting under an independent chair. The formality of these negotiations could be contrasted with the position in the woollen and worsted sector, where until recently a series of negotiations took place with a number of relatively small unions, like the Dyers and Bleachers Union, on a much more informal basis (the position in this sector changed somewhat in the mid-1980s after the Dyers and Bleachers union amalgamated with the Transport and General Workers' Union) with 'lead' negotiations dictating their pattern for later ones. In some sectors of the industry, like the cotton, man-made and allied fibres, the national negotiations have been limited in scope, with the employers' side keen to leave as much as possible to local negotiations, whereas in other sectors, like knitting and hosiery, the national negotiations have been much more comprehensive and although some variations have occurred in individual companies, such variation typically has been the result of local productivity deals rather than a renegotiation of national terms. In many of the sectors a single trade union negotiates with a single employers' federation, but in the yarn and fibre products sector five unions are party to the negotiations with one taking the lead. There are also substantial overlaps in the parties to the negotiations between the sectors. Some unions negotiate in more than one sector (for example, the Transport and General Workers' Union negotiates in a number of sectors with the same national official taking the lead) as do some employers' associations (the British Textile Employers' Association negotiates in both the yarn and fabric production and dyeing and finishing of cotton and woven fabrics sectors). The complexity of negotiations in the textile industry increased in the 1980s as some of the main firms left the national negotiating machinery. In some cases, the negotiations within those firms were clearly influenced by those conducted for the rest of the sector, but in others, firms devolved bargaining to 'profit centres' leading to a variety of substantive and procedural agreements within the sector.

DEVELOPMENT OF COLLECTIVE BARGAINING IN BRITAIN

The origins and early development of collective bargaining in Britain have been discussed at length by a number of authors.[13] Although differences of emphasis exist, the outline is broadly accepted. For example, most writers accept that although there is evidence of collective bargaining in Britain in the eighteenth century (particularly in the silk weaving and shipbuilding industries) and of negotiations between employers and groups of workers where internal contracting was common (Littler [14]), major and sustained development did not take place until the middle of the nineteenth century, and even then was concentrated in certain areas. Thus, it has been argued[15] that by the late nineteenth century collective bargaining had only become well-established practice in two groups of industries and occupations. The first of these groups were the skilled trades (such as shipbuilding, engineering, building, furniture making and printing); the Webbs estimated that

> in all skilled trades, where men work in concert, on the employers' premises, ninety per cent of the workmen find, either their rate of wages or their hours of work, and often many other details, predetermined by collective bargaining.[16]

The second group consisted of predominantly piece-work occupations in the coal mining, iron and steel, cotton textiles, boot and shoe and hosiery and lace industries.

It is also generally accepted that even though collective bargaining had been extended to other groups of workers (particularly manual and unskilled) by the outbreak of the First World War, it was still essentially locally based. Thus, Clegg has argued that before the First World War 'it was difficult to discern a definite trend towards industry-wide pay settlements'.[17]

However, a move towards industry-wide settlements occurred during and immediately after the First World War. It is not easy to say precisely why it happened, but it appears that at least four developments acted as catalysts.

The first was the rapid rise in the cost of living during the war which meant that wages had to be constantly adjusted. Thus it has been argued that in 'these circumstances the settlement of rates of pay separately town by town and district by district seemed cumbersome and dilatory'.[18] The second was the decision by the government to take control of many industries for the period of the war (coal and railways are good examples). This meant that there was one central employer who was able to, and would probably find it more convenient to, bargain on a national basis. The third was the decision of the government to introduce the Munitions of War Act in 1915. The Act effectively prohibited strikes and lockouts and introduced a system of compulsory arbitration throughout a wide range of industries. Arbitration, because it normally concerned national terms, clearly encouraged bargaining over such issues.

However, in many ways, the most important catalyst was the fourth, the Whitley Committee. The Committee, established in 1916 partly as a response to the industrial unrest of the first few years of the war, had been asked to make suggestions for securing a permanent improvement in the relations between employers and workmen and to recommend ways of systematically reviewing industrial relations in the future. The Committee produced five reports[19] in all, and in the process suggested major innovations in bargaining machinery. Two of these innovations were particularly important. First, the Committee argued for the establishment of joint industrial councils in well-organised industries where national bargaining could take place (these councils were to be supported by a range of district and local bodies). Second, it suggested extensions to the system of statutory wage regulation in badly organised trades and to the powers currently held by the government to conciliate and arbitrate in industrial disputes.

The Committee's recommendations were well received by the government and both sides of industry. Between January 1918 and December 1921, 73 joint industrial councils and 33 interim reconstruction committees (set up by the Ministry of Reconstruction to provide some representative body in industries where organisation was insufficiently developed to enable a joint industrial council to be proposed) were established. The statutory regulation of wages in unorganised industries suggested by the Committee was achieved in 1918 through the extension of the Trade Boards Act of 1909 which had empowered trade boards (composed of representatives from both sides of industry) to fix minimum wage rates, and the facilities for arbitration and inquiry recommended were introduced through the Industrial Courts Act of 1919.

The reports of the Whitley Committee can be said to have provided the basis for much of the present-day national bargaining machinery in Britain, though it should be noted that much of the machinery set up during this period fell into disuse in subsequent years; for example, by 1924 only 47 of the joint industrial councils were still operating and by 1938 there were only 45. There were also attempts on the part of a number of employers to move back to local negotiations. In the coal mining industry, for instance, the employers reintroduced local bargaining after the general strike and maintained it for the whole of the inter-war period (the Coal Mines Act of 1930 set up the Coal Mines National Industry Board, designed to provide a platform for national negotiations, but the employers refused to nominate members and as a result it was never able to operate).[20]

Of course, there were exceptions to this general rule. For example, collective bargaining altered little in the relatively small number of industries sheltered from the depression; these included those not subject to foreign competition (such as building and the railways) and a number operated by prosperous combines (such as chemicals, cement and flour milling). Similarly, collective bargaining escaped more or less unscathed in the public sector; joint industrial councils were maintained and in some instances extended in the manual, public and civil service sections. These exceptions, however, merely point up the general decline in national bargaining machinery in this period.

In many ways, though, the inter-war period might be regarded as a temporary setback, for during the Second World War much of the machinery and techniques that had fallen into disuse were revived. For example, joint industrial councils again flourished; fifty-six were established or renewed in the wartime period. Similarly, the government again introduced a form of compulsory arbitration, this time through the Conditions of Employment and National Arbitration Order of 1940 (which prohibited strikes and lock-outs and set up a new body, the National Arbitration Tribunal, to arbitrate in disputes and to issue binding awards). Further, the system of statutory wage regulation, which had been started in its current form through the trade boards and consolidated after the Whitley Report, was extended through the Wages Council Act of 1945, the Catering Wages Act of 1943 and the Agricultural Wages (Regulation) Act of 1947.

As a result, by the end of the Second World War, the bulk of workers in British industry were covered by some kind of national collective bargaining machinery. Indeed, the Ministry of Labour estimated that only 2 million of the 17.5 million workers in industry and services at this time were not covered by voluntary or statutory negotiating machinery. In succeeding years coverage was extended to two of the most important remaining groups, non-manual workers and professional employees.

Progress in these areas was partly the result of increased government activity in the industrial and service sphere. The Nationalisation Acts put a statutory responsibility on the new authorities to set up negotiating machinery for all their employees; as most manual workers were already covered this requirement had most effect on the non-manual sector. Government involvement in the provision of services, particularly social services, encouraged the development of bargaining machinery to cover professional groups. In the past, professionals had maintained that bargaining machinery was inappropriate because normally contracts were made with individual employers; when the state took over as the major employer and the third party between the client and the professional, then collective bargaining became more feasible and desirable.

Descriptions of bargaining machinery written in the 1950s and 1960s tended to conclude with the assumption that Britain had a comprehensive system of national collective bargaining; little was heard of local machinery or local bargaining. In fact there is little doubt that such descriptions were inaccurate. Clegg[21] has pointed out that local bargaining and local workgroups had been important for many years, and he refers, for example, to the importance of workgroups and shop stewards in the engineering industry at the end of the nineteenth century. Nevertheless, when the Donovan Commission reported in 1968[22] that local collective bargaining was more important than anyone had ever realised, it was treated as a major revelation. In their report, the Commission argued that there were two 'systems' of bargaining: one the formal system based on the often-described national negotiating machinery, the other the informal system based on local activity. Local bargaining was often unstructured and was not based on any formal machinery (there were, of course, exceptions to this rule – the bargaining machinery for the coal mining industry provided a detailed structure at the local level); maybe this is one of the reasons why it had been so studiously ignored by earlier commentators. Yet, the Donovan Commission argued, local bargaining was now of crucial importance.

The review of the Donovan Commission came out at a time of ferment within British industrial relations in general and collective bargaining in particular. The traditional system of industrial relations was being modified by increased state intervention. This will be looked at in detail in Chapter 11. However, it is worthwhile noting that it led to a debate about the desirability of 'free' collective bargaining. Most trade unions fiercely defended their right to bargain with employers free from the control of the state. Incomes policies which sought to establish norms for wage rises became the focus for trade union opposition. Some union leaders recognised that the achievements of free collective bargaining had been limited and that more state intervention might be necessary if the position of the low paid were to be significantly changed. Even those leaders, though, were concerned at the attention paid to wages rather than other sources of income and profits and at the differential rate of success of 'incomes restraint' in the public and private sector. The employers, in particular the view presented for them through the CBI,[23] were less critical of government intervention as such. They were more concerned, though, to encourage government action to rectify what they saw as an imbalance of power between unions and employers and with what government could do to improve 'realistic' bargaining rather than with rigid controls on incomes.

In the 1980s the position of trade unions came under attack and as was noted in Chapter 3, the extent of unionisation of the workforce was reduced. In some areas this meant a reappraisal of bargaining machinery. Nevertheless, collective bargaining remained of major importance for industrial relations in Britain. The British Workplace Industrial Relations Survey[24] estimated that 71 per cent of all employees were covered by collective bargaining in 1984. This, of course, is much more than the proportion in trade unions at the same date. There were, though, significant differences within this overall total. In the public sector the nationalised industries can be distinguished from public administration. In the former, virtually all employees were covered by collective bargaining, whereas in the latter, only about three-quarters were covered. In the private sector, a distinction might be drawn between manufacturing and services. In the former, collective bargaining was used to determine the pay of manual workers in a majority of establishments (55 per cent in 1984), although in only a minority (26 per cent in 1984) where non-manual workers were concerned. In the latter, collective bargaining was used to determine the pay of manual workers in a lower proportion of establishments (38 per cent in 1984) but in a higher proportion of establishments for non-manual workers (30 per cent in 1984). Such differences to a large extent reflected differences in unionisation, but the size of the undertaking was also an important factor (of course, unionisation rates are also linked to size). For example, in private manufacturing industry collective bargaining was used to determine rates of pay of manual workers in less than 40 per cent of establishments with fewer than 50 workers, but in 99 per cent of establishments with more than 500 employees. Another survey of the extent of collective bargaining, in this case by the Confederation of British Industries,[25] reached broadly similar conclusions. Although it recognised significant differences between sectors and companies, it noted that the coverage of collective bargaining, in aggregate, had changed little between 1979 and 1986. Of manufacturing establishments, 70 per cent were reported as having collective bargaining in 1986 compared to 71 per cent in 1979. The CBI survey also allowed changes in the use of collective bargaining in individual firms to be noted. Thus, a range of firms that reported collective bargaining in 1979 were asked whether these arrangements had changed in 1986.

> This matched sub-sample enabled a clear picture of the extent of change amongst those establishments over a period of recession. Of the 249 establishments that had collective bargaining in 1979 only ten no longer had collective bargaining by 1986. Indeed by 1986 nine of those establishments previously without collective bargaining had introduced it. As a result although there were some minor shifts in the extent of collective bargaining at the margins, the total number of establishments covered was effectively unchanged.[26]

INTERNATIONAL COMPARISONS

The British model of collective bargaining probably can be contrasted most vividly with its US counterpart. Traditionally the hallmark of British collective bargaining was its 'voluntary nature'; although it was encouraged by the state (especially during wartime), generally unions and employers were left to establish their own bargaining machinery. However, in the USA the bulk of collective bargaining has a long-standing legislative base. Perhaps the most important piece of legislation in this context is the Wagner Act of 1935 which laid down the procedure for the registration of bargaining units and the recognition of bargaining rights. The central role was given to a National Labor Relations Board, with the power to ballot employees to discover which union should be given bargaining rights and to compel an employer to bargain effectively over a specified range of issues. Some indication of the impact of this legislation can be obtained by looking at the figures relating to the extent of collective bargaining in the USA; whereas in the early 1930s only about 10 per cent of employees were covered by collective bargaining, the proportion was in excess of 50 per cent by the 1960s.[27] Although it would be erroneous to argue that collective bargaining would not have been extended at all had it not been for the Wagner Act it is worthwhile noting that collective bargaining covered a considerably higher proportion of the workforce than do the trade unions.

Two important consequences of the Wagner Act might be mentioned. First, it resulted in extensive litigation over bargaining rights and bargaining units. Throughout the 1960s, on average, about 7,000 elections were conducted annually to determine bargaining rights under the auspices of the NLRB; it is also worth noting that in about 40 per cent of the cases the union concerned lost the contest.[28] There are also provisions which enable a union to be divested of current bargaining rights. Although overall such provisions have been used far less frequently than those governing the granting of bargaining rights (on average there have been only between 200 and 250 elections each year over the decertification of unions for bargaining purposes) the position has been different at certain times, particularly during harsh economic conditions, and the proportion of cases in which the unions have lost their rights has been high.[29]

Second, it has meant that in the USA bargaining machinery has been centred traditionally on the firm and the enterprise rather than the industry. This is related to the interpretation of the bargaining unit used by the NLRB. Of course, this does not mean that industry-wide agreements are unknown (Weber[30] has noted developments in this area), nor that informal arrangements do not exist to encourage comparability between different firms in the same industry (Chamberlain and Kuhn[31] discuss the development of 'pattern bargaining' and 'key bargains' through which settlements reached within a major bargaining unit become the pattern for other enterprises), but it does mean that local bargaining is far more the centre of the formal system than it is in most other countries.

The important role played by the law in collective bargaining in the USA is also well illustrated by the Taft–Hartley Act of 1947. Whereas the Wagner Act dealt with the parties to and conditions for bargaining, the Taft–Hartley Act concentrated on its consequences. Under the terms of the 1947 Act the President has been able to intervene in bargaining if stalemate has been reached and he has felt that the resulting dispute would be likely to imperil national safety or health. After seeking a report on the dispute, the President has been able to take out an injunction against the strike or lock-out and order the two sides to cooperate with the Federal Mediation and Conciliation Service to try to find a solution. A period of sixty days has been set aside for this stage, after which a report has been made by the mediators and the National Labor Relations Board have balloted the workers concerned to see whether they would accept the employers' latest offer. Once this had been done, if the workers still refused to accept the offer, then the dispute could continue unhampered.

The Taft–Hartley procedure clearly was not intended to be widely used: it is only suitable for major disputes where protracted negotiations have failed to find a solution. Further, in most of the cases in which an injunction has been taken out, a voluntary agreement has been reached between the parties and the compulsory ballot has been unnecessary (it is worth noting, though, that when a ballot has been held compulsorily it has invariably resulted in a vote against the latest offer). Nevertheless, the Taft–Hartley procedure has been an important element in US bargaining, if only because it has existed as a threat and shown the extent to which the law could be used in the final resort.

Collective bargaining in Britain and the USA has also been markedly different in the substantive nature of agreements reached. Two examples might be cited. The first is the difference in terms of the length of the contract. Traditionally in the USA collective agreements have been fixed term, usually for a year or longer;[32] crucially they have all had a definite date on which they have to come to an end. Traditionally in Britain, agreements have been open-ended. In the 1960s and 1970s there was a move in Britain towards the US (and generally European) procedure; fixed-term contracts were negotiated, for instance, in the engineering, building, shipbuilding, cotton textile and railway industries. Nevertheless, the fixed-term contract is still not as widely accepted in Britain as in the

USA with the result that British bargaining is not as clearly geared, as in the USA, to the annual bargaining round (the time when a number of major contracts come up for renewal). This difference has been important for it has meant that in the USA there has been a period, known well ahead, when major disputes were likely to occur. On the other hand, in Britain, it has been far more difficult to predict disputes or to assume that they will fall within a fairly well-defined period.

The second example concerns the range of issues covered by collective bargaining. Traditionally trade unions in the USA have sought, and been much more successful than their British counterparts in obtaining, fringe benefits for their members through collective bargaining. Partly, this has been due to the policy of the National Labor Relations Board in the USA which has insisted, with its legal powers, that employers bargain over a wide range of issues; however, it has also been the result of other factors, such as the restricted role of the state in the provision of welfare benefits, the relatively weak political links of the unions and so on. There has been some movement in the situation in Britain in recent years. For instance, whereas in 1961 only 3 per cent of full-time workers had a holiday with pay entitlement of more than two weeks a year, by 1986 all full-time employees had an entitlement of at least four weeks. Similarly, by 1982 more than 49 per cent of male and 57 per cent of female employees were covered by occupational pension schemes.[33] Nevertheless, the benefits gained for workers in Britain are still more restricted in scope and certainly far more recent than those gained for their US counterparts. Thus, it was estimated[34] that as early as 1960 over 14 million US workers were covered by pension schemes.

In recent years the proportion of workers in the USA covered by collective bargaining has declined markedly. In the private sector the number of workers covered has fallen from 10.8 million in 1970 to about 6.5 million in 1987. This has been compensated for to a small extent by an increase in the number of workers covered by collective bargaining in the public sector, though despite this increase the 1987 total for the public sector was only 2.3 million. The decline in the coverage of collective bargaining in the private sector in part mirrors the decline in union membership (about 2.5 million of the 4.3 million decline can be accounted for by the drop in union membership). At the same time as the coverage of collective bargaining has declined unions have faced a more difficult bargaining climate and pressure for different types of agreement. Thus, there has been pressure to agree to lump sum payments rather than increases in basic wage rates, backloading of contracts (that is, when agreements last for more than a year, higher wage rises are concentrated at the end of the period) has become much more common and the use of pattern bargaining has declined. Much of this pressure for different types of agreement can be linked to adverse economic conditions, and the particular problems caused by those conditions in the early 1980s led to the growth of what became known as 'concession bargaining' where employers negotiated wage and other concessions from unions in return for job retention (a survey by *Business Week* in the spring of 1982 reported that a quartet of firms settling achieved wage and benefit concessions from workers). Some of this pressure eased as economic conditions improved in the late 1980s, but the continued weakness of trade unions has meant that there has been little recovery in the coverage of collective bargaining in the private sector.

In some ways collective bargaining in Europe has reflected a mixture of British and US styles. For example, bargaining has been based on national negotiating machinery, as traditionally was the case in Britain (though, as will be noted in Chapter 7, this has been changing in recent years), rather than on local machinery as in the USA. This has probably been most visible in West Germany, where nearly all bargaining has been on an industry basis and virtually none has been at plant level (the only major exceptions have been found in Volkswagen and the sugar industry where plant bargaining has a long history). It also has been broadly true of most other European countries: in particular in Denmark (where bargaining has been highly centralised between the main employers' organisation, the DAF, and the main trade union organisation, the LO), the Netherlands (where centralised bargaining has been used to underpin, until recently, a relatively 'successful' incomes policy) and in France (where until recently heavy reliance was placed on state-regulated minimum terms). One needs to add a caveat, though; in the past few years changes appear to have been taking place and there is more evidence of local bargaining. This has been especially noticeable in Italy and France; it is also noticeable in other countries like Sweden and West Germany where one might have expected more resistance.

However, while the level of bargaining in most European countries has had some similarities with the traditional position in Britain, in most cases its legal framework has more clearly resembled the US model. Perhaps the best example can be found in France where collective bargaining has been based on the Collective Agreement Act, passed in 1950 and amended in 1971. The 1950 Act, together with its amendments, has provided a comprehensive legal framework for collective agreements. It has established that agreements must be written not oral; they must contain the minimum terms of social legislation as a collective contract cannot restrict the statutory rights of employees; non-union workers benefit from the terms of the agreement and further parties must not be barred from acceding to it at a later date; and all agreements are legally binding on their signatories.[35]

Similar comments might be made about Germany, where collective bargaining has been based on a series of Collective Agreement Acts (1949, 1952 and 1969), which have established that all collective agreements are legally binding and circumscribe a worker's right to strike. The major exceptions to this rule are Denmark, where relations between employers and workers, despite certain legislative provisions, have been based on a strong tradition of 'voluntary' cooperation ('the emphasis in the system is on voluntarism and legal regulation is at a minimum'[36]) and Italy, where the state has intervened relatively little in collective bargaining in recent years, the only exception being the Workers Statute of 1970 which was designed to promote the development of collective bargaining 'by virtue of the positive support [it] gave to the position of the unions'.[37]

There are other similarities between collective bargaining in Europe and the USA. For example, collective agreements have tended to be for fixed terms (although in some cases for more than one year, on occasions for as long as three or four) and have had a wider coverage of conditions than has been the case in Britain (in many senses British unions were unique in their lack of interest in fringe benefits for so long). However, in other aspects collective bargaining in Europe resembles neither the British nor the USA model. Perhaps the feature which best exemplifies this is the operation of works councils in most European countries.

The role of works councils in many Western European countries was noted in the discussion of trade unions. They are particularly important in Germany where they have to be established by law (through a series of Acts dating from 1952) in all joint stocks companies with over 500 employees; in France where an enterprise committee has to be set up (through an Ordinance introduced in 1945) in all enterprises employing more than 50 workers; in Belgium whose works councils have been required under legislation passed in 1948 in all private sector enterprises employing 200 persons or more, and in Italy, the Netherlands and Denmark. The precise role of these councils and committees varies but most include a mixture of items, some of which are covered by collective bargaining in Britain. As a result the relationship between works councils and collective bargaining is not always clear. In some circumstances works councils can be seen as a separate method of worker participation; a supplement rather than a partial alternative to collective bargaining. However, a report issued by the Commission on Industrial Relations argued that most works councils in European countries were 'effectively collective bargaining institutions at plant level'.[38]

Possibly the most important implication of the work undertaken by the councils from the point of view of collective bargaining is the extent to which that can lead to a split in collective bargaining between the national and local level. This is especially likely to occur when the trade unions are responsible for negotiations at the national level but have no representation on the works council. This is not true in all countries (in Italy, for example, only trade unions may submit lists for election to the council), but a number of instances were noted during the discussions on the role of trade unions where this was the case.[39]

The variations in collective bargaining machinery from one country to another could be listed, almost *ad infinitum*. For example, in Sweden[40] collective bargaining is even more strongly centralised than in most European countries. Effectively wage norms are agreed by the main employers and union organisations with the government, and all bargaining takes place within these guidelines. In Eastern Europe[41] bargaining again has been highly centralised, but the bargaining has been between the unions and the government, not private employers. As a result, bargaining probably has been a misleading term to use in this context; trade unions have agreed to fulfil a role which fits into the national plan. The main bargaining (analogous with that carried on in the West) in Russia, for instance, occurred at the local level where unions were involved in negotiating over plant interpretation of national rules and individual grievances. At the time of writing changes were taking place to the role of trade unions in Eastern Europe but in the USSR, for instance, the traditional model still dominated. In Australia 'collective bargaining as understood' in Europe and the USA 'applies only to a very small proportion of the workforce'.[42] Instead the majority of the workforce finds its terms and conditions fixed by industrial tribunals. Thus, Isaac has said:

> One of the outstanding features of industrial relations in Australia is the important place occupied by industrial tribunals in settling disputes and fixing the terms of employment by legally binding awards and determinations. The influence of these tribunals is so deep and so pervasive as to distinguish the character of Australian

industrial relations markedly from that of most other countries where collective bargaining operates.[43]

In Japan, and some South-East Asian countries, enterprise bargaining dominates and although there are some examples of industry bargaining, in practice very little takes place.

However, the immense variation in collective bargaining machinery from one country to another should by now be abundantly clear. It also needs to be stressed, though, that there are in addition some important variations within countries; in some cases these internal variations are just as marked as the cross-national differences. One might note, for instance, the variations in Britain between industries covered by joint councils and those covered by wages councils; in the USA special provisions affect bargaining in craft industries; whilst in Western European countries there are often major divergences in forms of bargaining in the public and private sectors. Consequently, while it is important to appreciate the extent of differences between countries, it is important to appreciate that national boundaries are not the only reasonable unit of analysis. Equally significant conclusions can be derived from comparisons based on industry boundaries.

DETERMINANTS OF BARGAINING MACHINERY

An examination of variations in bargaining machinery inevitably leads one to question why such variations exist and why particular industries, firms or countries have adopted one form of bargaining machinery rather than another. Many writers base their explanation on the context in which the machinery has to operate.

It has often been argued that collective bargaining machinery is essentially a reflection of a particular social and political climate; for example, by Blanpain in his discussion of the origin of collective bargaining machinery in Belgium. He says: 'The phenomenon of collective bargaining cannot be fully appreciated without taking into account the cultural and historical environment in which the system has its roots.'[44] It is also evident in Beal and Wickersham's discussion of variations in bargaining machinery between countries.[45] They explicitly adopt a systems theory perspective. This leads them to argue that bargaining machinery is largely a product of the industrial relations system in which it operates, and in turn the industrial relations system itself is crucially influenced by its environment, the wider social system. Thus one would account for variations in bargaining machinery by looking at the differences in the power relations of the actors who make the rules (the unions, employers and government), different market contexts and so on.

A similar line of reasoning is evident in the work of Ross and Hartman.[46] They attempt to classify industrial relations systems and in so doing point out the regularities they perceive. Yet underlying their approach is the assumption that one needs to look at 'characteristic configurations' of labour/management relations. In other words, one does not look at collective bargaining machinery in isolation; it can only be understood if examined as part of a wider network of relationships and institutions.

Some writers have highlighted not industrial relations systems in general, but more particular aspects. For instance, the centralisation of unions and employers' organisations in Sweden might be seen as one part of the explanation for the importance of economy-wide bargaining in that country, though one has to be aware of the danger of a circular argument in that the importance of economy-wide bargaining can be seen to reinforce the centralisation of unions and employers' organisations. The local bargaining in the USA is sometimes linked to the importance of the local union organisation and if that again is open to the charge of being a circular argument it can be suggested that there is less of a push towards national union organisation and bargaining in the USA than in, say, Western Europe, because USA unions – unlike their Western European counterparts – do not have major political aspirations. At the same time, it needs to be recognised that other factors can help to explain the importance of local bargaining in the USA earlier, the importance of the definition of the 'bargaining unit' by the National Labor Relations Board was noted.

All of these examples have centred on differences in bargaining machinery between nations. However, the line of reasoning is by no means constrained in this way; it can easily be applied to differences between industries in the same country, between different firms in the same industry and between the same firm at different periods of time. The level of analysis is relatively unimportant; the method, which stresses the importance of viewing collective bargaining machinery as part of a wider system, is applicable to all levels.

Of course, as such, this kind of analysis is merely a variant of structural explanation which covers a much wider field. For example, one might also note the argument developed by writers such as Kuhn[47] that technology plays an important part in determining the type of bargaining (this kind of theory is particularly useful when looking at differences between industries rather than differences between countries). Others have pointed to the importance of the structure of industry in determining the shape of the bargaining machinery: Scandinavian countries, for example, are relatively heavily dependent on a small number of export-based industries and it has been argued that this has been important in the pressure for centralised bargaining structures. Further, one can discuss the part played by social and economic conditions in determining the type of bargaining machinery without necessarily suggesting that these conditions are interrelated in a social system. However, structural explanations, whether constrained by the systems notion or not, present problems if they ignore the possible importance of particular events or particular personalities.

The important role of particular events was stressed by Isaac in his discussion of the development of collective bargaining machinery in Australia.[48] He argues that a particular series of strikes (often referred to merely as 'the strikes of the 1890s' although the most important one was the maritime strike which commenced in August 1890) played a crucial role. Isaac described the outcome of the strikes as a 'crushing defeat' for labour, but he also records that they had a much wider impact; they resulted in 'financial losses, economic dislocation, violence and human misery, not only to those directly involved in the struggle but also to the general public'. Further, he argues that 'the failure of conciliation and voluntary arbitration imposed an inescapable duty on the government to regulate industrial relations'.[49]

The basis of his argument, then, is that if 'these strikes had not occurred and if unionism and collective bargaining had been allowed to become more firmly established, as they showed every sign of doing in the 1880s, the course of Australian industrial relations might well have been different'. Indeed, he says, Australian industrial relations could well 'have followed the British system of collective bargaining, with government regulation through wages boards taking root only in those areas where, for reasons of lack of union strength, collective bargaining cannot be expected to operate effectively'.[50]

Of course, this line of reasoning can be applied outside the Australian context; it could be extended to cover collective bargaining in any country. The essence of the approach is the attempt to identify a crucial point or points in the development of machinery; one particular event which could be said to have determined the one of the infinite number of possible futures which was realised.

However, it would probably be as much a mistake to view these particular events in complete isolation as it would be to argue that bargaining machinery is the inevitable result of changes in the social structure. Both of these positions would be an oversimplification and an exaggeration. To return to the Australian case study, it would be difficult to view the strikes of the 1890s as completely isolated phenomena; they were clearly influenced by existing power relationships, the market position and so on. Further, one should inquire into later developments. How and why were they constrained; was the system initially established, challenged or reinforced, and why? Collective bargaining machinery may have been strongly influenced by a particular event but it is inevitably moulded by a series of events and personalities over time.

It is being argued, therefore, that collective bargaining machinery can best be viewed in a historical perspective as the outcome of the interaction of social and economic conditions and the motives and perceptions of individuals. Social and economic conditions limit the action and influence the attitude and perceptions of individuals at any particular point in time. However, the individual retains a degree of 'non-determinacy' through which he or she contributes uniquely to the creation of the social conditions of the future which will in turn limit, but not completely constrain, the actions of others.

EFFECTS OF COLLECTIVE BARGAINING ON INCOMES AND DIFFERENTIALS

Collective bargaining is often treated in a fairly formal and neutral fashion in industrial relations textbooks. Bargaining structures are described and machinery analysed but often there is little attempt to examine the effect and implications of collective bargaining. However, with the growing challenge to the use of collective bargaining, with some employers arguing (though it has been suggested in Britain, relatively few pressing this point so far) that collective bargaining is 'outmoded' and that they want to move from collective to industrial bargaining, a number of important questions need to be asked about its economic and social consequences.

The first is, what effect has collective bargaining had on the distribution of the national income? The evidence on this question is not as clear as one might hope. For example, while it appears that the share of the national income accruing to labour has increased in Britain and the USA over the last eighty or so years (in Britain, the proportion of the Gross National Product claimed by labour increased from 55 per cent just before the First World War to over 78 per cent in the late 1970s, and similar, though not identical, trends can be noted in a number of other countries), the reason for this is less than clear. There is some evidence that trade unions may have been able to increase the incomes of their members though estimates of the effect have varied: Lewis[51] in a USA study, suggested 15 per cent, but Pencavel[52] in a British study suggested up to 10 per cent and Blanchflower[53] using information from the British 1980 Workplace Industrial Relations Survey argued that many earlier studies had overestimated the size of the effect and failed to take account of variations between sectors in the labour market. However, it is not clear that any such increases have been at the expense of profits rather than other workers. It is also certainly possible to argue (though the argument is by no means conclusive and many would disagree with it[54]) that changes in taxation policy have been just as important in bringing about the increase in the proportion of national income accruing to labour, as action taken by trade unions. Of course, if this were the case, then it would be important to note that some, like the Harvard school,[55] have suggested that trade unions can have a positive effect on productivity (thus increasing the national income) and in preventing the proportion of the national income accruing to labour from falling, and that trade union political activity, in part at least, may have been responsible for persuading governments to take action on items like taxation.

A second and related question, is what effect trade union action through collective bargaining has had on differentials between groups of workers. Again, the evidence is less than fully satisfactory or conclusive. It appears, for example, that there has been a degree of long-term stability in wage differentials. Of course there have been some important shifts; and some which may appear relatively minor when looked at as part of the overall structure may nevertheless appear extremely important to the workers concerned. Such shifts may form the basis for the framing of a wage claim and industrial action, or for the decision to seek unionisation on the part of a section of the workforce. In Britain, for example, coal miners lost their place in the wages league over the late 1950s and 1960s (in 1956 coal mining wages were 25 per cent higher than the average in manufacturing industries whereas by 1970 they were marginally lower). In the early 1970s miners sought to recover their position with the aid of improved economic conditions in the industry and were able to achieve their central objective (a number of writers[56] have noted the importance of a combination of factors like trade union action and improved economic conditions, rather than just one factor in isolation). More generally, the erosion of the salaries of public compared to private sector employees has led to a build-up of discontent and associated industrial action on a number of occasions, particularly in the late 1970s and 1980s.

SOCIAL IMPLICATIONS OF COLLECTIVE BARGAINING

In the early stages of industrialisation, employers often resisted union attempts to gain recognition and bargaining rights. Taft and Ross[57] note that in the USA employers, often aided by governments, fought (sometimes literally) pitched battles to prevent the spread of unionism and deny bargaining rights. Similar examples, although often not as extreme, could be drawn from the history of most other nations. By the post-Second World War years, though, matters had changed and collective bargaining was seen in a different light. What, then, led to this change of heart and to this general acceptance of collective bargaining?

At one level this change of heart probably represented nothing more than a belief that the fight to prevent the spread of trade unionism and collective bargaining was not worth the effort; in essence, to oppose collective bargaining was causing more problems than might be expected if it were accepted. This line of thought was evident in the preamble to the 1935 Wagner Act; it said that 'the denial by employers of the right of employees to organize' and their refusal 'to accept the produce of collective bargaining' had been the cause of strikes and other manifestations of industrial conflict. From this point of view, employers and governments merely 'learned to live' with collective bargaining.

However, there were other more positive reasons for the acceptance of collective bargaining. These centred on the notion that collective bargaining can help to regularise and institutionalise industrial conflict. There were a number of elements to this belief.

First, collective bargaining is the means by which a 'normative system' is created for regulating industrial conflict and ensuring that it is kept within acceptable bounds. Collective bargaining does not prevent industrial conflict, but it provides a forum for discussion and a 'means for systematic social change in the working code governing management–men relations'.[58]

Second, collective bargaining enables parties to a dispute to view the situation more dispassionately than might otherwise be the case; it allows time for thought and to review the consequences of possible courses of action. In particular, the costs as well as the benefits of violent conflict may come to be appreciated. Thus, Kerr argued that collective bargaining can aid 'rationality-knowledge of costs and consequences – and thus the diplomatic resolution of controversies'.[59] Similarly, Dubin noted how collective bargaining could help to introduce a time perspective into industrial conflict and suggested that this

> time perspective can have an important tempering influence towards limiting disorder. It is significant that in the United States strike violence has been inversely related to the permanence of unionism. As collective bargaining becomes an established feature of our society both sides come to recognise that each conflict-created disorder is inevitably succeeded by a re-established order and that permanently disruptive disorder may materially impede the resolution of the conflict.[60]

Third, collective bargaining absorbs energy which might otherwise be more destructively directed. Thus, Harbison[61] argued that collective bargaining provides a 'drainage channel' for worker dissatisfaction. In essence, if workers and their leaders devote a considerable proportion of their time to scoring bargaining points and winning concessions at the bargaining table this is likely to divert attention from questioning more fundamental aspects of industrial society.

Fourth, collective bargaining, by providing a forum for meetings between management and unions, can help to facilitate improved relations and gradual change. Thus Dahrendorf argued that 'by collective bargaining the frozen fruits of industrial conflict are thawed. If the representatives of management and labour meet regularly for negotiations, gradual changes of social structure replace the tendency toward revolutionary explosions and civil war'.[62]

The above argument is in essence the pluralist justification for collective bargaining. In the 1960s and 1970s it came under attack from those who portrayed pluralism as a means of perpetuating 'the myth' of a rough equality of power of the two sides of industry. Thus, Eldridge argued that one should not assume 'either a view of bargaining parity between the antagonists or of rough equality of skills'[63] as some writers have suggested. Employers and trade unions have different weapons at their disposal and their ability to make full use of what power they have differs.

It also needs to be noted that even writers who broadly supported the pluralist thesis accepted that there might be limitations to the extent to which collective bargaining might institutionalise conflict. In some ways its own success might be the source of its own downfall. For example, trade union leaders, through collective bargaining, might accept that open conflict is undesirable and agree to follow the rules of the game. However, if in so doing they move too far away from the interests and views of their members then they might find themselves being challenged by unofficial leaders who are not part of the bargaining machinery, and are willing to urge their constituents to adopt more aggressive and violent means.

In the 1980s, though, the pluralist view of collective bargaining came under threat much more from the radical right. The desirability of collective as opposed to individual bargaining or unilateral imposition of terms and conditions of employment came to be challenged. The desirability of 'compromise' needed more justification and although collective bargaining remained of major importance, support for it, and the pluralist basis on which it rested, could not be assumed.

SUMMARY

Flanders argued that the Webbs's definition of collective bargaining was erroneous. They saw collective bargaining as being exactly what the words imply – a collective equivalent to individual bargaining. Flanders argues that it is a different, more centrally political activity. Fox attacks Flanders's interpretation and defends the Webbs. Essentially Fox believes that Flanders overestimated the differences between individual and collective bargaining and paid insufficient attention to the economic motivation behind a great deal of such activity.

In Britain the major development of collective bargaining did not occur until the end of the nineteenth century and it was not until after the First World War that it became firmly established on a national rather than a local basis. By the 1960s national bargaining machinery of some form covered almost all workers.

There have been major contrasts between collective bargaining in Britain and the USA. In Britain, traditionally, collective bargaining has been 'voluntary' whereas in the USA it has had a firm legal base, epitomised in the Wagner and Taft–Hartley Acts. Similarly, in Britain, traditionally, collective bargaining has centred on a fairly restricted range of issues and resulting agreements often have had no time limit, whereas in the USA collective bargaining has covered a far wider field and agreements have tended to be for a fixed term (resulting in the phenomenon of the bargaining round).

In some ways, collective bargaining in European countries seems to be a mixture of both British and US systems. For example, as was the case in Britain until relatively recently, most bargaining machinery seems to be concentrated at the national level, while as in the USA, most bargaining seems to have a strong legislative base. However, in other ways collective bargaining machinery in Europe is unique because of the existence of works councils (and their equivalents) which seem to perform a mixture of bargaining and consultative functions. Bargaining machinery outside Europe also has its own distinctive flavour: in Australia it is dominated by the system of compulsory arbitration while in Japan it is concentrated on the enterprise, and in Eastern Europe bargaining in the Western sense only seems to take place at the local level.

Many writers have tried to account for the differences between the bargaining machinery of different nations by referring to the different social and economic conditions in which the machinery has developed (some have located these conditions within the framework of systems theory). Others have taken a different approach and stressed the way in which individuals and particular events have played a crucial role in the development of bargaining machinery. However, it has been argued that it would be just as much a mistake to view these individuals or events in isolation as it would be to argue that the bargaining machinery is the inevitable result of changes in the social structure. Collective bargaining machinery, rather, should be viewed in an historical perspective as the outcome of the interaction of social and economic conditions and the perceptions of individuals.

It is difficult to say with certainty what effect collective bargaining has had either on incomes or on differentials. The evidence is patchy and difficult to evaluate. Few would argue, though, that it has resulted in wage-earners obtaining a substantial increase in their share of the national income. On the other hand, there is rather more evidence to support the views put forward concerning the social consequences of collective bargaining. Harbison has described it as 'one of the major bulwarks of the capitalist system', though care needs to be exercised in making a judgement, even on this issue; it is by no means certain that collective bargaining will always fulfil this function no matter what form it takes or no matter what the attitude of the parties involved.

7 Major developments in collective bargaining

Three issues are highlighted in this chapter: first, local bargaining; second, productivity bargaining and the growing popularity in the 1980s of profit and performance related pay; and third, final offer arbitration. The discussion builds on the more general review in Chapter 6, seeking to identify some of the major developments that have taken place in the last twenty years or so.

THE REDISCOVERY OF LOCAL BARGAINING

Discussion of collective bargaining in Britain used to concentrate on the national machinery. This was viewed as being of prime importance, and although local bargaining was not totally ignored[1] it was seen as having a limited and secondary role. This position started to change, however, in the 1960s, particularly as the result of the work of Flanders.[2] His evidence to the Donovan Commission was influential in persuading it to highlight developments in local bargaining as being of critical significance. It is worthwhile, therefore, looking briefly at the argument and evidence Flanders put forward.

The critical feature of local bargaining, as identified by Flanders, was that it had developed 'not as a deliberate policy, but haphazardly as a result of the pressure of the moment'. It was 'forced upon employers and unions, at first largely against their will, by the logic of the prevailing situation'. They had been concentrating on national negotiations rather than recognising the inadequacy of that machinery. As a result, workplace bargaining was 'largely informal, largely fragmented and largely autonomous'.[3] It was informal because while there may have been 'some jointly agreed or tacitly accepted rules regulating relations between management and workers',[4] they usually remained uncodified, and if they appeared in writing at all it was usually merely in the minutes of meetings. It was fragmented because it was conducted in such a way that different groups in the works secured different concessions at different times. It was autonomous because neither trade unions nor employers' associations had any real control over it.

In so far as Flanders attributed blame, he argued that management must accept the greater share; he said that the 'excessive informality and fragmentation' of local bargaining was 'mainly a reflection on managements'.[5] Management alone, he argued, was in a position to take the initiative and place local bargaining on a 'more satisfactory foundation'. However, management, Flanders suggested, was ill-prepared to do this job for three main reasons. First, management training; few managers had been well prepared for the social aspects of their job with the result that labour relations in the firm had been conducted

> in almost complete ignorance of the social sciences and frequently on the basis of the most primitive dogmas about the determinants of behaviour. In these circumstances the reactions of workers and their representatives could hardly appear other than unpredictable, and the natural desire of those who have been trained as technicians to fight shy of labour relations has been fortified by the apparently baffling nature of the behaviour observed.[6]

Second, management structure; personnel management had been separated from management in general, in part because of the differences in training and background and in part because of the difficulty general management encounters in trying to understand personnel questions. This had inhibited management initiative because the personnel manager had been seen as a trouble-shooter rather than as someone who could suggest long-term policy. Third, management ideology; any division or sharing of authority traditionally had been rejected by management. Thus, when management was faced with a challenge to its authority from the shop-floor it preferred to treat this as a 'temporary aberration' which could best be dealt with informally.

Flanders's evidence to the Donovan Commission was broadly supported by the findings of specially commissioned research. This research was published separately and two of the papers are of particular importance. Research Paper 1 reviewed existing information on the role of shop stewards in British industry.[7] It argued that although shop stewards had a very restricted formal role (evidence was taken from Roberts's study[8] of 134 union rule books, which showed that many made no reference at all to shop stewards and others referred to them merely as collectors of union dues) in practice they were much more important. They negotiated with local management over a wide range of issues; for example 'shop stewards and managers [settled] disputes concerning piece work prices, bonuses, plus payments, job descriptions, workloads, overtime [and] the introduction of new machinery'.[9] This extension from 'the minimal de jure rights of shop stewards' was achieved by the 'development of a network of informal de facto privileges enabling them to consult members, meet with other stewards, move freely about the firm and so on' and by the 'proliferation of unwritten agreements and understandings that arise as a result of the day to day settlement of substantive grievances and claims in the shop'.[10]

Research Paper 10[11] presented the results of a new survey of shop stewards and workplace relations in Britain. This special survey confirmed the impression gained after the review of existing information in Research Paper 1. For example, it showed that, despite considerable variations, most shop stewards negotiated on a wide range of issues at the local level. The issues concerned are shown in Table 7.1, and for purposes of comparison the bargaining records of works managers, personnel officers and foremen are also given. From this table it can be seen that the vast majority of shop stewards bargained over wages and working conditions; fewer, although still a majority, bargained over discipline and employment issues. The authors of Research Paper 10 went on to argue that the 'stewards survey [also] supports the view that the growth of shop floor bargaining leads to the development of informal contacts which supplement and to some extent circumvent, more formal methods of approach'.[12] They suggested that direct evidence of what was happening was provided by shop stewards' replies to a question asking them if they had ways of approaching management outside the formal procedure:

> seven out of ten said that 'unofficial' channels existed and almost all of them thought these were very important. Almost half of those who had a foreman said that in this way they could bypass him if they needed to, and one in four claimed that they were able to approach top level management without going through the lower levels.[13]

It was also noted that shop steward activity had become far better organised: one indication was the growth of the workshop committee. The committee functioned as a meeting ground for shop stewards throughout the plant and frequently officers were elected or leadership roles assigned. In many cases this took the form of the appointment

Table 7.1 Items on which shop stewards and others negotiated

Groups of issues	Respondents who negotiated (%)			
	Works manager	Personnel	Foremen	Stewards
Wages	82	80	72	83
Working conditions	88	89	79	89
Hours of work	78	73	62	75
Discipline	76	76	61	67
Employment issues	71	76	43	67

Source: W. E. J. McCarthy, S. R. Parker, *Shop Stewards and Workshop Relations* (HMSO, London, 1968)

of a senior shop steward or a convener. In the Royal Commission's survey of workshop relations, two-thirds of the personnel officers interviewed said that senior shop stewards operated in their plant.

The Donovan Commission,[14] not surprisingly, strongly supported the line of reasoning presented to it and the evidence of the systems of industrial relations. The Commission argued that there were two systems of industrial relations. One was the formal system which was embodied in the official institutions; it assumed that industry-wide organisations were capable of imposing their decisions on their members and was centred on national bargaining machinery. The other was the informal system which was created by the actual behaviour of trade unions, employers' associations, managers, shop stewards and workers. The informal system consisted largely of tacit arrangements and understanding and custom and practice, rather than formal machinery.

However, in some ways the Donovan Commission's comment that the 'formal and the informal systems are in conflict' was more important than these comparisons. They said that the informal undermined the formal system. For example, the 'gap between industry-wide agreed rates and actual earnings continues to grow' and procedure agreements 'fail to cope adequately with disputes arising within factories'. Nevertheless, collective bargaining in Britain, it was argued, was still based on the assumption that national bargaining was of prime importance and this prevented

> the informal system from developing into an effective and orderly method of regulation. The assumption that industry-wide agreements control industrial relations leads many companies to neglect their responsibilities for their own personnel policies. Factory bargaining remains informal and fragmented, with many issues left to custom and practice. The unreality of industry-wide pay

agreements leads to the use of incentive schemes and overtime payments for purposes quite different from those they were designed to serve.[15]

A number of studies of workplace relations in Britain[16] were undertaken in the years following the Donovan Report to see whether the trends noted in the Commission's report had been maintained or whether significant changes had occurred. A number of them noted an increase in both the number and importance of shop stewards; they were better organised and frequently were offered better facilities at the workplace. At the same time such studies noted little evidence of any increase in the importance or role of full-time officials at the shop-floor level. One of the surveys noted that the overwhelming majority of their respondents said there had been an increase in local bargaining since the Donovan Report.

However, possibly the most interesting comments were those on the nature of workplace bargaining and agreements. Although the authors of one of the surveys recognised that there had been some increase in the number of formal agreements at the local level they concluded that informal relations were still of prime importance. Thus, they said that despite 'the increase in written agreements, it is clear that informality still played a large part in the conduct of industrial relations in 1972'.[17]

The development of local bargaining in Britain in the 1960s and 1970s has parallels in other European countries. Perhaps the closest parallel is with Italy. Thus, Balfour argued that the changes in collective bargaining in Italy were 'rather similar to the shift in bargaining in Britain described by the Donovan Report as the "two systems"'.[18]

The changes began to be noticed in Italy in the late 1950s. Guigni commented that

> relations at the level of the undertaking developed in a direction that contrasted with the strict observance of the principles of exclusive national bargaining. In principle any improved conditions enjoyed by workers in an undertaking should have been granted freely by the management, but in practice they were very often negotiated with the works committee although those representative bodies . . . had and still have no authority to conclude agreements.[19]

Such breaches in official procedure first came to light in the iron and steel industry in 1958 although subsequently they were also noted in most other industries.

The response of the national unions and employers' associations was the development of what was termed 'articulated bargaining'. This involved the recognition of a number of different bargaining levels, one of which was based on the plant. As such, the development of 'articulated bargaining' can be seen as a recognition of existing trends and an attempt to develop machinery to deal with them.

However, 'articulated bargaining' was not as successful as was at first hoped. One of the reasons was that although local or plant bargaining was given recognition the role assigned to it was very restricted; essentially it was not to extend beyond a discussion of piece-work rates and productivity bonuses. Further, it was meant to work within strict guidelines set down by national negotiators; crucially these guidelines usually included a fixed duration for all agreements and the stipulation that the agreement could not be renegotiated during the time period.

In fact, local bargaining very quickly developed well beyond these constraints: it was given new impetus by the events of 1968/69, usually referred to as the 'hot autumn'. The catalyst, as in the late 1950s, was a dispute in the metal industries which soon spread to most other groups of workers. The result was a period of 'industrial ferment' and 'continuous bargaining'. These events had a major impact on the development of local bargaining. This can be seen by recalling that in the two following years, 1970 and 1971, 4,400 new plant agreements were signed in Italy, covering more than 1.5 million workers. It also can be seen through the emergence of the shop delegate as a critical force within the union organisation and the development of a 'new powerful form of organisation generally known as the factory council or "consiglio di fabrica"'. The councils became particularly strong in the metal, textile, clothing and rubber industries (in the metal industries alone, more than 1,400 committees were established) but they emerged throughout Italian industry in all but the smallest firms. They bargained over a wide range of issues and did not appear to be constrained by any framework established at the national level; they emerged in the late 1960s, almost spontaneously. They effectively bypassed the existing union organs, works committees and bargaining machinery; they appeared to be operating independently and often in opposition to established workers' organisations and machinery.[20]

Bargaining in Italy provided the closest parallel to developments in Britain. However, over the same period, similar developments were taking place, to some extent, in most other European countries. For example, although in Denmark wage levels were formally determined at the national level, piece-work and bonus rates were left to local negotiations and increasingly they were used as a way of altering nationally agreed rates. A survey[21] of collective bargaining in Denmark published in the mid-1970s, concluded 'that a surprisingly high proportion of the total pay packet was locally determined'. One company examined operated a form of measured day-work which gave bonus payments on time saved that amounted to 60 per cent of total pay. In three other firms the proportions involved were 40 per cent, 30 per cent and 20 per cent. Further, it was noted that negotiations at the local level over bonuses and the like were conducted directly between shop steward and management.

Similarly, although many commentators have noted that collective bargaining in France has been remarkably slow to develop (most put this down to the weakness of French trade unions), a number have argued that there was a trend towards increased plant and local bargaining in the 1960s, particularly after the turmoil of 1968. In subsequent years the number of plant agreements concluded increased dramatically – from 52 in 1968, to 91 in 1969, to 658 in 1970.[22] In 1970 legislation was introduced to provide rules to cover plant bargaining and to control its future development. Slack[23] referred to evidence of earnings drift in France, though he added a note of caution about interpreting the developments in plant bargaining in France as being too closely modelled on the British example because of the way in which the shop-floor representatives still saw themselves much more as a union than a workforce representative.

Again, although in Belgium the formal system of collective bargaining stressed the importance and primacy of national agreements, Blanpain noted the growth in the extent of bargaining at the local level over this period. He said that in many cases 'the national agreement only [constituted] the first round of bargaining' and in practice, 'the minimum terms established by national agreements [remained] applicable only to marginal employers'.[24] He also noted a significant growth in unofficial strikes towards the end of the 1960s which subsided in 1970 but surfaced again in the early 1970s and could well be seen as a sign of disapproval of national negotiations.

Plant level bargaining probably developed least in West Germany and the Netherlands. In West Germany wage bargaining was largely in the hands of national union officials; the law successfully prevented works councils from intervening in this area. In the Netherlands attention focused on national bargaining and the incomes policy. However, Reichel[25] believed that the series of wild cat strikes in the autumn of 1969 in the German metalworking industry was an indication of a growing disillusionment with national bargaining and there was further extensive unofficial action in 1972 and 1973. Similarly, Albeda, in an article on developments in the Netherlands,[26] suggested that the breakdown of the incomes policy was accompanied by increased pressure for local bargaining. This was not fully recognised because of the weakness of Dutch unions at the local level (contrasted to their strength at the national level) though the appointment of shop stewards in certain sections of industry (they were almost completely absent before) changed the position somewhat.

It is also worth noting that in Australia, where many commentators[27] have argued that collective bargaining in the European sense does not exist (instead there is a formal system of compulsory arbitration) there were signs of a growth in local bargaining. Yerbury and Isaac, commenting on developments in Australia[28] pointed out that there were indications that collective bargaining, in the European sense, was showing signs of gaining a foothold, if not acceptance (they recognised that it still had a long way to progress before it could be considered to be established) and that formal national settlements were being supplemented by informal local agreements. Similarly, although local bargaining has been much better developed in the USA there was evidence of increased unofficial bargaining at the local level.

Naturally, such a widespread development of local bargaining stimulated attempts at explanation. Why did local bargaining develop at this particular time and why did it develop in some countries and in some industries more than in others?

One type of explanation which figured in many accounts stressed the importance of changes in the economic climate. 'Buoyant' economic conditions meant that there was a shortage of labour in many industries. This increased the ability of employees to bargain effectively at the local level. Thus, Roberts and Rothwell noted that whereas under 'conditions of mass unemployment the task of the shop steward was largely confined to maintaining trade union membership and endeavouring to prevent employers from undercutting agreements negotiated at the industry level' under full employment the bargaining power of shop stewards increased substantially: 'shortage of labour made the employers vulnerable to pressure from employees for increases in wages greater than those negotiated nationally'.[29] However, buoyant economic conditions also meant that employers felt better able to offer more than nationally agreed wages; they realised it was fairly easy, in such circumstances, to pass increased costs on to the consumer in the form of higher prices. This kind of explanation was explicitly offered by Guigni in his discussion of developments in Italy. He argued that as a result of improved economic conditions employees acquired sufficient power to negotiate locally over matters like incentives; for the employers 'it was a question of realistic adaptation to changing conditions'.[30]

Others pointed to the importance of the increased use of piece-work and incentive methods of payment. There is evidence that there was a general increase in the use of such methods throughout industry in the immediate post-war years; it is also clear that it remained important in particular industries. A survey of the use of piece-work in Britain[31] in the early 1960s found that 90 per cent of employees in the steel industry, 90 per cent in the ports, 85 per cent in the paper industry and 70 per cent in the construction industry had piece-work payments as an element of their wages. The importance of piece-work and bonus payments in Denmark has already been noted. Although national agreements could determine these rates, frequently such agreements accepted the necessity for local variations and in practice the bulk of decisions on incentives were made at the local level.

Other writers have noted that while such arguments may appear persuasive they ignore essential elements. For example, Coates and Topham[32] suggested that the growth of local bargaining should be seen as a move by workers to gain greater control over the work situation. This kind of argument can be linked to the challenge over managerial prerogatives. The approach suggested by Banks[33] has some similarities. He argued, like Coates and Topham, that the development of local bargaining could be viewed as an attempt to gain greater control over work conditions. However, he argued, that the stimulus to such action was not the desire for greater workers' control as such but the need to combat the increasing remoteness of decision taking centres, itself a function of the growth in the size of the enterprise.

One limitation of such a discussion is that it gives the impression that only employees saw local bargaining as advantageous. There is evidence that this was not the case. Roberts and Rothwell noted that the 'growth of plant and company bargaining [in Britain] could not have been achieved without the willingness of employers to play their part in this development'. They argued that one of the reasons for the employers' acceptance of company bargaining was the influence of US companies. Thus, they said that the 'change in the policy of management towards plant and company bargaining was encouraged by the example of large scale American-owned companies. These companies have tended to bring with them attitudes and practices developed in the United States'.[34] Similarly, McCarthy and Parker in their study of local bargaining in Britain[35] argued that these developments were supported as much by the employers as by the employees. Employers believed that problems could be solved more readily and more satisfactorily by local agreement; they also appeared to like the informal style of bargaining at this level because it meant that they could make a decision to cover a particular situation without it becoming part of a formal written precedent (the comments of Flanders on this issue, noted on p. 163, support this view).

Very few people who commented on these developments opposed local bargaining in practice. The Donovan Commission which strongly criticised local bargaining in Britain opposed merely the informal and unstructured nature of such bargaining. The Commission believed that the way in which it operated led to 'piecemeal' decisions and competitive agreements (in particular in the field of earnings). Further, it was argued that 'these characteristics of collective bargaining provided the explanation for the pattern of strikes'[36] in Britain, a pattern which emphasised relatively short, local and unofficial strikes.

The remedy suggested by the Donovan Commission was not the abolition, but the restructuring, of local bargaining; it was viewed as a 'fact of life' which unions and management had to come to terms with. Collective bargaining machinery had to be changed to take account of this; essentially the aim was for the introduction of formal machinery at the local level.

Again, this line of reasoning was by no means unique to Britain. In those European countries where local bargaining became important the central concern of the government and the two sides of industry was to try to keep control of developments. This was probably best exemplified in Italy where the trade unions made considerable efforts to retain control over local bargaining by changing their attitude towards local strikes. Increasingly they were willing to give recognition to strikes initiated by local work groups because they saw this as a useful way of keeping control of developments rather than because they carefully examined the nature of the disputes and felt them to be worthy of support. The same could be said of events in most other European countries; for example, the 1970 law in France can be seen in this context, as can the growing interest of trade unions in Denmark in discussions on issues other than those concerned with national incomes policies.

The thesis put forward in the Donovan Commission's report and echoed in the moves made in other European countries was necessarily pitched at a fairly detailed practical level. However, it was supported at a theoretical level by Fox and Flanders[37] using the concept of anomie (as put forward by Durkheim, in outline, 'this describes a state of normlessness resulting from a breakdown in social regulation').[38]

According to Fox and Flanders every system of industrial relations is a normative system regulating employment relations. 'A norm can be seen as a "a rule, a standard, a pattern for action" and a set of integrated norms – i.e. norms consistently related according to certain principles – constitutes a normative system.'[39] The institutional basis of such a normative system in industry, of course, is collective bargaining. Thus, they said that 'historically collective bargaining has been the principal method evolved in industrial societies for the creation of viable normative systems to keep manifest conflict in employment situations within socially tolerable bounds'.[40]

However, in certain situations collective bargaining has not been totally successful in the regulation of conflict. The position they noted in Britain is an example, but others might be quoted from a number of European countries. The principal reason for this was that the machinery was not altered to take account of changes in power relationships, and in particular the growth in the power of employees at the workplace.

Fox and Flanders argued, therefore, that because of the inadequacy of bargaining machinery in Britain (and elsewhere in Europe) there existed a state of 'anomie'. In other words there was no adequate system for developing norms which could regulate behaviour in the field of industrial relations.

The solution proposed by Fox and Flanders closely followed that put forward in the Donovan Report. It centred on the 'construction of agreed normative systems covering the company or plant'[41] and their harmony with the normative systems at the industry level. The stimulus to such action would come mainly from within the plant or within the industry. Nevertheless, there would be a role for bodies like the Commission on Industrial Relations to give encouragement.

The Fox and Flanders thesis was subject to critical review by Eldridge.[42] The crucial question posed by Eldridge was whether the solution put forward by Fox and Flanders was adequate to deal with the problem. He believed that it fell into the familiar pluralist trap of supposing that only marginal adjustments were needed to remedy the problem. In fact, he suggested, the adjustments needed were more fundamental; change was required in a whole range of social and economic inequalities. The problem, then, was not merely one of the tidying up of machinery or the discovery of new ways to re-establish the equilibrium, but concerned the moral basis of society.

Although it would be wrong to argue that the growth and development of local bargaining in the 1960s and 1970s was simply a reflection of particularly conducive economic circumstances – for as was argued earlier a range of other factors need to be taken into account – it would be wrong to underestimate the importance of economic conditions in providing a climate in which the other factors that were important in encouraging local bargaining could be influential. It is worthwhile recording, then, that after the first quarter of the 1970s these economic conditions began to change and by the beginning of the 1980s the climate looked very different. It is worth while asking whether these changed economic conditions were accompanied by a reversal of earlier trends which had suggested the growing importance of workshop groups and local bargaining.

Lindop,[43] writing at the end of the 1970s, suggested that there was a range of evidence which while not necessarily conclusive, all pointed towards a reduction in the importance of local bargaining. For example, he referred to a study by Daniels[44] in which it was shown that many managements in manufacturing industry were pointing to the importance of bargaining at other than the local level.

In practice, the picture painted by Lindop at the end of the 1970s did not survive into the 1980s. Some of the conditions that led Lindop[45] to assume it would, persisted – in particular the adverse economic environment; however, others changed, the most critical being the political context. The Conservative government which gained power in 1979 led a determined assault on the size of the public sector and argued that pay should be related to what companies could afford, rather to a national 'going rate'. In so far as Lindop recognised the growth of company bargaining as being important his prediction for the 1980s could be sustained. However, national bargaining has decreased in importance and workplace bargaining has by no means faded away.

In summary, what appears to have happened in the 1980s is that in substantial parts of British industry (though as will be noted later, not all), employers started to withdraw from national bargaining machinery. Instead they relied on company or workplace bargaining. Of the two, the former seems to have been particularly strongly supported. This cannot be seen, though, as a return to the position of the 1960s. In the 1960s employers still formally bargained through national machinery; bargaining at lower levels was largely informal. In the 1980s the devolution of bargaining was frequently accompanied by a withdrawal from national machinery and the company or workplace bargaining that replaced it was formally constituted. Along with this was a noticeable trend for employers to bargain at fewer levels.

One of the difficulties with a summary such as this is that while trends can be correctly identified they have not affected all sectors identically. Some of the evidence to support the trends is little more than anecdotal. However, there have been a number of substantial surveys which allow one to identify in more detail what has been happening.

The British Workplace Industrial Relations Survey[46] allows one to make an assessment of the extent to which changes in bargaining levels occurred in the early 1980s. As Brown notes[47] the survey, comparing as it does practice in 1980 and 1984, allows one to look at a period when economic conditions were rapidly deteriorating, the level of nominal wage rises declining and trade union density falling. It also allows one to look at differences between sectors and categories of workers within sectors. Table 7.2 summarises some of this evidence and shows that the decline in national bargaining was only really noticeable for manual workers in private manufacturing industry. The same table indicates an increase in company/divisional bargaining throughout private industry, but only in a major way for non-manual workers in private services (although there is other evidence from the survey to suggest that the growth in importance of company or divisional bargaining as opposed to both national and workplace bargaining might be more widespread). In all sectors of private industry there was evidence of some reduction in the number of levels at which bargaining took place, though this reduction was most noticeable in the case of manual workers in manufacturing industry (in that case, pay was subject on average to bargaining at 1.2 stages in 1984 compared to 1.4 in 1980).

The survey suggested that in manufacturing industry there was a link between the size and the ownership of the enterprise on the one hand and the type of bargaining on the other: the larger the enterprise the more likely it was for plant or company bargaining to be important, and plant bargaining was much more important in establishments owned by non-UK companies.

The 1984 Workplace Industrial Relations Survey went beyond earlier work by looking not simply at the level at which bargaining took place, but also at the extent to which local negotiations were really free from the effects of outside factors. It is quite possible, for example, for negotiations to take place at the plant level but for the stance taken by management in these negotiations to be influenced

Table 7.2 Collective bargaining and pay determination, 1980–4

| | Private manufacturing industry | | | | Private services | | | |
| | Manual workers | | Non-manual workers | | Manual workers | | Non-manual workers | |
	1980	1984	1980	1984	1980	1984	1980	1984
Pay result of collective bargaining	65	55	27	26	34	38	28	30
Most important level:								
National/regional	27	22	5	5	19	20	12	11
Company/divisional	10	11	8	9	10	12	10	15
Plant/establishment	26	21	13	11	3	4	2	3
Other	1	1	*	1	*	2	5	*
Pay not result of collective bargaining	35	45	73	74	66	62	72	70

Source: N. Millward, M. Stevens, *British Workplace Industrial Relations, 1980–1984* (Gower, Aldershot, 1986)

Note: * Less than 1.

by guidance from the main directors or by industry-wide agreements. In the case of the first of these matters the survey suggested that higher-level management had significant influence over plant-level bargaining (in the case of manual workers where management said that pay was determined at plant level, two-thirds of respondents reported that they consulted higher in the organisation before the start of negotiations). However, in the case of the second of these matters the survey suggested that company level and workplace bargaining was only influenced by multi-employer bargaining in a minority of cases (around 25 per cent of cases for manual workers, but only around 15 per cent for non-manual).

Other evidence of the changes which took place in bargaining over roughly the same period can be gained from a Confederation of British Industries[48] survey of the private sector for 1979–1986. Two important trends were noted in the case of manufacturing industry. The first was a decline in the use of national multi-employer bargaining. In 1986 single-employer bargaining dominated for all issues, but particularly over basic wage rates, bonuses, sick pay and pensions, whereas in 1979 the picture had been much more varied (for example, in 1986 single-employer bargaining was used for 87 per cent of all employees covered for basic pay, whereas the proportion had been 53 per cent in 1979). This shift towards single-employer bargaining was noticeable throughout manufacturing industry but was particularly strong in metal manufacture, mechanical engineering and instrument and electrical engineering.

In a further breakdown of the total sample, the group of companies that claimed in 1979 that they relied solely on multi-employer agreements were looked at separately and it was found that in 1986 only 56 per cent of that group continued to do so.

The second trend to note is the decentralisation of bargaining in the case of subsidiaries of larger enterprises. Over a quarter of the respondents from subsidiaries said that their pay arrangements had become more decentralised, and while this was countered by some pointing to a move in the other direction, it was a much smaller proportion. The move towards decentralisation was much more pronounced in larger establishments.

The British Workplace Industrial Relations Survey and the CBI survey both offered a degree of detail on the position in the private sector. The former of these covered the public sector as well, but little detail was offered when discussing bargaining structures and strategies; the latter was specifically a private sector survey. In practice, national negotiations have always been much more dominant in the public than the private sector and their position has continued throughout the 1980s. Nevertheless, there have been some moves towards decentralisation of bargaining even if on a more tentative and limited basis than in the private sector. The 1983 Water Act encouraged such moves and although suggestions that national pay bargaining should be completely abolished were resisted, changes have now been made to allow for separate negotiations for individual companies.[49] In a number of parts of public administration moves have been made to allow greater regional variations, both in terms and conditions of employment. This met considerable opposition in the case of the DHSS, though in parts of the civil service it has been accepted. In 1989 the British Rail board announced its intention of moving towards local bargaining, an announcement which led to a series of strikes. Other moves taking place within the public sector have put national negotiations under pressure. Privatisation and contracting out inevitably put pressure on uniform national terms and conditions of employment.

The move away from national negotiations in the public and private sectors has been encouraged by government. The argument has been that national bargaining inevitably means that less attention can be paid to the needs and performance of individual firms, profit centres and plants. The Conservative government after 1979 pushed negotiators away from comparisons towards what the individual employer or workplace 'can afford'. This view has been embraced by many employers who have taken the lead in proposing changes to bargaining arrangements. Unions have been more cautious. They have seen the move away from national bargaining as a device to restrict their power in areas where they are weakest. National negotiations have been seen as providing a 'floor' of basic pay and conditions and while on occasions unions have been happy for supplementary bargaining to take place at company and workplace level they have been reluctant to see such negotiations taking place without this 'floor'. In some industries, nevertheless, unions have accepted the desire of the employers to withdraw from national negotiations, particularly if guarantees have been given on union recognition and on the maintaining of existing conditions as a minimum.

In Chapter 6, when the different levels at which bargaining can take place were being reviewed, it was noted that the level of bargaining could be related to the kind of individuals likely to be involved and the responsibilities they were likely to be asked to assume. Devolution of bargaining clearly has consequences in these terms and if it is to be successfully introduced, demands that training should be given so that individuals who in the past have either had no direct responsibility for bargaining or who have had only limited responsibility in the area can fulfil their new role. Further, if withdrawing from national bargaining is intended to ensure that debates take place about what a company or a workplace itself 'can afford' then this has implications for the provision of information, again normally to an extent and to a range of people, not practised before.

PRODUCTIVITY BARGAINING

Chamberlain and Kuhn[50] have drawn a distinction between what they term 'conjunctive' and 'cooperative' bargaining. The former deals with matters over which the aims of employers and labour diverge; essentially they are each pulling in a different direction. In the end the parties may recognise the need to compromise to enable the enterprise to continue in operation; however, 'the resolution of divergent interests through conjunctive bargaining provides a basis for operation of the enterprise – and nothing more'.[51] The outcome of conjunctive bargaining, or the precise nature of the compromise reached, will depend on the relative bargaining power of the parties concerned and coercion 'is the principal ingredient of conjunctive bargaining power'.[52]

The basis of cooperative bargaining is rather different; it is the fact 'that each party is dependent on the other and, as a matter of fact, can achieve its objectives more effectively if it wins the support of the other'.[53] The aim of the bargain is not to persuade one party to give up something but to persuade both parties to take action so as to increase the total available. Thus, Chamberlain and Kuhn argue that the parties approach cooperative bargaining 'with the realization that the better the performance of each, the better the joint performance. Further, each understands that the better the joint performance, the greater the advantage for both'.[54]

The work of Chamberlain and Kuhn in this area overlaps with that of Walton and McKersie[55] who draw a distinction between when they term distributive and integrative bargaining. Distributive bargaining is similar to what Chamberlain and Kuhn have termed conjunctive bargaining; it refers to joint decisions for resolving conflicts of interest. Essentially it is a way of dividing limited resources. On the one hand integrative bargaining is similar to what Chamberlain and Kuhn have termed cooperative bargaining; it refers to a joint problem-solving search process which results in benefits for both sides. The distinction between conjunctive and distributive bargaining on the one hand, and cooperative and integrative bargaining on the other is sometimes also referred to, in games theory, as a difference between a zero-sum and a positive-sum game, the implication being that in the latter, unlike the former, there is additional product from the game.

Cooperative (or integrative) bargaining first began to be noticed in the USA in the late 1950s. 'As the fifties grew to a close, unions and management found themselves confronted with the large and difficult problems of adjusting to rapid economic change in a lagging economy, automation, and a quickening shift of the workforce from blue to white collar workers'. Chamberlain and Kuhn argue that these problems were the main spur for the development of cooperative bargaining. They say that management and workers 'developed a new willingness to try to resolve their divergent interests through continuous attention to problems in order to evoke a cooperative effort to improve their joint performance in specified areas'.[56]

One of the most spectacular of the early cooperative bargains was that on the mechanisation of the US Pacific coast port transport industry. The difficulty was that mechanisation involved a relaxation of working rules and, crucially, a reduction in the size of the workforce. The unions decided that they would not fight management plans in principle – rather they would demand a price for their cooperation. They took the view that working rules (or as the management referred to them 'restrictive practices') were their 'property rights' which management would have to buy if they wanted to introduce mechanisation. They also decided that if management wanted their cooperation to make moves which would increase profits then the workers must be given a share of those profits. In the end the agreement reached allowed for changes in working rules to permit mechanisation in return for the establishment of two funds: one to establish a wage guarantee, another to establish a pension scheme.

In Britain, cooperative bargaining was discussed under the title productivity bargaining. The first British productivity bargain of any note occurred in 1960 at the Esso Oil Refinery at Fawley, near Southampton. Flanders, who has written a detailed account of the agreement, argues that it was 'without a precedent or even proximate parallel in the history of collective bargaining in Great Britain'.[57] However, he recognises that the agreement in the US port transport industry provides a close analogy.

There were two major parts to the agreement. The first was what Flanders has termed the 'productivity package deal'. Briefly the unions agreed to accept certain changes in working practices (such as the relaxation of job demarcations, the withdrawal of craftsmen's mates and their redeployment to other work, and greater freedom for management in its use of supervision) in return for pay increases in the order of 40 per cent. The second was an agreement dealing with 'systematic overtime'. Overtime caused particular problems at Fawley; because it had been permanently maintained at a high level it had been built into the firm's wage structure (by 1959 it had reached an average of 18 per cent of total hours worked). The agreement provided for a reduction in the high level of overtime (in the case of maintenance workers it was to be reduced to a level of 2 per cent) in return for wage increases to compensate for lost earnings.

Although these were the most important parts of the agreement, two other aspects might be mentioned. First, the company agreed that there would be no redundancy as a result of the other provisions. Second, the wage increases were to be accompanied by the introduction of a 40-hour week in place of the previous 42 or 42½ hours.

The other notable feature of the Fawley agreement was the way the deal was negotiated. In many cases bargaining is exclusively between the trade union and management officials; consequently the agreement may be misunderstood, mistrusted or even rejected by the rank and file union members. In this instance, attempts were made to involve as wide a section of the workforce as possible in the negotiations at one point or another.

In the early 1960s Esso followed the Fawley agreement by negotiating similar settlements at a number of other undertakings. This proved to be an important lead to the rest of the petrochemical industry. However, the major spur to productivity agreements in British industry generally was the activity of the National Board for Prices and Incomes established by the Labour Government in 1965 to police its incomes policy. 'Unions and employers were encouraged to negotiate productivity agreements, since the promise of achieving above-average increases in output was accepted as a justification for above norm pay increases.'[58] In the three years, 1967 to 1969, a total of 5,185 productivity agreements were registered with the Department of Employment and Productivity.

The link between productivity agreements and incomes policy, though, complicates the discussion a little. In Britain in the late 1960s a number of agreements were made which attempted to link pay increases to rises in productivity. There was not necessarily a specific package deal to change working rules, or the like; rather, productivity increases were expected in the future (possibly because of new technology) and such increases were to act as the measure for wage rises. Such agreements closely paralleled those of a number of European countries, especially the Netherlands. In 1959 in the Netherlands, the government introduced a new system of wage control which directly linked the productivity of each industry to the level of wages paid.[59] Such bargaining and agreements differ considerably from those discussed by Chamberlain and Kuhn under the title 'cooperative bargaining' and by Flanders under the title 'productivity bargaining'. The essence of the bargaining discussed by Chamberlain and Kuhn and Flanders was that management and unions should reach an agreement about measures to be taken to increase production; the essence of much productivity bargaining linked to incomes policy was an agreement on the appropriate level of wage increase and how any gains in productivity should be shared. Indeed, if one takes the definition of productivity bargaining proposed by McKersie it is possible to argue that the productivity-linked wage rises were not in reality an example of productivity bargaining. McKersie suggested that the 'distinctive feature of productivity bargaining is its specificity, with respect both to the nature of achievement and rewards and also to the time period during which extra rewards and extra achievements are coupled'. He contrasts it with other methods of wage payment which 'tend to be openended, and the exact amount of extra achievement is determined by the motivational effectiveness of the system rather than by collective bargaining'.[60]

The growth in the popularity of productivity bargaining inevitably leads one to question why it gained such widespread acceptance. Why did employers, governments and unions support the idea of productivity bargaining? In this instance the motives of employers are not difficult to understand. Reference has already been made to the observation of Chamberlain and Kuhn that the first cooperative bargains in the USA were inspired by the search for a way out of economic problems. R. F. Banks has offered a similar explanation for employers' support for productivity bargaining in Britain in the 1960s. Thus, he said:

> The main initiating force behind productivity bargaining has come from management as a result of the growing awareness of the need to improve efficiency in British industry. In the last five years this need has been demonstrated repeatedly by continual increases in unit labour costs resulting from inflationary wages settlements, the identification of extensive underutilisation of manpower associated with a heavy reliance on overtime work, and the awareness that traditional working practices were fast becoming irrelevant to the demands of new technologies.[61]

Chamberlain and Kuhn recognised that in many instances workers and trade union representatives might be less enthusiastic about cooperative and productivity bargaining than management. Workers, they said, might find it difficult to think in 'cooperative' terms when they were used to 'conflict'; trade union leaders might be afraid that their members would not accept a bargain struck and that because of the need to discuss work practices in detail they might be drawn too closely into the management function.

Nevertheless, many union leaders accepted productivity bargaining in the 1960s and pursued it enthusiastically. There is no doubt that such union leaders sincerely believed that this was an important device for substantially improving the standard of living of their members.

There is also no doubt that productivity bargaining was supported by many rank and file members. However, Daniel[62] has shown that there were a variety of reasons for the support given. He looked at the attitudes of workers following two particular agreements and found that they supported the agreements, both because of the accompanying financial benefits and because of the changes in work practice which gave them greater control over their work situation and greater intrinsic satisfaction. The crucial aspect of his account, though, was that these differences were not given by different workers or about different agreements, but by the same workers about the same agreement at different points in time. He argued that initially workers accepted the agreement because it offered higher economic rewards. After a while these rewards were taken as 'given' and the workers looked for other advantages, in this case, greater intrinsic work satisfaction.

Governments also supported productivity bargaining for a number of different reasons. Many, like employers, saw it as a way of increasing the efficiency of industry; many also saw it as a useful element in an incomes policy, although it has already been noted that this often led them to support a kind of productivity bargaining different from that envisaged by writers like Chamberlain and Kuhn and Flanders. However, the link between incomes policy and productivity bargaining also led governments to modify their support in the late 1960s and early 1970s. Many governments felt that productivity bargaining was being misused: it was being adopted by employers and unions as a device for obtaining wage increases above those permitted by the pay policy, but the productivity element was often more apparent than real.

It is also important to note that other major criticisms were made of productivity bargaining; they centred on the balance of benefits and sacrifices of employees. Thus, it was suggested that productivity bargaining could be seen as a method used by management to regain control over work behaviour and practices. Such a viewpoint was put forward by Topham.[63] He argued that with the development of workplace bargaining and the growth of the shop steward movement workers were able to regain some initiative and control over work practices; management was attempting, through productivity bargaining, to buy back this control. Thus, on this basis, what management termed 'restrictive practices' were seen as important inroads into managerial prerogatives, inroads which management wanted to reverse.

Another item of concern over cooperative and productivity bargaining was the extent to which such bargaining was undertaken on an equal basis. In many bargains, management offered to 'open its books' to the workforce but it is questionable whether management always gave all available information to the unions, or whether the unions were able to analyse the information they were given satisfactorily. The end product of productivity bargaining, therefore, may have been an agreement which benefited management and owners more than it benefited the employees.

Finally, cooperative and productivity bargaining was attacked because it is seen as a way of maintaining the *status quo*. Its use in this regard was specifically noted by Fox[64] who argued that within the pluralistic frame of reference productivity bargaining could be seen as a way of reconciling conflicting objectives. Hyman argued, though, that an incomes policy which included the notion of productivity bargaining meant that at best

> the relative shares of rich and poor – labour and capital – will be frozen; that the privileged position of the wealthy minority will be consolidated; and if the 'productivity' criterion is rigorously enforced, that workers will have to pay for their own pay improvements through more dehumanising conditions of labour.[65]

These reservations do not mean that productivity bargaining has been abandoned. Far from it, in the 1980s the pressure on wages and profits has meant that productivity bargaining has been held out by the employers as the only way that unions can secure wage increases. Nevertheless, there has been caution on all sides and the pressure to conclude productivity agreements has produced its own conflicts. In Britain in early 1982, the railway industry was regularly brought to a halt as the result of a disagreement between the Railways Board and one union, ASLEF, over productivity bargaining.

Productivity bargaining faced another problem in the 1980s. The adverse economic conditions and the high rates of unemployment meant that unions became acutely sensitive to the impact of such bargaining on employment opportunities. Insistence from employers on reductions in employment levels and redundancies were difficult to accept. Yet, at the same time, they were often difficult to resist. Employers were frequently able to push through changes in employment practices and to introduce new technology without the agreement of unions. The News International dispute over the transfer of work to the Wapping plant was a good example of the ability of an employer to force through changes without the agreement of previously recognised unions. In some cases then, productivity bargaining gave way to employer imposition of changes designed to increase productivity.

The popularity of productivity bargaining was retained in one form, however, through discussions on labour flexibility. Functional flexibility, or multiskilling, came to be seen as a key development in the 1980s. A survey by ACAS[66] found that between 1985 and 1988, 25 per cent of firms had made changes to enable production workers to do routine maintenance tasks, 34 per cent had made changes to allow craftsmen to do work usually performed by other craftsmen, and 25 per cent relaxed divisions between manual, technical and clerical staff. The extent of moves towards functional flexibility has also been documented by the Institute for Manpower Studies,[67] although they caution the assumption that such moves are evidence of genuine 'multiskilling'. In practice the moves to break down skill boundaries had a lot in common with productivity bargaining of the 1960s. In return for changes in working practices employees were offered a range of benefits, not just wage increases, but higher status, better job security (than those not covered by such agreements), and better fringe benefits. Interestingly, many of the firms that had been at the forefront of developments in productivity bargaining in the 1960s were at the forefront of developments linked to functional flexibility in the 1980s.

Two other developments which have gained favour in the 1980s might also be mentioned in this context, merit pay and profit sharing. Of course, neither is a new idea. As Fowler has argued: 'Paying more to employees who work well than to those who work less well is a practice as old as employment itself.'[68] However, merit pay has gained in popularity considerably in recent years, and significant changes have taken place in the way it has been used. Conventional merit rating, which concentrated on scoring an individual's qualities by looking at items like commitment, cooperation, initiative and dependability, has declined while performance assessment has increased. Performance assessment places much greater emphasis on 'setting individual objectives within the context of departmental and company goals', on using qualitative as well as quantitative judgements, and on distinguishing between short-term and long-term goals. Merit rating is still used, for example in some parts of the civil service, but performance assessment has also been popular in parts of the public sector (such as the health service) as well as throughout the private sector.

The growth in the popularity of merit and performance related pay in the 1980s can be explained in part because it fits in well with the view that employees should not be paid simply 'the going rate' for the job, a view that also found expression in the move away from nationally negotiated pay scales. The aim of individualised payments systems have been stated as being 'to ensure that every pound spent on payroll gives good value in terms of attracting, retaining and motivating employees – particularly the good performers'.[69]

The growing popularity of such a method of payment should not allow one to overlook that it has critics from both sides of industry.

Trade unions are sceptical because merit pay has been introduced in many non-union firms. They also have expressed concern about the subjectivity of some of the assessments made and because of the way that performance related pay is often linked to the development of appraisal systems, so the argument goes, to the detriment of both. Others have pointed out that performance and merit related pay can sometimes get intertwined with special payments designed to retain staff with scarce skills.

> the tightening of the southeastern labour market and the growth of skill shortages has meant that individualised payments have often become intertwined with recruitment supplements, allowances for workers in special locations, and ad-hoc payments to retain key workers.
>
> This has meant that even at companies where all the annual increase in pay is determined by 'merit', labour market pressures have predominated.[70]

It also needs to be recognised that there is a great deal of evidence to suggest that if the aim of the exercise is to motivate workers then pay may not be the most effective mechanism. On the other hand, failure to award a merit pay rise might give a signal to a worker that will demotivate.

> There is also this warning from Mr Len Peach, a senior personnel executive with IBM, and for the last two years chief executive of the National Health Service management board: 'Pay is rarely a good motivator for people who are already motivated. But a bad pay decision can be an excellent demotivator'. How will companies cope with the disillusionment of staff whose performance review delivers a resounding zero?[71]

Profit sharing, like merit pay, is far from a new idea, but interest in it has expanded in the last decade or so. Since 1978 a series of initiatives by governments have provided encouragement to profit sharing. In 1978 the Finance Act allowed for the introduction of Approved Deferred Share Trusts. In such schemes a company allocates profits to a trust fund which buys shares and then holds them on behalf of employees although the employees themselves do not receive the shares as such for two years (they need to hold them for five years at least if they want to gain maximum tax benefit). Two years later the 1980 Finance Act allowed for the introduction of 'save as you earn' share options. Under this scheme employees who agree to save for five or seven years are allocated shares which they can opt to buy at the end of the period or which they can cash to realise their savings. The attraction of this scheme is the tax exemptions that are offered. Another scheme was introduced through the 1984 Finance Act, in this case the Discretionary or Executive Share Option Scheme. This allows a company to offer shares to selected employees, in most cases senior employees, with considerable tax benefits. The restricted coverage of that scheme can be contrasted to another, introduced through the 1987 Finance Act, Profit Related Pay. This could only be operated if at least 80 per cent of a firm's employees participated. However, in return, considerable benefits were offered, for half of the profit-related pay, up to 20 per cent of total pay or £3,000 were to be free of income tax. The range of schemes was completed in 1989 by the backing given in the Budget to Employee Share Ownership Plans. In this case a bank, or other similar body, lends money to an employee benefit trust, which then acquires shares in the company on behalf of the employees. The cost of the loan may be met either by the company or the employees. Shares acquired by the trust are then distributed over time to employees. ESOPs have been used for some time in the USA and were used to some degree in Britain prior to the 1989 Budget. They were particularly popular in employee buy-outs, and thirteen were established in the two years prior to the 1989 Budget. However, that Budget gave added impetus to them by allowing companies to claim corporation tax relief for the funds they put into an ESOP. In order to be able to claim such relief, though, they had to show that the ESOP would lead to greater individual rather than common ownership. This was because of the suspicion of the government that some plans were collectivist, a view that to look at matters from a different perspective made them more attractive to trade unions (Unity Trust, a bank closely associated with the trade union movement has been one of the institutions giving strongest support to ESOPs).

The introduction of such schemes had a range of objectives. At one level, there was a general political objective of widening share ownership and an understanding of the importance of profitability. Firms that introduced schemes have had a number of particular objectives, including increased employee motivation, retention of staff, an identification of staff with the firm, and a willingness of employees to accept changes in work organisation.

Evidence on the operation of some of these new schemes has raised a degree of scepticism about their effectiveness. Duncan has argued that the 'widespread interest' in profit-related pay has been for the wrong reasons; he describes them as 'little more than an expensive tax dodge in favour of the higher earners'[72]. Crainer has referred to the American experience with ESOPs where, he argues, 'companies can create an ESOP as much to take advantage of the tax incentives as to benefit the workforce'.[73] Others have voiced concern that the fastest growing of the profit-sharing schemes by far, has been the Discretionary or Executive Share Option Scheme: by 1988 the number of companies participating in such schemes was 3,174 compared to 756 for the Approved Deferred Shares Trust and 742 for the Save As You Earn Share Option Scheme. This rapid growth in discretionary schemes has worried even some who support the principle of profit sharing.

> If the growth of ADST and SAYE schemes has been steady, then the upsurge in discretionary schemes since 1984 has been nothing short of spectacular. The rapid growth of those schemes has, however, been a course of concern, not elation, on the part of some of the strongest advocates of profit sharing schemes. The Wider Share Ownership Council believe that companies should not be permitted to operate discretionary schemes on their own and have urged the Chancellor to amend the legislation to this effect. They argue that the existence of executive-only schemes cut across the objectives of integration and involvement which employee share ownership is meant to generate.[74]

Others have been more optimistic particularly about the effect of profit sharing on the motivation of employees, their attachment to the firm and their willingness to accept changes in established methods of organisation. Thus, Price and Nicholson, reviewing their research of firms which had developed a significant degree of employee ownership, said that it appeared 'to have a beneficial effect upon performance where it made workers more willing to accept any rationalisation and changes in working practice'.[75] Poole and Jenkins were more cautious in their claims for profit sharing arguing that 'it is unlikely that the more grandiose claims for schemes, such as increasing levels of profit-consciousness among the workforce, will be fulfilled'. Nevertheless, they suggested that profit sharing may be 'accompanied by improvements in satisfaction and in communications in the firm' and may be likely 'to improve attitudes and the "climate" in companies', concluding that 'the development of profit sharing and share ownership is likely to prove valuable so long as expectations of benefits are realistic'.[76]

The impact of all these matters can be glimpsed if one looks at the current methods of determining pay. A number of recent surveys have shown the importance of flexibility, performance and profit sharing as items that help to determine the size of the pay packet of many workers. Three surveys might be referred to, all of which are based on different samples and therefore show different detailed results, but all of which allow one to identify common themes.

The Workplace Industrial Relations Survey[77] asked a range of questions of managers designed to discover what factors influenced the level of pay. In 23 per cent of establishments, managers said manual workers' pay was influenced by productivity/profitability and 8 per cent by the individual merit of the person concerned. The percentages were somewhat higher for non-manual workers, 25 per cent for productivity/profitability and 16 per cent for merit. There were some important variations within the total sample. Thus, the proportion of manual workers whose pay was influenced by productivity/profitability rose to 31 per cent when only establishments that did not recognise unions for that group of workers were considered, for individual merit it rose to 18 per cent (it is worthwhile recording nevertheless that the number of employees in such a category is relatively small, 14 per cent of manual workers in manufacturing industry). In the case of non-manual workers, the proportion whose pay was influenced by productivity/profitability was 37 per cent in establishments where unions were not recognised for this category of workers, though the number whose pay was influenced by merit in such circumstances, at 11 per cent, was lower than for the total sample.

Another survey, in this case by the Confederation of British Industries,[78] looked at similar issues. In the case of manufacturing industry, it was suggested that 61 per cent of establishments used 'additional payments' of one form or another; these ranged from 'profit sharing' to 'triggered payments' to 'discretionary bonuses' (this latter form of payment was particularly important in establishments without collective bargaining). In the service sector performance-related payments were widespread. Only 8 per cent of the companies surveyed did not relate pay to the performance of their employees, although there was considerable variation in the way the relationship between pay and performance was drawn. A majority of companies (57 per cent) linked pay of the same employees to both individual and company performance, but a significant minority (28 per cent) used only individual performance. Relatively few used only company-wide schemes.

A third survey, by the Advisory, Conciliation, and Arbitration Service[79] looked at the use of payment systems which attempted to achieve some flexibility in labour costs and rewards. A number of different methods of payment were covered under this heading: payment systems which reward the acquisition of new skills, merit pay, profit sharing and share option schemes, integrated job evaluation and integrated payment systems. Of this range of measures, profit sharing seemed to be the most important (26 per cent of companies having introduced schemes over the previous three years and a further 18 per cent planning to do so) with merit pay close behind (24 per cent of companies had introduced merit pay over the previous three years with a further 19 per cent planning to do so). A significant number of firms had also introduced or were planning to introduce payment systems which rewarded the acquisition of new skills (21 per cent had done so and 17 per cent planned to do so).

FINAL-OFFER ARBITRATION

Many collective agreements specify that if the two sides fail to resolve their differences in the normal course of negotiations, then some kind of third party intervention may or should take place. The state has a major role to play in providing such third party intervention and that role, in its own right, and the mechanisms adopted, will be discussed later, in Chapter 11. However, third party intervention is not synonymous with the state and in recent years there have been interesting developments in the kind of third party intervention accepted. The most widely debated innovation has been final offer or pendulum arbitration. Essentially (though there are variations) this constrains the arbitrator to accept the final position of one side or another, rather than finding a middle way between them. As Singh points out,[80] something like final offer arbitration has been used in the UK for a long while when dealing with 'rights' disputes (the distinction is made between 'rights' and 'interest' disputes, with the former being concerned with the interpretation of existing agreements or legislation and the latter being concerned with the views of the partner about, say, the level of pay that should be offered, or the hours that should be worked) for almost inevitably in such cases an arbitrator has to choose one interpretation or another, although in theory a third view might be possible. Sir John Wood also notes that the arrangements for wages councils have provisions rather like final offer arbitration in that after a period of 'bargaining' a vote may take place in which the position taken by the 'independent' members is critical and their support for one side or the other effectively will resolve any dispute. However, final-offer arbitration is seen as novel because it is frequently associated with a package of measures on industrial relations, like single-union agreements and no-strike deals, and has been pioneered in the UK by foreign-owned firms.

The attractions of final-offer arbitration are that it is seen as being one way of overcoming the disadvantages associated with more traditional forms of arbitration. Two such disadvantages have been highlighted, particularly in the USA literature. The first, is what Feuille has referred to as the 'chilling effect'.[81] This suggests that employers and unions will frequently hold something back during negotiations for fear that their dispute has to go to arbitration, because of the belief that the arbitrator will always 'split the difference'. While that may be an exaggeration, the view that in what have been called 'interest' disputes an arbitrator will often give both sides a little more than the last offer, may be realistic and is probably widely believed. Final-offer arbitration is likely, so it is argued, to reduce 'the chilling effect' because both sides will be under pressure to adopt a position most likely to be seen as 'reasonable' by a third party. The second disadvantage noted for traditional forms of arbitration has been referred to by Wheeler as the 'narcotic effect'.[82] This suggests that the use of arbitration might be seen by the parties bargaining as an easy way of resolving problems with the result that they might grow to rely on it rather than exhausting their own efforts. In so far as arbitration takes matters out of the parties' own hands it can be seen as undesirable, and final-offer arbitration might lessen this possibility. It might do so in that the parties might be less likely to submit to arbitration if it is a 'winner-takes-all' situation. Final-offer arbitration also lessens the relevance of third parties in that the solution found is one put forward by one of the parties themselves; the arbitrator does not put forward the solution, merely judges between the alternatives put forward.

The evidence for these disadvantages is less than clear (in the case of the 'chilling' effect, one can presume that this would only occur where the parties believed that arbitration was not only possible but also a likelihood). There are also complications, if not disadvantages, associated with final-offer arbitration. One is that it is not always easy to determine what was the 'final offer'. Should this be seen as the position adopted at the last round of bargaining or should it be seen as the position presented, maybe in a written submission, to the arbitrator? Linked to this, one needs to ask whether the parties are ever to be permitted to revise their 'final' offer, say after seeing new evidence, and how are the 'final' positions to be determined when the 'two sides' are made up of a number of separate parties, such as a number of trade unions or a number of employers organisations, all of whom may have adopted different positions. Such complications explain why in the UK, final offer arbitration has frequently been associated with single-union agreement. Another complication is that many disputes are not just about one issue; frequently also they are not just about 'rights' or 'interest' issues but are a mixture of the two. If final-offer arbitration implies that the third party has to accept the full package of one side or another, it might involve deciding in favour of some items with which the third party profoundly disagrees simply because the package as a whole is more acceptable. One way round this is to allow for a separate decision on each item in dispute, but this could merely lead to another way of 'splitting the difference' by ensuring that each side wins at least some of its points.

One of the real problems with final-offer arbitration arises from one of its advantages: by removing the ability of the arbitrator to put forward a new 'third' view it overcomes some of the problems associated with the 'narcotic' effect but by doing so it also stops the knowledge and good sense of the arbitrator being put to use. In their reviews of final-offer arbitration both Singh and Sir John Wood[83] referred to a variation used in the USA which seeks to overcome this difficulty. In the state of Iowa final-offer arbitration is preceded by mediation, and crucially, 'fact-finding'. The process of 'fact-finding' allows a third view to be put forward on a way in which the dispute might be resolved. The arbitrator is then able to award either of the views of the two sides or the suggestion of the fact finder and can do so on an issue by issue basis. Experience with this method of using final-offer arbitration suggests that it gives further encouragement to the parties to resolve the dispute before formal consideration by an arbitrator, and when disputes go to arbitration the recommendations 'of the fact-finders' are more likely to be accepted than those of the two sides.

Although final-offer arbitration has been widely discussed in the UK, so far its use has been limited. Singh noted a number of examples[84]: the agreements between the EETPU and Hitachi, Sanyo and Toshiba; and the agreement between the AUEW and Nissan. There are others, but they are concentrated in the 'high-tech' industries. There are even fewer examples of final-offer arbitration actually being used. One of the most interesting occurred in the motor vehicle industry in 1988 at IBC Vehicles. It was interesting because it involved a number of unions, including the TGWU and the MSF who have been vocal in their opposition to such arrangements, and because its results were legally binding on both unions and employers (so that failure to accept the ruling would have led the parties to be open to claims for damages through the courts). In the event, the arbitrators decided in favour of the unions. The issue, compensatory time off in lieu of sickness absence during holidays, was minor, but the decision was of some importance as an illustration of the use of final-offer arbitration none the less. Other examples have produced different results so that at the time of writing there was an almost even split between the judgements in favour of the union and those in favour of management. Many trade unions (including as indicated above, the TGWU and the MSF), have been reluctant to accept pendulum arbitration, in part because of its association with other industrial relations initiatives. The unions that have supported it most strongly have been those associated with other measures, like single union deals. Thus, the AEU has supported pendulum arbitration and one of its officers voiced his union's support despite the fact that it has been one of the unions to lose a claim as the result of a judgement. Speaking on the dispute at which the union which lost its case at Bonas Machine, Sunderland (over an annual wage rise and performance related pay) the district secretary involved said:

> While we are obviously disappointed with the result, we feel that we went down the correct road with pendulum arbitration, and given a similar set of circumstances we would do so again.[85]

SUMMARY

Although formal bargaining machinery in Britain and Europe (unlike that in the USA) traditionally has been centred at the national level, local bargaining, nevertheless, has always been important. In Britain, the development of informal local bargaining was discussed by Flanders in the early 1960s and taken up by the Donovan Commission whose report was published in 1968. The Donovan Commission argued that Britain had two systems of industrial relations (the formal and the informal) which frequently were in conflict.

Explanations for the growth in the importance of local bargaining varied. Some authors pointed to economic conditions while others referred to the use of the piece-work method of payment, or the result of the effort of workers to establish control over the work situation. It also needs to be recognised that local bargaining during this period was frequently supported by local management who saw it as a more flexible and speedy method of operation.

The Donovan Commission suggested that in Britain unions and management should attempt to exercise greater control over local bargaining; they should not attempt to eliminate it, but they should try to regularise it. A similar point was made by Fox and Flanders when they argued that the problems of collective bargaining might be seen as a result of anomie, or the lack of normative regulation. However, others argued that the Fox and Flanders solution, because it failed to deal with basic inequalities in society, would make conflict worse rather than better.

Productivity bargaining usually takes place at the local level. However, authors like Chamberlain and Kuhn, and Walton and McKersie argued that it had special characteristics. Whereas traditionally bargaining has been based on the belief that for one side to gain the other has to lose, productivity bargaining has been based on the assumption that through joint effort both sides can benefit.

Productivity agreements first began to be noticed in the USA in the late 1950s; they appeared in Britain and the rest of Europe at about that time or a little later. For a while some people believed that they held the promise of a way through the constant conflict which seemed to (and some would argue necessarily must) pervade industrial life. Productivity bargaining began to lose some of its popularity in the late 1960s partly because attempts to link it to incomes policies appeared to fail and partly because some union leaders and sympathisers questioned its benefits, though it remained an important and influential practice in the 1980s.

The 1980s, though, saw important developments in both local and productivity bargaining. As far as local bargaining is concerned, the important development was the withdrawal by employers from national bargaining in a number of industries. Thus, local bargaining came to be more important not simply as a supplement, but also as an alternative to national bargaining. Productivity bargaining, as has been noted, far from disappeared in the 1980s but more frequently productivity changes have been enforced by management and where negotiations have taken place frequently they have been part of a broader move towards greater 'flexibility'. Profit and performance related pay have also gained in popularity.

One other development has been noted in this chapter, the increasing discussion of final-offer arbitration. It is a method of third party intervention that has been widely used in the USA, and increasingly it has been incorporated in the UK, though examples of the operation of such arbitration in the UK are still very limited.

8 Industrial democracy and participation

USE OF THE TERMS

There has been a great deal of debate, and confusion, over the use of the terms 'industrial democracy' and 'participation'. One of the best discussions of these terms is provided by Pateman. She not only seeks to distinguish between industrial democracy and participation but also between different kinds of participation.

Pateman identifies three kinds of participation. The first is what she calls 'pseudo participation' where management uses participation as way of persuading workers to accept decisions that have already been made.

> A typical example would be the situation where the supervisor, instead of merely telling the employees of a decision, allows them to question him about it and discuss it. In fact, many of the so-called 'participation' experiments with small groups were of this form . . . often the concern was not to set up a situation where participation (in decision making) took place, but to create a *feeling* of participation through the adoption by the leader (supervisor) of a certain style or approach . . .[1]

The second is what Pateman calls 'partial participation'. In this case two or more parties are able to influence the decision that is made but the final power rests simply with one of them.

> The use of the word parties . . . implies an opposition between two sides, which is in fact the usual case in the industrial situation, the parties in question being the management and the men. Furthermore, the final power of decision rests with management, the workers if they are able to participate, being able only to influence that decision. Because they are 'workers' they are in the (unequal) position of permanent subordinates; the final

'prerogative' of decision making rests with the permanent supervisors, with management.[2]

The third is 'full participation'. She defines this as a 'process where each individual member of a decision-making body has equal power to determine the outcome of decisions'.[3] Examples include situations where workers operate virtually unsupervised by management as self-regulating groups, making their own decisions about the work process. The crucial difference between this situation, and that described as partial participation, is that in this case there are not two 'sides' with unequal decision-making powers but one group of individuals who effectively make their own decisions about how work is allocated and carried out.

Pateman also makes a distinction between 'lower level' and 'higher level' participation. In the former, participation relates to the control of day-to-day shop-floor, activity while in the latter, participation relates to the running of the whole enterprise (such as decisions on investment and marketing).

This distinction between 'higher' and 'lower' level participation has relevance for Pateman's definition of industrial democracy. She argues that industrial democracy implies a system which allows for full higher-level participation by employees. Pateman does not rule out the possibility of a representative system but her emphasis on full participation, which she earlier defined as each member having equal power to determine decisions, suggests that the currently prevailing power relationships in most Western enterprises would have to be changed.

> In either case whether the democratic system was representative or direct it would mean that the present distinction between management, permanently in office, and the men, permanent subordinates, was abolished.[4]

Pateman's distinctions are by no means universally accepted. For example, Brannen draws attention to some of the difficulties in separating out different kinds of participation. Certainly it cannot be done simply by looking at the formal structure. Thus, he argues that some 'institutions which have a formal participative goal become or operate as institutions of "pseudo participation"; other institutions which are set up on the basis of pseudo participation can, in fact, become participatory'.[5]

Pateman's definition of industrial democracy is also very clearly at odds with that adopted by Hugh Clegg. Whereas Clegg believed that industrial democracy was maintained through a system of opposition in which the ownership of industry was irrelevant, Pateman argues that industrial democracy implies a significant change to the traditional authority structure in Western nations. Pateman suggests that in Clegg's formulation unions would be a permanent opposition and management a government; there would, as a result, be no opportunity for the governed to change the government. Thus she says: 'It would be a most curious kind of democratic theorist who would argue for a government permanently in office and completely irreplaceable.'[6]

Pateman, then, would see Clegg's definition[7] as too restrictive and not meeting the basic requirements of a democratic system. At the same time others would see Pateman's definitions as being too restrictive. For example, Elliott has argued that industrial democracy is not just restricted to the authority structures of the enterprise but should also cover the wider range of structures that affect a worker's position.

> The term 'industrial democracy' means many things to different people and has been much abused . . . The first thing to say about it therefore is that it is a far wider and older issue than just about worker directors, possessing both industrial and political dimensions. Broadly, industrial democracy involves workers (normally through their trade unions) claiming rights to have a greater say over matters affecting their working lives. This involves the running of the country's economic and industrial affairs which in turn involves those who are in positions of authority handing over some of their powers to representatives of workers.[8]

Elliott's point is well made, though in practice is not taken on board in most discussions of industrial democracy which rely on schemes whose point of reference is the firm or the workplace rather than broader political structures. For our purposes we will not venture as far as Elliott in this chapter, not because the issues he refers to are unimportant, but because for ease of presentation they are dealt with in Chapter 7.

As far as participation and democracy in the firm is concerned the above discussion suggests a variety of possible types of arrangement. A number of examples are given in Table 8.1. They are placed along a continuum, rather than categorised just into three different types, as suggested by Pateman. The continuum reflects the stated structure of the arrangements concerned and Brannen's point, essentially about the enormous variety between theory and practice, needs to be remembered. Nevertheless, the continuum serves to draw to the attention the variety of different arrangements that can be considered.

The continuum also has value in that it allows for recognition that the sponsors of schemes of industrial democracy and participation might vary. The distinction between management and worker inspired schemes was used by Poole,[9] although his examples ranged wider than those covered in Table 8.1. The distinction is useful because it allows attention to be paid to the motives behind the introduction of schemes of industrial democracy and participation. The aims and aspirations of management are likely to be very different than those of workers and union. Whereas the former might see them as means of increasing efficiency and by involving workers helping to legitimate their position and their control, the latter are likely to see them as a way of taking control from management and as a way of recognising a separate and different interest.

The different objectives of labour and management are stressed by Ramsey.[10] He seeks to explain the 'cycles' of interest in participation. Management's interest occurs when their authority is being challenged and is a way of securing the compliance of labour. Thus, management interest in participation rises and falls according to the extent of the challenge they face. Participation schemes when introduced almost always emphasise a 'consensual unitary philosophy'. However, Ramsey also recognises that it is not simply management that has supported participation. Support has also been given by workers and their representatives on the basis that it has offered an opportunity to extend their influence and control. It may fail to do so, and following Ramsey's argument almost always does, and as a result workers may loose interest in the particular initiative put forward. The key to understanding the support that is given to participation at the height of its popularity in any particular cycle, though, is that the conditions that allow workers to challenge managerial authority seem to mean both that management needs to look to participation to meet its own aspirations and workers feel that they have a good chance of using participation for their own different ends.

INDUSTRIAL DEMOCRACY AND PARTICIPATION IN THE UK

Brannen[11] comments that issues of participation and industrial democracy are far from new but have been fought over since the earliest times of industrial society. Examples can be found in the UK of a number of different attempts to further worker participation and industrial democracy which date back many years, some to the

Table 8.1 Industrial democracy and participation

Management inspired and controlled schemes						Worker/union inspired and controlled schemes	
No participation	Financial participation	Communications	Employee involvement	Consultation	Joint decision-making	Worker representation on final decision-taking bodies	Self management
Job roles	Profit sharing	Briefing groups	Job enlargement quality circles	Joint consultative committee	Collective bargaining	Worker directors	Worker cooperatives

nineteenth century, and the examples come from different points on the participation continuum. At one extreme, examples of profit sharing can be noted that date back to the middle of the nineteenth century and examples of joint consultation can be pointed to which had gained considerable momentum by the beginning of the twentieth century (spurred on, in particular, by the publication of the report of the Whitley Committee). At the other extreme one can point to examples of workers cooperatives which date back to early in the nineteenth century and examples of worker directors, particularly in the gas industry, which date back to the nineteenth century and continued in one form or another in that industry until nationalisation in 1948.

In the twenty years or so that followed the end of the Second World War, however, participation, for most UK workers, meant little more than joint consultation and collective bargaining. There were some novel schemes which were well discussed at the time. The Glacier Metal Company introduced a complete system of work councils which was the subject of research by Jaques and Brown,[12] and the John Lewis Partnership introduced a system of councils and profit sharing which was studied by Flanders, Pomeranz and Woodward.[13] Although both allowed for higher-level participation neither allowed for full participation. In the port transport industry the Dock Labour Scheme introduced in 1947 gave workers, through their trade unions, joint decision making over the size of the dock labour register and discipline. However, the private employers remained and the scope of joint decision making was limited.[14] On occasions, moves to increase worker participation in decisions relating to their own jobs were introduced in a number of firms as were schemes of job enlargement, job enrichment and eventually quality circles. However, the dominant view was that relatively little that was new was happening and some of the major opportunities for extending worker involvement in decision making at the highest levels were not pursued at the time of nationalisation, after the Second World War, because the union movement had turned against their earlier support for radical measures like workers' control.

A number of important developments occurred, however, from the 1960s. First the trade union movement started to alter its stance towards involvement in management of enterprises. The TUC in its evidence to the Donovan Commission[15] argued that the independence of unions would not be impaired by the involvement of worker representatives at board level of companies. In succeeding years it put forward specific plans for a two-tier board system with representatives on the supervisory board from trade unions. Not all unions accepted this new stance, but the majority and some of the most influential ones did so. A second important development was the entry of Britain into the EEC in 1973. In the three years proceeding Britain's entry a number of attempts were made to develop EEC policy on industrial democracy, including the preparation of a draft statute submitted to the Council of Ministers in 1970 and the draft fifth directive on company law of 1972 which provided for worker representation on the supervisory boards of public companies with more than 500 employees. Although these EEC proposals were still under discussion, and a long way from being approved when Britain joined the EEC, they provided an important background and spur to activity in Britain.

The Labour Party which gained power in 1974 was elected with a manifesto commitment to take action to increase industrial democracy. In 1975 the Bullock Committee was established to take this matter forward. The Committee was headed by Lord Bullock, Master of St Catherine's College, Oxford (and a former vice-chancellor of Oxford University), and included amongst its members, three trade union representatives (Mr Clive Jenkins, Mr Jack Jones and Mr David Lea), two academics (Professors George Bain and K. W. Wedderburn) a solicitor (Mr N. Wilson) and three employers' representatives (Sir Jack Callard, chairman of British Home Stores, Mr Barrie Heath of Guest Keen and Nettleford, and Mr Norman Biggs of Williams and Glyn's Bank). It could be argued, fairly, that given the composition of the Committee and given the Committee's terms of reference (they began: 'Accepting the need for a radical extension of industrial democracy in the control of companies by means of representation on Boards of Directors, and accepting the essential role of trade union organizations in this process . . .') a move towards greater employee representation could have been forecast. When the majority report was published in January 1977[16] the contents fulfilled such expectations, for the Committee suggested major changes in the government of British industry. In summary, the majority report suggested that in future, in private firms with more than 2,000 employees, existing company boards should be radically restructured so that instead of being controlled by shareholders' representatives alone they should be composed of three groups of people: one representing existing shareholders, another (of equal number) representing workers, and a third (a smaller number) of co-opted people. This became known as the 2X plus Y formula. Clearly, in such a set up, the third (Y) group and its composition could be vital. The majority report said:

> Our intention is that the co-opted directors should be individuals who can make a valuable contribution to the work of the Board. We do not propose, therefore, any restriction as to eligibility for co-option or any stipulation that they should be independent or neutral.[17]

The report anticipated that this third group would be composed of bankers, solicitors, accountants, union officials not operating in the firm, and the like. The co-opted members should be chosen by agreement, but in the absence of agreement a procedure was laid down for arbitration. The majority report's proposals did not envisage the same size board in all companies; broadly the size of the board and the size of the representative groups were to vary according to the size of the company. For example, in companies with between 2,000 and 10,000 employees, 4 directors would be elected as worker representatives, 4 as shareholder representatives and 3 would be co-opted, whereas in firms with more than 25,000 employees the board would be comprised of 7 workers and 7 shareholder representatives plus 5 co-opted members. Possibly the most important aspect of representation on the board, however, lay not in the crude numbers or proportions, or even the make-up of the co-opted group, but in the source of worker representation. Under the terms of the majority report all would be chosen directly by the unions operating in the firm, not by shop-floor employees. Disagreements between unions over representation would be settled by an Industrial Democracy Commission, a new body to be established with the overall responsibility for the introduction and implementation of the plans. Further, it was stated that schemes would not be introduced in individual companies without the prior approval of a majority of employees in a secret ballot, initiated again by the unions negotiating (and this time also organising at least 20 per cent of the workforce) in the firm.

However, it is important to record that not all of the Bullock Committee supported the majority recommendations, and the employers' nominees issued a dissenting minority report.[18] At the end of the day the government adopted a cautious approach. The following year, they published a White Paper[19] outlining their plans on the subject. They suggested that initially the matter should be left to the parties concerned to make their own arrangements, but if this proved impossible, legislation would provide a mechanism to enforce a solution. This solution would include the provision that in all private companies with more than 500 employees, trade unions, through Joint Representation Committees, should have the right to require the board to discuss company strategy with them. Further, in companies with more than 2,000 employees, after three or four years of operation, the Joint Representative Committees could require a company to ballot employees on whether they wanted employee directors. If the vote went in favour then the company had the right to make voluntary changes or it could be compelled to accept a system of government which gave employees the right to appoint directors to a 'top policy' board.

The government's proposals represented a considerable shift from the recommendations of the Bullock Committee, in that they allowed for the gradual introduction of industrial democracy through voluntary agreement. In addition, they opened the possibility for non-union representation in the Joint Representation Committees (or a parallel committee) and for non-unionists to stand for election as employee directors. Nevertheless, even these proposals were abandoned when the Labour Party lost the election in 1979.

The Conservative Party which gained power in 1979 took a very different line on industrial democracy. Schemes for boardroom participation were abandoned in favour of lower-level participation, consultation and communications. Few private companies, for example, tried to move to introduce 'worker directors', and the public sector schemes ran into difficulties. The British Steel Corporation had introduced worker directors to their regional boards in the mid-1960s and their main board in 1976. Initially the worker directors were kept at a distance from the trade unions operating in the industry and anyone appointed as a worker director had to resign union office. Later unions were involved in the selection of worker directors and those selected were allowed to retain union office, but the choice of worker directors continued to be controversial with management retaining the final say. Research evidence suggested that worker directors had limited effect[20] partly because they tended to identify with the business needs of the industry (thus, Bank and Jones[21] reported one worker director as justifying redundancies on the basis of the need for greater efficiency) and partly because they did not have access to the same range of information as other directors. The experiment with worker directors in the Post Office started in 1978 and allowed for union representatives on the main and regional boards. The scheme was abandoned two years later because of management opposition, but also with research evidence from Batstone *et al.*[22] which suggested that although union representatives were able to make some impact on industrial relations matters their overall impact was negligible partly because of management opposition and the strategy of discussion of bodies where unions were not represented.

One piece of legislation, the 1982 Employment Act, appeared at first sight to give some encouragement to greater worker participation. A Liberal/SDP amendment to the original proposal meant that companies with more than 250 employees were required to report on action taken during the previous financial year to introduce or develop employee involvement. A detailed analysis of these requirements, though, makes it clear that the legislation was in a very different mould from the ideas of the Bullock Committee. The reports made by companies had to cover matters like the provision of information, methods of consulting with employees, financial involvement and schemes to increase the economic and financial awareness of workers rather than board-level representation. Further there was nothing to stop companies reporting nil progress, which some did.

The major developments in the UK in the 1980s followed the ideas favoured by the 1982 Act. Thus, joint consultation which suffered in the 1950s and 1960s with the growth of workplace bargaining, regained some of its popularity in the 1970s and 1980s. The nature of the available evidence makes it difficult to follow though and shows changes over a period of time. Nevertheless, it appears that the number of workplaces with a consultative committee increased in the 1970s in particular, and may have continued to increase in the 1980s. This was the conclusion, for example, of a Scottish study by Cressey *et al*. published in 1981.[23] The Workplace Industrial Relations Survey[24] suggested that overall the proportion of the workplaces with consultative committees stayed constant at about 34 per cent between 1980 and 1984, although when 'higher level' committees were added to the total then the proportion of workplaces either with a committee or with a representative on a committee rose to 41 per cent (covering 62 per cent of employees). The survey also suggested, however, that the constant overall figure for 1980 and 1984 concealed some changes in its composition. In particular, it suggested a decline in the use of committees in private manufacturing industry matched by an expansion in the public sector, although the decline in manufacturing seems to have been linked to structural changes in that industry rather than a tendency of establishment with committees to abandon. Edwards,[25] in a study of large manufacturing enterprises, seemed to contradict the Workplace Industrial Relations Survey findings for he reported an increase in the use of such committees between 1978 and 1984, but this apparent contradiction may be explained by Edwards's concentration on large enterprises and by the possibility that most of the expansion he noted occurred in the early part of his period. One of the other issues about consultation committees brought up by many surveys is the extent to which such committees frequently do not restrict themselves solely to consultation; sometimes one single committee is responsible for both consultation and negotiation.

At the same time other developments were taking place which sought to involve employees in discussion on their work tasks. For example, quality circles, where a group of workers (usually no more than 10 or 12) meet voluntarily on a regular basis to solve problems related to the quality of their work, were extended. Quality circles, to be effective, need to have the support of senior management who, in certain circumstances, may delegate to the group of employees the right to implement their decisions. However, it should be stressed that the decisions concerned are very much related to an employee's own work, and in many instances workers have to submit ideas for approval by senior management before they can be implemented. Senior management will also encourage middle level and supervisory management to become involved in quality circles, with the latter frequently playing a leadership role.

Many British companies supported quality circles in the 1980s, including British Telecom, Wedgwood and Jaguar. The ideas behind quality circles have been taken further, by companies like IBM, with the move to 'Total Quality Management'. Their aim is to ensure quality not by checking it after production but by building it in during production, and to do so using participatory techniques similar to those adopted in quality circles.

A related development is that of 'team briefings'. In British industry team briefings have been championed by the Industrial Society.[26] Essentially this is a means of communication with the workforce, but a highly structured one. Employees are briefed by line management in small groups and on a regular basis. The aim is to ensure that they are kept fully informed about the policy of the enterprise and how it relates to their jobs. Meetings are generally fairly short, ideally half an hour, and should concentrate on the specific items that management wishes to communicate rather than degenerate into a general discussion. Management control of such meetings is crucial and much depends on the ability of the team leader. Much also depends on the ability of the organisation to ensure that team briefings inform employees before informal structures take over. The aim is to control the flow of information and to do this timing is important.

At the same time as these developments have been noted, considerable effort has also been put into encouraging financial participation by employees. The Finance Acts of 1978, 1980, 1984 and 1987 gave a major boost to such initiatives and have been responsible for an extension of schemes, in one form or another, to a number of British firms. This issue overlaps with consideration of pay bargaining and is dealt with more fully in Chapter 7 (see pp. 186–8).

The most important pressure on the UK to take matters further at the end of the 1980s and in the early 1990s came from the EEC. It has already been noted that the draft Fifth Directive first produced in the early 1970s provided for worker representation on supervisory boards of large companies. In practice, these proposals were modified after their first version and rather than putting forward just one model of worker participation allow choice from a number, including an arrangement that would not necessitate worker board membership. A second piece of proposed EEC legislation, the Vredeling Directive would require multinationals with Head Offices outside the EEC, but substantial activity within it, to consult with employees, and agree to disclose a range of information to them. A third proposal is for the introduction of the Social Charter. This would give workers the right to information consultation and participation. In practice, with all of these proposals, it may be the threat of EEC intervention rather than the detailed provision that has caused most concern.

EXPERIENCE IN OTHER COUNTRIES

A number of other countries have made more radical moves in the area of industrial democracy and participation than in the UK. There are a wide range of examples that could be examined, though three have been selected: co-determination in West Germany, workers control in Yugoslavia and workers cooperatives in Mondragon, Spain. Each have been widely discussed: the West German example, by some, as a possible model for the UK, and the Yugoslavian and Mondragon examples much more as instances where more imaginative developments have taken place on a large scale.

In West Germany the system of co-determination has been in existence in the coal and steel industries since 1951. Essentially it provides for workers and shareholders to have equal representation on a supervisory board and for the election of the management board (which deals with executive matters in a similar way to a Board of Directors) by the supervisory board. It also provides that one of the members of the managing board will be the labour director whose appointment can only be made with the support of the employee representatives on the supervisory board. Legislation introduced in 1976, which took effect in 1978, extended co-determination to all companies which employed more than 2,000 workers. This was an important development as it extended co-determination to a large section of the workforce (about 4 million). However, under this extension one of the employees representatives has to be of managerial status, and the chairman is appointed by the shareholders and given a casting vote. Further the labour director on the management board does not have to have the support of the employee representatives but simply has to be able to attract the support of a majority of the members of the supervisory board (which may be possible without the majority support of the workers' representatives given as Toscano notes[27] the frequent alliance of white collar workers' representatives and management.

The system of workers' control established in Yugoslavia is far more radical and dates back to the immediate post-Second World War period. Under this system private enterprise has been removed from the scene, to all intents and purposes, ownership of industry now being held by all in the community (there are exceptions but they are relatively minor). Control, rather than ownership of the enterprise, is vested initially in a body known as the workers' council. This is a body directly elected by the whole of the workforce, although there have been restrictions on the method of nomination for election which have meant that trade union nominees have captured most vacancies; there are also restrictions on the proportions of representatives permitted from different sections of the workforce (to prevent domination by, say, white collar or managerial personnel) and the number of times a candidate might stand for re-election (to ensure the maximum possible breadth of participation in the council's work). The executive functions of the enterprise are delegated by the workers' council to a body known as the management board, which itself is elected by the council. In recent years a number of other management bodies have been introduced in an attempt to increase efficiency, and enterprises have been sub-divided so that power can be given directly to mass meetings of workers.

The Mondragon experiment offers the largest concentration of industrial producer cooperatives in the West. It dates back to 1956 when a priest Jose Maria Arizmendi-Arrieta, initiated the organisation of a bankrupt factory for an experiment in worker cooperatives.

The initiative was extremely successful and the number of

cooperatives and the range of activity steadily increased. The largest, Ulgor, employs about 3,500 people though the smallest employs less than 50 and there have been moves in recent years to ensure that enterprises do not grow too large. The enterprise is aimed at those working within it and control is formally exercised by the workforce. The typical enterprise has a general assembly which elects on a one person one vote basis a board of directors and a social council which operates rather like the works council with a representative function. The board of directors appoint the chief executive or general manager. The system of remuneration is linked to the performance of the enterprise and there are differentials between jobs though the differentials are less than in a typical Western firm. When a worker joins an enterprise he or she has to make a capital contribution. The share in the enterprise thus gained cannot be sold and there are restrictions on withdrawing capital on leaving the enterprise. Considerable efforts have been made to recruit workers who accept the cooperative spirit, and discipline is tight once in employment with severe penalties for striking. In return, although workers are not guaranteed a job for life there are rules which provide considerable job and income protection. The Mondragon cooperatives now include manufacturing enterprises producing a range of goods from refrigerators to furniture, but also what are referred to as 'second degree cooperatives', such as banks, social security and training facilities.

These systems of industrial democracy cannot, of course, be divorced from the social, cultural, economic and political background in which they operate. This is true of all industrial relations institutions but may be more so in the area of industrial democracy. Dahrendorf[28] argues, for example, that the West German system of co-determination is the result of a German tradition which emphasises the establishment of mechanisms which prevent the emergence of conflict rather than trying to contain it once it is manifest. In the case of Yugoslavia the system of workers' control has to be seen in the context of the attempt to develop a different approach to socialism than that adopted in the USSR so as to distance Yugoslavia from the USSR. Also important has been the degree of decentralisation in Yugoslavia which can be seen in part as a result of ethnic differences within the country and the associated opposition to central control, and in part as a result of the problems of communications and geography. The Mondragon experiments have clearly been influenced by Basque nationalism and the distinctive features of the region. Bradley and Gelb[29] have argued that one of the important factors for the

Mondragon experiment has been the relatively low labour mobility in the area.

Assessing the impact of these initiatives is necessarily more contentious. In theory the system of co-determination in West Germany, particularly as introduced in the coal and steel industries, gives workers considerable power. Thus Lane argues that any 'decision on major business changes, such as expansion, major cutbacks, relocation of production, appointment or dismissal of members of the executive, is made by a majority vote of members of the supervisory Board'. She goes on to suggest that in 'theory this form of co-determination gives the employed a genuine chance to participate in the determination of major company goals or, at least, to block policies which are perceived to be against their interests' and it should afford 'some direct influence on the executive or management Board, through the person of the Labour Director'.[30] However, Clegg[31] saw the practical position as being very different to the theoretical one suggesting that employee representation was much weaker, partly because it was split between the trade union and the works council. This split is particularly important because the works council often adopts a more 'conservative' approach than the union. For example, legislation prohibits their involvement in strike action. Further, Reich[32] has shown that on occasions not only will they fail to support strike action but they will also take the employers' side and oppose it. Lane also recognises some limitations in practice and, now talking about the 1976 variant for co-determination introduced outside the coal and steel industries, she comments that because of the role of representatives of managerial grades on the supervisory board and because the chairman who is not neutral has a casting vote, that 'contentious issues can thus still be decided in favour of the shareholders'. This does not of course negate the value of co-determination entirely and the unions have fought to retain it, if only as a way of obtaining information and to warn about developments they may want to debate.

There has been a great deal of research on the Yugoslavian system of workers' control. An early piece of research by Kolaja[33] drew attention to the problems that workers' council representatives had in making an impact on major decisions, partly because of their lack of technical knowledge, and partly because the system of elections provided for the rotation of office. His research centred on two particular factories. In one he found that managerial personnel participated in discussions twice as frequently as non-managerial personnel on the workers' council and three times as frequently on the managerial board. In the same factory the suggestions of managerial personnel were accepted nearly three times as frequently as those of non-managerial personnel on the workers' council and nearly four times as frequently on the managerial board. Furthermore, Kolaja pointed out that suggestions of non-managerial personnel that were accepted tended to be about non-production matters, frequently about welfare. In the second factory a similar, though not such extreme pattern, was found. That study was obviously based on a very limited range of observations and was criticised by Blumberg[34] on that basis. Other later researchers, though, have echoed the general line of some of Kolaja's findings. Obradovic and Bertsch, and Obradovic

> have shown that even with the Yugoslav system in which the executive authority (management and staff) are supposed to implement decisions formulated by the policy authority (the workers' council and other forms of self-managerial), in practice the deliberations within these councils are largely dominated by high level managers and specialist technical experts.[35]

There is, however, a danger in exaggerating this conclusion. While it is undoubtedly the consensus that on many matters, particularly technical, non-managerial employers routinely play only a limited role, they can and do play a more important role on occasions. Reviewing the literature, Bean concluded that 'despite the discrepancies between formally prescribed participation and its actual practical execution, enterprises seem to provide for a more equal distribution of power and industrial involvement in decision making than those elsewhere'.[36]

The Mondragon experiment, like Yugoslavian workers' control, has been subject to considerable research. One of the issues which has been raised is the extent to which the need for technical and economic efficiency in the cooperatives has meant that workers have found themselves operating in the same kind of environment and under the same kind of pressures as they would outside the system. Johnson and Whyte[37] argued that the superviser can act just as autocratically in Mondragon as in a private firm, and while Oakshott[38] has pointed out that the general manager can be dismissed by the board of directors, and thus is subject ultimately to the control of the workforce, in practice most general managers appoint their own staff and are able to operate much as management would do elsewhere. The role of the cooperative bank, the Caja Laboral Popular, is also important in keeping the enterprise to economic disciplines. As well as providing finance it also offers professional assistance designed to ensure the economic success of the enterprise. Brannen comments that the protection of the management function has not taken place without creating some strain between management and worker members[39] and there has been one strike at Mondragon, in 1974, when 19 strike leaders were expelled and other penalties were imposed on 397 strikers (but to date that is the only one) Bradley and Gelb, though, have taken a more optimistic view and have argued that the cooperative model allows the gulf normally seen between management and workers to be narrowed and in a later article they have argued that it has had some advantages if necessary adjustments have to be made: 'Mondragon provides evidence that abolishing the capital–labour distinction and localising adjustment within smaller groups can result in greater pay flexibility, less change in employment and smoother adjustment.'[40]

THE POSITION OF TRADE UNIONS

While most trade unions support any move towards greater industrial democracy few have been unaware of one major danger: that through their involvement in such schemes they might find themselves drawn into undertaking managerial functions to such an extent that they lose their independence and their ability to protect their members' interests. Clearly unions face a real dilemma; one of their central aims is the extension of employee control over the work situation, yet by allying themselves too closely with such moves they may impair their ability to defend workers' interests in other ways.

This argument has been forcefully advanced by Clegg.[41] He suggests that a free, independent trade union movement is the best guarantee of industrial democracy. Employees are likely to gain less rather than more control over the work situation if unions become so engaged in the process of management that they lose their independence.

This danger has been noted by a number of people who have written on the Yugoslavian system of workers' control. For example, one of the reasons why Kolaja[42] argues that workers' interests in the Yugoslavian enterprise may have suffered is because the union is too closely identified with the workers' council; the trade union is directly financed by and organises most successful candidates for election to the council. The result is that the shop-floor worker has no independent champion and therefore is unable to challenge assertions and decisions of management successfully.

It has already been noted that fears about the loss of independence also led British trade unions to adopt a cautious approach on the question of involvement in the management of nationalised industries.

In the early twentieth century British unions had expressed support for the idea of workers' control of industries after nationalisation (this can be seen in the Labour Party programmes 'Labour and the New Social Order' and 'Labour and the Nation'). However, by the late 1920s the climate of opinion started to change; for example, in 1928 Shinwell and Stacy produced a memorandum on the nationalisation of the coal mining industry in which they abandoned the notion of workers' control and argued instead that management should merely be regarded 'as a business' matter. This point of view was consolidated in the 1930s with the Morrison doctrine and in the 1940s with the TUC's plans for the post-Second World War reconstruction of industry; trade unions, they said, might nominate people to serve in the administration of a nationalised industry but anyone appointed would not be a union representative and would be required to relinquish their trade union membership on appointment. This is the main reason why the boards established to govern industries nationalised in Britain after the Second World War contained no direct union representation. Recently, as has been noted, some unions have taken a more direct role in the government of nationalised industries. However, their experience has not been entirely happy.

It is also clear that the Bullock Committee's majority report, although welcomed by many trade unions, was not welcomed by all. Three of Britain's major unions, the General and Municipal Workers Union, the Amalgamated Engineering Union, and the Electricians Union, in varying degrees, were hostile to the proposal. The essence of the remaining trade union hostility was still the fear that through cooperation with shareholders' representatives, they might become too closely identified with management.

The majority report of the Bullock Committee, however, believed that it was possible to guard against this danger. One of the major ways in which it was suggested that this might be achieved was to give the workers' representatives freedom of action. Thus, the majority report said:

> We are quite clear that an employee representative would be in breach of his duty if he voted in a particular way solely because of instructions of his trade union. He must be a representative free to express his own opinions and to reach his own conclusions about which policies will work for the greater good of the company, not a delegate told how to vote by his constituents.[43]

It was not made quite so clear, though, how this would work in practice, for the majority report also argued that a representative must not be cut off from his constituents and would have to establish an efficient feed-back system. One of the comments made on the system of trade union representation in the port transport industry in the UK has been that the theory of independence of action for representatives has not always been seen as such by the workforce no matter what the principle or practice. The same kind of question mark must be attached to the Bullock Committee's proposals.

However, there is a danger of over-emphasis on this issue: complicated formulas for representation of trade unions may be unnecessary for trade unions may be able, themselves, to adapt successfully, different attitudes towards different aspects of their work. Thus, a union may play a cooperative role in certain of its relations with management but reserve the right to disagree on other matters.

Further Blumberg[44] argues that Clegg and others have placed too much emphasis on the importance of trade union independence; he suggests that it is no guarantee of industrial democracy. Clearly one of the important issues is the basis of the quid pro quo; what kind of benefits can the union gain for its members through participation in schemes of industrial democracy and what kind of sacrifice does it have to make to obtain these benefits? If the union is merely being asked to 'participate' in capitalist management so that it can 'police' its members then the disadvantages may well outweigh the advantages.

Coates and Topham[45] though, recognised that industrial democracy is unlikely to be achieved in one single operation. It is much more likely to be a gradual process. As a result unions and workers may have to accept arrangements which are not satisfactory in themselves but which can be used as a stepping stone to something better. It is also clear that industrial democracy can be advanced without the union necessarily being directly involved in the arrangements. Workers' representatives can be elected directly and the unions can remain relatively free from managerial functions.

This, however, raises another danger. Many unions have long been afraid that if they allowed worker representation on managerial bodies to be organised separately then there was a possibility that an alternative source of worker allegiance would be created which could be a rival to the unions. Richardson argued that unions have reason to beware of such a possibility.

> The unions aim to be the only body to protect and represent the workers' interests . . . They therefore tend to react unfavourably to proposals by employers to form works councils, unless they are sure

that they can control the representation of the workers. Their fears of works councils have certainly not been groundless. This was particularly true in the United States in the 1920s and 1930s where in many industries trade unionism was weak and still struggling to establish itself. Among the weapons which many undertakings adopted to fight the trade union movement was the formation of works councils, often called employee representation schemes or company unions. While some employers used these methods for genuine consultation and co-operation, others introduce them in the hope that their workpeople would accept them as an alternative to trade unions.[46]

As has been noted, it has been claimed that one of the reasons for the weakness of co-determination in the German coal and steel industries seems to be a split in labour representation on the supervisory board between the union and the works council.[47]

This experience was clearly in the mind of the Bullock Committee on Industrial Democracy in Britain when it argued that worker representation on boards in Britain would be solely through trade unions. Thus, the majority report said:

Since unions are necessary to ensure that employees have an effective voice in decision taking both within the company and within the wider society, we wish to ensure that board level representation is designed in such a way that it does not undermine the union's representative capacity. The best way of ensuring that board level representation and collective bargaining do not in practice become confused and conflict is to insist that both processes be firmly based on the single channel of trade unionism.[48]

The dangers facing worker organisations bring one back to consideration of internal democracy. If the object of industrial democracy is to enable workers to gain more control over their work situation then little will be achieved by agreeing to systems which place a union leader on the board or committee if that leader is not influenced by membership needs and demands. From this point of view it might be argued that the ability of members to influence policy in worker organisations is an essential prerequisite for effective 'representative' industrial democracy.

This argument might be taken a stage further. It might be suggested that internal democracy in worker organisations will provide members with the kind of experience and education which is essential if they are to be effective in any system of industrial democracy. It would also enable the base of worker representation to be widened; if this were done then the dangers of trade union involvement in managerial functions might be lessened.

SUMMARY

There has been much debate about the definition of the terms 'participation' and 'industrial democracy'. However, most would recognise that there is a major difference in the aims of schemes put forward by management and those put forward by workers.

In the UK recent experience with participation and industrial democracy has been limited. Since the demise of the Bullock Committee recommendation most of the initiatives have been initiated by management and offered workers little real power. In some other European countries more radical experiments have been attempted.

Trade unions themselves are clearly interested in 'industrial democracy'. Such interest, to many, seems to embody the true *raison d'être* of trade unionism: the extension of the control of the worker over the working environment. Yet this interest is not without its own dangers, for it can result in a trade union becoming closely involved with management and as a consequence losing its own independence. The extent to which this is likely to happen may depend, in part, on the type of internal organisation and participation in the union concerned.

9 Industrial conflict

WHAT IS INDUSTRIAL CONFLICT?

Many discussions of industrial conflict simply refer to strikes. Strikes are probably the most visible and the most spectacular aspect of industrial conflict, but they are only part of the phenomenon. Kornhauser has argued that a study of industrial conflict needs to examine 'the total range of behaviour and attitudes that express opposition and divergent orientations between individual owners and managers on the one hand and working people and their organisations on the other'.[1]

Kornhauser goes on to list a number of manifestations of industrial conflict. His list is divided into two sections; one covers organised conflict, essentially group behaviour (usually between union and management), while the other covers unorganised and individual conflict. Examples include strikes and lockouts, output restrictions, removal of plant, conflicts in contract negotiations (all organised conflict), labour turnover, absenteeism, autocratic supervision, unnecessary firing and unofficial speed-ups (all unorganised conflict). Through these examples, Kornhauser makes it clear that conflict is not always manifest in (and certainly not always the result of) employee behaviour, as might be implied by merely studying the strike; conflict can just as easily be manifest in employer behaviour, such as the lockout and the removal of plant.

However, on the basis of this discussion alone one might imagine that industrial conflict has to occur between the two sides of industry. It is clear, though, that conflict can occur, for example, between members of the management team as well as between manager and worker. This is stressed by Fox,[2] who presents a four-category classification of conflict. The first category is conflict between individuals; the second is conflict involving an individual who is not a member of a collectivity and management; the third is conflict between a collectivity or one of its members and the management group or the manager; the fourth is conflict between collectivities. As presented, the first and fourth categories could involve conflict which does not cross the management/worker divide; in the first category this might be conflict within the management or union hierarchy, while in the fourth category this might be interunion conflict over job demarcation. However, Fox recognises that the third category might profitably be broadened to cover conflict between a workgroup and some higher level of its own union outside the organisation.

MEASUREMENT OF INDUSTRIAL CONFLICT

A wide range of different measures could and have been used for industrial conflict. However, the most common are statistics on strike incidence, labour turnover, absenteeism and accident rates. It is not difficult to appreciate their attraction. They are often easily available or fairly easy to collect, and they facilitate comparison, at least on a superficial level. Nevertheless they are not without problems.

At first sight the measure of strike incidence may seem fairly straightforward; but what is meant by the term 'strike'? For example, can one distinguish between a strike and a lockout (the Ministry of Labour used to try to do so in Britain but it is a difficult exercise to undertake); can one distinguish between a strike and a short stoppage of work (many countries try to do so by using guidelines like the length of the stoppage – half a day in some countries, a shift in others – or the number of workers involved, but nearly every country has a different guideline); can one distinguish between a strike and a stoppage to further political aims (the Department of Employment tries to do so in Britain by referring to stoppages of work relating to industrial disputes, but the distinction has been difficult to make because of the frequent overlap between industrial and political issues – for example, disputes over the Industrial Relations legislation or strikes over Privatisation proposals)? Further, there is the problem of the kind of measure of strike activity one should use; should one use the number of strikes, the number of workers involved in strikes or the number of working days lost? Frequently the different measures give very different results. The implications of these matters will be discussed in Chapter 10, but some of the questions raised are of sufficient importance to be noted here.

Labour turnover, absenteeism and accident rates have all been used as measures of industrial conflict because it has been argued that they are alternative ways in which a worker may express dissatisfaction with employment conditions and relations. Thus, it has been suggested that if workers dislike their jobs or feel aggrieved about action taken by management or management personnel, they may decide to leave the job altogether, or if that possibility is not open (because of the absence of alternative job opportunities) then they may merely stay off work for a short while (when they do so they may give no explanation, in which case the absence is likely to be classed as 'voluntary', whereas if they say they were ill their absence may be classified as 'involuntary', although this distinction may be difficult to make in practice and in many cases will not be very meaningful), or they may take less interest in and care over their work, which might lead to an accident. It is clear, however, that there are many other reasons why workers might leave their jobs or absent themselves from them, or why an accident might occur; for example, they might have to move to another area because of family commitments, they might be genuinely ill, or safety precautions at the place of work might be inadequate. Studies which have used such measures of industrial conflict have tried to guard against these fairly obvious problems by looking at general trends and taking factors like the state of the labour market, sickness and accident rates in comparable occupations into account. Yet, in the end, there is still a limit to the extent to which it is possible to control the effect of these 'external factors'.

Many writers have argued that it is dangerous to use just one of these measures of industrial conflict because they are really alternative ways of expressing similar feelings to a particular situation and the method of expression may not be determined by the strength of feeling but by the opportunities available to the people concerned. Handy,[3] in his study of conflict in the British coal mining industry, has shown how strikes, absenteeism, labour wastage and accidents can be used as alternative ways of expressing discontent. He argued that some miners used absenteeism, labour turnover and accidents as a form of output restriction because economic conditions meant that it was undesirable for them to use the strike weapon. Thus, merely to look at one measure of industrial conflict would be a mistake because low scoring on this measure may well be compensated for by a higher scoring on another.

On the other hand, there is a view that where there is a high incidence of one of these forms of conflict there is likely to be a similarly high incidence on others. The argument is that a particular kind of industrial relations climate is one in which conflicts of all kinds are likely to occur. The debate on this matter is far from concluded[4] and it is not necessary to try to resolve it here. Both views assert a link between strike and industrial conflict and the value of looking broadly at a variety of measures rather than just one.

It is also important to recognise that none of these measures does more than 'scratch the surface'. They merely examine the dramatic manifestations of conflict. Yet as Fox points out,[5] at any one time, conflict may be suppressed, and there they may be no obvious outward manifestation. However, conflict may still exist in that workers and managers, to use Kornhauser's phrase, may hold 'divergent orientations'. Consequently, studies of industrial conflict might be validly extended to include those dealing with attitudes towards industrial work and morale.

EXPLANATIONS OF INDUSTRIAL CONFLICT

Human relations school

One of the most influential explanations of industrial conflict which embodies an essentially functionalist view of industrial society is that suggested by the work of the human relations school. This viewpoint has its origins in the Hawthorne experiments and the research of Elton Mayo[6] although it has undergone considerable revision since that time. In this work Mayo highlighted the importance of social relationships in the workplace, and particularly the role of informal groups. Two different types of group were discovered. The one that was found during the relay assembly test room experiments both provided personal satisfaction for its members and furthered management aims. In this latter connection the members of the group believed that they had a favoured position in the plant and that this could only be maintained by a high level of production. The group, therefore, chided members if they fell behind with their production quotas and helped to maintain discipline. The second kind of group was found in the bank wiring room experiment. In this case also, the group provided personal satisfactions, but unlike the other group it acted against management aims. Production was restricted by informal agreement and output was regularly below what could have been achieved. The means used by the group to control those who produced too much included damaging complete work, hiding tools, and threats of physical violence.

The recognition of the importance of informal groups for the worker, then, was allied to a recognition that such groups could operate in line with, or counter to, management aims.

The role of management, from this standpoint, was not to try to deny the social needs of the worker, but to try to work within the boundaries they imposed and ensure that informal groups worked for, not against, them. Thus, some members of the human relations school have held that managers should assist in the strengthening of informal groups and in protecting them from disruption. Management should encourage its lower-level supervisors to enter these groups, and, if possible, to become their leaders, in order to direct them 'consonant with the aims of the formal organisation'. Sometimes control of the informal structure will be impossible. In such circumstances the manager should aim to prevent the growth of the more harmful type of group, 'perhaps by encouraging a multiplicity of informal groups cutting across lines of potential conflict or disruption'.[7]

Perhaps the most authoritative review of the Hawthorne experiments is that of Roethlisberger and Dickson. They sought to identify the lessons that should be drawn for management and drew attention to what they saw as the essential link between the economic purpose of the enterprise and its social organisation. Thus, they said that the social and economic functions of the organisation are interrelated, and failure 'to obtain satisfaction from cooperation will prevent in time the effective achievement of the common economic purpose of the organisation'.[8]

A successful manager, then, needs to treat workers, not as 'economic men', as traditionally was the case, but as 'social men': any attempt to see workers, supervisors and executives without taking their social setting into account will be inadequate. As far as industrial conflict is concerned the failure to meet social needs and the failure to harness them effectively can present real dangers.

One particular emphasis which was taken out of the early work of the human relations school (and which was highlighted by Roethlisberger and Dickson) was the emphasis on good communications as a way of avoiding conflict. This was an important element, for instance, in the study by Scott and Homans, mainly of car workers in post-war Detroit. They argued that, especially in large organisations, poor communications meant that workers felt they were being given the 'run around'. Workers 'use that phrase when they feel that what they consider is important is not being treated as such by people in authority'.[9] Some of the reasons suggested for poor communications were language problems, lack of time and the difficulties facing the 'link men' – foremen.

A number of other studies have drawn attention to the importance of the foreman. For example, Dalton argued that providing 'he learns to function flexibly and work out accommodations in response to imperatives playing on him' the foreman can be 'one of the major influences for reducing conflict within the organisation'.[10] However, it was recognised that foremen face major problems: they are expected, as members of the management team, to share in the responsibility for management decisions, but usually they have had no part in making them and may not even have been consulted about them. Later work has suggested that frequently foremen are bypassed by both management and unions: management, for instance, may talk directly to the union representative on the shop-floor, going over the head of the foreman. The problems relating to the foremen are part of a more general concern about supervision. In this context they link with the argument put forward in Whyte's study of a steel container factory, where he suggested that conflict arose because of the autocratic attitude of the works manager.[11]

Many would accept the points made by the human relations school. Workers have social as well as economic needs; as a corrective to the assumptions of 'economic man' made by scientific management they were making an important point and it was generally taken. Even Carey who was strongly critical of the Hawthorne studies and argued that the evidence was surprisingly consistent with a rather old world view about the value of monetary incentives, driving leadership and discipline rather than conclusions put forward by the Hawthorne researchers, was more concerned to attack the methodology than to argue for the view of 'economic man'.[12] Thus, he said:

> To make these points is not to claim that the Hawthorne studies can provide serious support for any such old-world view. The limitations of the Hawthorne studies clearly render them incapable of yielding serious support for any sort of generalisation whatever.[13]

Similarly, few would argue with the desirability of 'good communications', though the words of caution of Kerr and Siegel[14] that improved communications will only 'solve' industrial conflict if that is where the real problems lie are important (if the problems lie elsewhere, improved communications may make the basic disagreement more visible and conflict worse). However, many have been concerned to point to the inadequacies of particular studies within the human relations school, to the proposition that not all workers want to gain social satisfaction from the workplace (or to be members of social groups) and, critically, to the other needs as well as to the social needs of workers. As far as industrial conflict is concerned the argument has been that meeting supposed social needs alone will not be a solution. In essence, the problem with the human relations school was that they did not consider the other sources of conflict in the workplace.

The early human relations studies were followed by others which are sometimes grouped under the heading of the 'neo-human relations school'. The argument is still that workers look for more than economic rewards from the workplace; however, now it is suggested that they may look for more than social rewards as well. One of the main propositions is that they will seek satisfaction from the work itself (writers who have put this forward are sometimes referred to as the 'self-actualisation school').

There are a variety of different interpretations of this point. For example, McGregor put forward his theory X and theory Y thesis.[15] This holds that managers frequently assume that workers seek financial reward from their work (theory X) and can only be motivated by the consideration of such factors. He contended that managers should pay more attention to the demands of workers and recognise that expenditure of effort is natural and will be readily accepted by workers providing certain conditions are met (theory Y). It is only, so the argument proceeds, by paying more attention to theory Y that managers will be able to motivate workers properly.

Similarly, Hertzberg[16] has argued that a two-factor approach to worker motivation should be adopted – it should be recognised that satisfaction and dissatisfaction are not merely opposite sides of the same coin:

> the factors involved in producing job satisfaction were *separate* and *distinct* from the factors that led to job dissatisfaction. Since separate factors needed to be considered, depending on whether job satisfaction or job dissatisfaction was involved, it followed that these two feelings were not the obverse of each other. Thus the opposite of job satisfaction would not be job dissatisfaction, but rather no job satisfaction; similarly the opposite of job dissatisfaction is no job dissatisfaction, not satisfaction with one's job.[17]

Hertzberg distinguished between hygiene factors (such as good wages and working conditions) and satisfiers (responsibility, recognition, interesting work). Both hygiene factors and satisfiers are important, but they fulfil different roles. Hygiene factors prevent dissatisfaction but management cannot motivate workers simply by paying more attention to them; to motivate workers, attention also has to be paid to satisfiers.

Again, Maslow has discussed workers' 'needs' in terms of a hierarchy, ranging from needs that are essential for survival to those which enable workers to make full use of all their resources.[18] Self-actualisation is at the top of the hierarchy. Once lower-level needs have been met to a reasonable degree then managers will have to look further up the hierarchy if they are to motivate workers. The emphasis on 'met to a reasonable level' rather than 'met completely', though, is important. Maslow recognised that 'most members of our society who are normal are partially satisfied in all their basic needs and partially unsatisfied in all their basic needs at the same time'. Similarly, the emergence of a new need after a lower-level one has been satisfied 'is not a sudden salutory phenomenon but rather a gradual emergence by slow degrees from nothingness'.[19]

Recognition of the 'needs' of workers has an explicit management objective; it is not simply an academic matter. The aim, as with the early human relations school, is quite clearly to harness workers' energy to support management aims. McGregor explicitly argued that management should organise work so that employees would achieve their own aims 'by directing their own efforts towards organisational objectives'.[20] Another writer from the same 'school', Likert, linked worker satisfaction to increased efficiency probably more clearly than anybody else.[21] The new system of management was one in which motivational forces were recognised and used to ensure that the objectives of the organisation were achieved.

The view that workers are concerned to obtain satisfaction from the work itself has led to the proposal that work should be restructured to allow it to resemble more closely the principles of 'craft work'. Such principles imply that workers should be able to identify with the product they are making and that they should have more control over it when they work. Ideally it should also mean that the worker sees little distinction between work and leisure. A number of moves have been suggested to try to achieve this goal and make modern industrial employment more like craft work; these include job enlargement, job enrichment and flexitime.

Few would oppose the move to make work more interesting. Nevertheless, major criticisms have been made of the assumptions of the self-actualisation school. Some have been made by other social psychologists who have questioned the idea of a set agenda for motives; rather, it has been argued, motives can vary according to the situation of the person concerned. One writer from the Massachusetts Institute of Technology, Bennis, has questioned the assumption in the work of the self-actualisation school about basic human needs.[22] Other objections have been raised by trade unions, who have been concerned that job satisfaction might be seen by management as an alternative rather than as a supplement to workers' other needs.[23] Another criticism has developed from a major British study. The 'Affluent Worker' studies of Goldthorpe *et al.* have questioned the extent to which all workers seek intrinsic satisfaction from their work.[24] In their study Goldthorpe *et al.* claimed to find an instrumental orientation to work: the principal aim was to earn sufficient from work to gain satisfaction elsewhere. Although the 'Affluent Worker' studies have not themselves escaped criticism (some USA studies,[25] for example, have been able to point to aspirations for jobs that offer a high skill and interest content while others have questioned the whole notion of 'orientations to work'[26]) they served to draw attention to the fact that not all workers see obtaining an interesting job as their only or main aim; other needs have to be met if worker dissatisfaction is to be lessened, and some of these may be generated outside as well as within the workplace.

Other critics of the self-actualisation theories have questioned the assumption in much writing that the restructuring of work can be achieved to meet the needs of both the worker and the employer. Experiments, like those at Volvo's Kalmar plant in Sweden, it has been argued, do not prove the ability to meet both sets of needs in quite the fashion assumed by some of the more optimistic commentators. While it is accepted that Volvo has been able to modify the traditional system of work in the car industry without sacrificing efficiency or competitiveness in the market, it is suggested that the changes have not been as radical as is often assumed: the work is more varied in that an opportunity is given to perform a larger number of tasks, but the skill level of the work is not much greater.

Technology and industrial conflict

The concerns of the human relations school to recognise and harness the social needs of the worker, and of the self-actualisation school to modify the nature of modern industrial work, have links with the view that the kind of technology employed in an industry will help to determine worker satisfaction and the level of industrial conflict. The clearest link is through the concern about the impact of assembly-line production. A great deal of work designed to show the impact of assembly-line technology was undertaken in America in the 1950s. Studies of the motor vehicle industry by Walker and Guest[27] and Chinoy[28] pointed out that extreme specialisation led to fragmented and repetitive work tasks. They also showed how the technology used restricted the opportunities for social intercourse: for instance, noise and brevity of spare time between job cycles restricted any conversation between operators, while the range of people to whom an operator could talk was determined by the position on the line.

Such views of assembly-line technology led the authors to propose changes which have been associated with the human relations and neo-human relations schools. Walker, for example, considered ways in which the foreman could become a group leader and harness the group's social needs for managerial ends; Chinoy suggested job rotation and job enlargement in an effort to overcome the monotony of assembly-line production. These views of assembly-line production, though, also have a link with the proposition that the kind of technology used helps to determine worker satisfaction. In this case, one particular kind of technology was being examined but the way in which this technology was seen to determine social relationships, which in turn could affect satisfactions derived from work, is more generally important.

A variety of work fits into this school of thought. Again, many of the same issues recur, particularly the importance of social relationships and work groups. For example, Sayles tried to categorise work groups and explain differences between them in terms of the kind of technology used.[29] Sayles looked at 300 work groups, in a number of different industries in the USA. Four different types of group were distinguished. The first was what he termed the 'apathetic' group. Such groups had no clear leadership, little internal unity, played little part in union affairs and were not seen as cooperative with management or as high producers; they also had low levels of grievance activity. The second type of group was termed 'erratic'. Such groups were more united internally, leadership was often highly centralised, members often played an active part in unions and they were seen as unsatisfactory employees by management; they frequently engaged in grievance activity but it was not controlled well or necessarily linked directly to the goal of the group. The third type of group was called the 'strategic' group by Sayles. They tended to be composed of key workers and had a high degree of internal unity. Members of such groups participated regularly in union activities, frequently taking leadership roles, although they were also often viewed positively by management. This type of group had the highest level of grievance activity and such activity was clearly directed towards the group's own ends. The final kind of group was termed 'conservative'. These groups were highly united internally and highly valued by management. At the same time they paid little attention to union affairs and used 'restrained' pressure in support of their grievances.

Sayles sought to explain the differences between the groups not by reference to factors like the skills of the supervisor or management but by reference to the kind of technology employed. Technology, he argued, influences the extent to which the division of labour can be taken, and in turn the division of labour influences the formation and nature of work groups. Thus, Sayles argued, a division of labour 'which separates or eliminates workers doing identical tasks, reduces their tendency to engage in concerted activity'. The number of problems on which there can be consensus can be reduced 'by the simple expedient of reducing the number of similar jobs, or separating them in space so that communications barriers are created among the job-holders'.[30]

Work groups and technology both have an important role to play as well in the analysis of Kuhn.[31] He looked at workers in the rubber tyre and electrical equipment industries in the USA; his aim was to discover why workers in the rubber tyre industry participated more in fractional bargaining (the unauthorised pursuit of demands backed up by unoffical action) than workers in the electrical equipment industries. His argument centred on the idea that the type of technology used in the industries determined the willingness of workers to formulate, and their ability to press, demands; in the case of the rubber tyre industry it encouraged and aided workers to press demands whereas the opposite was the case in the electrical equipment industry.

In detail, and as a general hypothesis, Kuhn suggested that technology with the following four characteristics was more conducive to fractional bargaining. First, that which 'subjects a large proportion of workers to continued changes in work methods, standards or materials as they work at individually paced jobs'. Second, that which permits interaction between workers in the same task group. Third, that which 'groups most of the workforce into several nearly equal-sized departments'. Fourth, that which 'requires continuous rigidly sequential processing of materials into one type of product'. Kuhn argued that the first two characteristics stimulated the workforce to engage in fractional bargaining while the fourth increased their ability to press home demands by ensuring that the cost of work disruption would be much greater for management than workers. The third characteristic weakened the power of the union over the work group and as a result helped to ensure that action taken would be unofficial.

A simple view, though, that the kind of technology employed in an industry determines the level of conflict faces problems, for there are variations in the level and nature of conflict within industries. Goldthorpe's study of a 'deviant case' in the British motor vehicle industry (Vauxhall) drew attention to this problem.[32] Goldthorpe's solution was to place emphasis away from technology on to the orientations of workers. Technology was not discarded altogether as an explanation, but it was not seen as *the* explanation. The type of technology placed constraints on the behaviour but did not determine it. Different meanings can be attached to the same 'objective factors' by different workers and if one is to understand these different meanings then one has to look beyond the workplace itself, to the social lives of the workers involved.

Sayles and Kuhn both recognised the problem that had to be faced if their explanations were to be tenable. Sayles, in particular, seemed to move away from technological determinism at one stage. He noted the importance of leadership within work groups and, as Eldridge has argued, this 'would seem to lead us away from the doctrines of technological determinism when discussing the question of strike-proneness as between firms'.[33] However, Sayles's conclusion is fairly rigid thus, he argues that 'the conclusions of the study' show that the technology of the plant 'moulds the type of work groups that evolve', and 'the human element, so-called, is a resultant of the technological decisions and, in part at least, predictable from them'.[34]

Other writers have been much clearer in their attempt to move away from technological determinism. For example, Woodward, in an early study, looked at the organisational structure of a hundred British firms.[35] This suggested that organisational characteristics were not directly related to factors like size, broad industrial classification or the degree of business success enjoyed, but were directly related to the technology used. Three main groups of technology were identified: those producing units or small batches for customer orders, those working on the basis of large batch or mass production and those operating on the basis of continuous process production. 'When the organisational characteristics of firms were related to these technical categories, it was found that specific organisational patterns were associated with each category.'[36] The unit/small batch method of production and the continuous process method of production appeared to produce structure and behaviour 'more consistent and predictable' than large batch or mass production. Woodward went on to argue that the attitude and behaviour of management and supervisory staff and the 'tone' of industrial relations was determined by the type of technology. For example, pressures seemed to build up in an assembly-line technology and these adversely affected industrial relations.

However, Woodward took these issues further in a later study and recognised that the relationship between technology and behaviour might be more complex than initially thought. First, although the behaviour of an employee may be limited or constrained by technology 'these limitations will not be the only ones, for he will also be limited by the requirements of the administration, by the demands of his colleagues and by other factors'. Second, the interplay between the individual operator and his technological surroundings will not necessarily be one-way; 'often he may be able to bring about changes in his immediate technical situation, over and above those changes which he is expected to carry out as part of his job'.[37]

Woodward went on to argue that industrial organisations can best be studied through a socio-technical system approach. This approach implies that theories about industrial organisations will be incomplete and relatively unhelpful 'if they are limited solely to the technical aspects, or solely to the social aspects of organisations'[38] – the study of industrial organisations, rather, should give due regard to the interaction between the social and the technical. The socio-technical systems approach, however, also implies that study can be constrained within the boundaries of a social system. Woodward argued, explicitly, that technological systems can be isolated and their boundaries fairly easily determined.

A range of work has been produced utilising the concept of the socio-technical system; much has arisen from researchers at the Tavistock Institute of Human Relations. For example, Trist – *et al.* looked at labour relations in the coalmining industry.[39] This research centred on three main mining systems. The first was the traditional system of single-place working. In this

> the miner possesses the necessary range of skills to undertake all facework tasks in a self-contained work place. His role is that of a multi-skilled, self-supervising workman towards whom the deputy stands in a service rather than a supervisory relation. Groups of up to six men share a place, the men selecting their own mates. Since all members do all jobs, either on the same or different shifts, they share equally in the same paynote.[40]

The second was the conventional longwall system. This marked a sharp break with the single-place working for there was 'a formal division of labour with specialised tasks carried out by a number of groups of varying size'. Further, although there were task groups each had 'its own customs and agreements, including separate paynotes, so that each' was segregated 'from the other and bound within its own field of interest'. Since the groups did not spontaneously work together, coordination and control had to be provided 'entirely from outside – by management'.[41] The third mining system was the composite longwall system. This had some similarities with conventional longwall mining in that the same basic technological devices were utilised; however, it differed in the way the men were organised to carry out these similar tasks. Thus, although the task groups were the same as on conventional longwalls with regard to the activities they carry out, they were not segregated from each other, but interchangeable in memberships.

> As soon as the scheduled work of a shift is completed, men spontaneously carry on with whatever activity is next in sequence so that subsequent groups gain time in hand against unpredictable interferences with the progress of the cycle, always to some extent likely in the underground environment.[42]

Such a method of work organisation, Trist argued, results in the development of self-regulation and continuity characteristics which parallel those of single-place working.

Trist drew two important conclusions from this analysis. The first was that the kind of organisation associated with the single-place system and the composite longwall system has both technical and social benefits; it was found to possess characteristics conducive 'to productive effectiveness, low cost, work satisfaction, good relations and social health'.[43] They appeared to be able to overcome the disadvantages associated with conventional longwall mining, such as work isolation, conflict, supervisory problems, and low productivity. The second, and probably even more important conclusion, was that the technical system need not determine precisely the form of work organisation. The same basic technical system, longwall mining, could be used in a number of different ways, two of which have been highlighted. The aim, therefore, should be to recognise the consequences of different methods of work organisation and to select the one which provides the best fit between the social and technical objectives.

The emphasis in this writing on the way in which technical systems can be affected by other variables, and the move away from a deterministic stance, is welcome. Nevertheless, it is open to question whether too much emphasis is still given to the importance of social satisfaction. The criticism here has to return to the kinds of issue discussed in the analysis of the human relations school: other sources of conflict need to be considered.

Marxist explanations of industrial conflict

A clear challenge to the assumptions of both the human relations school and the technological school is provided by the Marxist approach to industrial conflict. The central problem from this point of view lies in the economic rather than the social sphere. In essence the problem lies in the division of economic resources and the existence of a capitalist class.

One of the leading exponents of the Marxist view of industrial conflict has argued that industrial relations occur 'within a dynamic conflict situation which is permanent and unalterable so long as the structure of society remains unaltered'.[44] The conflict situation is viewed as a product of the labour market, in which on the one hand there are workers who have to sell labour power in order to subsist, while on the other hand there are buyers of labour power who own the means of production and purchase labour power (for them the cost of labour power is an important factor in the cost of production).

> These two interests are irreconcilable. They are engaged in a perpetual conflict over the distribution of revenue. It might be stated that the interests have a common purpose increasing total revenue and so they have. But the conflict over distribution is in no sense lessened by this for the actual distribution of additional increments of revenue is determined by the power situation. Employees with no power may get nothing. There is no automatic distribution based on a sense of fairness or equity. Shares have to be fought for sometimes bitterly.[45]

Of course, this picture may well not be recognised by all of the participants, crucially by all of the workers; they may view conflict on a much narrower front and on a more parochial basis. However, this does not invalidate the picture that has been drawn, it merely draws attention to the problem of 'consciousness' which is highlighted in a great deal of Marxist writing. Absence of consciousness on the part of the workers, and false class consciousness, may affect the outcome, but it does not affect the assessment of the basic cause of conflict.

When one turns to look at the strike and the role it plays, though, the Marxist view becomes more difficult to state in a straightforward fashion. Marx and Engels clearly saw a role for strikes in raising consciousness; Engels described strikes as 'the military school of the working man in which they prepare themselves for the great struggle which cannot be avoided'.[46] Yet Marx and Engels both saw dangers as well in the 'injudicious use of power'. There was a danger, they argued, that workers would be limited to 'petty warfare against the existing system' rather than attempting to change it. There was also a danger, so it was argued, in adopting elements of the syndicalist tradition which elevated strike action, particularly the general strike, to a critical role in bringing about revolutionary social change. Support for the general strike frequently paid insufficient attention to the organisational demands for successful action. Engels portrayed this position as too simple and unrealistic. It assumed that

> one fine day all the workers in a country or even maybe throughout the world will stop work and force the wealthy classes in at most four weeks either to give in or attack the workers, who in turn will have the right to defend themselves and so can overturn the whole of the old society.[47]

In practice Marx and Engels took a view in between the two extremes put forward: they saw strikes neither as meaningless nor as the single important weapon. Yet their middle way has not always been accepted, and in the years since their writing was first published there have been many debates within the Marxist tradition about the value of strike action.

In a similar fashion Marxist writers have debated the role that trade unions can and do play. Early Marxist writers clearly saw a role for trade unions: trade unions were seen as an expression of the common interest of the working class (recognition that workers had a common interest in fighting the ruling class, rather than fighting amongst themselves was an important stage in the movement towards revolutionary social change). However, Marx and Engels recognised some dangers in trade union activity and this caution was taken up by later writers. Lenin, for example, argued that trade unions tended to concentrate on economic matters which were only of sectional interest (such as the improvement of conditions in their own factory or industry).[48] This was a mistake because it meant that workers often ignored non-economic issues and it hindered the development of class consciousness. Others, writing at the same time, expressed similar reservations. Trotsky, for example, argued that trade unions might be ineffective because they would be 'incorporated' into the state: trade unions in all societies competed with capitalists to obtain the favour of the state.[49] However, both Lenin and Trotsky stopped short of adopting the position put forward by some others – that trade unions were at best irrelevant, and at worst their action was counterproductive in the drive to achieve radical social change. Writing in 1938 Trotsky said that the 'powerful growth of trade unionism in France and the United States is the best refutation of the preachments of those ultra-left doctrinates who have been teaching that trade unions have "outlived their usefulness"'.[50]

The debate within the Marxist tradition, while important and worth stressing, has still been less critical than the debate between the Marxist tradition and other schools of thought. This is well exemplified in the discussion of alienation, in which divergent approaches and even definitions of the term can be seen in the positions taken by Marxists and non-Marxists.

Alienation was one of the important themes in the early writings of Marx. It was central to his argument that alienation arises from the fact that in the capitalist system labour is sold; it is bought by the capitalist and used to satisfy their needs rather than those of the worker. Thus the worker is estranged from the things he creates and this, in turn, violates the essential nature of man. Marx wrote:

> the alien character of work under capitalism emerges clearly in the fact that as soon as no physical or other compulsion exists labour is shunned like the plague. External labour, labour in which man alienates his self, is a labour of self-sacrifice, of mortification.[51]

Alienation is most vividly seen in modern industrial labour. Two aspects are particularly crucial. The first is the division of labour, which is seen by Marx as a means of promoting wealth for the capitalist but restricting even more closely the freedom of the worker. The second is the factor system of production, which is viewed as the most complete method of domination of the worker by the capitalist, for the capitalist can control in detail every activity of labour. However, it is crucial to appreciate that neither the division of labour nor the factor system were seen by Marx as important in their own right; they were only important because they represented the most developed form of treating workers as a commodity.

Discussion of alienation frequently becomes confused, because when the term has been used by other writers it has been interpreted in a different fashion. For example, although Weber rarely used the term he clearly had an interest in the area and commented on related issues at length. Yet Weber differed fundamentally from Marx in his analysis of the subject. As has already been noted, for Marx alienation was a consequence of capitalism; for Weber it was much more a product of industrialism and bureaucracy. As a result, although the abolition of private property is crucial in order to overcome alienation from the Marxist viewpoint, it is of little moment from the Weberian perspective.

Blauner[52] has also given a different emphasis in his discussion of alienation; he has linked it to particular types of technology. His starting point is to suggest that there are four dimensions of alienation, each of which can be contrasted with non-alienative states. One is powerlessness, which is contrasted with control; a second is meaningless which is contrasted with purpose; a third is isolation which is contrasted with social integration; and fourth is self-estrangement which is contrasted with self-improvement. Each of these dimensions is, in Blauner's view, linked, for each inhibits an essential and basic activity of man. Alienation was studied by Blauner in four industries (printing, textile, motor vehicles and chemicals) which were viewed as examples of four different technologies (craft, machine tending, assembly line and process respectively). His conclusion was that alienation in these different technologies could be looked at on the basis of an inverted 'U' curve; craft technology represents maximum freedom for the worker, a freedom which is sharply diminished in machine tending and assembly-line production, but which is largely regained through process technology. In this latter system, the progress of the division of labour is halted and may even be reversed, while automation enables the employee to increase his control over the work process.

Blauner's thesis is in many ways essentially optimistic. Although he adds caveats, such as that further automation may not necessarily reduce alienation because it may take forms other than process technology, he nevertheless holds out hope for improvements in the future. However, Blauner is only able to do so because of the particular view he adopts on the nature of alienation. For him it centres on a conception of 'basic human needs' which views the craft ethic as the ultimate aim; he is, in other words, taking the view put forward by the 'self-actualising' and 'neo-human relations' schools. This means that Blauner is able to postulate a reduction in alienation without fundamental changes to the ownership of industry or the nature of work organisation.

It is worthwhile referring here to the distinction made by Wright Mills,[53] and supported by Eldridge,[54] between objective (structural) and subjective (feeling states) factors. Blauner's discussion concentrates on subjective factors, assessing feelings of powerlessness, meaningless, normlessness and isolation; if a worker expresses satisfaction on these issues then he is assumed to be non-alienated. However, other sociologists would want to argue that the social structure may affect the individual in ways they would not perceive. Thus,

> if the sociologist wants to argue that social structures affect people's lives in ways which the people themselves only partially comprehend, then the actor's definition of the situation, whilst of great importance in sociological analysis, does not exhaust the sociologist's task.[55]

Wright Mills clearly adopts this latter position. Workers may express satisfaction with their present job, he says, but this does not mean that they have power, economic or political. Neither does it mean that the basis of alienation or industrial conflict has been removed. It merely means that employers have been able to manipulate workers into believing that they are satisfied: in fact, he says, 'the satisfaction thus expressed may be nothing other than "the morals of the cheerful robot"'. Similarly, he goes on to argue that 'current managerial attempts to create job enthusiasm . . . are attempts to conquer work alienation within the bounds of work alienation. In the meantime, whatever satisfaction alienated men gain from work occurs within the framework of alienation'.[56]

The issues outlined above again highlight the debate between structural and ethnomethodological/phenomenological views of society. Should one stress the importance of the influence of structure or the influence of the actors' interpretation, on behaviour? Of course, the question is much wider than the form in which it has been presented. It extends well beyond the issue of alienation, and, as has been seen in earlier chapters, well beyond industrial conflict or even sociology. It has also been argued earlier that one of the central challenges facing students of industrial relations is not to judge between these competing explanations but to find ways of bringing them together.

The study by Benyon[57] of workers at Ford's Liverpool factory is a recent illustration of research which accepts the importance of both structure and social consciousness. Benyon clearly accepts the importance of the structural position of the workers concerned when he emphasises the dehumanisation of assembly line production and the exploitation of workers. Yet he says that the picture he presents 'is painted in [the workers'] own words and the dynamism of the story is taken from their actions'. He was, he says, concerned not to write about the men 'as if they were the mechanical products of economic and technological forces' but to show that because of the way such forces constrain and limit people's lives 'they reveal the seeds of an alternative. For while classes are dependent upon economic forces they find their expression in the lives of real people.'[58]

It is also instructive to look at the way Benyon characterised workers' perceptions of their position. They all, he said, recognised the problems they faced and reacted to them; they all talked about the boredom, the monotony of their work, and so on. Yet Benyon stresses that while they saw their problems in much the same way as an academic analyst might have done they did not view their action or its consequences in the same way. Thus Benyon argues that the shop stewards at Fords adopted a belligerent yet essentially pragmatic attitude to their problems. They would demand action to deal with a particular irritant, but they would not view the irritant or the action in broader terms. For example, they have no desire to change the nature of industry or society. Looking at this issue in particular, Benyon says:

> As far as changing the nature of society goes, or even the organization of an industry, they don't know: 'If we thought about that we'd go crazy, I just can't afford to think about things like that. Sometimes I ask myself: Where are we going? What does all this add up to? Then I'm in another meeting, or on a case.'[59]

THE DESKILLING DEBATE

Blauner's use of the term alienation was a link back to the discussion of technology. Another, and one which links more clearly to the Marxist perspective, is provided by Braverman.[60] His book, published in 1974, has had a major impact. Braverman quite explicitly acknowledges his reliance on a Marxist perspective: as he says the 'intellectual influence under which [the] work was composed [was] that of Marx'.[61] However, it is also worthwhile noting that although Braverman explicitly acknowledged his Marxist perspective he said he owed little debt to anything that has been written by Marxists since Marx. He argued that in his writing Marx

shows how the processes of production are, in capitalist society, incessantly transformed under the impetus of the principal driving force of that society, the accumulation of capital. For the working population, this transformation manifests itself, first, as a continuous change in the labor process of each branch of industry and second, as a redistribution of labor among occupations and industries.[62]

However, since Marx completed his work in the 1860s, it is suggested that Marxists have added little to his body of work in this respect. 'Neither the changes in productive processes throughout this century of capitalism and monopoly capitalism, nor the changes in the occupational and industrial studies of the working population have been subjected to any comprehensive Marxist analysis since Marx's death.'[63]

Braverman's Marxist perspective was used for a survey of development of capitalism in the USA. Considerable emphasis was placed on the impact of Taylors' scientific management and the way that its principles have been used to guide the introduction of new production techniques. One particularly important and distinctive feature of scientific management was the concept of control. Braverman recognised that the issue of control was not new but had been an essential feature of management throughout its history; the argument was that with Taylor the issue of control assumed unprecedented dimensions. Taylor, it was argued, 'raised the concept of control to an entirely new plane when he asserted an *absolute necessity for adequate management the dictation to the worker of the precise manner in which work is to be performed*' [emphasis in original]. That management had the right to 'control' labour was generally assumed before Taylor, but in practice this right usually meant only the general setting of tasks, with little direct interference in the worker's mode of performing them. Taylor's contribution was to overturn this practice and replace it by its opposite. Management, he insisted, could only be a limited and frustrated undertaking so long as it left to the worker any decision about the work. His 'system' was 'simply a means for management to achieve control of the actual mode of performance of every labour activity, from the simplest to the most complicated'.[64] The application of Taylor's principles meant that the labour process was divorced from the skill and autonomy of the individual worker; it also meant a clear break between manual and mental labour and the monopoly of knowledge by management of every step of the labour process. The result, according to Braverman, has been the progressive degradation and deskilling of labour.

Braverman also recognised the impact of new technology. Methods of production have been revolutionised: 'modern production constantly overhauls all aspects of its performance, and in some industries has completely reconstituted itself more than once in the space of a hundred years'.[65] The drive for greater productivity has led to faster and more efficient methods and machinery. However, it is the way that new technology is used by management within capitalism, and the implications for control, that are important. In the capitalist mode of production

> new methods and new machinery are incorporated within a management effort to dissolve the labor process as a process conducted by the worker and reconstitute it as a process conducted by management. In the first form of the division of labor, the capitalist disassembles the craft and returns it to the workers piecemeal, so that the process as a whole is no longer the province of any individual worker . . . (But it) is in the age of the scientific-technical revolution that management sets itself the problem of grasping the process as a whole and controlling every element of it without question.[66]

The changes that Braverman noted are not restricted to manual labour in factory production. Increasingly, Braverman argued, the nature of both clerical and service work is being changed. The use of new technology in offices has transformed the work of clerks, and the use of new technology in shops is now being developed so that 'a revolution is now being prepared which will make of retail workers, by and large, something closer to factory operatives than anyone had ever imagined possible'.[67] These changes have implications for control, but also for the class structure. For example, when looking at clerical workers, Braverman argued that the problem of white-collar workers 'which so bothered early generations of Marxists, and which was hailed by anti-Marxists as proof of the falsity of the "proletarianization" thesis'[68] has been unambiguously clarified. The conditions of work of the clerk have lost all their former superiorities and the clerk has become part of a large proletariat in a new form.

The Braverman thesis has excited considerable debate. Hill has reviewed the Braverman thesis and noted a number of the criticisms made of it.[69] Initially three are highlighted. The first is that it is too single-minded in its emphasis on the conflict of interests between labour and capital as the source of managerial control needs, and of those needs as determining productive technique.

Capitalism is concerned with the making of profit, and to this end it has increasingly transformed the forces of production. One way of improving profitability is to create a production process which prevents the conflicts of interest in industry from hindering accumulation. But this is by no means the only impetus towards new techniques.[70]

Second, Braverman exaggerates the extent to which managers actually succeed in imposing control through the design of new work methods, at least in the short and medium term. Third, Braverman is too concerned with the consciously intended consequences of management activity. The origins and the outcome of the use of new technology are more complex than he imagines.

Hill goes on to suggest that there are 'alternative explanations of why managers have transformed the work process which are more appropriate in most instances than Braverman's'.[71] Senior managers obviously aim to use the resources at their disposal in the most efficient manner, so as to increase profit and the rate of capital accumulation. However, increasing their control over the workforce is only one means of doing that. New production techniques may be put forward, not because they increase control, but because they allow production to be carried out more efficiently than if human capability had to be relied on.

Hill also argues that Braverman exaggerated the inevitability of the transformation of the work process and 'underestimates the potential resistance of workers to work degradation'.[72] He points to evidence, particularly from Western Europe, of worker resistance to new production methods in the 1960s and 1970s. The resistance of workers in the car industry, for example, was manifest through recruitment difficulties, high rates of labour turnover and absenteeism. In the Swedish car industry such resistance forced management to move back from the strict application of assembly-line techniques.

Similarly, Hill argues that Braverman made an error in interpreting the tendency of production technology to give management responsibility for the organisation of the work process to mean that technology allows for management control of the whole of work in its broadest sense. 'In Britain, for example, where organised labour has rarely disputed the *principle* of management's right to extend its direction of work processes and rationalise production, there have been challenges to managerial control over other aspects of work.'[73]

One of the most wide-ranging reviews of the Braverman thesis has been undertaken by Littler.[74] He recognised that Braverman had made a major contribution by updating Marx and attempting to link the phase of monopoly capitalism and the transformation of the labour process. Nevertheless, Braverman, according to Littler, has created a number of impediments to further analysis. First, while

> Braverman appears to offer an historical argument starting with the development of management in the late nineteenth century, in fact the work is largely devoid of historical or empirical content. This has a number of consequences, of which the most important is that the work is permeated by an idealized conception of the traditional craft worker.[75]

Second, Braverman assumes that the separation of the conception and execution of work tasks is inimical to the essential character of human work, with the result that labour will continuously try to subvert such arrangements. Workers therefore come to their job opposed to capitalist authority. This means that Braverman 'ignores the fact that areas of influence and control may be the school, the family and other non-work social institutions' so that workers come to the factory prepared to work within the established arrangements. It also means that by assuming a universal recalcitrance on the part of labour he is able to avoid consideration of specific trade union or shop-floor existence and minimise the role of class struggle in shaping the labour process. Third, Braverman presents a view which has within it a strong strain of Marxist functionalism.

> Reorganisations of the labour process are presented 'as the outcome of a conscious design rather than of the product of the struggle of contending groups'. This perspective leads to an almost conspiratorial concept of capitalism in which every event is planned by the capitalist class and is in the interests of each and every unit of capital.[76]

Finally, Braverman equates the logic of Taylorism with the logic of capitalism. He seems to assume that what Taylor argued in theory actually happened on the shop-floor.

These impediments lead Littler to suggest the need for a less rhetorical and better grounded theory of labour process. The elements of this theory involve a concern for employer strategies, a recognition of the diversity within capitalism and the need for any system of control to take account of the consciousness of workers.

> Within capitalism there is a perpetual tension between treating workers as a commodity to be hired and fired and harnessing their

ingenuity and cooperativeness. Thus there is a twofold nature to the capital/labour relationship. If the contradictory nature of the capital/labour relationship is accepted, then this changes the nature of the control relation. Control should be seen in relation to conflict and sources of conflict and in relation to the potential terrain of compromise, bargaining and consensus.[77]

Littler's comparative study of USA, Britain and Japan serves to emphasise and illustrate this approach. It shows, for example, variations in the impact of Taylorism and in the strategies developed by employers.

Littler's criticisms follow those of a number of other writers who took part in the debate over Braverman in the 1970s. For example, both Friedman[78] and Edwards[79] drew attention to the way in which worker resistance can mean that managements have to develop fresh strategies to maintain control. Friedman talked about the way in which managements can develop 'responsible autonomy strategies' which have meant that the direct control approach of Taylorism has not been necessary. Edwards has pointed to different types of management strategies, such as the use of industrial relations procedures, attempts to channel and contain conflict, and the use of labour market strategies which divide and segment the working class.

Wood has edited a volume designed to evaluate the deskilling thesis.[80] In his introduction Wood argues that the Braverman thesis was accepted with excessive enthusiasm in Britain. He also argues that the Friedman and Edwards criticisms do not go far enough: 'the kinds of omission which critiques of Braverman have highlighted in his analysis involve fundamental questions: to incorporate worker resistance, labour and product markets and extra-economic factors involves more than simply extending one's analysis; it amounts to a theoretical reconsideration'. The deskilling which has occurred 'must be located in a context which is far broader than Taylorism and certainly more complex than a straightforward managerial conspiracy'.[81]

Wood's argument, then, is that the flaws in the Braverman thesis are more fundamental than has frequently been recognised. He also suggests that the Braverman thesis was not so novel as the author suggests and that in fact other Marxists have paid attention to the issues Braverman discusses. Wood's overall judgement is perhaps a little harsh. Braverman raised an area of debate and pertinent questions. A conclusion which suggested that he drew attention to some important processes rather than *the* important process might be a better summary of the debate which has surrounded his work.

THE INSTITUTIONALISATION OF CONFLICT

From a radical perspective the crucial question concerning industrial conflict is not why it occurs but why it occurs so infrequently. Of course, explanations vary. One is bound up with the notion of authority, which has been discussed at length by writers like Bendix[82] and Fox.[83] Briefly, authority is seen as legitimated power; that is, the person who receives the command accepts that it is legitimate for the person giving it to do so (for that particular issue). Workers might be persuaded by a variety of means (these are examined by Bendix) to accept the legitimacy of managerial control. Another explanation introduces the notion of the institutionalisation of conflict. It should be noted, though, that interest in this area is by no means confined to those who accept a radical perspective of industrial conflict, but covers a wide range of writers on industrial relations.

Although many people view conflict as disruptive and dangerous (this view was certainly present, for instance, in much of the writing of the human relations school) there are others who have argued that it need not be seen in this light. For example, Coser,[84] using the work of Simmel,[85] argues that conflict can be 'functional' (for the social system). For instance, it can have a group binding function (it can strengthen the cohesion of the group by uniting it against a common enemy); it can act as a safety valve (without an 'outlet' stress could build up within a group which might eventually lead to its destruction); and it can have a boundary-making function (it shows people in a group just how far they can go without expecting some reaction from the rest of the group).

Coser, however, also makes the distinction between communal and non-communal conflict. The former implies that there is a 'community of interests' (that is, there is basic agreement on what the parties are aiming at) while the latter implies that there are no common interests or common ends in view. Coser makes it clear that non-communal conflict can be disruptive for the system because, in the end, a compromise cannot be expected; it is communal conflict which is potentially functional. If conflict is to be functional, therefore, it has to be kept within certain bounds and there has to be some basis of agreement; thus the importance of the institutionalisation of conflict.

Two agents crucial for the institutionalisation of conflict are trade unions and collective bargaining. Wright Mills,[86] commenting specifically on US unions, has shown how trade unions can help to institutionalise conflict. He has done so by tracing the development of unions and analysing their role during different periods of time; he highlighted four stages. First, he argues, labour unions arose as a counterforce to the corporate form of business enterprise. The unions were 'economic attempts to equalise the bargaining power of the workers and the corporations'.[87] As a result the typical businessman saw labour unions as a threat; they challenged his freedom of action and his economic position. The second stage of development, therefore, saw the business community forming trade associations of their own, to counter 'union power'. This drove unions to bargain and take action on a national basis; it also incidentally increased the pressure on small businessmen because they were not efficient enough to meet the demands of industry-wide agreements. The end product was growing centralisation both within the business and labour hierarchies. The third stage of development saw the entry of the state into the arena in a major fashion. The state intervened increasingly in disputes between labour and business and on occasions took over the control of industries. This led on to the fourth stage during which political questions increasingly dominated discussion and action. However, in many ways union leaders were ill-suited to the new situation; they were used to taking short-term pragmatic economic decisions, not debating in the political arena. Therefore, in the final stage of development union leaders are faced with a problem. They have to deal with a situation which is alien to them and they have to find some way to defend the gains they have made. They have no long-term political strategy; neither for that matter do most of their members. In an attempt to stabilise their positions, therefore,

> the labor leaders allow their unions to evolve into institutions which integrate the industrial worker into a political economy that is changing from laissez-faire to monopoly and to state capitalism with many corporate features. The labour leaders become part of a machinery which keeps them as leaders but makes them the go-betweens of the rank and file workers and the class of owners and managers.[88]

The labour leader, therefore, maintains his role by bargaining on behalf of labour. He offers to make a contract with the owners and managers; he will provide labour for a certain price. However, if he is to maintain his credibility then he must supply that labour when it is required and see that it does not rebel. As a result, he has to act as a discipliner of the labour force and a manager of discontent.

Thus, Wright Mills concludes that although the union leader may be seen, and at times act, as one who 'whips up the opinion and activity of the rank and file and focuses them against the business corporation', because of 'his timidity and his fear and eagerness to stay alive in a hostile environment',[89] in fact, he serves to hold back rebellion.

> He organises discontent and then sits on it, exploiting it in order to maintain a continuous organisation; the labor leader is a manager of discontent. He makes regular what might otherwise be disruptive, both within the institutional routine and within the union which he seeks to establish and maintain.[90]

Although the comments of Wright Mills were drawn from the history of unions in the USA there is little doubt that he saw them as having a more general application. Allen, in his study of British trade unions, has painted a picture which has many similarities. Although Allen argues that militant trade unionism is possible (after a process of 'resocialisation'), at the moment most British trade unions are required to fit, and succeed in fitting, neatly into the capitalist system.

> At every point of their involvement unions are accommodated comfortably within the system of distribution they are struggling against . . . In the main they have evolved equipped to struggle in a limited short-term fashion and, though many pay lip-service to socialist aims, they accept the capitalist system largely for what it is.[91]

Allen also comments on one other way in which the activity of unions in Britain may be seen as helping to maintain the present system. They have, he says, accepted the capitalist norms of peaceful competition, to such an extent that now 'they are competing against each other in a wasteful, resource-consuming and fruitless activity, of benefit only to employers'.[92]

The way in which collective bargaining can help to institutionalise conflict has been dealt with already in Chapter 6. It was mentioned that it could do so by encouraging labour to work under certain guidelines, by persuading them to accept, ultimately, the need for a compromise, and by leading them to believe that gains can be made within the confines of the present system.

The regulation of industrial conflict, however, can be encouraged not only through the use of the trade unions and collective bargaining: it can also be encouraged in a much less tangible way. For example, there is considerable evidence[93] which shows the way in which moral pressure and persuasion can be used to reduce the level and extent of overt conflict. The appeal to 'the national interest' is probably the most outstanding instance, although such notions as 'a fair day's work for a fair day's pay' clearly also encourage people to accept the justice of a wage labour system and thereby reduce the likelihood of serious challenge.

Dahrendorf[94] has brought another important dimension to this discussion. He contrasts industrial conflict in capitalist with that in post-capitalist society (this latter concept indicates the belief that many Western industrialised nations have moved beyond the crude 'capitalist' phase with the stark divisions between owners and employees). In capitalist society 'industrial conflict was exceptionally intense' because 'the lines of industrial and political conflict were superimposed. The opponents of industry – capital and labour – met again, as bourgeoisie and proletariat in the political arena'. However, in post-capitalist society, industry and society have been dissociated. 'Increasingly the social relations of industry, including industrial conflict are . . . institutionally isolated, i.e. confined within the borders of their proper realm and robbed of their influence on other spheres of society.'[95]

However, Dahrendorf, while recognising the way in which the isolation of industrial conflict has led to a reduction in its violence and intensity also notes that there are limits to the extent to which industrial conflict has been and can be institutionalised. He points to a number of circumstances which may militate against the institutionalisation of conflict. For example, he argues that for conflict to be institutionalised all parties have to accept that it exists, or as he says, 'the necessity and reality of the conflict situation'. Fox[96] has shown that many managers do not accept conflict as inevitable even today. He argues that many managers hold a 'unitary frame of reference' which suggests that conflict is abnormal and undesirable. More generally, in the 1980s the whole approach by the government has underscored the unitary approach and has challenged the ability of unions to engage in open conflict. Legal compulsion in industrial relations is an attempt to impose a settlement; there is no recognition of basic and inevitable differences. The result is likely to be increased pressure, discontent and conflict.

Similarly, Dahrendorf argued that the effective coordination of interest groups is important for the institutionalisation of conflict. In particular, if there is fragmentation of worker representation then the ability of the union leaders to 'manage' conflict will be weakened. This is the challenge presented by the growth of the rank and file movement. In so far as this movement is separated from the official union leadership, and autonomous, it presents a real threat. Further, it is possible that the very success of the official union leadership in managing conflict may itself provide the motivation for the growth of the unofficial movements. The danger is that the official union leadership will become so engrossed with the national issues and national negotiations that they will omit to persuade their constituents of the value of their actions.

It could be claimed that in the past this has occurred in many Western nations. At times in the 1970s, national union leaders were persuaded after detailed discussions with governments of the need for pay restraint in order to combat the effects of inflation. However, in many cases they did not persuade their members to accept this point of view. This may be because they neglected this aspect of their work or because the rank and file membership accepted a different analysis of the situation and believed that wage restraint was not the key to the control of inflation. Whatever the reasons, the outcome was the growth of unofficial movements which have provided an alternative source of allegiance. It also needs to be noted that there is a view[97] that the capitalist system may not be able to deliver even the limited economic demands of trade unions. If this became true then workers may become disillusioned with settling conflict in the currently established fashion, and others may decide that in order to persuade them to do so, some kind of control or force may be necessary. As was noted earlier, this in itself could be a challenge to the institutionalisation of conflict, though, of course, taking things this far depends on accepting the basic premise about the problems of meeting 'limited economic demands'.

SUMMARY

Strikes are the most visible but only one aspect of industrial conflict. In order to examine the phenomenon fully, it is necessary to look at range of behaviour, a search which leads one into studies of morale and attitudes towards industrial work.

Explanations of industrial conflict have been attempted by a host of writers. Some of the most influential, who have adopted an essentially functionalist view of society, can be grouped under the heading, the 'human relations school'. They centre their explanation on poor social relations, such as inadequate communications. The neo-human relations school are a later development who have widened the search for work satisfactions; many stress the importance not only of social relations, but also of 'self actualisation'.

One of the other extremely influential schools of thought which attempts to explain industrial conflict is subsumed under the heading of 'technological determinism'. Writers like Kuhn have stressed the way in which the type of technology used can determine the pattern of work relations and thus the emergence of conflict. The socio-technical school is a later development which accepts that, although technology alone may not crudely determine behaviour, it may form an important part of a socio-technical system.

Conflict is endemic in the industrial situation for the Marxist: it is an inevitable part of the wage system. Alienation plays a crucial role in this line of thought. Labour is alienated in the capitalist system essentially because it is treated as a commodity, to be bought and sold. Other writers have adopted a different approach to alienation, and have defined it in a different fashion. Weber seems to have believed that dissatisfaction (if not alienation as such) was a consequence of industrialisation and bureaucracy rather than capitalism, while Blauner relates it much more centrally to the kind of technology used.

Some writers would argue that such a discussion focuses too much on structural factors and that more attention ought to be paid to the way in which the individual interprets what he experiences. However, such a view need not directly conflict with all branches of Marxism, much of which places considerable emphasis on the importance of 'consciousness' as a variable. It is also argued that there are ways of integrating structuralist perspectives with those which rely more on individual motivation and interpretation and that these may well provide the most useful avenues of thought.

One of the most interesting recent debates from the Marxist perspective has concerned the 'deskilling' of work. The Braverman argument has received considerable attention, particularly by UK writers, though it has not been reviewed entirely uncritically.

To many writers, and certainly to the Marxist, one of the most important questions is not why conflict occurs, but why it occurs to such a limited extent. One of the answers lies in the institutionalisation of conflict through devices like collective bargaining and the trade union movement. Dahrendorf, however, notes the limitations and constraints on the institutionalisation of conflict and reminds us that the experience of the past need not necessarily be mirrored in the future.

10 Strikes

Although strikes are only one manifestation of industrial conflict they are in many periods the most spectacular and easily visible. As a result a great deal of attention has been focused on the strike. Most major industrial nations collect strike statistics and while most people recognise their inaccuracy and volatility they have formed the basis of much of the academic and political discussion of the subject.

UK STRIKE STATISTICS

The Ministry of Labour have published, and the Department of Employment still regularly publishes, figures relating to strikes in the United Kingdom. They are collected by the Department's local officers and supplemented by information gained from a variety of other sources (including newspaper reports, employers and trade unions).

Not all stoppages of work noted by the Department's officials will, in the end, appear in the official figures for they only relate to certain types of stoppages and those of a certain size or duration. Thus, the figures only refer to stoppages caused by industrial disputes (not those classified as 'political'), which either last for a full working day and involve ten workers, or lead to a loss of 100 working days or more.

A number of different measures of strike activity are published; the three most widely quoted are the number of strikes, the number of workers involved in all strikes and the number of working days lost through strikes. From these figures two further measures can be calculated. The average number of workers involved in each strike can be computed simply by dividing the number of workers involved in all strikes by the number of strikes. The average duration of each strike can be computed by dividing the number of working days lost by the number of workers involved in each strike and the number of strikes.

As this last calculation has been undertaken by the Department of Employment already (the number of workers involved in all strikes is simply the number of strikes multiplied by the number of workers involved in each strike) the answer can be arrived at easily by using official figures. Data is also available which looks at various measures of strike duration more directly, though there is some problem with changes of categorisation over the years.

UK STRIKE INCIDENCE: MEASURES FOR COMPARISON

The two measures of strike activity most commonly used for comparative purposes are the number of strikes and the number of working days lost through strikes. The decision as to which measure should be used, however, can be crucial for the two measures frequently give different results and indicate different trends (as will be shown later).

The use of the number of strikes as a measure of strike activity is justified on the basis that this is more crucial than the length of the strike (which would be stressed by the number of working days lost) because a large number of small strikes can be more damaging to industrial production than a small number of long strikes. This notion was supported by the Conservative Party in their policy document *Fair Deal at Work*[1] when they argued that short strikes tended to be unofficial and unpredictable; thus they were likely to have an important impact on production because management would be unable to take action to minimise their effect. A similar conclusion (although supported by different reasoning) was reached by the Donovan Commission.[2] They argued in their report that a large number of short strikes had a greater than proportionate effect on production because they undermined management confidence.

Turner[3] has disputed these arguments; like the Conservative Party and the Donovan Commission he examined the effect of strikes on production, but concluded that long strikes have a greater than proportionate effect than short strikes, and that as a result the number of working days lost should be seen as the most crucial measure of strike activity. He used evidence presented by Clack[4] from the motor vehicle industry to support his case. In essence, his argument was that after a certain length of time a strike tends to have an impact beyond its immediate environment; to take the case of the motor vehicle industry, a strike in a factory supplying components will initially only have an impact in that factory (the vehicle manufacturer probably will have a stock of the components which will keep him in business for a short while), but later it will have an impact beyond the immediate factory and start holding up production at establishments which use their products. Turner, therefore, postulated a threshold effect for strikes; once the threshold had been crossed the strike tends to have a greater than proportionate effect on production.

Turner's views have been given support by writers like Vanderkamp[5] and Silver[6] who have suggested that the number of working days lost is the best guide to the economic cost of strikes, both for those concerned in the strike and for the economy more generally. However, although such writers have suggested that the number of days lost is the best single guide to the economic cost of strikes, still it is not necessarily an entirely accurate one. An alternative might be to suggest that a composite index of a number of different measures of strike activity might be more satisfactory. Such a composite index has been produced by Galambos and Evans.[7] However, even this may not be entirely satisfactory, as a composite index may obscure important variations within its component parts.

The decision about which measure of strike activity to use should be influenced by the needs of the exercise. Much of the above discussion has centred on the impact that strikes have on management and production. Of course, strikes have an impact on many other people and aspects of life and one can be interested in strikes from a variety of different perspectives. One also suspects that the decision about which measure of strike activity is used, is influenced by the nature of the case being made. Sometimes the trends gained from different measures point in different directions and the choice of measure may be determined by which provides most support for the argument being advanced.

STRIKE INCIDENCE: HISTORICAL COMPARISON OF STRIKES IN THE UK

Table 10.1 shows the number of strikes, the total number of workers involved in all strikes, and the number of working days lost through strikes in the UK in every year from 1911 to 1989. Table 10.2 shows the same figures grouped into five-yearly periods. Table 10.3 shows the average number of workers involved in each strike and the average duration of each strike, for five-yearly periods, between 1911 and 1989.

An examination of these tables allows a number of patterns to be identified. As far as the number of stoppages is concerned the very much higher level in the post- than the pre-Second World War period

Table 10.1 Industrial disputes in the UK – number of disputes, number of workers involved in disputes, and number of working days lost through disputes, 1911–89

Date	Number of disputes	Number of workers involved in disputes (000s)	Number of working days lost through disputes (000s)
1911	872	952	10,155
1912	834	1,462	40,890
1913	1,459	664	9,804
1914	972	447	9,878
1915	672	448	2,953
1916	932	276	2,446
1917	730	872	5,647
1918	1,165	1,116	5,875
1919	1,352	2,591	34,969
1920	1,607	1,932	26,568
1921	763	1,801	85,872
1922	576	552	19,850
1923	628	405	10,672
1924	710	613	8,424
1925	603	441	7,952
1926	322	1,154	47,233
1927	308	108	1,170
1928	302	124	1,390
1929	431	533	8,290
1930	422	307	4,400
1931	420	490	6,980
1932	389	379	6,490
1933	357	136	1,070
1934	471	134	960
1935	553	271	1,960
1936	818	316	1,830
1937	1,129	597	3,413
1938	875	274	1,133
1939	940	337	1,356
1940	922	299	940
1941	1,251	360	1,079
1942	1,303	456	1,527
1943	1,785	557	1,810
1944	2,194	821	3,710
1945	2,293	531	2,835
1946	2,205	526	2,158
1947	1,721	620	2,433
1948	1,759	425	1,944
1949	1,426	433	1,807
1950	1,339	302	1,389
1951	1,719	379	1,694

Table 10.1 continued

Date	Number of disputes	Number of workers involved in disputes (000s)	Number of working days lost through disputes (000s)
1952	1,714	415	1,792
1953	1,746	1,374	2,184
1954	1,989	450	2,457
1955	2,419	671	3,781
1956	2,648	508	2,083
1957	2,859	1,359	8,412
1958	2,629	524	3,462
1959	2,093	646	5,270
1960	2,832	819	3,024
1961	2,686	779	3,046
1962	2,449	4,423	5,798
1963	2,068	593	1,755
1964	2,524	883	2,277
1965	2,354	876	2,925
1966	1,937	543	2,398
1967	2,116	733	2,787
1968	2,378	2,257	4,690
1969	3,116	1,656	6,799
1970	3,906	1,801	10,980
1971	2,223	1,173	13,558
1972	2,497	1,722	23,816
1973	2,873	1,513	7,089
1974	2,922	1,626	14,750
1975	2,282	809	6,012
1976	2,016	668	3,284
1977	2,703	1,166	10,142
1978	2,471	1,041	9,405
1979	2,080	4,608	29,474
1980	1,330	834	11,964
1981	1,344	1,513	4,266
1982	1,538	2,018	5,313
1983	1,364	574	3,754
1984	1,221	1,464	27,135
1985	908	791	6,402
1986	1,074	720	1,920
1987	1,016	887	3,546
1988	781	790	3,702
1989	701	727	4,128

Source: Various

is evident: before the Second World War the number of stoppages averaged less than 1,000 (only 357 between 1926 and 1930, though 1,077 between 1916 and 1920) whereas following a decline in the late 1940s the average rose to over 2,000 from the mid-1950s onwards, only falling below this number in the 1980s. The trend, as far as the number of workers involved in strikes, shows some similarities. The average number of workers involved before the Second World War was frequently between 300,000 and 500,000, though on occasions it rose much higher (between 1916 and 1920 it rose to over 1,300,000). After the Second World War the total dipped but then the average started to rise from the early 1950s, though it did not reach the 1 million level until the 1960s (the highest average was over 1.6 million for the period 1976 to 1980). The trend in the case of the number of working days lost through stoppages has been rather different. The highest averages were recorded in the immediate post-First World War years, with a peak of over 26 million between 1921 and 1925. In the years following the Second World War the averages were lower, at around 2 million. The average increased somewhat from the early 1950s, though it was the 1970s before the major increase occurred (between 1971 and 1975 over 13 million working days were lost and the average for the following five years was much the same). The five-year average for working days lost declined in 1981–5 to around 9 million, and more markedly in the following time period to around 3 million.

Some care needs to be taken, though, in interpreting these figures. In part, this is because of the way that averages mask significant variations between years. This is particularly the case when considering the number of working days lost. For example, the 1921–5 average masks the fact that the total for 1921 was about 86 million, more than three times greater than the preceding year and more than four times greater than the succeeding year. Again the 1976–8 average masks the fact that the 1979 total was over 29 million, about three times greater than the totals for the preceding and succeeding years, and the 1981–5 average masks the fact that the 1984 total, at over 27 million was more than seven times the total for the preceding year and four times the total for the succeeding year. The yearly totals for working days lost are particularly likely to be affected by major strikes, even one major national strike: the 1972, 1974 and 1984 totals were dominated by strikes in the coal mining industry, while the 1979 total was affected not by one major strike but by a series of strikes in the public sector referred to as the 'winter of discontent'. If the years 1960 to 1979 are taken then 46 per cent of all days lost were a result of 64 large strikes.[8]

Care also needs to be taken in interpreting these figures because of the impact of trends in particular industries on the national figures. The obvious example is provided by the coal-mining industry. This will be discussed in more detail later but for the moment it is important to recall that in some years that industry accounted for over 80 per cent of all days lost through strikes in the UK (in 1926 and 1984) and for one fifteen-year period coal mining never accounted for less than half of all strikes. If one excluded the coal-mining industry from consideration then changes in strike trends that occurred between say 1961 and 1980 would look very different. Over that period the number of strikes including coal mining rose in the late 1960s but fell back in the late 1970s so that by 1976–80 the yearly average was about 12 per cent lower than it had been in 1961–5. However, if coal mining is excluded, then the yearly average was approaching 50 per cent higher in 1976–80 than it had been in 1961–5.

The differences noted in the trends of strikes in the UK between different measures is in part a reflection of changes that occurred in the size and duration of stoppages. Table 10.3 presents the simplest measures of size and duration by the same five-year periods used for

Table 10.2 Stoppages of work due to industrial disputes in the UK, 1911–89

Period	Number of stoppages	Number of workers involved in stoppages (000s)	Working days lost through stoppages (000s)
1911–15	962	795	14,736
1916–20	1,077	1,357	15,101
1921–25	656	762	26,554
1926–30	357	445	12,497
1931–35	438	282	3,492
1936–40	937	365	1,774
1941–45	1,765	545	2,408
1946–50	1,690	461	1,946
1951–55	1,917	658	2,382
1956–60	2,612	771	4,450
1961–65	2,416	1,511	3,160
1966–70	2,691	1,398	5,531
1971–75	2,559	1,369	13,045
1976–80	2,120	1,663	12,854
1981–85	1,274	1,290	9,374
1986–89	893	781	3,324

Source: Department of Employment, *Gazette*

Table 10.2. This information suggests that both the average number of workers involved in stoppages and the average duration of stoppages declined after the inter-war years. Between 1921 and 1930 on average over 1,000 workers were involved in each stoppage, and stoppages lasted for around 30 days. Each average fell in the 1930s and continued at a relatively low level in the post-Second World War years: between 1946 and 1960 on average around 300 workers were involved in each stoppage and stoppages lasted for 4–6 days. The average number of workers involved in each stoppage rose in the 1960s, and subsequently continued at a higher level than seen since the 1920s, and the average duration rose in the 1970s and continued at a relatively high level (though not as high a level as the 1920s and early 1930s) until the mid-1980s.

The Ministry of Labour and Department of Employment have, for many years, produced further information on the duration of stoppages though as has been noted it suffers from changes in categorisation. Nevertheless, broad trends can be identified. It is clear, for example, that over most of the periods covered the short stoppage has dominated. Between 1935 and 1951 over half

Table 10.3 Stoppages of work due to industrial disputes in the UK, 1911–89: average number of workers involved in, and average duration of, each strike

Period	Average number of workers involved in each strike	Average duration of each strike (days)
1911–15	826	19
1916–20	1,260	11
1921–25	1,161	35
1926–30	1,247	28
1931–35	644	14
1936–40	390	5
1941–45	309	4
1946–50	273	4
1951–55	343	4
1956–60	295	6
1961–65	625	2
1966–70	520	4
1971–75	535	10
1976–80	784	8
1981–85	1,010	7
1986–89	875	4

Source: Department of Employment, *Gazette*

of the workers involved in stoppages took part in strikes that lasted under one week; between 1946 and 1971 over half of the totals were accounted for by stoppages of six days or less; and between 1972 and 1975 over half of the totals were accounted for by stoppages lasting five days or less. The position changed somewhat in the mid-1970s: between 1976 and 1980, on average less than 30 per cent of the total was accounted for by stoppages that lasted for five days or less. The second half of the 1970s also saw an increase in the proportion of relatively long stoppages: stoppages lasting over fifty days accounted for over 20 per cent of the total between 1976 and 1980. Table 10.4 shows more detailed information for the period 1979 to 1988. This allows one to appreciate the volatility in this measure of strike duration in recent years. For example, whereas only 12 per cent of the total in 1979 was accounted for by stoppages of 5 days or less the total rose to 50 per cent in 1981. In fact the 1981 total was closer to the average for the 1980s which was in excess of 40 per cent. The

Table 10.4 Stoppages of work by duration, UK, 1979–89

Workers involved in stoppages	Percentages										
	1979	1980	1981	1982	1983	1984	1985	1986	1987	1988	1989
Not more than 1 day	3.7	18.5	30.0	21.2	16.7	22.0	25.6	29.4	19.7	29.4	11.5
Over 1 day, not more than 2	2.9	7.4	8.4	6.3	12.6	6.1	10.6	8.2	7.8	6.2	7.5
Over 2 days, not more than 3	1.3	7.8	4.5	2.0	6.8	4.9	2.2	3.4	2.8	2.5	3.3
Over 3 days, not more than 4	3.1	4.1	1.8	1.7	4.3	2.0	2.3	2.4	2.3	2.4	1.7
Over 4 days, not more than 5	1.6	2.8	5.3	1.7	5.4	14.1	1.5	8.0	2.0	7.7	2.5
Over 5 days, not more than 10	4.2	18.2	4.8	4.3	11.1	8.9	8.4	6.5	7.5	35.3	13.3
Over 10 days, not more than 15	35.3	4.9	6.6	3.1	7.4	7.4	3.0	2.7	0.9	1.9	50.9
Over 15 days, not more than 20	0.9	7.1	2.2	3.6	4.7	1.9	2.0	0.6	16.3	0.5	2.5
Over 20 days, not more than 30	2.8	2.3	4.1	1.7	6.0	2.4	21.6	8.0	2.8	2.8	1.1
Over 30 days, not more than 50	10.1	2.0	0.5	0.6	10.9	15.3	1.7	2.3	2.6	7.2	1.7
Over 50 days	34.1	24.9	31.8	53.8	14.1	15.0	21.1	28.5	35.3	4.1	4.0

Source: Department of Employment, *Gazette*

volatility can also be seen in the number of longer stoppages: those lasting for more than 50 days accounted for over 50 per cent of the total in 1982 but only about 14 per cent the following year.

The volatility of the figures and the somewhat different impressions given by changes from one year to the next make it difficult to identify major trends and developments. However, in the post-Second World War years two major developments have been highlighted for discussion. The first is that in the early 1960s there was an absence of large strikes and a decline in the duration of strikes. Durcan, McCarthy and Redman noted that a major change occurred in the 1960s. 'Between 1960 and 1970 the macro-strike virtually disappeared again – apart from the single event of the seamen's strike in 1966.'[9] The growing importance of the short strike was one of the main features of the analysis of the Donovan Commission.[10] The number of short strikes reached its peak in the first half of the 1960s and fell back from 1965; consequently by the time the Donovan Commission reported (in 1968) the trends seemed to have changed, though it is likely that this apparent change was largely if not entirely a reflection of the reduction in the number of strikes in the coal-mining industry, and it is at least arguable (though the data are not available to permit a precise examination of the thesis) that the proportion of short strikes continued to rise outside coal mining throughout the 1960s.[11]

The second development that might be highlighted is the increase in the number of large strikes and the increase in the average length of strikes in the 1970s. Many of the large strikes occurred in the public sector when government tried to restrict pay increases in line with incomes policy guidelines and as an example to the private sector. Some, though, occurred in the private sector, like the national engineering stoppage of 1979. This trend continued into the 1980s and was best exemplified by the national strike in the coal-mining industry, though in fact this was only one of a number in the public sector. There is little doubt that government pay policy, particularly towards its own employees, was an important explanatory factor, though other aspects of government policy were important as well, as were worsening economic conditions.

However, Edwards offers a word of caution on this interpretation. He accepts that a significant change took place in the 1970s but argues that short strikes nevertheless still predominate in Britain. This is particularly so, he argues, if one includes those strikes that escape inclusion in the national figures.

258 An introduction to industrial relations

The typical British strike is, thus, extremely short. Any tendency for strikes to have grown longer must be seen in this context. It is possible to point to certain tendencies in the economic and industrial relations climates which may have led to longer strikes. With the growing importance of very large disputes it is easy to give the impression that the whole strike picture has dramatically altered. In a way this is true, and it would be wrong to ignore the upsurge of the large national strike. But most strikes remain extremely short and limited affairs, of significance only in the workplaces in which they occur.[12]

THE REASONS GIVEN FOR STRIKES IN THE UK

Considerable attention has been focused in the UK on the reasons given for strikes. In his analysis of strikes between 1911 and 1947 Knowles regrouped the then official classification to try to determine trends. The regrouping left him with a threefold classification:

1 *Basic issues* – including wage increase questions, wage decrease questions, other wages questions, hours of labour.
2 *Frictional issues* – including employment of certain classes of person, other working arrangements, rules and discipline.
3 *Solidarity issues* – including trade union principles, sympathetic action, miscellaneous causes.

Knowles distinguished between two periods, with the break being made in 1926, the year of the General Strike. The very general trend he highlighted was a decline in strikes over basic issues and an increase in strikes over frictional issues. Knowles made an initial assessment of the reasons for these trends. First, he argued that the reduction in the importance of basic issues was largely accounted for by the reduction in one of its sub-categories, wage increase strikes, which in turn might be linked to the realisation by unions that the strike 'is not an instrument by which the wages problem can be solved'.[13] Second, he suggested that the relative increase in frictional issues was largely accounted for by the increase in the sub-category 'other working arrangements' which in turn might be linked to workers' demands to be consulted by management over a wide range of matters. Third, the position of solidarity issues, which showed a decrease in terms of the number of strikes but an increase in terms of the number of workers involved, might be accounted for by changes in the sub-category of 'trade union principles', which in turn might be linked to the fact that such strikes were no longer about the right to organise or about recognition but were concerned with the closed shop.

In fact the trends identified by Knowles started to change after the period covered by his study. In particular the decline in stoppages accounted for by wage disputes was halted and reversed. Table 10.5 shows that the percentage of stoppages accounted for by wage disputes rose steadily from the mid-1950s until the mid-1970s, and although the average for the following decade fell back a little it remained at over 50 per cent for the number of stoppages and over 80 per cent for the number of days lost until the mid-1980s. If the effect of the changing pattern of strikes in the coal-mining industry is excluded (relatively few strikes in coal mining were over wages and the number of strikes in that industry declined dramatically from the 1960s) then the trend is in the same direction but less erratic. In particular the sharp decline in days lost as the result of pay disputes in 1985–9 would be modified. The 1985 figure was dominated by the stoppage in the mining industries over pit closures; the percentages for pay disputes for subsequent years when stoppages in coal mining were much less important were 59 (1986), 82 (1987), 51 (1988) and 80 (1989).

The position with respect to all the categories of causes of stoppages between 1979 and 1988 is summarised in Table 10.6. This table again uses the official classification of the causes of stoppages though in this instance without regrouping them. It should be stressed that these figures, like those used by Knowles, report what the parties involved in stoppage said was the principal cause. Of course, this may be different than the real cause and so the figures can be taken as no more than a guide to the issues in dispute; nevertheless they are worthwhile looking at on that basis. The dominance of wage disputes is again

Table 10.5 Stoppages of work over pay, UK, 1915–88

Period	Percentage of stoppages over pay	Percentage of days lost over pay
1915–24	66.9	–
1925–34	53.1	87.5
1935–44	52.7	60.2
1945–54	44.4	49.7
1955–64	47.1	70.9
1965–74	56.1	82.3
1975–84	50.4	81.0
1985–89	38.8	54.5

Source: Department of Employment, *Gazette*

noticeable though it should be recorded that it is less so than it had been in the 1970s. The other interesting aspect of the recorded causes of stoppages shown in Table 10.6 is the importance of factors like working conditions and supervision, manning and work allocation, and dismissal and other disciplinary matters. Together they were the recorded cause of 38 per cent of all stoppages and over 7 per cent of all working days lost. The very high proportion of days lost accounted for by redundancy questions is largely, though not entirely, a result of the 1984–5 miners' strike.

Interunion disputes (which have been recorded primarily under the heading of trade union matters, though this category covers other issues as well) generally have not been recorded as a major cause of stoppages in the UK in recent years. From Table 10.6 it can be seen that only around 6 per cent of stoppages and less than 2 per cent of days lost were accounted for by 'trade union matters' and in fact less than a third of these were interunion disputes.

OTHER TRENDS IN STRIKE ACTIVITY

It was noted earlier that consideration of strike trends in the UK has to be undertaken with a recognition that for a substantial period the

Table 10.6 Principal causes of stoppages in the UK, 1979–88

	Number of stoppages (%)	Number of working days lost (%)
Pay – wage rates and earnings	43.0	54.1
Pay – extra wage and fringe benefits	2.2	1.5
Total pay	45.2	55.6
Duration and pattern of hours worked	3.7	1.2
Redundancy question	7.9	34.3
Trade union matters	5.2	1.8
Working conditions and supervision	9.6	0.9
Manning and work allocation	18.2	4.1
Dismissal and other disciplinary matters	10.2	2.1
Total	100.0	100.0

Source: *Employment Gazette*, various issues

influence of one industry, coal mining, was considerable. This issue might now be explored a little further. It might be noted that from the General Strike until the 1960s the coal-mining industry dominated stoppage activity in the UK. General Strike year, 1926, was clearly atypical, yet from 1937 to 1964 coal mining never accounted for less than 35 per cent of all stoppages and between 1931 and 1945 it only accounted for less than 40 per cent of all days lost on four occasions. The domination of the coal-mining industry started to fade, as far as days lost are concerned, in the 1950s, and as far as the number of stoppages are concerned, in the 1960s. The reduction in the number of stoppages in coal mining from about 2,000 in the mid-1950s to around 250 in the mid-1970s, and in the number of working days lost from about 0.5 million in the mid-1950s to around 75,000 in the mid-1970s, had important implications for overall strike trends in the UK. It is worthwhile noting, that despite the general reduction in the proportion of stoppages in the UK occurring in the coal-mining industry, in particular years this general trend has been reversed. In 1972, 1974 and 1984–5 a very large proportion of days lost through stoppages in the UK were accounted for by strikes in the coal-mining industry. The same is not the case if the number of stoppages rather than the number of working days lost is looked at because in each of these years the coal-mining industry was the scene for a major national strike. An additional consideration is put forward by Winterton. He argues that the proportion of stoppages qualifying for inclusion in the published statistics declined over the 1960–78 period. 'This accounts,' he says 'for a significant amount of the apparent decline in coal mining strike proneness since 1960.'[14]

A broader view of strike activity in the UK by industry is offered in Table 10.7. Information is given per 1,000 employees in each industry list for the period 1982 to 1989. The dominance of certain industries over this period is clear from this table, although there are some variations from year to year. The importance of the coal-mining industry in certain years (1984 and 1985) has already been noted. Motor vehicles has also been highly strike prone in a number of years: in practice motor vehicles has been relatively highly strike prone throughout the post-Second World War years (its high strike proneness, along with shipbuilding and port transport was noted by the Donovan Commission[15] and was the subject of a number of specific studies[16]). In 1988 the three most strike-prone industries (by the number of days lost) were sea transport, other transport equipment, and other transport and communications. It is interesting to note, however, that the prominence of these industries is explained

Table 10.7 Stoppages of work due to industrial dispute, UK, 1982–9 (by industry group)

Industry group	Working days lost (per 1,000 employees)							
	1982	1983	1984	1985	1986	1987	1988	1989
Agriculture, forestry, fishing	–	2	3	–	–	–	–	–
Coal extraction	1,395	1,901	97,849	19,248	781	1,413	1,833	488
Extraction and processing of coke, mineral oil and natural gas	49	1,854	21	23	–	–	1	33
Electricity, gas, other energy and water	148	2,252	102	167	20	30	52	59
Metal processing and manufacture	406	637	94	285	618	65	77	87
Mineral processing and manufacture	110	131	126	225	89	53	37	24
Chemicals and man-made fibres	61	62	187	14	48	28	76	–
Metal goods not elsewhere specified	237	91	185	125	86	85	107	74
Mechanical engineering	316	406	228	107	252	223	63	179
Electrical engineering and equipment	276	236	284	93	38	52	41	96
Instrument engineering	670	150	348	18	148	33	13	–
Motor vehicles	1,710	1,775	3,575	245	478	60	1,968	496
Other transport equipment	480	573	1,634	866	1,467	255	3,283	1,214
Food, drink and tobacco	255	127	372	201	52	70	85	57
Textiles	113	61	74	85	55	75	309	28
Footwear and clothing	97	58	167	36	78	104	49	32
Timber and wooden furniture	35	20	129	147	4	7	7	16
Paper, printing and publishing	200	180	277	143	116	36	7	65
Other manufacturing industries	242	342	169	16	32	18	21	17
Construction	39	67	340	52	33	21	16	120
Distribution, hotels and catering, repairs	6	5	4	2	3	1	2	1
Railways	6,641	20	127	140	3	17	87	2,269
Other inland transport	393	137	377	149	137	201	90	397
Sea transport	462	224	800	865	1,630	109	5,343	41

Table 10.7 continued

Other transport and communications	541	248	141	147	147	3,204	2,480	37
Supporting and miscellaneous transport services	451	448	1,641	62	55	56	60	521
Banking, finance, insurance, business services and leasing	2	6	11	3	2	–	–	1
Public adminis-tration sanitary services and education	109	32	214	265	120	243	65	569
Medical and health services	618	4	17	24	9	15	25	102
Other services	14	74	107	29	2	32	16	95
All industries and services	249	178	1,283	298	89	162	166	182

Source: Department of Employment, *Gazette*

in each case by a single strike, a fact which shows how a single year's figures can be dramatically affected by just one dispute. In the case of sea transport, a five-day strike over a no-redundancy guarantee and a week-on-week-off rota led to the loss of 168,000 days and a total of 184,000 for the industry that year; in the case of other transport equipment, a lengthy strike by shipyard workers and caterers in Cumbria over a proposal for fixed holidays led to a loss of 754,000 days out of a total for the industry of 803,000 for that year; in the case of other transport and communications, a strike by postal workers over the use of cohort labour led to the loss of 1,036,000 working days over an eight-day period and further associated strikes at other times leading to the loss of another 127,000 working days out of an industry total of 1,242,000 for that year.

One of the most interesting developments in strike activity in recent years has occurred outside the major strike-prone industries. In the public sector a number of groups, like health-service workers, civil servants, teachers and the local-authority workers, who historically have not readily engaged in strike activity, have started to do so. A study by Terry of thirty British local authorities in 1979 suggested that 60 per cent had experienced a strike of one day or longer, and some form of industrial action (not necessarily a one-day strike) seemed to have occurred in every authority over a two-year period.[17] Although in general, local authorities experience less strike action than industry as a whole (Smith suggested that the incidence of strikes in local authorities was less than that for all industries[18]), this does not detract from the increasing use of strike activity amongst some workers in local authorities. Until recently, for example, teachers would not have been expected to engage in strike activity. Although one of the 'teachers' unions', the Professional Association of Teachers, still refuses to undertake such action, the rest of the teachers' unions do not take such a stance and in 1984 and 1985 engaged in a series of strikes (bolstered by other forms of industrial action) throughout Britain. The same kind of picture emerges if one looks outside the local authorities but still within the public sector. One of the nurses' representative organisations, the Royal College of Nursing, still refuses to engage in strike activity, but other organisations representing more nurses do not share that view. In the early 1980s nurses, along with other health-service workers, engaged in a prolonged series of strikes, which was controversial but nevertheless gained support from large sections of the profession. In 1990 ambulance workers embarked on a lengthy national strike. In part, the growing militancy of the public sector can be linked to the growth in unionisation; however, it can also be linked to a change of tactics by trade unions and a recognition by groups of workers who would not have seen strike activity as appropriate, that it may be necessary to achieve their objectives.

Discussion of the strike record of different industries is to some extent complicated by the recognition that most strikes occur in a relatively small number of workplaces rather than in the whole of an industry. Smith noted, for example, that in manufacturing industry in Britain only 2 per cent of workplaces had a recorded strike in any one year.[19] Of course, over a longer period of time a higher proportion of workplaces will experience recorded strikes and others will experience industrial action that is never recorded. Creigh and Makeham noted that although a small number of plants may be affected in any one year, this is a changing set and they may thus reflect the general characteristics of an industry.[20] Nevertheless, suggestions have been made that highly strike-prone workplaces frequently differ from others in the same industry (for example, they tend to be larger) and this issue clearly makes the whole discussion of strike activity within industries more complex.

Regional variations in strike propensity have been identified in analysis of the strike records of most industrial nations, and the UK is no exception to the general rule. They have received considerable attention: the earliest study, by Bevan, dates back to 1880;[21] the matter was examined by Knowles in his book published in 1952;[22] and more recently a number of projects have sought to examine matters further, the most substantial being Durcan, McCarthy and Redman's study of strikes in Britain between 1946 and 1953.[23] They noted that two regions appeared to have been most strike-prone in terms of worker involvement: Wales and Scotland. Five regions appeared to have been moderately strike-prone: the Midlands, Yorkshire and Humberside, the North West, the North, and Northern Ireland. The least strike-prone regions were the South West and South East. If time lost per 1,000 employees were to be considered then a similar pattern would emerge. The most strike-prone regions were Wales and Scotland, followed in rank order by the North, North West, Midlands, Yorkshire and Humberside, Northern Ireland, the South West and South East. Durcan, McCarthy and Redman offer a word of caution, though, about examining these variations, which echoes that made when considering strikes by industry:

> the regions themselves are far from homogeneous and . . . only a small minority of employees in each region was involved in stoppages e.g. even in Wales 90 per cent of employees were not, on average, involved in stoppages at any time in the course of the year.[24]

The most comprehensive study is that by Smith, in which part of the time period examined by Durcan, McCarthy and Redman was considered. Smith's study of regional variations between 1968 and 1973 went below the major regional units to look at 61 subdivisions. A procedure was adopted to allow account to be taken of the most obvious explanation for regional variations – differences in industrial structure. It was found that even after variations in industrial structure had been allowed for, substantial differences remained in strike incidence between different parts of the country. The analysis suggested that two factors were particularly strongly associated with high strike-proneness: higher than average plant size and a rapid rate of earnings growth. Nevertheless, problems still remain. A considerable amount of the variation still has to be explained (if differences in industrial structure are discounted). Smith accepts that his study may have failed to find such explanations either because the range of economic variables employed was inadequate or because social-cultural factors (which were not looked at in this study) are important. The problems with the statistics being affected by strikes in a small number of plants also recurs yet again. Smith reported that in the analysis of manufacturing industry in Britain it was found that variations between areas were due to the better or worse performance of a small minority of plants.

The position as far as regional variations are concerned is updated by Table 10.8. This looks at seven years: 1982–8. The breakdown of regions is different to that used by Durcan, McCarthy and Redman. Nevertheless, some similarities with the earlier period can be pointed to. For example, Wales lost more days per 1,000 workers than the UK average in each year apart from 1988, while the South East and South West both lost markedly fewer than the UK average. However, there are some differences, including the markedly lower strike figures for Scotland (in three years the Scottish totals were lower than the UK average). The position of Scotland has been looked at elsewhere and while comprehensive explanation for the recent change in the Scottish position has not been attempted one factor of interest noted was the increase in the level of female economic activity, an increase which outstripped that in the rest of the UK.[25]

A great deal of attention has been focused on the unofficial or wildcat strike. In the UK the assumption was often made that a majority of strikes and days lost through stoppages were the result of unofficial action. The Donovan Commission estimated that in the post-Second World War years up to 95 per cent of all strikes and 80 per cent of all days lost through strikes were the result of unofficial stoppages. At the time they compiled their report there were no published statistics on the matter. However, subsequently,

Table 10.8 Stoppages of work in the UK, by region, 1982–9

	Working days lost (per 1,000 workers)							
Region	1982	1983	1984	1985	1986	1987	1988	1989
South East	174	138	212	67	41	148	130	125
East Anglia	163	86	126	60	38	106	55	109
South West	113	58	258	56	39	128	74	105
West Midlands	243	152	713	142	88	150	185	203
East Midlands	222	140	2,061	333	39	126	121	137
Yorkshire and								
Humberside	322	236	5,339	1,179	138	188	132	179
North West	414	331	587	169	172	166	198	299
North	407	232	4,065	859	216	182	762	288
Wales	314	395	3,914	1,035	90	235	130	313
Scotland	328	162	1,210	348	165	225	106	276
Northern Ireland	216	170	112	87	67	236	108	71
United Kingdom								
average	252	180	1,283	298	89	163	164	182

Source: Department of Employment, *Gazette*

statistics were published for the period 1960 to 1980. These showed that although the Donovan Commission estimates were of the right order, particularly as far as the number of strikes are concerned where the proportion of unofficial strikes never fell below 92 per cent in any year between 1960 and 1980, there were major variations from year to year as far as the number of working days lost through stoppages were concerned, largely as the result of the enormous impact in particular years of individual strikes. For example, whereas in 1967 85.9 per cent of days were lost as the result of unofficial stoppages the total for 1980 was 15.7 per cent. It also needs to be borne in mind that the interpretation of the term 'unofficial strike' should be exercised with care. In practice the term covers a wide variety of different kinds of action. It is clear, for instance, that while some unofficial strikes may be disapproved of by union national executives not all will be viewed in this way.

COMPARISONS WITH OTHER INDUSTRIAL NATIONS

All major industrial nations publish statistics on strikes. Although the hopes of the International Labour Organisation have not been met, virtually all countries collect data on the number of stoppages, the number of workers involved in stoppages and the number of working days lost through stoppages. These statistics enable some comments to be made about the broad trends within countries (and in certain instances for Western nations in general) and comparisons to be made between them. Strike statistics, however, need to be interpreted with care. Attention needs to be paid to differences in the method of collection, different practices used in the consideration of statistics, and differences in the definitions used for strikes.

One of the most important issues in this context is exactly what is meant by the term 'strike'. In practice what are often referred to in shorthand as strike statistics are more accurately described as stoppages of work resulting from industrial disputes. They therefore include both strikes and lock-outs. The latter are believed to be less important than the former, though only West Germany publishes separate figures. (In West Germany over the period 1972 to 1981 lock-outs accounted for 24 per cent of all workers involved in disputes and 44 per cent of working days lost, though many claim that such percentages are unusually high even for West Germany, where the lock-out is generally recognised to be more important than in many other countries.)

It needs to be borne in mind, as well, that the distinction between a strike and a lock-out, and between a strike and other kinds of industrial action, is not easily made. Many disputes involve a mixture of different forms of action, the balance between which varies over time, and whether a dispute should be classified as a strike or a lock-out may depend as much on who is doing the defining as on the particular course of events. It is by no means unknown for workers to define a dispute as a lock-out at the same time as the employers are defining it as a strike.[26]

In this context, then, the method of collection of strike statistics and the sources used become important. The normal practice is for the state employment or labour relations agency to be responsible for the collection and publication of information, although there are exceptions (in Belgium and Italy the police are the responsible agency, and in Denmark the state is only responsible for publication not collection). In most countries employers are the principal source of information (in West Germany employers are legally obliged to report strikes to the local office of the federal Employment Service), though in a small number of countries (such as Iceland and Austria) information is collected solely from trade unions. In practice most countries claim that they use a number of different sources of information. For example, in the USA information is collected 'largely from newspaper accounts',[27] though these accounts are also supplemented by information from local offices of the state social security agencies, state and federal mediation and conciliation agencies, as well as trade unions, individual employers and employers' federations.

Other difficulties in any analysis of strike statistics include the extent of under-reporting (evidence of the extent of under-reporting is limited, though some is available from West Germany, the United Kingdom and Sweden[28]); the classification of a dispute as industrial, compared to say political (in France, Japan, New Zealand and the United Kingdom political stoppages are concluded from dispute statistics); the minimum criteria for the inclusion of stoppages in the statistics (varying from the Netherlands where there is no restriction to Australia where a stoppage has to lead in total to the loss of at least ten working days, to the USA where since 1981 a stoppage has had to last for a day or a shift and involve at least 1,000 workers), and the treatment of workers indirectly affected (many, though not all, countries cover workers indirectly affected at the same establishment, but none cover the indirect affects at other establishments). A summary of the position on these matters is given in Table 10.9.

Table 10.9 Industrial disputes: comparisons of coverage and methodology

	Minimum criteria for inclusion in statistics	Are political stoppages included?	Are indirectly affected workers included?	Sources and notes
Australia	10 or more days lost	Yes	Yes	Information gathered from arbitrators, employers and unions.
Austria	No restrictions on size	Yes	No	Trade unions provide information.
Belgium	More than one working day's duration	Yes	No	Local police reports sent to National Conciliation Service. Follow-up questionnaires sent from National Statistical Institute.
Canada	10 or more days lost, or of more than half a day's duration	Yes	No	Reports from Canada Manpower Centres also Press and Provincial Labor Departments.
Denmark	100 or more days lost	Yes	Yes	Voluntary reports from employers' organisations sent annually to Statistical Office.
Finland	More than 4 hours' duration unless 100 or more working days lost	Yes	Yes	Returns from mail questionnaires to employers and employees.
France	No restrictions on size. However, public sector and agricultural employees are excluded from statistics	No	No	Labour Inspectors' reports.
Germany (FR)	More than 10 workers involved and more than one day's duration, unless 100 or more working days lost	Yes	No	Compulsory notification by employers to labour.
Ireland	10 or more days lost, or of more than one day's duration	Yes	Yes	Reports from local employment office.

Table 10.9 continued

	Minimum criteria for inclusion in statistics	Are political stoppages included?	Are indirectly affected workers	Sources and notes
Italy	No restrictions on size	Yes	No	Local police reports sent to Central Institute of Statistics.
Japan	More than half a day's duration	No	No	Interviews by Prefectorial Labour Policy section or local Labour Policy Office of employers and employees.
Netherlands	No restrictions on size	Yes	Yes	District Employment Offices inform Central Bureau of Statistics. Public servants are forbidden to strike.
New Zealand	More than 10 working days duration. Statistics exclude public sector strikes	No	Yes	Information gathered by district offices of Department of Labour.
Norway	More than one day's duration	Yes	No	Questions to employees' and employers' organisations.
Portugal	Up to 1985: no restrictions on size. 1986 onwards: excludes firms with fewer than 5 employees. However, statutes exclude disputes which involve more than one company	Not known	No	1986 and onwards: figures exclude Madeira and the Azores.
Spain	No restrictions on size	Yes	No	Returns by local province delegates of Ministry of Labour and Social Security, and by some local communities up to 1985: figures exclude: Catalonia. 1986 onwards: figures exclude Basque country.

Table 10.9 continued

Sweden	More than one hour's duration	Yes	No	Press reports compiled by State Conciliation Service are checked by employers' organisations and sent to Central Statistical Office.
Switzer- land	More than one day's duration	Yes	No	Federal Office for industry, crafts, occupations and employment collects press reports and checks with trade unions and employers.
United Kingdom	More than 10 workers involved and of more than one day's duration, unless 100 or more working days lost	No	Yes	Local unemployment benefit offices make reports to Department of Employment HQ, which also checks press, unions and large employers.
United States	More than one day's or shift's duration and more than 1,000 workers involved	No	Yes	Reports from press, employers, unions and agencies, followed up by questionnaires.

Source: *Employment Gazette* (June 1989), p. 312

Many comparative studies of strike statistics are based not on all industries and services but on the mining, manufacturing construction and transport sectors. The argument for such concentration in part is that these sectors have dominated strike activity; in part, though, it is also that it aids comparability between countries, for without the use of such a restricted point of departure variations in strike figures might tell the reader more about the industrial structure of the country than about its strike record. This point of view has been put forward by the International Labour Organisation.

However, by no means all studies have adopted such an approach, and there are arguments for not doing so. One is that the main industrial sectors are becoming less important in terms of employment opportunities. In many countries the service sector dominates or is coming to dominate. Predictions suggest an increasing role for service and a decreasing role for manufacturing industry as far as employment is concerned. While it is clearly true that in general most strike activity occurs outside the service sector, the growth of white-collar unionisation, and changes in the aims and methods of professional organisations, make it important to examine their record in industrial disputes. In some particular cases the strike propensity in the service sector is greater than in some other traditional sectors of the economy. Walsh notes,[29] for instance, that in Italy between 1970 and 1979, while 430 working days were lost through strikes per 1,000 workers in the primary sector, and 608 in the construction industry, 622 were lost in the service industries; the manufacturing industry total of 1,647 per 1,000 workers was well above that for the service industries, but this does not detract from the surprisingly high ranking for service industries in Italy. Similarly in France, service industries with 90 working days lost per 1,000 employees experienced more strike activity than the primary sector and the construction industry. This suggests that in particular instances failure to take account of the service sector could give a totally misleading impression of strike activity.

Such arguments are gaining increasing recognition. A number of individual academics have sought to produce statistics for the broader range of all industries and services, while the EEC has started to produce such statistics for member countries. As a result statistics using both bases are presented here.

Table 10.10 shows the number of working days lost through stoppages in 21 OECD countries over a ten-year period, 1978 to 1987, along with an indication of the position in the first five and last five years of that period. The first part of the table shows the number of days lost in all industries and services while the second part of the table concentrates on some of the generally most strike-prone industries.

Two comments might be made about this table. First, it shows that there has been a general tendency towards a reduction in the number of working days lost in most countries between the first and last five-year periods covered. Only five of the 21 countries did not follow that trend: Denmark, Finland, Germany, New Zealand and Norway. Second, one can identify a group of countries that appear to be relatively highly strike prone by this measure, and another that appear to be relatively lowly strike prone. The first group of countries includes Greece, Spain, New Zealand, Finland and Italy if all industries and services are looked at, and Spain,

Table 10.10 Industrial disputes in selected countries, 1978–87

	Days lost per thousand employees*					
	All industries and services			Mining and quarrying, manufacturing, construction, transport and communications		
	1978–82	1983–87	1978–87	1978–82	1983–87	1978–87
United Kingdom	540	400	470	1,080	960	1,020
Australia	600	250	420	1,290	560	930
Austria	–	–	–	–	–	–
Belgium	(200)	n/a	n/a	(360)	n/a	n/a
Canada	820	440	620	1,670	820	1,250
Denmark	120	250	190	250	560	410
Finland	300	520	420	500	740	620
France	120	50	80	230	110	170
Germany (FR)	40	50	50	80	110	90
Greece	950	590	760	(940)	n/a	(940)
Ireland	800	400	600	1,390	510	980
Italy	1,160	510	840	1,600	730	1,190
Japan	20	10	10	40	10	30
Netherlands	30	10	20	60	30	50
New Zealand	350	550	450	740	1,240	990
Norway	60	140	100	140	230	180
Portugal	(210)	120	(160)	(360)	230	(260)
Spain	1,110	560	850	(1,850)	600	(1,150)
Sweden	250	60	150	470	10	240
Switzerland	–	–	–	–	–	–
United States†	200	100	150	(440)	270	(330)

Source: Department of Employment, *Gazette* (June 1989)

Notes: * employees in employment;
– less than 5 days per thousand;
figures in parentheses are based on incomplete data;
n/a (not available);
† significant changes to threshold for inclusion in statistics introduced in 1981.

Canada, Italy, Ireland and Australia if the more restricted range of industries is looked at. The second group of countries includes Switzerland, Austria, Japan, Netherlands, France, Germany, Norway and Sweden for both all industries and services and the more restricted industry coverage. The United Kingdom is at neither extreme by these measures though it appears to be above the average for stoppage incidence. It is noticeable that in most cases the restriction of the statistics to the more strike-prone industries means that the strike incidence generally doubles. The relative position of most countries does not change a great deal though Canada seems markedly more strike prone when the restricted industry measure is used.

These comments need to be read bearing in mind the earlier discussion on the collection and interpretation of strike statistics. One of the most important instances is provided by the USA. A change in the threshold for inclusion in strike statistics significantly affected internal comparability over this period, and the new level adopted has made comparisons with other countries very difficult to follow through.[30] Another important example is provided by the exclusion of public sector and agricultural strikes from the statistics in France.

It also needs to be borne in mind that the statistics referred to so far simply relate to the number of days lost through disputes. There are advantages in looking at this measure for comparative purposes for the impact of different thresholds for the inclusion of strikes are minimised; large strikes, which make the most significant impact on these figures, will be included through most thresholds (the same is not true, though, of differences in the inclusion, for example, of political strikes and public sector strikes). However, there are arguments that it is at least worth considering one of the other measures of strike activity: the number of strikes. Interestingly, if this is done, then while there are differences with the rank order produced (some of which might be accounted for by different thresholds for the inclusion of strikes and related matters) there are broad similarities. For example, the countries in the most strike-prone group are Finland, Australia, New Zealand, Spain, Italy and Iceland while the countries in the least strike-prone category are Switzerland, Austria, Netherlands, Norway, Japan and Sweden (comparable figures are not available for West Germany).

EXPLANATIONS FOR STRIKES

The variations in strike patterns and trends, both over time within countries and between countries, have excited considerable interest. A vast amount has been written on the subject which is difficult to summarise. However, possibly the best approach is to group the work that has been completed into one of a small number of categories. This allows general approaches to be identified and some examples of particularly important work to be quoted. Initially, three categories will be identified: explanations which are based on institutional, political and economic factors. Later studies of inter-industry variations in strike propensity will be examined, followed by the way that case studies of strikes can be used.

Institutional factors

One of the first major attempts to provide an explanation for strike activity came from Ross and Hartman.[31] They concentrated on analysing two measures of strike activity – the membership involvement ratio (the sum of all workers involved in strikes in a year divided by the average number of union members in that year) and the strike duration ratio (the number of workers involved in strikes divided by the number of working days lost through strikes). Data were collected for fifteen countries between 1900 and 1956.

Two main themes can be discerned from this study. The first is the general reduction in strike activity over the period concerned: what Ross and Hartman referred to as the 'withering away of the strike'. The second is the identification of distinctive patterns of industrial conflict and the linking of them to different industrial relations systems. In particular they argued that it was possible to classify the fifteen countries they had looked at into 'several distinct patterns of industrial conflict'. The four groups they isolated were termed the North European pattern first variant (Denmark, Netherlands and West Germany with the UK on the borderline), the North European pattern second variant (Norway and Sweden), the Mediterranean/Asian pattern (France, Italy, Japan and India) and the North American pattern (Canada and USA). They argued that the North European pattern first variant was characterised by a nominal propensity to strike and a low or moderate duration of strikes; the North European pattern second variant was characterised by infrequent but long stoppages; the Mediterranean/Asian pattern was characterised by high participation in strikes but short duration; and the North American pattern was characterised by a moderately high propensity to strike as well as a relatively long duration. Three of the original countries – Australia, Finland and South Africa – were excluded from this classification because they were 'special cases'.

Ross and Hartman argued that the distinctive strike patterns they had identified were associated with particular kinds of industrial relations systems. Five key characteristics of such systems were identified and are shown in Table 10.11. In the North European pattern first variant the countries were said to have mature labour movements with firm and stable memberships; leaderships conflicts were subdued; there was a widespread acceptance of the role of trade unions in industry with centralised collective bargaining; there was

Table 10.11 Principal features of industrial relations system used for comparison

---

1   Organisational stability
   (a) Age of labour movement
   (b) Stability of membership in recent years
2   Leadership conflicts in the labour movement
   (a) Factionalism, rival unionism and rival federations
   (b) Strength of communism in labour unions
3   States of union–management relations
   (a) Degree of acceptance by employers
   (b) Consolidation of bargaining structure
4   Labour political activity
   (a) Existence of labour party as a leading political party
   (b) Labour party governments
5   Role of the state
   (a) Extent of government activity in defining terms of employment
   (b) Dispute settlement policies and procedures

Source: A. M. Ross, 'Changing Patterns of Industrial Conflict', in G. G. Sommers (ed.), Proceeding of the 12th Annual Meeting of the Industrial Relations Research Association, 1959

an important labour party; and governments rarely intervened to regulate the terms of employment though they frequently intervened in collective bargaining. The North European pattern second variant showed many of the characteristics of the first variant but there was less active intervention in labour–management relations. The Mediterranean/Asian pattern countries were said to have relatively young labour movement (either they had just become mass organisations or were reorganised after 1945); union membership was often an 'ephemeral phenomenon'; internal leadership conflicts were endemic; labour–management relations were weak and unstable with unions too weak to conduct long strikes; left-wing parties were divided; and there was considerable state direct intervention in industry. In the last of the four patterns, the North American, Ross and Hartman argued that while labour movements were older than in the Mediterranean/Asian pattern they were younger than in the other patterns; union density had become more stable in recent years and interunion rivalry had subsided; unions were increasingly accepted by employers; bargaining structures were decentralised; terms and conditions of employment were largely determined privately; and there was not a successful labour party.

Ross and Hartman, in their discussion, put forward particular arguments. However, others have taken up not just the particular arguments but more importantly the general themes.

The first theme can be seen, for example, in the work of Kerr *et al.*[32] In their discussion of the 'logic of industrialism' they sought to highlight the consequences of industrialisation. In this context they argued that there was a link between industrialisation and industrial conflict. The earlier stages of industrialisation would lead to conflict connected to adjustment to new methods of production, but as industrialisation proceeded conflict would lessen. Union organisation would develop, eventually becoming accommodated within the system, and mechanisms such as collective bargaining would be established to bring order into industrial relations. Kerr argued that the influence of industrialisation would be so strong and pervasive that all industrial countries would move in the same direction and come to discover similar ways of dealing with problems. The 'convergence' of industrial societies to which Kerr referred, despite differences in the social, political and economic backgrounds of the countries, has been widely debated. Nevertheless, the issue raised in this context – the effect of industrialisation on industrial conflict – has found echoes in the work of many.

The second theme developed by Ross and Hartman – the importance of institutional arrangements – has similarly been taken up by many writers and continues to be the source of controversy. It has much in common with the general approach of Dunlop.[33] More specifically, a number of writers have sought to explain particular aspects and patterns of industrial conflict by reference to industrial relations institutions, in particular to collective bargaining. In Britain the analysis of the Donovan Commission fits into this context.[34] In Chapter 7 it was noted how the Donovan Commission sought to explain the rise in the number of strikes, particularly short workplace stoppages in the 1960s, by centring on the problems surrounding the collective bargaining machinery.

The discussion introduced in the Donovan report, of course, was specifically designed to highlight and explain the experience of British industrial relations in the 1960s. The broader arguments, though, of which this is just one example, have been applied in different contexts by many others. For example, Kassalow sought to compare industrial conflict in the United States with that in Western Europe by examining the level and the scope of collective bargaining,[35] and Clegg's study of industrial conflict in six countries (Australia, France, West Germany, Sweden, the UK and the USA) in which he sought to relate strike proneness to the structure of bargaining.[36]

Ingham's study is an interesting bridge between those who criticise and those who try to extend the themes of Ross and Hartman, for while Ingham offered specific criticisms of Ross and Hartman's themes and tried to make important changes to their theoretical underpinning he did not abandon the themes as such altogether. Some of the criticisms related to detailed aspects of the study. For example, Ross and Hartman conducted their analysis on the basis of averages for three different periods of time, 1900–29, 1930–42, and 1948–56. They gave no reason for the selection of the periods concerned nor for the fact that the first period covers thirty years, whereas the second period covers only thirteen years and the third period only covers nine years. Ingham points out that the selection of different time spans would have produced different results. However, the main thrust of Ingham's analysis was not on the detail of Ross and Hartman's study but was concerned with an attempt to move away from the 'functionalist' towards a Marxist approach. Ingram characterised the functionalist approach as one which saw manifest variations in the levels of institutionalisation between industrial societies as a consequence of diverse 'cultural' and 'historical' factors 'which are not intrinsic to capitalism as such but are features of the pre-industrial social order which are more entrenched in some countries than others'.[37]

Ingham's alternative was to 'account, in general terms, for observed variations in the levels of institutionalisation by reference to important differences in the industrial infrastructure of the societies in question'. The industrial infrastructure was taken 'to refer to those features of a society's economic and technological system which shape the organisation of and the social relationship between those groups engaged in the process of production'.[38] Three dimensions of the infrastructure were isolated as particularly important in this context: the degree of industrial concentration, the complexity of this technical and organisational structure, and product differentiation and specialisation.

> Each of these closely related dimensions sets a framework on the nature of the power relations between the respective organisations of capital and labour which, in turn, determine to a large extent a society's capacity for developing centralised institutions for the regulation of conflict.[39]

> High levels of concentration, relatively simple technical and business structures and high levels of product specialisation in the small-scale Scandinavian countries supported the growth of highly centralised employers' associations and labour movement, which, after a period of intense and widespread conflict result in their

highly regulated system of industrial relations. On the other hand, the fragmented bargaining structure and low level of normative regulations in Britain [should be seen] in the context of the low levels of industrial concentration, product specialisation and infrastructure complexity which shaped its distinctive character.[40]

Other critics of the Ross and Hartman themes have put forward objections which would lead to a significant change of direction. They have argued that the emphasis on the institutions of industrial relations is misplaced. The attempt by Ingham to change to theoretical underpinning does not get over this. Thus, Korpi and Shalev[41] have argued that Ingham misinterpreted the true position of industrial relations in Sweden (which is not as tightly centralised as claimed, gave the unions an entry to political decision making, and meant that they were able to pursue their interests in this fashion rather than through more restricted dispute with employers). Korpi and Shalev argued that 'Swedish labour in effect renounced the strike weapon in order to more effectively pursue its . . . class interests in the political arena; what Pizzorno[42] has called a "political exchange" took place'. It is also noted that the institutional arrangement, of which much has been made by both Ingham and Clegg, dates back to the beginning of the twentieth century, but it was only after the political changes that industrial conflict declined. If one looks outside Sweden then the problems identified with Ingham's analysis, and those of others taking an institutional approach, can be exemplified. A number of writers have pointed to the relatively late development of the Canadian economy and to the concentration of industrial activity.[43] The Ingham thesis would place Canada in the same category as Sweden though in fact its strike record is very different.

These detailed criticisms, however, are less important than the general point that is being made. Essentially the argument is that the institutional arrangements themselves are not a satisfactory explanation for variations in the level of strike activity. Institutional arrangements cannot be seen as independent variables. This is not to deny them any importance but it is to argue that they need to be seen in a broader context, particularly in the context of the power relationships that exist and develop in a society.

Political factors

The criticisms made of those who try to explain strike patterns by reference to institutional arrangements find concrete expression in an alternative school of thought. In essence this 'school' starts from the position that conflict is endemic in capitalist society because of the different interests of particular sections of society. The question to be addressed is how these different interests can be, or are, pursued, and in what circumstances strike action will occur.

Shorter and Tilly's work, initially on France but extended to cover other countries, is one of the best-known examples of this approach.[44] There are two central themes behind their work. The first is that organisation is essential for strike activity. Trade unions have a crucial role to play. They take worker dissatisfaction and translate it into strike action. The second theme is that strikes have political aims and implications. When the labour movement does not have political power, strikes are a way of putting pressure on those who do.

Shorter and Tilly specifically challenge the view that strikes are to be seen simply as an expression of economic interest. Major accumulations of strikes and disturbances occur

> when it becomes apparent to the working classes as a whole that a point of critical importance for their own interests is at hand in the nation's life, and when the latticework of organisation suffices to transform these individual perceptions of opportunity into collective action.[45]

In their study of France, Shorter and Tilly identify a number of 'strike waves' where action spread from one group and one region to the next. According to Shorter and Tilly, strike waves 'march as exclamation marks in labour history' in France from late in the nineteenth century to 1968. The timing of these strike waves depends to a large extent on the timing of political crises. It is argued for example that the 1968 strike wave 'came in the immediate wake of the severest political crisis since 1947'.[46] However, in line with their main theme, Shorter and Tilly argue that 'organisation is essential to the successful launching of such forms of large-scale political action as strike waves'.[47]

In seeking to extend their analysis beyond France, Shorter and Tilly tried to explain differences in strike records by reference to the extent to which the labour movement had gained political power. In the pre-war years 'the working classes in all western countries mobilised themselves for political action, with varying degrees of effectiveness and within disparate constellations of national politics; their mobilisation generated everywhere a great wave of strike activity'.[48] Strike activity before the Second World War, then, was of a similar kind throughout the countries they looked at.

After the Second World War, though, patterns started to differ.

In European countries, where labour gained political power (such as Scandinavia), strike activity declined, whereas in those countries where labour did not gain political power (such as France) strikes continued at a higher level and as an expression of political aspirations.

In North America strikes in the post-war era did not differ greatly from those in the pre-war era. This was despite the fact that during the depression 'the North American working classes succeeded to political power'.[49] Strike activity did not wither away in North America as it had done in Northern Europe, according to Shorter and Tilly, because the government failed to intervene in shop-floor conflicts on the side of the working class. Eventually American labour became reconciled to a watertight division between job action, where free collective bargaining unhindered by government intervention operated, and political action executed through 'interest-coalition political parties'. Shorter and Tilly comment that the North American case is important because it shows that 'admission to the polity need not automatically lead to the withering away of the strike; other variables such as national tradition interpose themselves'.[50]

The issue of political power is clearly seen by Shorter and Tilly as a crucial variable. Strikes can be used as a way of gaining political power or at least fostering political aspirations, but whether they are used in this way or not will depend on the extent of political power already held by the labour movement. Korpi and Shalev, in their criticisms of the institutional explanation of strike action, referred to the importance of political power in the Swedish case. They argued that the rise to power of the Social Democratic Party was crucial. In the same way as Shorter and Tilly, however, they have tried to use their ideas outside the context in which they were originally expressed.

The general assumption of Korpi and Shalev was that where labour can be effectively mobilised to gain political power there will be a reduction in strike activity. Labour will renounce the strike weapon because it believes it can more effectively pursue its objectives through the political arena. In order that this can happen the political power of labour has to be secure and enduring. Labour is also likely to need to be organised effectively internally with a high degree of centralisation. On the other hand where labour is fragmented and fails to gain political power, strikes will remain at a high level. Two sets of examples of countries at the opposite extremes of their continuum are cited, which seem to fit the assumptions. Austria and Norway follow the Swedish model in that labour has been effectively organised and Social Democratic parties have gained power. As a result strikes have been renounced as a method of achieving broad objectives. At the other end of the spectrum, in countries like Canada, USA and the Republic of Ireland, labour movements have been much less effective. Socialist parties enjoy little support and labour movements are not centralised or coordinated. Korpi and Shalev argue that in these cases 'the working class person has never played a significant role in national politics'. There has not been

> any long run decline in conflict, which in addition retains a degree of intensity unknown in other countries since the war. In these instances, conflicts between buyers and sellers of labour power continue to be manifested primarily within the employment context, something which is no longer the case elsewhere. The long duration of strikes in these countries has contributed to give them very high relative volumes of strikes (man-days idle) in the post-war period.[51]

If one leaves the two extremes, however, then there are three other groups of countries which also have to be accounted for. In some cases Korpi and Shalev are able to develop explanations in line with their central theme. However, others do not fit easily into the basic model. For example, in Switzerland, despite the absence of a strong labour movement, overt conflict has remained low; the explanation offered by Korpi and Shalev is the integration of the working classes into public policy making through extra-parliamentary action.

The line of argument followed by both Shorter and Tilly and Korpi and Shalev has centred on the extent to which the labour movement has been able to gain power at the central political level. Hibbs's work fits into this theme but offers a variation on it by arguing that it is not simply the assumption of power by the labour movement that is important, but that the critical factor is the policy pursued.[52] (In particular, the emphasis is placed on policy on the development of welfare provision.) Hibbs argued that a high level of expenditure on the public sector, particularly on social services, will shift the centre of debate to the place where decisions on these matters are made – the central political arena. In such situations industrial conflict will subside. In other countries where parties of the 'right' or 'centre' have dominated, and where public/social expenditure has been maintained at a low level, then conflict will be concentrated on the private market and strike activity will be maintained at a high level.

It would be wrong to characterise Snyder's model as one which simply demonstrated the importance of political issues and power in determining strike activity.[53] Snyder had a broader aim: a range of issues were recognised as potentially influencing strike activity. However, one of the points of his explanation was to determine when political factors would be crucial. The interest and comment on political factors, particularly on the work of Shorter and Tilly, makes it sensible to discuss his work in this context.

Snyder distinguished two different kinds of situation. In the first, labour organisation will be relatively strong and the labour movement as a whole will be effective politically. The institutions of collective bargaining will have been well established. In this kind of situation strikes will be determined by economic factors. In the second situation trade unions are weaker, with fewer members, and they are less stable organisations. The labour movement has little influence over general political matters. In this instance the institutions of industrial relations are less well developed. Economic matters will have a less important role in strikes. The incidence of strikes will vary according to the basis of union organisation and political changes. In general, though, labour organisations will not be sufficiently strong in organisational terms to be able to take advantage of economic conditions. Strikes, in such circumstances, will have a political role, since unions will concentrate on longer-term aims rather than shorter-term economic considerations.

Snyder tested his thesis in three countries: France, Italy and the USA. He encountered some difficulties both in operationalising his variables consistently between countries and in the results of the analysis. Nevertheless, he argued that this data broadly supported his thesis.

There have been a number of criticisms of specific aspects of studies reviewed under this heading.[54] More general criticisms have been made which apply to a number, not just one, of the studies reviewed. For example, one of the themes developed by a number of writers is the importance of a strong and coordinated labour movement. This can be a determinant of ability to take action and gain political power. However, the direction of such links can be questioned. While it may be the case that a strong labour movement is able to take advantage of favourable conditions, whether to pursue political power or to take industrial action, in practice strength may also be the consequence of such action. If a union is able to show that it can take effective action either against an employer or in the political arena then it may help that union, or the union movement, to recruit members, coordinate activities, and organise more effectively.

At a similar level of generality it can be argued that care needs to be taken about interpreting the implications of a labour or socialist party gaining power. There are examples where it has resulted in more not fewer strikes. Creigh, Poland and Wooden point out that 'in Australia the highest levels of strike activity in the post-war era were recorded under the Labour Governments of the late 1940s and early 1970s'.[55] Similar examples might be quoted from the British experience. The 'winter of discontent' (1978–9) saw an explosion in strike activity in direct opposition to the policy of the Labour Government. In many cases left-wing governments, when they gain power, are forced to take actions which are opposed by the trade unions; this may be because their election to office in itself drives the financial institutions to adopt postures which threaten stability, or it may be because after long periods in office a left-wing government has ceased to pursue the ideals it espoused before it gained power. In this context it is interesting to record that a study by Paldam and Pederson, which will be reviewed in more detail later, found that one of the 'political' variables included in their analysis – the political orientation of the government – showed a significant and negative relationship with strike activity.[56] This suggested that there were more strikes under left-wing than right-wing governments. In particular, significant negative correlations were found for Australia, Canada, the Republic of Ireland, Finland and Norway.

The kind of criticisms made of those who adopted the approach that the 'institutions' determined strike action can also be made of those who would argue that political and organisational factors would do so. At their extreme, either position would seem to be placing too much emphasis on simply one factor. It is not necessary to argue that such a factor has no role to play in explanation – simply that it does not by itself provide an explanation. In fact, as has been noted, a number of writers have suggested that one factor alone has not been adequate to explain strike trends. Some have recognised the importance of a combination, including institutional arrangements, political, and economic factors.

Economic factors

The discussion of economic factors as a way of explaining strike trends is the most extensive of the approaches considered.

The first major study within this approach was undertaken by Hansen in the early 1920s. He attempted to link strikes to the business cycle in the USA between 1881 and 1919. He suggested that analysis might be aided by splitting the period looked at into two the first would then cover 1881 to 1897 during which there was a long-run trend towards falling prices, while the second would cover 1898 to 1919 during which there was a long-run trend towards rising prices. Such a split would be useful, he argued, because the explanation for strike trends might be different during a period of falling prices than during a period of rising prices.

In the period of long-run falling prices, Hansen argued, labour is on the defensive. It therefore follows that 'in a period in which the secular trend of prices is downward the struggle between labour and capital may be expected to become most severe and the number of strikes greatest in the years of depression'.

On the other hand, Hansen argued, in a period when the general trend is for prices to rise one should expect labour to be particularly aggressive. 'The struggle between labour and capital now becomes most bitter in the years of prosperity.' There are two reasons for this: first, it is in the prosperous years that prices and living costs rise; and second, 'the large profits accruing in years of prosperity give rise to a contest over its distribution'.[57]

The analysis undertaken, Hansen claimed, supported the hypotheses. 'Strikes correlate inversely with the business cycle in periods of long-run falling prices, while they correlate directly with the business cycle in periods of long-run rising prices.'[58]

Hansen's attempt to link strikes to the business cycle was enormously influential. Of course, there were debates even between those who held that the relationship between strikes and the business cycle was crucial. Rees pointed out that there was disagreement between such writers 'on the nature of the relation between strikes and business fluctuation'.[59] He exemplified the point by comparing the work of Hansen to that of Griffen,[60] Yoder,[61] Burns and Mitchell[62] and Jurkat and Jurkat.[63] Rees himself introduced another dimension to this debate by suggesting that the strike peak consistently preceded the peak in the business cycle. His explanation centred on the differing expectations of employers and unions. Despite those differences the central idea of a link between strikes and the business cycle remained.

The economic analysis of strikes was given new impetus in the late 1960s through the publication of the work of Ashenfelter and Johnson.[64] They did not discard the idea that the business cycle had a role to play but introduced a new element by looking centrally at the relationship between union members and leaders. The study was based on USA strike statistics for the 1952–67 period. Their argument was that in many instances member expectations of a wage demand may be greater than the union leaders are able to deliver from an initial negotiation with employers. Union leaders can try to lower expectations during the negotiations and thus be able to propose an agreement which is acceptable to members and employers. If they are unable to do so then they may be forced either to try to conclude an agreement even though they know that it will not be acceptable to members, or to organise a strike. One of the functions of the strike may be to lower the aspirations of their members so that eventually an agreement may be signed.

The rank and file expectations it is argued, will be influenced by economic factors, like the level of demand for labour and the level of profits. The aggregate level of strike activity will be related to the degree of tightness of the labour market and previous rates of change of real wages. However, the introduction of discussion about relationships between union leaders and rank and file members was an important extension of earlier work, and they returned to the policy implications of this matter in their conclusion. Thus, they argued that policies which are geared to induce labour leaders to convince their constituencies to be satisfied with 'more reasonable' wage settlements are likely to result eventually in political turmoil in trade unions. It does not, therefore, seem likely that such a policy can continue for long without encouraging the growth and power of more militant leadership and a subsequent decline in the effectiveness of the original policy.[65]

The Ashenfelter and Johnson approach was followed by a number of studies which further explored the relationship between strikes and economic variables in a variety of countries. Pencavel, for example, examined strikes in the United Kingdom, outside mining, between 1950 and 1967.[66] Although he recognised that differences between the systems of industrial relations in the United Kingdom and the United States meant that the Ashenfelter–Johnson model would need adapting, the basic approach was retained. The specific adaptation proposed arose from the high proportion of unofficial strikes in the United Kingdom, which meant that leadership positions had to be seen as resting with the branch official or shop steward.

> In short . . . officials lower down in the echelon of authority take on much of that function of trade unionism which relates to the welfare of the member at his place of work, and in this capacity they operate much like the union leadership described by Ashenfelter and Johnson.[67]

Paldam and Pederson's study is attractive because not only is it comparative (it covered seventeen OECD countries) but it also (unlike many other studies) looks at post-1960s strike trends: their analysis covered 1948–76.[68] The study is also interesting because it raises questions about the general applicability of the Ashenfelter and Johnson model. Three of their conclusions seemed to refute the Ashenfelter and Johnson model. First, they argued that nominal wage changes 'have a superior overall explanatory power compared to real wage changes'.[69] (Ashenfelter and Johnson had placed emphasis on the importance of real wage changes.) Second, they argued that the dominating signs on both nominal and real wage changes are positive (Ashenfelter and Johnson argued that a decline in real wages was associated with an increase in strikes). Third, they argued that the relationship between unemployment and strikes was unstable. The relationship between unemployment and strikes was only significant in one-third of the cases. Further, the direction of the influence varied between countries. Ashenfelter and Johnson had suggested that a decrease in unemployment was associated with an increase in strikes.

The relationship between strikes and unemployment has been examined further in a number of studies. Following a study of fifteen OECD countries Creigh and Makeham suggested a positive relationship between unemployment and strike activity. The argument was that during periods of high unemployment employers may be less willing than they would be in more buoyant conditions to take what action was necessary to avoid the disruption likely to be caused by strike action. Consequently, if strikes occurred during periods of high unemployment they would be likely to last longer.

In another study, this time with Poland and Wooden; Creigh took an even wider spread of countries (twenty OECD countries, though evidence was not available on all variables for all countries) and a longer time period (1962–81).[70] A large number of possible explanations for stoppage incidence (number of working days lost) were tested, but standardised unemployment rates were found to be the most important single explanatory factor. 'The variable accounted statistically for 18 per cent of total stoppage incidence variation, with a percentage point higher unemployment rate being associated with an increase of over 91 days lost in the stoppage incidence rate.' Critically, they also added that the 'result supports the argument that higher unemployment rates raise stoppage incidence since those stoppages which do occur tend to be of long duration'.[71]

This issue is clearly a difficult one on which to reach a conclusion. Some writers like Creigh and Makeham have found a positive association between unemployment and strikes, others, and Hibbs might be cited as an example, have found a negative relationship. Further, a third group of writers have concluded that there is no relationship at all. For example, one study that looked at strike trends in the UK in considerable detail concluded that unemployment was not helpful in explaining patterns or variations.

> Given the general level of success of the econometric models tested it is of some interest to note that there does not appear to be any general relationship between strike measures and unemployment rates, either at the level of industries or at the level of subdivisions of regions.[72]

This conclusion was echoed by others, like Shorey[73] who also looked at strikes in post-war UK.

Inter-industry variations

The studies looked at so far have concentrated on explaining economy-wide strike trends. It has long been recognised though that there are major variations in strike incidence between industries. Kerr and Siegel sought to examine variations between industries across countries. They argued that a league table could be constructed of strike propensity by industry which held across countries. This league table (reproduced as Table 10.12) was based on an analysis of strikes in eleven different countries. They found that certain industries (notably mining and maritime and longshore) were highly strike-prone in all of the countries looked at, whereas others (notably railroad and agriculture) were lowly strike-prone in every country. From this basis, they looked in more detail at the industries concerned to see if they could discover any reason for the different strike propensities.

Their explanation centred on two theories. The first was that the location of the worker in society determines their propensity to strike, and that their location is heavily influenced by their industrial environment. In summary this theory stated that industries will be highly strike prone when workers form a relatively homogeneous group which is usually isolated from the general community and which is capable of cohesion; on the other hand, industries will be relatively strike free when their workers are individually integrated into larger society, are members of trade groups which are coerced by government or the market to avoid strikes, or are so individually isolated that strike action is impossible. On this basis the high strike proneness of groups like miners, sailors, dock workers, and to a lesser extent textile workers, would be explained by reference to the type of communities they live in. They all live apart in their

Table 10.12 General pattern of strike propensities

Propensity to strike	Industry
High	Mining
	Maritime and longshore
Medium high	Lumber
	Textile
Medium	Chemical
	Printing
	Leather
	Manufacturing (general)
	Construction
	Food and kindred products
Medium low	Clothing
	Gas, water and electricity
	Services (hotels, restaurants, etc.)
Low	Railroad
	Agriculture
	Trade

Source: C. Kerr and A. Siegel, 'The Interindustry Propensity to Strike – an International Comparison', in A. Kornhauser, R. Dubin and A. Ross (eds), *Industrial Conflict* (McGraw-Hill, New York, 1954)

separate communities and these communities have their own codes, myths, heroes and social standards. There are few neutrals in such a community and all members are subject to the same grievances. The union plays a crucial role; not only is it an industrial organisation but it is also a kind of working-class solidarity which is reinforced by the support of the community.

The second theory looked at by Kerr and Siegel was that the character of the job and the worker influenced the strike propensity. Stated briefly it argued that the nature of the job determines, by selection and conditioning, the kind of workers employed and their attributes, and these workers in turn cause conflict and peace. Thus, if a job is physically difficult and unpleasant, unskilled, casual and fosters an independent spirit, it will attract tough, inconsistent and combative workers who will be inclined to strike. On the other hand, if the job is physically easy, skilled, performed in pleasant surroundings and subject to close supervision, it will attract women or the more submissive type of men who are unlikely to strike.

Kerr and Siegel argued that the most satisfactory explanation could be gained by an amalgamation of the two theories. This led them to outline two polar opposites as far as strikes are concerned: the isolated mass of workers undertaking unpleasant work who will be highly strike prone, and the dispersed workforce engaged in more attractive work who will be less strike prone.

Kerr and Siegel's work has attracted criticism as a study in its own right. For example, they have been criticised for the way they left certain industries out of their final analysis. Thus, the steel industry was initially examined by Kerr and Siegel but was omitted from their final league tables. In fact, the steel industry is difficult to fit into the Kerr and Siegel pattern because its strike record is not consistent in different countries. It has also been argued that while the Kerr and Siegel thesis may be persuasive in explaining the exceptional strike records in a small number of industries (like mining and dock work) it is less persuasive as a general explanation of strike proneness. Nevertheless, these criticisms do not detract from a fairly general acceptance that there are important variations between the strike records of different industries which seem to endure across many if not all countries.

In recent years the issue of inter-industry strike variations has been taken up by economists. In some cases the studies have concentrated on variations within a particular group of industries. Thus, McLean[74] examined variations in strike activity across USA manufacturing industries. Other studies[75] have looked beyond manufacturing industry. For example, Kaufman's study sought to examine strike trends among all major industries in the United States.[76] The data covered the years 1960 to 1969. For the purposes of his exercise he grouped the industries into four categories. In the majority of cases he found that factors like unemployment change and inflation accounted for the patterns highlighted. However, in other cases they were affected by unique industry-specific developments:

> These include the creation of the Construction Industry Stabilization Committee by President Nixon in 1971, the adoption of the Experimental Negotiating Agreement in Basic Steel in 1972, the breakdown of contract administration machinery in coal and the political turmoil in the United Mine Workers Union, and in apparel, the movement of firms to the non union South and the growing threat from foreign competition.[77]

One of the most detailed examinations of inter-industry variations in strike activity, across the whole range of industries, has been attempted on UK data for the years 1966–73. The study was published as part of a Department of Employment research paper.[78]

Twelve different possible explanations for variations between industries were examined. These ranged from the proportion of white-collar employees (white-collar workers have been less well organised and less forceful in bargaining and generally are less strike prone than manual workers), to trade union density (it is assumed that unorganised workers are less likely to take collective action), to the state of the labour market (the bargaining power of labour will be high in industries with low unemployment and, assuming that employers do not simply respond with higher wage offers, there will tend to be more strikes). At the end of the analysis it was claimed that four variables appeared to be particularly important and consistent as explanations. These were:

1 Earnings levels. Industries with relatively high earnings levels also tended to be those with high strike proneness. One explanation might be that 'workers in industries which pay relatively high wages will be likely to strike, according to a "probability-of-success" theory, because they have the economic resources to endure a stoppage. They also have a greater interest in developing the earnings potential of their jobs since they are less likely to find financial improvement by seeking jobs in other industries'.[79]
2 Labour intensity. Industries where labour costs account for a high proportion of total costs appeared to be more strike prone. It might be that in such industries employers' cost levels are more sensitive to wage costs, and other things being equal, a given wage claim will be more likely to meet with employer resistance.
3 Establishment size. Industries with above-average establishment size appeared to be subject to more strike activity. One explanation may be that large plants or establishments appear to experience more industrial conflict because of the increased problems of communication and control.
4 Female workers. A high proportion of female workers was negatively correlated with strike incidence. This is consistent with the view that, for a number of reasons, female workers are less likely to engage in strike activity than male workers.

Two other factors, the extent of trade union membership and the state of the labour market, appeared to work as explanations in certain, but not all, circumstances.

CASE STUDIES

The literature, a sample of which has been reviewed above, seeks to explain strike trends and patterns by reference to the institutions of industrial relations, to political factors, or to economic factors, as an aid to a better understanding of the causes of strikes. There is not, however, a single view coming from within, let alone from between categories. One of the reasons for this is that explanations which seem helpful for a particular time period or a particular society do not hold for all time or for all countries. Another important consideration, though, is that in discussing strikes one is not talking about a single phenomenon. The brief downing of tools by a small number of workers in one part of a factory over a decision taken by a supervisor is clearly different to a national strike of workers in many industries over proposed new industrial relations legislation. This suggests that one should not look for a single explanation for all strikes. The broad study can help to identify factors that may appear important in a number of different circumstances, but the broad study should not obscure the role that can be played by the more detailed study of an individual strike. This can help one to understand not only the specifics of that particular action but it also allows one to examine the motives and attitudes of participants.

There are a number of well reported case studies of strikes, some of which have gained classic status. Probably the best known is Gouldner's *Wildcat Strike*, in which he attempted to explain the cause of a strike at a gypsum mine at Oscar Centre, a small rural community near the Great Lakes.[80] The explanation he put forward was not one that could reasonably have been expected from a macro-level study of strike patterns in that it centred on a detailed analysis of relationships between workers and management at one particular mine. According to Gouldner, what he termed the 'indulgency pattern' was crucial to this relationship (the indulgency pattern essentially meant that management did not supervise workers too closely and also included the idea of the 'second chance' when workers transgressed). Gouldner saw the break-up of the indulgency pattern, which occurred when a new manager was appointed at the mine, as the beginning of a period of increasing resentment against management and the company. This resentment eventually led to the strike, although the strike was actually called over a wages issue: the wages issue, though, was merely a more convenient and acceptable explanation.

The ability to look in detail at working relationships has many attractions. It allows new possibilities to be examined and evaluated. Case studies can, though, also be used to take account of the same kind of factors as those considered in macro studies. There is no reason, for instance, why case studies cannot take account of the impact of changed economic conditions. For example, this was one of the factors looked at in Liston Pope's study of the Loray textile mill strike.[81] One of the 'environmental' factors that he highlighted as being important to an understanding of the cause of the strike was the severe decline in the market for cotton textiles in the 1920s. This led to a budgetary and technological reappraisal in the industry. Costs were lowered by rationalisation (including mill mergers, greater bureaucratisation of individual enterprises and changes in labour policy) and new machinery was introduced which heralded increased working speed and closer management supervision of work tasks. One of the other 'environmental' factors was the increasing power of the union, the National Union of Textile Workers. The point that is being made is that the kind of factors looked at in this case were not all that different from those examined in macro studies. The difference was in the detail with which they were examined and the ability to look at the way in which national conditions had an impact at the local level.

Other studies of strikes have concentrated quite explicitly on the perceptions of those involved in the action. Lane and Roberts,[82] in their study of a strike at Pilkington's glass works near St Helens, argued that in attempting to understand the causes and progress of the strike it was crucial to appreciate that each group of participants viewed the dispute and strike in different ways. 'What was sincerely felt to be a real issue by one party was genuinely felt to be irrelevant by others.' Lane and Roberts went on to argue that interpretations of what the strike was really about help to explain the large number of conspiracy theories sustained before, during and after the seven weeks strike. For example, the firm and the union 'both suspected that they were being challenged by a subversive plot in which alien political forces were playing a manipulative role'.[83] On the other hand, the unofficial strike committee 'in turn, strongly suspected that it was facing an unholy alliance of the firm, the union and (at times) the police in which plots and strategies to deceive the strikers were being hatched'.[84] Neither conspiracy theory, Lane and Roberts comment, had much basis in fact, yet they help to explain how a small-scale, isolated wage miscalculation dispute escalated into a major seven weeks strike.

Elsewhere[85] I have looked in some detail (as have others) at the miners' strike of 1984/5. A variety of factors need to be taken into account in explaining that strike, including the threat to jobs in the industry resulting from rationalisation proposals, the economic and the political climate. However, two other factors are crucial to an understanding of the strike. First, the earlier 'successful' strike in 1974 which has been seen as partly responsible for the fall of the then Conservative-government. This resulted in a view about the power of the miners' union which might be seen to have encouraged their action and the decision on the part of the Coal Board and the government to plan more carefully than they might otherwise have done. Second, some attention has to be paid to personalities, in particular the miners' leader Arthur Scargill and the chairman of the coal board Ian MacGregor. This is not to suggest that the strike can simply be seen as a battle of personalities in the way frequently portrayed in the press. Nevertheless, it is difficult to resist the view that personalities, the style adopted by the leaders and some of the key decisions they made, had an impact on the conduct of the strike.

SUMMARY

Strikes are the most visible and spectacular manifestation of industrial conflict. Consequently considerable attention has been focused on the strike figures published regularly by the governments of most industrialised nations. Such figures enable one to make historical and international comparisons of strike incidence. However, comparisons like this have to be treated with caution. For example, what measure of strikes (the number of strikes, the number of working days lost through strikes or the number of workers involved in strikes) is the most valuable or apt guide? Similarly, particularly in the case of international comparisons, one needs to be aware that different countries define strikes in different ways and that this can have a major impact on the figures recorded. Nevertheless, such comparisons are made and in Britain have in the past been used as the basis for public concern and government action on industrial relations.

In the UK official statistics are also regularly published on strike causation. Again, these need to be treated with caution for they only refer to the immediate reported cause of the strike; nevertheless they have been used as a starting point for more detailed investigation.

In this chapter considerable attention has been paid to different attempts to explain strike pattern and trends. Three main categories of explanation were looked at, along with studies which have focused particularly on inter-industry differences in strike propensity.

Other authors have examined strikes not through strike statistics but through the use of a case study. This method of working enables the researcher to examine the complex interrelationships that characterise any social situation more fully and to pay more attention to the motives and attitudes of participants. Three case studies were looked at, the

Loray textile mill strike, the wildcat strike at the Oscar Centre gypsum mine, and the strike at Pilkington's. All three studies can be used to show how explanations of strikes have to take as their starting point the fact that the same action or situation may be interpreted differently and have a different meaning for the different groups of participants.

11 The role of the state in industrial relations

VOLUNTARISM AND LEGAL REGULATION PRIOR TO THE 1960s

Many writers have argued that prior to the 1960s Britain had a 'voluntary' system of industrial relations.[1] Flanders has noted[2] that in its pure sense the application of the term 'voluntary' should imply that the state plays no part whatsoever in industrial relations. Thus it might be argued that the American Federation of Labor under the leadership of Samuel Gompers supported a voluntary system of industrial relations; they opposed state intervention of any kind, including the introduction of social insurance and unemployment benefit as well as legislation dealing with wages and hours of work. However, the British 'system' of industrial relations has never been 'voluntary' to that extent, nor have any of the major parties (including the trade unions) supported such an approach. The state in Britain has always intervened on certain issues.

For example, the state has intervened through the Factory Acts and associated legislation (such as the Mines Acts and the Offices, Shops and Railways Premises Act). These regulate working conditions by laying down rules for the notification of accidents and industrial diseases, the provision of proper ventilation and sanitation and maximum hours of work. The earliest Mines Acts were concerned to regulate and then prohibit the employment of women and children underground and this concern is still evident in recent legislation such as the 1961 Factory Act (which limited the working hours of women in factories to nine each day and forty-eight in a week as well as prohibiting the employment of women at night unless special exemption was obtained). Although much of the early legislation was inspired by a concern for the welfare of women and children the coverage was expanded to cover the work community as a whole.

Another example of government intervention in industrial relations in Britain prior to the 1960s can be seen in the field of wage regulation. One part of this wage regulation dates back to 1909 and the Trades Boards Act of that year. The 1909 Act set up trade boards (consisting of equal numbers of employers' and employees' representatives plus three independent members) for four trades (tailoring, paper-box making, machine-made lace and net finishing, and chain-making), where wages were so low and conditions of employment so poor that they had attracted almost universal condemnation. The boards were empowered to fix statutory minimum wage rates which were backed by an official inspectorate and the threat of legal penalties. The trade boards were strongly supported by the Whitley Committee[3] and as a result in 1918 a new Act was passed which enabled the Minister of Labour to extend their coverage (the criterion to be used for the selection of industries was that no adequate machinery existed at the time in the industry for the effective regulation of wages). After the Second World War the functions of trade boards were carried out by wages councils (bodies with a similar composition and powers) set up by the Wages Council Act of 1945. However, the powers and scope of wages councils started to be reduced in the 1980s. In particular, the Wages Act of 1986 limited wages councils to fixing wage rates for adults and made it easier to abolish councils altogether.

Another part of state wage regulation was to be found in statutes which provided that wages and conditions of employment generally accepted in an industry or an area should be applied to all workers. These statutes had a link with the compulsory arbitration introduced, temporarily, for the period of the wartime emergency (Second World War) though they could be seen most clearly in Section 8 of the Terms and Conditions of Employment Act of 1959. This said that where it could be shown that employers' and employees' organisations had agreed on the terms and conditions of employment to be applied to a particular industry (or part of an industry) then if an employer in that industry was not observing those conditions a case could be presented to the Industrial Court who would order that the employer should do so; enforcement would be by the Court stating that these provisions were to be an implied term of the contract of employment. The 1959 Act was replaced by the Employment Protection Act of 1975 (in which section 11 filled a similar role to section 8 of the 1959 Act), while the Industrial Court's role was taken over by a new body, the Central Arbitration Committee (though the aims and powers remained unchanged).

Governments also have been active in the field of wage regulation through the Fair Wages Resolutions of the House of Commons. These were first introduced in 1891 to deal with a dilemma of competing priorities. It is usually taken for granted that governments should place contracts so as to ensure that work is done efficiently; frequently, though not always, this means accepting the lowest tender. However, it is also recognised that strict observance of this rule might lead governments to contract with employers who are able to offer an attractive contract because of the poor conditions under which they employ labour. The dilemma, therefore, has centred around the conflicting principles of efficiency and fair treatment in relationship to government contracting on the one hand, and the desire to encourage 'generally accepted' conditions of employment on the other; by accepting the lowest tender for a contract the government could be seen to be encouraging an employer 'who was unfair not only to his own employees, but to other employees who were prepared to pay reasonable wages'.[4]

The Fair Wages Resolutions were designed to resolve this dilemma. They said that any employer who contracted with the government had to 'observe terms and conditions of employment not less favourable than those established for the trade or industry in the district where the work is carried out by machinery of negotiation or arbitration'.[5] Initially the Resolutions only applied to wages, but those passed in 1990 and 1946 extended the cover to other areas including hours of work and trade unions membership (an employer was not to prevent his workers from joining a trade union but he did not need to encourage them to do so). Although the Resolutions were not enforced by legal sanctions they were supported by the threat that the government would refuse to contract with an employer if he offended their provisions. It is also worthwhile noting that a number of other public agencies (in particular, local authorities and nationalised industries) adopted a similar standpoint.

Such examples of government intervention in industrial relations in Britain prior to the 1960s mean that the assertion that Britain had a voluntary system of industrial relations may be challenged. However, this does not mean that the claim should be ignored completely; rather it should be qualified and possibly restated. Somewhat more acceptable is Kahn Freund's often quoted statement, made in the early 1950s, that:

There is perhaps, no major country in the world in which the law has played a less significant role in the shaping of [industrial] relations than in Great Britain and in which today the law and the legal profession has less to do with labour relations.[6]

This claim is related to, but by no means the same as, the one that Britain had a voluntary system of industrial relations. It does not imply that the state did not take an interest in or intervene in industrial relations in Britain; rather it implies that the state played a restricted role and, crucially, tried to keep industrial relations and trade unions away from the courts.

Evidence to support this contention can be gained by examination of trade union law and the law of trade disputes in Britain prior to the 1960s. In the case of trade union law it is clear that the framers usually had a 'negative aim'. Thus, the Trade Union Act of 1871 was passed in an attempt to prevent trade unions from being declared 'unlawful bodies' and being sued for acting 'in restraint of trade'; it also tried, although not entirely successfully, to stop judicial interference in the internal affairs of trade unions. Similarly, the Conspiracy and Protection of Property Act of 1875 attempted to prevent unions being sued for 'criminal conspiracy' as the result of strike action. On occasions, the judiciary seemed intent on circumventing the will of Parliament by opening loopholes in legislation but these loopholes were usually quickly closed again (for instance, through the Trade Disputes Acts of 1906 and 1965 and the Trade Union Act of 1913).

In a similar way, prior to the 1960s no attempt was made to provide a legal framework for collective bargaining conciliation and arbitration. For example, there was no attempt to make collective agreements legally enforceable, to determine with whom an employer must bargain or over what they must bargain, or to provide compulsory arbitration. Of course this does not mean that governments did not take an interest in such questions; in fact they have offered conciliation and arbitration services since 1896 and through the Advisory, Conciliation, and Arbitration Service still do today. However, they have always left it up to the parties to a dispute to decide whether or not they wanted to avail themselves of the services and accept any recommendations that might be made. The only exception to this rule is that during both World Wars governments have temporarily introduced compulsory arbitration (in the First World War through the 1915 Munitions of War Act and in the Second World War through the 1940 Conditions of Employment and National Arbitration Order). In both cases, though, the moves to establish compulsory arbitration were seen as a response to wartime emergency and the legislation was revoked soon after the end of the war. The Second World War legislation lasted the longest; it was not revoked until 1950 and even then an element of compulsory arbitration, though not a prohibition of strikes and lock-outs, was retained until 1958 through the Industrial Disputes Order of 1951.

There is a clear contrast between such an approach and that adopted in most other countries over the same period. This is probably most vividly illustrated by reference to the position in the USA. Legislation has been introduced in the USA to cover a wide range of aspects of industrial relations and although it would be an exaggeration to claim that industrial negotiations are solely the province of lawyers, the legal profession comes close to dominating the scene. Earlier note was taken of legislation (primarily the National Labour Relations or Wagner Act of 1935) governing collective bargaining: the National Labour Relations Board can determine who shall have bargaining rights, and the constituency and issues over which they may bargain. The Labour Management Relations, or Taft–Hartley Act of 1947, made collective agreements legally enforceable, introduced the concept of a 'cooling off period' (during which strike action has to be suspended), enabled a district court to issue an eighty-day injunction against a strike or lock-out causing a national emergency, regulated the internal affairs of trade unions and provided protection for workers who refused to join a union. The provisions in the Taft–Hartley Act concerning the internal affairs of trade unions were extended and added to in the Labour–Management Reporting and Disclosure, or Landrum–Griffin Act of 1959.

Similarly, earlier discussion has noted how collective bargaining in Australia is dominated by the law. Compulsory arbitration is not reserved for exceptional cases (as it is in the USA) or for wartime emergency (as it was in Britain); rather, it is accepted as a normal part of industrial relations. This has led Isaac[7] to argue that collective bargaining, as it is understood in Europe, does not exist in Australia; so few decisions on pay and conditions of work are reached voluntarily by the two sides to a dispute that bargaining would be a misnomer.

Further, many European countries have procedures far closer to those of the USA than those of Britain. For example, a review of industrial relations in Germany argued that 'there is a strong legalistic basis to the German Industrial relations system'.[8] This can be seen in a number of areas: collective bargaining has a firm legal basis (through a series of Collective Agreements Acts in 1949, 1952 and 1969), collective agreements are legally binding, and it is illegal to strike for the duration of an agreement (a major trade union was successfully prosecuted in Germany in 1958 for breaking a no-strike rule and since then courts have issued interim injunctions to prevent strikes and violation of agreed procedures). Similar comments can be made about the Netherlands. Collective bargaining has been legally controlled since the beginning of the century. Collective agreements are legally enforceable and Albeda notes[9] that strikes are not legally recognised (they are forbidden in the case of government employees and railway workers). In addition, the Netherlands has had a central legally enforceable incomes policy since the end of the Second World War; 'it is probably no exaggeration to say that the Dutch system of wage control was more comprehensive than any other in the free enterprise economies'.[10] Again many commentators[11] have noted that in France, collective bargaining is based on a comprehensive legal framework which stipulates the issues over which bargaining should take place and the parties to whom collective agreements should apply.

A number of writers have argued that the law plays a less important role in certain other European countries. Thus, Blanpain argues that industrial relations 'in Belgium rely almost entirely on practice and on gentlemen's agreements between the social parties'.[12] He notes that Belgian trade unions have no legal personality and that they cannot be sued for breach of collective agreements. Similarly, it is claimed[13] that in Denmark legal regulation is at a minimum and that in Italy there is no legislation effectively governing collective bargaining.

Nevertheless, on closer inspection, it is hard not to conclude that even in Belgium, Denmark and Italy the law plays a more important role in industrial relations than it does in Britain. For example, in Belgium collective agreements – in certain circumstances – can be made legally binding, and a privileged bargaining position has been granted to parties who fulfil certain conditions stipulated by law. Similarly, in Denmark a system of labour courts has been in use since the beginning of the century (they were set up by the Labour Court Act of 1910), while collective agreements are legally binding. Again, in Italy legislation has been introduced to encourage the development of collective bargaining and the strengthening of trade unionism.

Hyman argues[14] that the role of the state in industrial relations in any country can be linked to the economic and social philosophy dominant during the formative period of trade unions. Thus, he notes that trade unionism became established in Britain during the heyday of *laissez-faire* liberalism,

> Initially this doctrine was interpreted in a manner extremely hostile to collective action by workers: their combinations were judged to be 'in restraint of trade', interfering with the right of the employer to make a 'free' contract with his employees as individuals.[15]

As a result legislation was passed to repress the growth of unionism. However, later influential employers came to terms with trade unionism and decided that it was not seriously disadvantageous. Consequently 'laissez-faire was reinterpreted to imply that union and employers should carry on their relations with the minimum of state interference'.[16] As a contrast, in most other countries stable industrial relations developed at a time when the state was actively involved in general economic affairs. 'In many countries where industrial development occurred later than and in competition with British capitalism, laissez-faire was inappropriate; the rapid accumulation of capital required to close the gap demanded active intervention and sponsorship by the state.'[17] As a result, state intervention in industrial relations has always been more generally accepted in such countries.

However, while such an explanation has support, for example from England and Weekes,[18] it needs further examination. In particular the suggestion that the role adopted by the state is a function of the period during which unions become established and that a dominant philosophy is associated with particular periods, seems too narrow. For example, it would be difficult to fit the Australian experience into this explanation. Trade unions in Australia developed and became established during the same period (which Hyman argues was associated with a *laissez-faire* social and economic philosophy) as their British counterparts, yet the role of the state in industrial relations in Australia is completely different to the British model. One possible explanation[19] for the different approach was noted in Chapter 6. A series of strikes in the 1890s brought about such disruption that it led to a clamour for government intervention in industrial relations. Consequently, while it might be possible to argue that the same dominant economic and social philosophy has had an influence on the role of the state in industrial relations, it would be unreasonable to rule out the possible influence of other factors.

In some ways, though, there is an even more important criticism to be made of the Hyman thesis: it is not sufficiently dynamic. It places too much emphasis on one formative period as far as the role of the state in industrial relations is concerned and pays insufficient attention to later developments. Although it is fair to argue that once a pattern has been set it is often difficult to change (many people have a personal interest in the preservation of current institutions and policies) it is by no means impossible to do so and significant modifications are certainly possible. Consequently, it would be better to view the role of the state in industrial relations as being the result of piecemeal development. Initial decisions will restrict and weight future choices but not determine them.

From this point of view, then, it is important to look not only at why the initial decision was made but also at why it was confirmed or amended at a later date. The British case might be taken as an example. Although the policy of minimum state intervention formulated during the latter part of the nineteenth century was never fundamentally changed during the succeeding 50 to 75 years this does not mean that it could not have been, nor that it was never, challenged. For instance, it was challenged during and immediately after the General Strike when the government adopted a far more interventionist strategy for a while. This strategy was not made permanent because of the later assessment and attitude of both employers and government who believed such a move to be unnecessary. They took this view because, first, the employers and the government thought that they had 'won the battle' and dealt a decisive blow against union power. Second, the General Strike was followed by economic conditions which by themselves severely hampered the operations of the trade unions and seemed to render government intervention unnecessary. Third, the majority of national union leaders were felt to be 'responsible' and 'moderate'. This belief had been encouraged by the way the union leaders had agreed to make sacrifices for the war effort during the First World War (for instance, accepting dilution) and confirmed by the way the TUC General Council had agreed to call off the General Strike after no more than a few days.

The policy of non-intervention was challenged again later during the Second World War. This time it was maintained largely because of the support of the unions. Flanders has argued[20] that 'voluntarism' retained its place in British industrial relations largely as a result of the efforts of one of the key trade union leaders during the Second World War. He argued that the Second World War was a triumph and a vindication for the principle of voluntarism, 'so much so that, for some years when the war was over and throughout the fifties, it became an almost unchallengeable article of faith'. The success of voluntarism, in turn, was to a large extent the result of the support it was given by Ernest Bevin (a major trade union figure) as Minister of Labour in the wartime coalition government. Flanders quoted the following passage from Bullock's biography of Bevin to show how strongly, and in what fashion, Bevin supported voluntarism.

> When Bevin talked about 'voluntaryism' (his own word for it) he meant something more than the traditional trade-union opposition to industrial conscription. He started with the question: how could a country with the democratic institutions of Britain hope to match the degree of organisation already achieved in Germany? Not, Bevin answered himself, by discarding its own traditions and trying to copy the totalitarian methods it was fighting against: this was the mistake of those who wanted to treat the whole nation in wartime as if it were an army and organise it on military lines. The right way was to stick to the basic principle of democracy, government by consent, and rely on the willingness of the people in an emergency to make greater sacrifices willingly than they could be dragooned into making by compulsion. This he believed, could be more effective than dictatorship, provided that besides appealing to people, you took practical steps to remove the obstacles which inhibited or impaired consent . . . Bevin had too much experience of organising men to suppose that the country would get through the war without having to apply some degree of compulsion to labour . . . 'Voluntaryism' did not rule this out, did not mean that the Government had to rely solely on appeals for volunteers; what it did mean was that, instead of starting with a full-blown system of industrial conscription, you began from the opposite end, demonstrating to people that it was not only necessary but fairer to employ compulsory powers and keeping their use to a minimum. When the time came Bevin proved that he was quite prepared to issue orders if he thought this necessary; but when he did, it is not playing with words to say that it was upon a basis of consent, and that consent was willingly given because he had plainly exhausted the possibilities of purely voluntary methods first.[21]

It is worthwhile noting that in other countries, where the role of the state in industrial relations has differed significantly from the British model, trade unions have played a major part in sustaining earlier developments. For example, there is little doubt that, although there was a degree of scepticism initially, evaluations of experience led the bulk of Australian trade unions and the Labour Party to accept compulsory arbitration and this has been important in sustaining the level of state intervention. Thus, when the Labor Party has gained office it has not tried to dismantle existing machinery; to the contrary – on occasions it has been instrumental in extending the present system. Similarly, although the American Federation of Labor initially opposed state intervention in industrial relations in the USA through the Wagner Act, it later changed this stand. Experience persuaded the AFL that state intervention could be beneficial and it abandoned its support of 'voluntarism'. Trade unions in the USA have on a number of occasions since that time pressed for greater, not less, state intervention in industrial relations.

RECENT DEVELOPMENTS

In many ways the 1960s mark the turning point in the role of the state in industrial relations in Britain. Earlier the state had pursued a policy emphasising minimum intervention; since the 1960s this policy seems to have changed. Governments of all political complexions seem to have accepted the need for more direct and sustained intervention.

The first signs of what was to happen can be seen in what might be termed fringe areas. In the early 1960s the government intervened for the first time in two areas, the termination of employment and industrial training. The former issue was dealt with in the Contract of Employment Act of 1963. This Act covered a wide area, centring on the need for an employer to give an employee a written statement of certain (though not all) of the terms of his or her contract (the written statement had to cover the scale or method of calculating remuneration, the intervals at which remuneration is to be paid, the conditions relating to hours of work, sickness and holiday pay and pension arrangements). Further the Act required an employee to be given certain minimum notice for the termination of the contract (on the basis of a scale which ran from one week's notice after half a year's employment to four weeks' notice after five years' employment). Although the periods of notice required were fairly minimal, and were already exceeded by many employers, they nevertheless marked an important break with precedent. Previously the period of notice necessary before the termination of employment had been a matter left to the two sides on industry; the 1963 Act meant that it had become an area of concern for the state.

Governments in Britain had expressed an interest in the other area, industrial training, as long ago as 1948; however, the Employment and Training Act of 1948 which marked the culmination of that interest was more concerned with placement services than training.

The Industrial Training Act of 1964 was a much more important and decisive piece of legislation as far as training was concerned. Under the terms of the Act the government was empowered to set up training boards, to cover particular industries, with the function of improving training facilities for people over school-leaving age. The boards were to consist of a chairman (appointed by the Minister of Labour), equal numbers of representatives of both sides of industry and a number of other people appointed after consultation with the Secretary of State for Scotland and the Minister of Education. The boards were given the power to impose a levy on all employers in the industry to finance their operations; the size of the levy was not specified but was to vary according to the needs of the industry. The Act also established arbitration machinery (based on industrial tribunals) to deal with disputes (usually over the payment of the levy) concerning the operation of the training programmes.

These first pieces of legislation in the areas of termination of employment and industrial training have been supplemented and amended since. For example, the provisions concerning the termination of employment in the 1963 Contract of Employment Act were supplemented two years later through the 1965 Redundancy Payments Act. Whereas the 1963 Act had dealt with the length of notice to be given before the termination of employment, the 1965 Act dealt with the payment of compensation to a worker made redundant. Compensation was to be based on a formula which varied according to age and length of employment (for instance, redundancy pay of one-and-a-half weeks for each year's employment during which the employee was over 41 but under 64 years old) with a financial limit on the total payment. Although the compensation was to be paid directly by the employer, part of it could be claimed back from the redundancy payments fund to which all employers had to contribute regularly.

Recently, further additions have been made to the termination of employment regulations. For example, the Industrial Relations Act of 1971 contained provisions designed to protect employees against unfair dismissal (a dismissal was to be regarded as unfair if the employer could not show that the cause of the dismissal was related to the employee's capability, qualification, conduct, or was a question of redundancy). The 1971 Act was repealed by the Labour government in 1974; however, the Employment Acts of 1980 and 1982 have returned to earlier trends and extended them in certain areas. The Wages Act of 1986, though, made an important change by restricting rebates from the Redundancy Payments Fund to employers with nine or fewer workers.

The changes introduced since the early 1960s in the area of industrial training initially were rather less dramatic than those dealing with termination of employment. They centred on the administration of the scheme (brought under the control of the Manpower Services Commission, although the training boards continued to operate, under the Commission's guidance) and the provisions for exemption from the payment of the levy. However, earlier trends have now been radically reversed with the removal of the statutory requirement for training boards and Enterprise Trusts taking over some of their work.

There were, undoubtedly, a variety of motives behind government intervention in the fields of termination of employment and industrial training. Nevertheless, it is clear that one of the motives was economic. For example, one of the aims of the termination of employment regulations was to cushion some of the worst effects of redundancy and thus reduce the fear it understandably created. In turn, it was hoped that this would help to increase efficiency by encouraging workers to give up protective practices and to consider more seriously the possibility of mobility between jobs and different areas of the country. Similarly, one of the aims of the training legislation was to improve the opportunities available to train in areas where there were shortages of skilled labour.

The 1970s also saw a number of important initiatives in other 'fringe' areas. For example, major changes were introduced with the Health and Safety at Work Act of 1974. This allowed for the progressive replacement of earlier out-of-date legislation and imposed a duty on every employer to ensure, as far as 'reasonably practical', the health and safety of all their employees or others who used their premises. The 1974 Act also led to the establishment of a tripartite body, the Health and Safety Commission, and a Health and Safety Executive which were given the responsibility for encouraging research and training about safety, disseminating information, enforcing safety laws and publishing codes of conduct; gave the Secretary of State powers to provide for recognised trade unions' safety representatives; and created a centralised inspectorate system with new powers. The provisions in the 1974 Act were the source of some debate (for example, over whether the same person should be both a shop steward and a trade union safety representative), but they have been seen as a 'determined effort . . . to use the law flexibly and effectively in the drive for safety at work'.[22] They were subsequently built on, recently for instance, with the Control of Substances Hazardous to Health Regulation of 1988 which for the first time conferred legal status on occupational exposure limits and required employers, by January 1990, to make an assessment of the health risks involved in the use of hazardous substances. The scope of the regulation was very wide indeed, ranging from solvents in correction fluid to large-scale manufacturing processes in the chemical industry, though some have argued that enforcement is more important than the scope of legislative provision in this area.

There were also important moves over much the same period on the question of discrimination in employment. A number of pieces of legislation which sought to secure equal pay for women (Equal Pay Act, 1970), remove sex discrimination in the workplace (Sex Discrimination Act, 1975) and remove race discrimination at work (Race Relations Act, 1976). The legislation allowed aggrieved individuals to take action against employers that practised direct or indirect discrimination (indirect discrimination was defined as policy which although applied to everyone would be likely to affect one group to a disproportionate extent). The Equal Opportunities and Race Relations Commissions were also established to carry out investigations into discrimination and to assist others in taking action against it or take action against it, as appropriate.

The importance of the moves made in this area are that they indicate the willingness of the state to say that certain policies practised in the employment sphere were unacceptable and the state should accept responsibility for ensuring that they did not take place. The implementation of such policies has not been without problems for there have been major difficulties over the interpretation of the legislation. However, with the modifications made to tighten up the early provisions, and in the 1980s in particular the use of European legislation, the policy in this area has been seen as an important development of the role of the state.

INCOMES POLICY

Government intervention in the areas reviewed above was important as an indication of a changed view of the proper role of the state. In their own right, as well, the measures were of some importance for the conduct of industrial relations. However, government intervention in the determination of wages brought the state even more centrally into the main business of industrial relations.

British governments took an interest in the level of incomes long before the early 1960s (Clegg argues that such interest can be seen as long ago as 1916 when the Asquith coalition tried to halt the tide of war bonuses[23]). However, Corina suggests that there is a distinction between 'the management of incomes', through traditional fiscal and monetary means, and the promotion of an 'active incomes policy' which is concerned with the details, timing and magnitude of changes in specific incomes and prices.[24]

Even if we take Corina's definition of an incomes policy then it is arguable that incomes policies in Britain date back well beyond the 1960s; the Labour government after the Second World War attempted (initially successfully) to enforce a wages freeze between 1948 and 1950, while the Conservative government, a decade later, attempted a rather less successful price freeze. Nevertheless, what can be argued is that such attempts were spasmodic and designed to deal with particular situations. Although the incomes policy attempts of the 1960s were also prompted by crisis (in particular, fear of the effects of inflation) they were accompanied by a belief, which gained ground in the 1960s, that government intervention in the fixing of income levels should be seen as normal and desirable. The feeling expressed was that if governments were to have any chance of success in achieving their often competing aims (full employment, slower price rises, faster growth, balance of payments equilibrium and high social welfare expenditure) then they had to be given the power to intervene in the fixing of income levels. Further, the 1960s were characterised by the establishment of government-sponsored agencies and bodies whose task was to implement government incomes policy in a wide variety of areas.

The history of incomes policy in Britain has been a chequered one. Specific policy initiatives have rarely lasted for more than a year or two. The tension between voluntary and compulsory measures has been apparent frequently as have been the differences in implementation between the public and private sectors.

The first attempts to introduce incomes policy were made by the Conservative government of the early 1960s. The 'pay pause' of 1961–2 was designed to apply directly to the public sector and also to set an example to private industry; later the National Economic Development council suggested 'the guiding light' policy under which pay increases were to average between 3 per cent and 3.5 per cent on the assumption of a 4 per cent growth rate.

Incomes policies became much more central and sophisticated, though, after the election of the Labour government in 1964. The history of incomes policies since 1964 illustrates well the tensions between voluntary and statutory enforcement.

When the Labour government came to power in 1964 it brought with it a commitment to promote economic planning, and George Brown, Deputy Leader of the Party, was appointed head of the new

Department of Economic Affairs. One of the Department's first tasks was the establishment of a new incomes policy. This was announced by the 'Declaration of Intent', an agreement signed by both sides of industry as well as the government, committing all parties to try to raise productivity, to keep money increases in incomes in line with increases in real national output and to maintain a stable price level. The policy was to be flexible; although a norm was established for pay increases it was recognised that variations from the norm were inevitable. It was also stressed that all incomes and prices were to be covered and that productivity was to play a crucial role. The watchdog of the new policy was the National Board for Prices and Incomes, a body which unlike its predecessor, the National Incomes Commission, had the support of both sides of industry.

The prices and incomes policy established by the Labour government was founded on the basis of voluntary agreement. The two sides of industry had voluntarily agreed to support the policy and the reports of the National Board of Prices and Incomes would gain voluntary acceptance: compulsion was not envisaged. However, it soon became clear that reliance on voluntary action was not producing the desired effect: the general level of wage rates and earnings rose faster than productivity and prices, while a number of reports by the Board on individual settlements were ignored.[25] By 1966 Britain was also facing an 'economic crisis'. In July of that year, therefore, the government introduced a prices and incomes 'freeze'; this was to be followed by a period of 'severe restraint' during which the norm would be zero, although exceptional increases would be permitted. The policy was no longer to be left to voluntary action; it was to be enforced by legal sanctions introduced by the Prices and Incomes Act. The Act required prior notification of price and pay increases and enabled the government to prosecute employers and employees who broke the policy; the penalties that could be imposed were restricted to fines and it was stated that such enforcement would only be available if brought into force by an Order in Council. Nevertheless, legal enforcement was part of the Act and was used within a few months of its passage.

The new policy was amended in succeeding years (in March 1967 a White Paper[26] was introduced outlining changes to take effect from the middle of that year and early in 1968 another White Paper[27] was introduced setting out the guidelines to be followed for the next two years) and the legal controls were slackened. Initially it appeared as if the policy was having some effect: both price and incomes rises slackened off and were lower than in the period before the freeze. However, both ran ahead of increases in productivity and the reduction may well have been influenced by factors unconnected with the incomes policies, such as the high rate of unemployment. Towards the end of the 1960s the rise in incomes speeded up once again and the Conservative government elected in 1970 declared that an incomes policy was unworkable and that it was determined not to use legal sanctions to enforce one.

In fact, the Conservative government soon changed its mind on this issue. Economic problems forced it to consider ways of controlling incomes and prices and it introduced its own policy. This eventually came to grief over the confrontation with the miners, and the new Labour government that gained office in 1974 asserted, as its predecessor had, that it would not resort to an incomes policy. Again, though, the new government was forced to make at least a partial change of direction and introduced, initially, an agreed package which included wage restraint (known as the 'social contract'), and later an incomes restraint backed by the threat of legal sanctions (interestingly, on this occasion, the sanctions were directed primarily against the employers rather than the employees in an attempt to avoid a direct confrontation with offending workers).

When the Conservative government was elected to office in 1979, like its Labour and Conservative predecessors, it was adamant that it would not seek to introduce an incomes policy and it has not explicitly reversed this stance. Nevertheless, it has intervened to influence pay settlements, particularly in the public sector. It has done so primarily by setting cash limits for spending areas that assume a certain level of wage rises. Initially the policy faltered because of the commitment to 'comparability settlements' agreed by the previous administration, but in recent years, aided by high levels of unemployment, it has been more successful.

The change in the stance of the government since 1979 has been important. Even though it is arguable that it has not abandoned an interest in levels of income, both in terms of its action over public sector pay and its exhortation to the private sector that high pay settlements threatened jobs, it has explicitly attacked the notion of incomes policies. This attack has been based in part on the practical problems of implementation. Previous policy initiatives, it has been argued, simply did not work. Whether one is considering the prices and incomes policy of the 1960s or the social contact of the 1970s, they all eventually broke down. The industrial action, the 'winter of discontent', that accompanied the breakdown of the social contact is used to illustrate the dangers of such a policy initiative. However, the attack has not simply been based on the practical problems of implementation. Much more important has been the attack linked to the disapproval of comparison in general and government attempts to control incomes in particular. The argument is put that government attempts to control incomes always face problems if they try to 'buck the markets'. Attempts to distort the market lead to short-term problems (like problems in recruitment, the use of 'unofficial' payments) and in the longer term are bound to fail. Such 'in principle' objections to incomes policy are not written on stone and with a change in political control could fall away. In such circumstances the debate about practical problems and the lessons of history once more would clearly come into focus.

It has already been stressed that there is a long history of Government intervention in industrial relations in many other countries. However, in most instances this was restricted to industrial disputes and collective bargaining; it did not deal directly with the determination of incomes. One of the few exceptions to this rule is provided by the Netherlands where incomes policies have a long history. However, by the end of the 1950s they had begun to break down and it was not until the latter part of the 1960s that the government tried to reintroduce controls. In 1969 the Dutch government introduced a new Wages Act; this enabled the government 'not only to require a general wage freeze in a national emergency but also to interfere in industrial agreements in the national interest'.[28] Later (in January 1974) further legislation was introduced concerning incomes; the Special Powers Act gave the government sweeping powers to regulate wages and prices and, using these powers, the government decreed a national incomes policy based on cash and percentage increases to current wages.

In most other countries which had little previous experience of incomes policies moves were made to introduce them in the 1960s and early 1970s. For example, in the USA the government introduced a ninety-day statutory price and wages freeze in August 1971. The aim of this measure (introduced along with others, including currency control and a partial import surcharge) was to 'correct the domestic and external imbalance' in the US economy; it was part of what was termed the 'economic stabilization programme'. At the end of the ninety-day freeze control was relaxed, but only to a limited extent, being replaced by a period of severe restraint. Phase II of the policy was guided by two new centrally appointed bodies – a price commission and a pay board. The latter aimed to keep wage rises to a limit of 5.5 per cent although in the first few months of the policy wage rises, in fact, averaged about 9 per cent (later the level was reduced to 7.2 per cent for the first nine months of 1972). Mandatory prices and wage controls were not finally removed until January 1973. Phase III of the policy depended on voluntary restraint, although Nixon threatened to reintroduce controls if the voluntary policy failed.

Many governments, then, have sought to control incomes, sometimes through formal incomes policies, sometimes through less formal strategies. Whatever the mechanics, it appears as if most governments have decided that the level of wage rises is too important for economic policy simply to be left to the parties concerned. However, as in Britain in the 1980s, interest in formal incomes policies has declined. The move against corporate solutions had not been as determined as in Britain, but in countries like the USA a similar adherence to the primacy of the market can be seen.

INTERVENTION IN BARGAINING AND DISPUTES: FIRST ATTEMPTS

British government intervention in the area of collective bargaining was explicitly sparked off by concern about its economic consequences. Stated simply and briefly, the belief was that one of the results of 'free' collective bargaining was that Britain suffered from too many strikes (for a discussion of this issue see the earlier chapters on bargaining and strikes), and that these strikes were economically damaging.

This view gained ground throughout the late 1950s and early 1960s, and was the major reason for the establishment of the Donovan Commission in 1965. The Commission's report was published in 1968. Its central argument has been outlined earlier; it was that Britain 'suffered' from 'too many strikes', most of which were a consequence of the outdated system of industrial relations. Action should be taken to bring the system more into line with the modern industrial situation. This might be achieved through the introduction of an Industrial Relations Act, under the terms of which all companies with more than 5,000 employees would be required to register their collective agreements, or if they had none to state why this was so. The agreements would be scrutinised by a new body, the Industrial Relations Commission, and improvements would be suggested where necessary. The majority of the Donovan Commission, however, came out strongly against the use of legal penalties to enforce compliance (although a minority of its members argued that legal penalties might be of value in certain cases). The essence of the Donovan Commission's approach was public scrutiny and persuasion.

The Donovan Commission's report was never acted upon. Instead the government brought out its own proposals in a White Paper called *In Place of Strife*.[29] Interestingly, the analysis of the problem presented in the White Paper did not differ significantly from that of the Donovan Commission. It confirmed that the main problem facing industrial relations in Britain was the prevalence of 'unofficial strikes', one of the main causes of which was the deficiency of the collective bargaining machinery. It also followed the Donovan Commission's proposals on certain issues; in particular, it accepted, in general at least, the proposal for the registration of collective agreements and the establishment of a Commission on Industrial Relations. Nevertheless, it differed fundamentally from the Donovan Commission in that it also suggested the use of legal penalties to enforce compliance with certain demands the government might make. For example, the Secretary of State would be given the power to enforce the recommendations made by the Commission on Industrial Relations. Following investigation of 'inter-union conflict', he would be able to order a 'conciliation pause' (strike action had to be suspended and the *status quo* accepted) for twenty-eight days, and he would be able to require that a strike ballot should be held. Further, trade unions would be required to register with a new Registrar of Trade Unions and Employers' Associations (the Registrar would have the power to require the revision of certain rules, notably those governing elections and discipline).

In the event the Labour government never translated the White Paper's proposals into law. The trade unions mounted a major campaign in opposition to them and in the end the government agreed to rely on voluntary action and abandoned its proposals for legal penalties. The TUC, for their part, agreed to take action, voluntarily, on a variety of issues, principally those concerning interunion conflicts.

The defeat of the Labour government's attempt 'to introduce the law' into industrial relations, however, did not spell the end of such moves, for the Conservative government which gained power in 1970 was pledged to introduce a similar package of measures. These formed the basis of the 1971 Industrial Relations Act.

When Robert Carr introduced the Industrial Relations Bill into Parliament he stated that it was based on three fundamental beliefs. The first was that the best way of determining pay and conditions of work in a free society was by a voluntary system of negotiations, free from state control. The second was that serious difficulties had developed in the voluntary system of collective bargaining being used at that time. The third was that 'vital and urgent' reform could only be secured by collective effort on the part of the government, management, unions and workers, within a new framework of law. The Industrial Relations Bill covered a variety of topics, from the right of the individual to join a trade union and an extension of the periods of notice required under the Contracts of Employment Act, to the outlawing of the 'closed shop', the specification that a collective agreement was to be legally binding unless stated to the contrary and the introduction of a new code of industrial relations practice. At a number of crucial points the Act provided for the use of legal penalties to counter 'unfair industrial practices', to enforce a 'cooling off' period (a device similar to the 'conciliation pause' proposed in the Labour government's White Paper) and to enforce the call for strike ballot. The Act also proposed the establishment of two new bodies: the Industrial Court (which would have the status of a High Court and whose president would be a High Court judge) to deal with the legal issues raised by the Act, and a Commission on Industrial Relations (with similar functions to the body proposed by *In Place of Strife*).

The trade unions fought just as determined a campaign against the proposals of the Conservative government as they had done against those of the Labour government two years earlier. However, they were less successful, because the Bill became law, despite the fierce opposition both inside and outside Parliament. In the longer term, though, the trade unions might claim some success, for within two years opinion within the Conservative Party turned against the Act: the CBI claimed that its effects had been divisive and the Conservative Party eventually accepted that its continuance would hamper the establishment of harmonious industrial relations. The imprisonment of dockers' leaders, 'The Pentonville Five', and the reaction to it, was critical in this regard. It showed the danger that action taken under the legislation could make trade union leaders martyrs and lead to an escalation of industrial action. The Act was repealed by the Labour Party following its victory at the general election in 1974 and the Conservative Party stated that when it regained power it would not try to reintroduce the Act.

The Labour Party, during the 1970s, was at great pains to argue that there were fundamental differences between their proposals – contained in *In Place of Strife* – and the Conservative government's Industrial Relations Act. The differences they referred to concerned matters like the attempt to 'outlaw the closed shop', to make collective agreements legally enforceable unless it was specifically stated to the contrary and to establish a new Industrial Court. However, while there were differences, there were also important areas of agreement. Crucially, both *In Place of Strife* and the Industrial Relations Act envisaged the law playing a much greater part in industrial relations, and proposed to give the Minister power to take action to force parties to accept his or her point of view on a variety of issues. Certainly the differences between the Donovan Commission's report on the one hand, and *In Place of Strife* and the Industrial Relations Act on the other hand, were much more important than the differences between the last two documents. Whereas the Donovan Commission accepted a pluralist position, suggesting merely that the bargaining machinery should be improved, the framers of the Industrial Relations Act and *In Place of Strife* adopted a position much nearer that described by Fox[30] as a unitary approach, for they seemed to believe that conformity to 'the national interest' should be enforced.

When the Labour Party gained power in 1974 there was no suggestion of it returning to the policy foreshadowed in its White Paper *In Place of Strife*. The whole of the Labour movement had been behind the attack on the use of legislation in industrial relations in the way it had been operated by the Conservative government through the 1971 legislation. The new Labour government was committed to repeal the 1971 Act and as has been noted it did so. However, the Labour government did not seek to return to the position that had existed prior to the 1960s. In practice, it extended state involvement in a significant way. Reference has already been made to increased involvement in health and safety and in sex and race discrimination. However it is not just in these 'fringe areas' that the state intervened, but also on matters more at the centre of industrial relations. Further, it did so in a way that strengthened rather than reduced the rights of employees and trade unions. The Trade Union and Labour Relations Act of 1974 and the Employment Protection Act of 1975 were key pieces of legislation which were built on later, particularly with the Employment Protection (Consolidation) Act 1978. The 1974 Act restored and extended the immunities of trade unions while the 1975 Act gave unions new rights in terms of recognition (these could involve ACAS intervention in disputes and reference of any recommendation for recognition which was not accepted to the Central Arbitration Committee, but there were still problems where an employer would not allow ACAS to ballot employees, as at Grunwick's), and in terms of the disclosure of information needed for collective bargaining.

INTERVENTION IN BARGAINING AND DISPUTES AFTER 1979

Although the Conservative Party promised not to try to reintroduce the 1971 Industrial Relations Act if they gained power, nevertheless, when they returned to office in 1979, they were still committed to greater state intervention in industrial relations. The main difference between the approach adopted after 1979 and that adopted in 1971 was that after 1979 the government dealt with issues gradually, building up a legislative base through a series of initiatives rather than in a single statute. The 1980s saw four major pieces of industrial relations legislation. Another important difference was that the government introduced the legislation but left much of the initiative on implementation to employers. The government was also keen to ensure that its legislation should target unions as organisations and avoid making industrial leaders martyrs.

The first piece of legislation was the Employment Act of 1980, introduced by the then Secretary of State for Employment Jim Prior. It was seen as only a limited move but some of its provisions were important and directly affected the conduct of industrial relations. The main provisions were:

1 Payments could be made by the government towards the cost of secret ballots held by trade unions on matters like strike action, the amendment of union rules and certain union elections.
2 The Secretary of State was empowered to introduce a code of practice on good industrial relations. The code was to be approved by Parliament (after consultation with ACAS) and although it was not to be treated as a statutory requirement it could be taken into account by tribunals and courts in determining questions to which it related.
3 Restrictions were introduced on the closed shop. New closed shop agreements had to be approved in a secret ballot in which at least 80 per cent of those covered supported it. Employees could refuse to join a union where there was a closed shop on grounds of 'conscience or other deeply held personal convictions', and employees who felt that they had been unreasonably expelled from a trade union where a closed shop operated, were to have a remedy – initially through an industrial tribunal.
4 Lawful picketing was restricted to a person picketing 'at or near his own place of work' and a trade union official accompanying such a person. An unemployed person was also permitted by the Act to picket outside his previous place of work if this was related

to a trade union dispute connected to his dismissal. Any picketing outside these limits would lose legal immunities and therefore be liable to be the subject of an injunction or a claim for damages.

5 Immunity for secondary industrial action (such as blacking and sympathetic strikes) was restricted to situations where the main purpose of the action was to interfere with the supply of goods or services during the dispute between the employer in dispute. Secondary action was also to be permitted where the aim was to prevent the transfer of work during a dispute to an associated employer.

6 A number of other changes were introduced relating to unfair dismissal and maternity rights, in both cases mainly aimed at restricting the impact of earlier legislation and easing the controls on 'small' employers.

Although far less radical than the 1971 legislation the 1980 Act still provoked considerable hostility, particularly from the union movement. As part of the campaign against the legislation most trade unions decided not to seek government finance for secret ballots. The code of practice envisaged by the Act was eventually introduced and in one of its most controversial provisions suggested that only six pickets should be needed to 'peacefully picket' during a trade dispute. Provisions like this in the code of practice had an uneven though not insignificant effect. Some of the other, less well discussed provisions, like those relating to unfair dismissals and maternity rights, were important as indicators of a reversal of earlier trends in employment policy.

Subsequently, James Prior lost his employment portfolio (moving to take on responsibility for Northern Ireland) and was replaced by Norman Tebbit. His approach was less cautious than that of James Prior, though still less direct than that adopted in 1971. For example, he decided not to try to introduce a new legal entity like the Industrial Court, which had been the focus for much union antagonism in 1971. Nevertheless, the legislation he introduced in 1982 was still much more interventionist and liable to have a greater impact on industrial relations than that adopted by James Prior.

The 1982 legislation covered six main areas:

1 It enabled the government to pay compensation to workers who were dismissed from their employment who would have been protected from dismissal as existing non-union members or 'conscientious objectors' had the closed shop provisions of the 1980 Employment Act been in operation. Essentially this

referred to those people who were dismissed because of the closed shop between 1974 and 1980 and who were not protected from dismissal because of the legislation introduced by the previous Labour government.

2 It extended the restrictions introduced by the 1980 Act on dismissal resulting from closed shop agreements. The 1980 Act had made it unfair to dismiss an employee for non-union membership in a closed shop brought into effect after 15 August 1980 if the agreement had not been approved in a ballot by 80 per cent of the workforce. The 1982 legislation extended this provision by insisting that any closed shop that had taken effect in the five years before 15 August 1980 had to be approved by a ballot of the workforce (it needed to be supported by 80 per cent of the employees covered or 85 per cent of those voting).

3 It insisted on regular reviews of closed shop agreements through ballots of the workforce every five years.

4 It made discrimination against non-union firms in the making or awarding of contracts illegal. It also removed the legal immunities from those who sought to put pressure (whether through industrial or other action) on an employer to discriminate against non-union firms.

5 It enabled trade unions to be sued for an injunction or damages (up to a specified limit) where they were responsible for 'unlawful action' by bringing the legal immunities from civil actions for trade unions into line with those for individual officials.

6 It restricted the definition of a 'lawful trade dispute' (on which the immunities from civil action are based) to disputes between workers and their own employer which are 'wholly or mainly related to the subjects of a trade dispute listed in section 29 of the Trade Union and Labour Relations Act 1974'.[31]

The impact of the 1982 legislation was greater than that of the 1980 Act. Nevertheless it was uneven, in part because many of its provisions depended on employers initiating action. Early indication suggested that few – particularly few large – employers would be willing to take such action and risk seriously damaging relations with trade unions. If this had persisted it would have been of some importance for as has been noted the 1982 legislation relied on employers rather than the government taking action. However, the position changed and gradually employers began to use the provisions of the legislation. Two main areas can be identified where the legislation had an important effect on trade unions. First, it allowed unions themselves to be sued in their own names for damages if unlawful industrial action (which has been defined to include secondary picketing, certain other secondary action and inter-union strikes) was organised or supported by union officials. Although the scale of damages was related to the size of the unions, for the larger unions the 1982 Act imposed a maximum of £¼ million. The legislation also made it more difficult for a union to 'disown' the actions of its own officials (as in some cases they were able to do under the 1971 Industrial Relations Act) and thereby to escape financial penalties. The ability of the courts to sequestrate union funds, illustrated in a number of disputes, further constrained the ability of unions to escape the impact of such legislation. The other important effect of the legislation on trade unions was that it weakened the ability of individual unions to extend unionisation. This was the result of the restrictions on the closed shop (although the legislation did not 'outlaw' the closed shop) and the restrictions on a union's right to insist that subcontractors only use union labour (a practice common in the engineering, construction and printing industries).

Apart from these two main areas, the 1982 legislation also substantially increased the damages that an individual could claim for unfair dismissal: where reinstatement was not possible or a reinstatement order was not complied with, damages of up to £20,000 could be awarded. Further, the legislation made 'political strikes' more difficult, a position which could affect the trade union movement in general, but which could have a particularly serious effect on workers in the public sector, where the distinction between 'political' and 'industrial' strikes is more difficult to determine.

The provision to enable people who were dismissed because of a closed shop agreement between 1974 and 1980 to claim compensation was an addition to the proposals originally made by Mr Tebbit in November 1981. The government saw this very much as a matter of principle. Thus, Norman Tebbit, introducing the additional provision in 1982, said:

> The Bill contains one entirely new proposal. It concerns those who lost their jobs because of the last Government's closed shop legislation.
>
> The 1974 and 1976 legislation first created and then consolidated a situation which was morally indefensible by sanctioning the dismissal, without compensation, of employees in a closed shop solely on the grounds of non-membership of a specified trade union, even when they were existing employees or when their objection to membership was based on grounds of conscience

or other deeply held personal conviction. The Government have always taken the view that this was wrong . . .

Mr Tebbit went on to state that the government ended what they saw as 'an injustice' in 1980, and now intended simply to compensate those people for this 'injustice'.

> We are now seeking in the Bill a power to enable the Government to compensate those who were dismissed in such circumstances while the 1974 and 1976 legislation was in force but who would have been protected if their case had fallen under the 1980 Act. I believe this will be widely welcomed.[32]

While this provision obviously was of considerable interest to the individuals concerned, its long-term implications were limited and linked more to an indication of attitude than anything else.

The government claimed that their proposals had 'widespread support' and undoubtedly there was some reason behind this argument. Most of the tests of public opinion that were available suggested a 'general view' at the time that there should be 'more controls' over industrial relations. However, whether one could argue that the detailed proposals of the 1982 Act were known let alone understood by most people is another matter. It is also worthwhile commenting that the general views expressed in tests of public opinion on industrial relations in general and trade unions in particular were simply what has been stated – 'general views' – and it does not mean that a particular view would be taken over a particular case. It is also quite possible that a person may argue that unions have 'too much power' yet at the same time defend the power claimed by his or her 'own union'.

The third major piece of legislation on industrial relations introduced since the election of the Conservative government in 1979 was the Trade Union Act of 1984. Headlined as legislation on trade union democracy it has three main provisions:

1 Members of a trade union's governing body (usually the national executive committee) and officers (such as the general secretary or president) who have a vote on the governing body would have to be elected in a secret ballot at least every five years. Although semi-postal and workplace as well as full postal ballots were permitted, if the first two forms were used then the conditions for the conduct of the ballot had to give the same protections and rights to individual members as were required of postal ballots.
2 If a trade union wished to retain legal immunities during an

industrial dispute then strike action had to be supported by those called on to take such action in a secret ballot held no more than four weeks before the start of the action.

3 A trade union's ability to maintain a political fund and levy was made conditional on a regular ballot of members, at least every ten years. An earlier suggestion to change the 'contracting out' to a 'contracting in' requirement was not pursued.

The first of these provisions is particularly interesting given the discussion in the literature on internal democracy in trade unions. It is a reasonable interpretation of one of the themes in that literature that a requirement for a national 'one person one vote' ballot for the election of national union officials does not guarantee greater internal democracy. In fact, in their pioneering work on this topic, the Webbs[33] argued that such a requirement was likely to lead to less rather than more real democracy in trade unions. A national ballot is likely to lead to established national leaders having a major advantage over challengers. The Webbs argued that the model adopted by the cotton operatives' union held out a much better likelihood of real representative democracy. In that model the union leaders were elected by a 'parliament' and it was argued that the members of that body were more likely to be able to properly evaluate the worth and contribution of potential national leaders than the rank and file member. Prior to the 1984 legislation British trade unions had a variety of different arrangements for electing their leaders. In part the variety reflected the different conditions in which the unions operated and in part different traditions. It is certainly open to question whether the replacement of this variety by a more standard requirement will lead to the aim of the legislation being met: that is, a trade union leadership more responsive to the needs and wishes of the union's rank and file members.

The second provision of the 1984 legislation relating to strike ballots, like much of the 1982 legislation relies, on others – mainly employers – taking action against trade unions. Its impact, therefore, was uneven initially, though after the evidence of the willingness of some major employers, like British Leyland, to use the legislation, it became much more widely used. This particular provision did not affect disputes started before 26 September 1984 and therefore could not be used in the 1984–5 miners' strike.

The third of the major provisions, relating to the political levy, was initially seen as something of a compromise. The results of the ballots could have led to a weakening of the link between the trade unions and the Labour Party. In practice this did not happen. All of the unions confirmed their support for political funds and some unions that did not have political funds prior to 1984 successfully balloted their members and established them.

The mid-1980s saw a number of major industrial confrontations. The most important was undoubtedly the miners' strike of 1984–5 which brought the use of new measures to prevent and reduce the impact of picketing. In practice, the legislation of the 1980s was not critical in this matter for much of the action taken against picketing was not dependent on specific industrial relations legislation. Other disputes, like those at the News International plant at Wapping and at P & O in 1987 and 1988, also caught the headlines and led to government determination to tighten up the provisions of the earlier legislation.

Early in 1987 the government published a green paper entitled *Trade Unions and Their Members*. This outlined a number of possible measures most of which were taken up in legislation proposed to Parliament later that year. Those proposals, with some alterations, became the Employment Act of 1988. That piece of legislation extended a number of the provisions of earlier legislation.

First, in section 1 of the Act, trade union members were given the right to apply to the High Court if their union sought to make official a strike or other industrial action (thus, an overtime ban or a decision to 'work to rule' would be covered, as well as a strike) if it had not been approved by a ballot that might meet the requirements of the law. The High Court, if it accepted the case of the aggrieved member, could order the union to withdraw its support for the strike, and take any action necessary to force the union to comply, although the Act did not allow the Court to order the strikers back to work, or to order the union to conduct a ballot. This approach, penalising a union that fails to comply, rather than dealing directly with strikers or ordering a ballot, is important, and in keeping with the tradition established by the earlier legislation of the 1980s.

Second, the Act strengthened the provisions on strike ballots introduced by the 1984 Act. It said that the ballot paper had to conclude without further qualification or comment the statement: 'If you take part in a strike or other industrial action, you may be in breach of your contract of employment.' It also said that members had to be asked specifically whether they were willing to take part in a strike or other industrial action (whatever was proposed, or a separate question for each if both a strike and industrial action were proposed). The Act also tightened up in the provisions about the constituency for a strike ballot, allowed the Secretary of State to issue codes of practice for promoting 'desirable practices' in relation to ballots and elections, and, through section 30, ensured that Crown servants, whom it might be argued did not have contracts of employment, should be deemed to have them for the purposes of the legislation on industrial action.

Third, the Act extended the earlier provisions relating to ballots on union political funds and the conduct of elections for union office. As far as election to union office is concerned, the 1988 Act provided that the requirement for periodic elections should extend to all non-voting members who attend and speak at meetings of the executive committee, and explicitly should extend to the union's general secretary and president. This extension was provoked by the example of the mineworkers' president escaping the provisions of the 1984 legislation by having his voting status on the national executive committee withdrawn. The rules for both elections and political fund ballots were tightened up in other ways, including the requirement for an independent scrutineer and the requirement that all ballots should be postal. Specific rules were introduced under section 13 governing election addresses.

Fourth, new controls were introduced under the Act over the use of union funds or property. Section 8 of the Act explicitly stated that it would be unlawful for a union to seek to indemnify individuals who had been penalised for contempt of court or for specified criminal offences. This was meant to deal with cases where unions had tried to indemnify members who had been fined in connection with picketing during an industrial dispute. It also raised questions, however, relating to hardship funds, and the answer as to whether their use would be restricted would depend on whether the fund was controlled by the union and whether it was used to indemnify criminal offences. The Act also gave members greater powers to control the action of union trustees, particularly where they proposed unlawful action (what is covered by unlawful action may not be as easy to determine as might be imagined, particularly when considering the day-to-day affairs of the union rather than the set-piece confrontation where a court order has been made).

Fifth, although the Act did not make the closed shop unlawful it made it impossible for a union to take lawful action to enforce such agreements. This means that even if there has been a strike ballot in accordance with the legislation the union will not be protected from action if enforcing of the closed shop is the objective, or even one of the objectives. The Act also extended the provisions with regard to unfair dismissal so that dismissal because of a closed shop would be automatically unfair.

Finally, the Act gave new rights to union members. The most controversial was the right not to be disciplined by a union for failing to support strike or other industrial action, even though the action was approved by a properly conducted ballot. This provision was not simply opposed by trade unions, but also by some employers' organisations, such as the Engineering Employers' Federation and the CBI. The argument against this provision was that it weakened the role of ballots. The employers were concerned that those who opposed a strike might not vote in a ballot if they knew they had the right to ignore the result. Further, the Act introduced the Commissioner for the Rights of Trade Union Members, who is able to assist the individual member in taking action against a union.

At the end of 1989 the government published proposals that became the 1990 Employment Act. Action was taken over three matters. First, the earlier moves against the closed shop were to be taken a stage further so that it would be unlawful to deny anyone a job either because they were or were not union members. Second, the provisions to withdraw amenities from secondary action were to be extended. This extension was prompted by the action of trade unions who opposed a single union agreement for a new Ford plant at Dundee. Third, it was to be made more difficult for a union to repudiate the actions of its members. If they wanted to avoid responsibility for unofficial action they would have to write to all members telling them that they gave no support and advising of risk of dismissal without compensation.

Increasing state intervention in British industrial relations undoubtedly has links with economic problems evident since the late 1960s. In a number of cases economic problems (inflation and balance of payments deficits) were cited explicitly as the reason for attempting incomes restraint. The same explicit connection was not always made for other types of intervention; nevertheless, there is little doubt that many were inspired by the belief that they would reduce the extent of strike action and as a result lead to improved economic performance.

Many writers[34] have used this evidence as the starting point for an argument that state intervention in industrial relations is general in Britain, and through incomes policy elsewhere, has been a reflection of a 'crisis in capitalism'. Thus it has been suggested that in an economic climate where there is a relatively small margin available for improvements in wages 'even the most modest trade union wage aspirations have a disruptive potential; indeed even resistance to a cut in living standards may threaten economic stability'.[35] As a result governments used whatever weapons they were able to find to try to control wage demands: incomes policies and wage freezes were attempts to do this directly, restrictions on the right to strike and the like were attempts to do it indirectly by limiting trade union and worker power.

However, it is worthwhile counselling caution in the interpretation of this argument. It is important to remember that the explicit is not always the full or even the main justification for action. While many politicians justified greater state intervention in industrial relations on the basis that it would lead to economic benefits, this does not necessarily mean that it was their only motive. There is reason to believe that moves to 'control' industrial relations also had an important political appeal. The evidence referred to earlier from opinion polls and the like, which showed that many people believed that trade unions were 'too powerful' needs to be interpreted cautiously but cannot be discounted as an incentive to political action. Certainly moves to curb trade union power promised to pay electoral dividends, especially if they could be given some kind of explicit economic justification.

One of the curiosities of the increasing role of the state in industrial relations in the 1980s is that it was undertaken by Conservative administrations that adopted a general approach which came close to a *laissez-faire* ideology. In most areas that meant reducing the role of the state, yet in industrial relations the opposite seemed the case. Two points might be made about this. The first is that the justification for government action in industrial relations was, in part, to curb the power of bodies like trade unions that were portrayed as interfering with the operation of the free market – for example by introducing rigidities into the labour market by keeping wages high and therefore preventing individuals from accepting what the market was willing to pay for the job, and interfering with individual freedom. Government action, then, was designed to restore the primacy of the market and as such fit in perfectly with the *laissez-faire* ideology. Attempts to reduce the power of trade unions were not simply meant to restore a 'balance of power' that some commentators felt had been undermined in the 1960s (an argument put forward by some pluralists who nevertheless took the view that a strong trade union market was important for democracy). The attempts to reduce union power in the 1980s were based on a view that trade unions were really unacceptable bodies interfering with the efficient operation of the market. Maybe they could not be outlawed but their power could be reduced. The second point is that the government policy in some areas was explicitly designed to remove restrictions, such as those imposed by wages councils and those imposed on small employers. These restrictions were seen as unnecessary, inhibiting the market and inhibiting enterprise. Although they were a less highly publicised aspect of government policy they were an important influence on employment relationships and were a much more straightforward adoption of the general philosophy of the government.

SUMMARY

It has often been argued that prior to the 1960s Britain had a 'voluntary' system of industrial relations. If a 'voluntary' system means that the state plays no part at all in industrial relations then the British system has never been truly 'voluntary'. The state has always intervened to a limited extent, often with the support of both trade unions and employers: the factory acts and statutory wage regulations are good examples. However, prior to the 1960s, the British system of industrial relations, although not based on completely voluntary action, was based on only a minimum of state and legislative intervention. In most periods, for example, collective bargaining was not based on legislation, collective agreements were not thought to be legally binding and there was no system of compulsory arbitration.

In many ways the system of industrial relations that existed in Britain prior to the 1960s was unique. Certainly there were few countries in the world where the state intervened as little in industrial relations as in Britain. In Australia industrial relations were grounded on compulsory arbitration, in the USA the state defined bargaining agents and bargaining rights and could intervene to prohibit strikes, while in most European countries collective relations had a firm legislative base.

Hyman argues that the role of the state in industrial relations in any country can be linked to the economic and social philosophy dominant during the formative period of trade unions. However, while such an explanation has some merit it places too great an emphasis on one formative period and pays insufficient attention to later developments.

The role of the state in British industrial relations appeared to change in the 1960s. First, the state intervened more decisively in the area of wages and salaries, a move crystallised in the notion of 'incomes policy'. In some circumstances this led the state not only to determine directly the level of incomes to be gained but also to take legal action against people who refused to accept their decision. Second, and possibly more decisively, governments attempted to introduce the law more centrally into collective bargaining, conciliation and arbitration. The Industrial Relations Act of 1971 marked the start, but by no means the conclusion, of this policy.

Notes

1 INDUSTRIAL RELATIONS AS A FIELD OF STUDY

1   J. H. Richardson, *An Introduction to the Study of Industrial Relations* (Allen & Unwin, 1965), p. 13.
2   Most of the early economists and political scientists referred to aspects of industrial relations. For example, Marx linked the growth of trade unions to the development of industry and the increasing misery of the proletarians. There are also useful essays in the Social Science Association's *Report on Trade Societies and Strikes* published in 1860. See, G. S. Bain, H. A. Clegg, 'A Strategy for Industrial Relations Research in Great Britain,' *British Journal of Industrial Relations*, vol.XII, no. 1 (March 1974).
3   S. and B. Webb, *A History of Trade Unionism* (Longman, London, 1896).
4   S. and B. Webb, *Industrial Democracy* (Longman, London, 1902).
5   V. L. Allen, *The Sociology of Industrial Relations* (Longman, London, 1971), p. 28.
6   Bain and Clegg, *op. cit.*, p. 98.
7   *Ibid.*
8   Royal Commission on Trade Unions and Employers' Associations, 1965–68, *Report* (HMSO, London, 1968, Cmnd 3623).
9   H. A. Turner, 'The Royal Commission's Research Papers', *British Journal of Industrial Relations*, vol. VI, no. 3 (November 1968).
10 J. Bugler, 'The New Oxford Group', *New Society*, 15 February 1968, p. 221.
11 H. A. Clegg, *A New Approach to Industrial Democracy* (Blackwell, Oxford, 1960).
12 A. Flanders, *Industrial Relations – What's Wrong with the System* (Faber, London, 1965).
13 See Bain and Clegg, *op. cit.*
14 J. E. T. Dunlop, *Industrial Relations Systems* (Holt, New York, 1958), p. vi.
15 D. Fatchett, W. M. Whittingham, 'Trends and Developments in Industrial Relations Theory', *Industrial Relations Journal*, vol. 7, no. 1 (1976), pp. 50–60.
16 *Ibid.*, p. 50.

17 H. Slichter, J. J. Healy, E. R. Livernash, *The Impact of Collective Bargaining on Management* (Brookings Institute, Washington, 1960).
18 Dunlop, *op. cit.*
19 T. Parsons, N. J. Smelser, *Economy and Society: A Study in the Integration of Economic and Social Theory* (Routledge & Kegan Paul, London, 1956).
20 Dunlop, *op. cit.*, p. 7.
21 *Ibid.*, p. 9.
22 *Ibid.*, pp. 16–17.
23 *Ibid.*, p. 17.
24 A. Flanders, *op. cit.*
25 *Ibid.*
26 *Ibid.*, p. 4.
27 Dunlop, *op. cit.*, p. 92.
28 J. E. T. Eldridge, *Sociology and Industrial Life* (Nelson, London, 1971), p. 22, quoted on p. 92.
29 Quoted by G. S. Bain and H. A. Clegg, *op. cit.*, pp. 92–3.
30 *Ibid.*, p. 92.
31 *Ibid.*, p. 95.
32 See, for example, J. A. Banks, *Trade Unionism* (Collier Macmillan, London, 1974).
33 S. J. Wood, A. Wagner, E. G. A. Armstrong, J. F. B. Goodman, E. Davis, 'The "Industrial Relations System" Concept as a Basis for Theory in Industrial Relations', *British Journal of Industrial Relations*, vol. XIII, no. 3 (November 1975), pp. 291–308. See also S. J. Wood, 'Ideology in Industrial Relations Theory', *Industrial Relations Journal*, vol. 9, no. 4 (1978/9), pp. 42–56.
34 C. J. Margerison, 'What Do We Mean by Industrial Relations? A Behavioural Science Approach', *British Journal of Industrial Relations*, vol. VIII, no. 2 (July 1969), pp. 273–86.
35 See Banks, *op. cit.*
36 J. H. Goldthorpe, D. Lockwood, F. Bechhofer, J. Platt, *The Affluent Worker: Industrial Attitudes and Behaviour* (Cambridge University Press, London, 1968) p. 184.
37 D. Silverman, *The Theory of Organisations* (Heinemann, London, 1970), p. 141.
38 *Ibid.*, p. 141.
39 Goldthorpe *et al.*, *op. cit.*
40 *Ibid.*, pp. 177–8
41 See, A. M. Bowey, 'Themes in Industrial Sociology', *Industrial Relations Journal*, vol. 6, no. 2 (1975), pp. 57–63.
42 Silverman, *op. cit.*
43 Eldridge, *op. cit.*, pp. 44–5.
44 See Banks, *op. cit.*
45 A. Fox, *Industrial Sociology and Industrial Relations* Research Paper 3 (HMSO. London, 1966).
46 Quoted by S. Hill and K. Thurley, 'Sociology and Industrial Relations', *British Journal of Industrial Relations*, vol. XIII, no. 2 (1974), p. 149.
47 Quoted by Fox, *op. cit.*, p. 2.
48 *Ibid.*, p. 2.

49 *Ibid.*, p. 3.
50 A. Fox, 'Industrial Relations: A Social Critique of Pluralist Ideology', in J. Child (ed.), *The Business Enterprise in Modern Industrial Relations* (Collier Macmillan, London, 1969), p. 189.
51 M. Poole, R. Mansfield, P. Blyton, P. Frost, 'Managerial Attitudes and Behaviour in Industrial Relations: Evidence from a National Survey', *British Journal of Industrial Relations*, vol. xx, no. 3 (November 1982), p. 304.
52 Ministry of Labour, *Final Report of the Committee of Inquiry under Rt Hon. Lord Devlin into Certain Matters Concerning in the Port Transport Industry* (HMSO, London, 1965, Cmnd 2734), pp. 42–3.
53 See, for example, the work of Elton Mayo.
54 See D. C. Miller, W. H. Form, *Industrial Sociology* (Harper & Row, New York, 1963), p. 245.
55 H. S. Ross in E. M. Hugh-Jones (ed.), *Human Relations and Modern Management* (1958), quoted by Fox, *Industrial Sociology, op. cit.*
56 *Ibid.*
57 H. A. Clegg, 'Pluralism in Industrial Relations', *British Journal of Industrial Relations*, vol. XIII, no. 3 (November 1975), pp. 309–16.
58 Quoted by Fox in Child (ed.), *op. cit.*, p. 203.
59 Quoted by Fox in Child (ed.), *op. cit.*, p. 215.
60 Quoted by Eldridge in Child (ed.), *op. cit.*, p. 146.
61 *Ibid.*, p. 162.
62 A. W. Gouldner, *The Coming of Western Sociology* (Heinemann, London, 1971).
63 J. Rex, *Key Problems in Sociological Theory* (Routledge & Kegan Paul, London, 1961).
64 C. Wright Mills, *The Power Elite* (Oxford University Press, New York, 1959).
65 A. Fox, in J. Child (ed.) *Man and Organisation* (Allen & Unwin, London, 1973), p. 231.
66 A. Fox, *Beyond Contract* (Faber, London, 1974).
67 S. Wood, R. Elliott, 'A Critical Evaluation of Fox's Radicalisation of Industrial Relations Theory', *Sociology*, vol. II, no. 1 (1977) p. 109.
68 Clegg, 'Pluralism in Industrial Relations' *op cit*, p. 311.
69 *Ibid.*, p. 312.
70 R. Hyman, 'Pluralism, Procedural Consensus and Collective Bargaining', *British Journal of Industrial Relations*, vol. XVI, no. 1 (1978), pp. 16–40.
71 G. Schienstock, 'Towards a Theory of Industrial Relations', *British Journal of Industrial Relations*, vol. XIX, no. 2 (1981), pp. 180–1.
72 R. Hyman, *Industrial Relations: A Marxist Introduction* (Macmillan, London, 1975), p. 26.
73 *Ibid.*, p. 28.
74 K. F. Walker, 'Towards Useful Theorising about Industrial Relations', *British Journal of Industrial Relations*, vol. XV, no. 3 (November 1977), p. 311.
75 D. Bell, *The End of the Ideology* (Collier, New York, 1961).
76 C. Kerr, F. Harbison and H. Myers, *Industrialisation and Industrial Man* (Heinemann, London, 1962).

77 Hyman, *Industrial Relations*, *op. cit.*
78 H. Braverman, *Labor and Monopoly Capitalism* (Monthly Review Press, New York, 1974).
79 A. Fowler, 'When Chief Executives Discover HRM', *Personnel Management* (January 1987).
80 *Ibid.*, p. 3.
81 M. Armstrong, 'HRM: A Case of the Emperor's New Clothes', *Personnel Management* (August 1987).

2 THE ORIGINS, GROWTH, AND DEVELOPMENT OF TRADE UNIONS

1 S. and B. Webb, *History of Trade Unionism* (Longman, London, 1896).
2 *Idem, History of Trade Unions* (Longman, London, 1920).
3 *Ibid.*, p. 1.
4 *Ibid.*, p. 22.
5 *Ibid.*, p. 22.
6 *Ibid.*, p. 22.
7 *Ibid.*, p. 180.
8 *Ibid.*, p. 218.
9 A series of measures taken by unionists against non-unionists in the Sheffield cutlery trade which culminated in an explosion at the house of a worker who refused to join a union.
10 S. and B. Webb, *op. cit.* (1920), p. 474.
11 *Quinn* v *Leatham* (1901), AC 495 (HL): 22, 24, 249, 258–60, 267, 269.
12 *Taff Vale Railway Co.* v *Amalgamated Society of Railway Servants* (1901), AC 426 (HL): (1900) *The Times*, 31 August, 22, 214, 226, 227–31, 235, 248, 318, 319.
13 S. and B. Webb, *op. cit.* (1920), p. 603.
14 *Osborne* v *Amalgamated Society of Railway Servants* (1911), 1Ch., 540: (1911–13) All ER Rep, 102: 80 LJ (CH) 315: 104 LT 267: 27, TLR 289, CA: 45 Digest (Repl) 530, 1132.
15 S. and B. Webb, *op. cit.* (1920), p. 594.
16 F. Tannenbaum, *The True Society: A Philosophy of Labour* (Jonathan Cape, London, 1964).
17 Quoted by J. A. Banks, *Trade Unionism* (Collier Macmillan, London, 1974), p. 3.
18 L. Brentano, *On the History and Development of Guilds and the Origins of Trade Unions* (Treubener, London, 1870).
19 G. Howell, *The Conflicts of Capital and Labour* (Chatto & Windus, London, 1878).
20 Banks, *op. cit.*, p. 4.
21 *Ibid.*, p. 4.
22 H. Pelling, *A History of British Trade Unionism* (Penguin, Harmondsworth, 1971).
23 A. E. Musson, *British Trade Unions 1800–1875* (Macmillan, London, 1972).
24 V. L. Allen, *The Sociology of Industrial Relations* (Longman, London, 1971).
25 *Ibid.*, p. 32.

26 *Ibid.*, p. 29.
27 See M. P. Jackson, *The Price of Coal* (Croom Helm, London, 1974).
28 Operating mainly in the Nottinghamshire coalfields, although later spreading to other areas. See *Ibid.* for details.
29 *Reports of the Committee on the Relations between Employers and the Employed* (HMSO, London, 1916–18, Cd 8606, Cd 9001, Cd 9002, Cd 9099, Cd 9153).
30 An alliance of the coal mining, railway, and transport unions.
31 See G. S. Bain, R. Price, 'Who is a White Collar Employee?', *British Journal of Industrial Relations*, vol. x, no. 3 (1972), pp. 325–39.
32 R. Lumley, *White Collar Unionism in Britain* (Methuen, London, 1973).
33 R. M. Blackburn, *Union Character and Social Class: A Study of White Collar Unionism* (Batsford, London, 1967).
34 See S. Lerner, *Breakaway Unions and the Small Trade Union* (Allen & Unwin, London, 1961).
35 See many industrial relations textbooks, for example, J. H. Richardson, *An Introduction to the Study of Industrial Relations* (Allen & Unwin, London, 1965).
36 H. A. Turner, *Trade Union Growth, Structure and Policy* (Allen & Unwin, London, 1965).
37 *Ibid.*
38 Trades Union Congress, Annual Report for 1966, p. 387.
39 See R. Buchanan, 'Mergers in British Trade Unions, 1949–79' for a full discussion, *Industrial Relations Journal* (May/June 1981), vol. 12, no. 3, pp. 40–50.
40 J. Hughes, *Trade Union Structure and Government*, Part 1, Research Paper 5 (Royal Commission on Trade Unions and Employers' Associations, HMSO, London, 1967).
41 R. Hyman, *Industrial Relations: A Marxist Introduction* (Macmillan, London, 1975).
42 *Ibid.*, p. 58.
43 *Ibid.*, p. 59.
44 *Ibid.*, pp. 59–60.
45 *Ibid.*, p. 41.
46 Allen, *op. cit.*, p. 143.
47 E. V. Schneider, *Industrial Sociology* (McGraw-Hill, London, 1971).
48 Campbell Balfour, *Industrial Relations in the Common Market* (Routledge & Kegan Paul, London, 1972).
49 *Kodaisha Encyclopedia of Japan* (Kodamamsha, Tokyo, 1983), p. 345.
50 For further details of union membership, see Y. Kuwahara, 'Japanese Industrial Relations', in G. Bamber, R. D. Lansbury (eds), *International and Comparative Industrial Relations* (Allen & Unwin, London, 1987).
51 *Ibid.*
52 B. M. Richardson, T. Keda (eds), *Business and Society in Japan* (Praeger, New York, 1981), p. 41.
53 There is evidence that this term was directly 'imported' from Britain.
54 R. A. Gollan, 'The Historical Perspective', in P. W. D. Matthews, G. W. Ford (eds), *Australian Trade Unions* (Sun Books, Melbourne, 1968).
55 Allen, *op. cit.*

56 Reported in C. Leggett, 'Industrial Relations and Enterprise Unionism in Singapore', *Labour and Industry*, vol. 1, no. 2 (June 1988), pp. 242–57.
57 J. England, J. Rear, *Industrial Relations and Law in Hong Kong* (Oxford University Press, Oxford, 1981).
58 Tannenbaum, *op. cit.*
59 Quoted by Banks, *op. cit.*, p. 51.
60 N. J. Smelser, *Social Change in the Industrial Revolution* (Routledge & Kegan Paul, London, 1959).
61 D. Lockwood, *The Black-coated Worker* (Allen & Unwin, London, 1958).
62 R. Price, G. S. Bain, 'Union Growth Revisited: 1948–1974 in Perspective', *British Journal of Industrial Relations*, vol. xiv, no. 3 (1976), pp. 339–55.
63 V. L. Allen, 'Trade Unions: An Analytical Framework', in B. Barrett *et al.* (eds), *Industrial Relations in the Wider Society* (Collier Macmillan, London, 1975).
64 *Ibid.*, p. 61.
65 Quoted by H. B. Davis, 'The Theory of Union Growth', in W. E. J. McCarthy (ed.), *Trade Unions* (Penguin, Harmondsworth, 1972), p. 214.
66 *Ibid.*
67 G. S. Bain, F. E. Elsheikh, *Union Growth and the Business Cycle: An Econometric Analysis* (Blackwell, Oxford, 1976).
68 Lockwood, *op. cit.*
69 R. Loveridge, 'Occupational Change and the Development of Interest Groups Among White Collar Workers in the UK: A Long Term Model', *British Journal of Industrial Relations*, vol. x, no. 3 (1972), pp. 340–65.
70 Banks, *op. cit.*, p. 54.
71 *Ibid.*, p. 54.
72 *Ibid.*, p. 55.

3 TRADE UNIONS: AN UNCERTAIN OUTLOOK

1 N. Millward, M. Stevens, *British Workplace Industrial Relations, 1980–1984*, (Gower, Aldershot, 1986).
2 E. Batstone, *Working Order* (Blackwell, Oxford, 1984).
3 S. Connock, 'Workforce Flexibility: Juggling Time and Task', *Personnel Management* (October 1985), p. 36.
4 E. Batstone, S. Gourlay, *Unions, Unemployment and Innovation* (Blackwell, Oxford, 1986).
5 P. B. Beaumont, *The Decline of Trade Union Organisation* (Croom Helm, Beckenham, 1987), p. 18.
6 *Ibid.*, p. 144.
7 Millward and Stevens, *op. cit.*, pp. 302–3.
8 B. Groom, D. Martin, 'The Greenfield Route to New Working Practices', *Financial Times*, 9 January, 1983.
9 *British Journal of Industrial Relations*, vol. xxii, no. 3 (November 1985), p. 452.
10 1984 TUC Report, p. 448.

11 *Ibid.*, p. 441.
12 J. Atkinson, 'Manpower Strategies for Flexible Organisations', *Personnel Management* (August 1984), pp. 28–31.
13 1984 TUC Report, p. 431.
14 *Ibid.*, pp. 439–40.
15 *Ibid.*, p. 578.
16 *Ibid.*, p. 578.
17 1985 TUC Report, p. 21.
18 Quoted by P. Bassett, *Strike Free: New Industrial Relations in Britain* (Macmillan, Basingstoke, 1984), p. 54.
19 R. E. Cole, 'Labor in Japan', in B. M. Richardson, T. Keda (eds), *Business and Society in Japan* (Praeger, New York, 1981), p. 35.
20 Y. Kuwahara, 'Japanese Industrial Relations', in G. Bamber, R. D. Lansbury (eds), *International and Comparative Industrial Relations* (Allen & Unwin, London, 1987), p. 215.
21 C. Leggett, 'Industrial Relations and Enterprise Unionism in Singapore', *Labour and Industry*, vol. 1, no. 2 (June 1988), p. 248.
22 A. A. Blum, S. Patarapanich, 'Productivity and the Path to House Unionism: Structural Change in the Singapore Labour Movement', *British Journal of Industrial Relations*, vol. 25, no. 3 (November 1987), pp. 399–400.
23 L. O'Brien, 'Between Capital and Labour: Trade Unionism in Malaysia', in T. M. Shaw, *Labour and Unions in Asia and Africa* (Macmillan, Basingstoke, 1988).
24 M. Gunderson, N. H. Meltz, 'Canadian Unions Achieve Strong Gains in Membership', *Monthly Labor Review* (April 1986), p. 49.
25 Court cases involving Radio Shack and Securicor.
26 S. Lash, J. Urry, *The End of Organised Capitalism* (Polity Press, Oxford, 1987).
27 Quoted *ibid.*, p. 3.
28 *Ibid.*, p. 5.
29 *Ibid.*, p. 269.
30 *Ibid.*, p. 272.
31 *Ibid.*, p. 274.
32 *Ibid.*, pp. 282–3.
33 Muller-Jentsch, 'Labour Conflicts and Class Struggles', in O. Jacobi *et al.* (eds), *Technological Change, Rationalisation and Industrial Relations* (Croom Helm, London, 1986).
34 A. Touraine, 'Unionism as a Social Movement', in S. Lipset (ed.), *Unions in Transition* (Institute for Contemporary Studies, San Francisco, 1986).
35 J. Kelly, *Trade Unions and Socialist Politics* (Verso, London, 1988).
36 *Ibid.*, pp. 284–5.
37 *Ibid.*, p. 285.

4 TRADE UNIONS: AIMS, OBJECTIVES, AND GOVERNMENT

1 Trade Union Act 1913 1(2) and 2(1).
2 S. and B. Webb, *History of Trade Unions* (Longman, London, 1920), p. 1.

3   T. Smith, 'Trade Union Education: its Past and Future', *Industrial Relations Journal*, vol. 15, no. 2 (summer 1984), pp. 72–90.

4   National Union of Mineworkers, *Rules, 1962* (as amended to 1969), quoted by N. Robertson and K. I. Sams, *British Trade Unionism: Selected Documents* (Blackwell, Oxford, 1972), vol. 1, p. 49.

5   Transport and General Workers' Union, *Members' Handbook, 1966*, quoted in *ibid.*, p. 51.

6   Amalgamated Society of Woodworkers, *Rules, 1964*, quoted in *ibid.*, p. 44.

7   H. A. Clegg, A. H. Killick, R. Adams, *Trade Union Officers* (Blackwell, Oxford, 1961).

8   J. H. Goldthorpe, D. Lockwood, F. Bechhofer, J. Platt, *The Affluent Worker: Industrial Attitudes and Behaviour* (Cambridge University Press, London, 1968), p. 113.

9   H. Pelling, *A History of British Trade Unionism* (Penguin, Harmondsworth, 1971).

10   See M. P. Jackson, *The Price of Coal* (Croom Helm, London, 1974), for wider discussion.

11   M. Poole, *Industrial Relations: Origins and Patterns of National Diversity* (Routledge & Kegan Paul, London, 1986).

12   H. A. Clegg, *Trade Unionism Under Collective Bargaining* (Blackwell, Oxford, 1976).

13   J. A. Banks, *Trade Unionism* (Collier Macmillan, London, 1974), p. 73.

14   Poole, *op. cit.*, pp. 89–90.

15   J. L. Porket, 'Industrial Relations and Participation in Management in the Soviet-type Communist system', *British Journal of Industrial Relations*, vol. VI (1978), pp. 70–85.

16   B. A. Ruble, *Soviet Trade Unions* (Cambridge University Press, London, 1981).

17   N. Millward, M. Stevens, *British Workplace Industrial Relations, 1980–1984* (Gower, Aldershot, 1986).

18   J. Goodman, 'The Role of the Shop Steward', in S. Kessler, B. Weekes (eds), *Conflict at Work* (BBC, London, 1971), p. 62.

19   *Ibid.*, p. 83.

20   D. C. Miller, W. H. Form, *Industrial Sociology* (Harper & Row, New York, 1963).

21   N. F. Dufty, 'A Typology of Shop Stewards', *Industrial Relations Journal*, vol. 12 (July/August 1981), pp. 65–70.

22   E. Batstone, I. Boraston, S. Frenkel, *Shop Stewards in Action* (Blackwell, Oxford, 1977).

23   M. Marchington, R. Armstrong, 'Typologies of Shop Stewards: A Reconsideration', *Industrial Relations Journal*, vol. 14, no. 3 (autumn 1983), pp. 34–48.

24   T. Schuller, D. Robertson, 'How Representatives Allocate Their Time: Shop Steward Activity and Membership Contact', *British Journal of Industrial Relations*, vol. XXXI, no. 3 (November 1983), pp. 330–42.

25   W. A. Brown (ed.), *The Changing Contours of British Industrial Relations: A Survey of Manufacturing Industry* (Blackwell, Oxford, 1981).

26 D. Watson, *Managers of Discontent* (Routledge & Kegan Paul, London, 1988), p. 21.
27 W. A. Brown, M. Lawson, 'The Training of Trade Union Officers', *British Journal of Industrial Relations*, vol. 11, no. 3 (1973).
28 Watson, *op. cit.*, p. 26.
29 *Ibid.*, p. 181.
30 *Ibid.*, p. 182.
31 G. J. Bamber, R. D. Lansbury, *International Comparative Industrial Relations* (Allen & Unwin, London, 1987), p. 156.
32 W. Albeda, 'Changing Industrial Relations in the Netherlands', *Industrial Relations*, vol. 16, no. 2 (1977), p. 137.
33 *Ibid.*, p. 137.
34 W. Korpi, 'Workplace Bargaining, the Law and Unofficial Strikes: The Case of Sweden', *British Journal of Industrial Relations*, vol. XVI, no. 3, (1978), pp. 355–68.
35 Watson, *op. cit.*, p. 189.
36 E. Stein, 'The Dilemma of Union Democracy', in J. M. Shepheard (ed.), *Organisational Issues in Industrial Society* (Prentice-Hall, Englewood Cliffs, NJ (1972).
37 R. Michels, *Political Parties* (Dover, New, York, 1959).
38 *Ibid.*, p. 16.
39 *Ibid.*, p. 16.
40 *Ibid.*, p. 17.
41 S. M. Lipset, M. A. Trow, S. Coleman, *Union Democracy, The Internal Policies of the International Typographical Union* (Free Press, Glencoe, 1956).
42 R. Martin, 'Union Democracy: An Explanatory Framework', *Sociology*, vol. 2 (1968), pp. 205–20.
43 J. Goldstein, *The Government of British Unions* (Allen & Unwin, London, 1952).
44 Goldthorpe *et al.*, *op. cit.*
45 W. W. Daniel, N. Millward, *Workplace Industrial Relations in Britain* (Heinemann, London, 1983).
46 H. A. Clegg, *The System of Industrial Relations in Great Britain* (Blackwell, Oxford, 1970), pp. 90–1.
47 P. W. D. Matthews, 'Trade Union Organisation', in Matthews, P. W. D., Ford, G. W. (eds), *Australian Trade Unions* (Sun Books, Melbourne, 1968) pp. 83–4.
48 R. Blanpain, 'Recent Trends in Collective Bargaining in Belgium', *International Labour Review*, vol. 104 (1971), p. 129.
49 G. Guigni, 'Recent Trends in Collective Bargaining in Italy', *International Labour Review*, vol. 104 (1971), p. 319.
50 Commission on Industrial Relations, *Worker Participation and Collective Bargaining in Europe* (HMSO, London, 1974), p. 98.
51 R. Hyman, *Industrial Relations: A Marxist Introduction* (Macmillan, London, 1975).
52 *Ibid.*, p. 73n.
53 H. A. Turner, *Trade Union Growth, Structure and Policy* (Allen & Unwin, London, 1962).
54 J. Hughes, *Trade Union Structure and Government*, Part 1, Research

Paper 5 (Royal Commission on Trade Unions and Employers' Associations, HMSO, London, 1967), p. 35.
55 Banks, *op. cit.*, p. 92.
56 *Ibid.*, p. 90.
57 Clegg, *The System of Industrial Relations*, *op. cit.*
58 W. E. J. McCarthy, S. R. Parker, *Shop Stewards and Workshop Relations* (HMSO, London, 1968).
59 G. Cyriax, R. Oakshott, *The Bargainers: A Survey of Modern British Trade Unionism* (Faber, London, 1960).
60 Banks, *op. cit.*
61 Hyman, *op. cit.*
62 Banks, *op. cit.*, p. 93.
63 *Ibid.*, p. 93.
64 V. L. Allen, *Trade Union Leadership* (Longman, London, 1957).
65 J. Hughes, *op. cit.*
66 Lipset *et al.*, *op. cit.*

5 THE INDUSTRIAL ENTERPRISE, MANAGEMENT AND EMPLOYERS' ASSOCIATIONS

1 H. A. Clegg, *The System of Industrial Relations in Great Britain* (Blackwell, Oxford, 1970), p. 158.
2 J. Child (ed.), *The Business Enterprise in Modern Industrial Society* (Collier Macmillan, London, 1969).
3 See Census of Production for 1963 and 1981.
4 S. E. Boyle, *Industrial Organisation* (Holt, Rinehart & Winston, New York, 1972).
5 Child, *op. cit.*
6 T. Ozawa, *Multinationalism, Japanese Style: The Political Economy of Outward Dependency* (Princeton University Press, Princeton, NJ, 1979).
7 M. and C. Norgren, *Industrial Sweden* (Swedish Institute, Stockholm, 1971), p. 55.
8 Quoted by G. Bone, '*The Structure of Industry*', British Economic Survey, vol. 5, no. 1 (Autumn 1975), p. 5.
9 Quoted *ibid.*, p. 5.
10 Quoted *ibid.*, pp. 5–6.
11 F. L. Pryor, 'An International Comparison of Concentration Ratios', *Review of Economics and Statistics*, vol. 54 (1972).
12 R. W. Revans, and 'Industrial Morale and Size of Unit', in W. Galenson and S. M. Lipset (eds), *Labour and Trade Unionism* (Wiley, New York, 1960), pp. 259–300.
13 Action Society Trust, *Size and Morale* (Action Society Trust, London 1953, 1957).
14 S. Talacchi, 'Organisational Size, Individual Attitudes and Behaviour: An Empirical Study', *Administrative Science Quarterly*, vol. 5 (1960), pp. 398–420.
15 G. K. Ingham, *Size of Industrial Organisation and Worker Behaviour* (Cambridge University Press, London, 1970).

16 S. J. Prais, 'The Strike-Proneness of Large Plants in Britain', *Journal of Royal Statistical Society, Series A (General)*, vol. 141, part 3 (1978), pp. 368–84.
17 P. K. Edwards, 'Size of Plant and Strike Proneness', *Oxford Bulletin of Economics and Statistics*, vol. 42 (May 1980), pp. 145–56.
18 P. M. Marginson, 'The Distinctive Effects on Plant and Company Size on Workplace Industrial Relations', *British Journal of Industrial Relations*, vol. XXII (March 1984), pp. 1–14.
19 A. I. Marsh, E. O. Evans, P. Garcia, *Workplace Industrial Relations in Engineering* (Kogan Page, London, 1971).
20 W. A. Brown, R. Ebsworth, M. Terry, 'Factors Shaping Shop Steward Organisation in Britain', *British Journal of Industrial Relations*, vol. XVI, no. 2 (1978), pp. 139–59.
21 N. Millward, M. Stevens, *British Workplace Industrial Relations, 1980–1984* (Gower, Aldershot, 1986).
22 A. L. Rainnic, *Industrial Relations in Small Firms* (Routledge, London, 1989).
23 *Ibid.*, p. 153.
24 N. J. Chalmers, *Industrial Relations in Japan* (Routledge, London, 1989).
25 *Ibid.*, p. 232.
26 Bone, *op. cit.*, p. 7.
27 G. K. Wilson, *Business and Politics: A Comparative Introduction*, (Macmillan, London, 1985), p. 115.
28 J. H. Dunning, 'Changes in the Level and Structure of International Production: The Last One Hundred Years' in M. Casson (ed.), *The Growth of International Business* (Allen & Unwin, London, 1983).
29 P. Hertner, G. Jones (eds), *Multinationals: Theory and History*, (Gower, Aldershot, 1986).
30 S. Hymer, 'The Efficiency (Contradictions) of Multi-national Corporations', *American Economic Review*, vol. LX, no. 2 (1970), pp. 441–8.
31 Wilson, *op. cit.*
32 See, R. E. Caves, 'International Corporation: The Industrial Economics of Foreign Inventions', *Economica*, vol. 38, no. 149, pp. 1–27; and R. E. Caves, *Multinational Enterprises and Economic Analysis* (Cambridge University Press, Cambridge, 1982).
33 E. Schoenberger, 'Multinational Corporations and the New International Division of Labour: A Critical Appraisal', in S. Wood (ed.), *The Transformation of Work* (Unwin Hyman, London, 1989), p. 95.
34 Dunning, *op. cit.*
35 Wilson, *op. cit.*, p. 115.
36 R. Bean, *Comparative Industrial Relations* (Croom Helm, London, 1985).
37 *Ibid.*, p. 184.
38 T. Servan-Schreiber, *The American Challenge* (Atheneum, New York, 1968).
39 C. J. McMillan, 'Corporations without Citizenship: The Emergence of the Multinational Enterprise', in G. Salaman, K. Thompson (eds), *People and Organisations* (Longman, London, 1973), p. 40.

40   *Op. cit.*, p. 8.
41   B. C. Roberts, 'Multinational Collective Bargaining: A European Prospect', in B. Barrett, E. Rhodes, J. Beishon (eds), *Industrial Relations and the Wider Society* (Collier Macmillan, London, 1975), p. 209.
42   Hymer, *op. cit.*
43   H. G. Perlmutter, 'Super Giant Firms in the Future', *Wharton Quarterly* (1986), pp. 40–6.
44   B. C. Roberts, J. May, 'The Response of Multinational Enterprises to International Trade Union Pressure', *British Journal of Industrial Relations*, vol. XII (1974); J. Hamill, 'Labour Relations Decision Making Within Multinational Corporations', *Industrial Relations Journal*, vol. 15 (1984); G. Hedlund, 'Autonomy of Subsidiaries and Formalisation of Headquarters – Subsidiary Relationships in Swedish MNCs', in L. Offerbeck (ed.), *The Management of Headquarters Subsidiary Relationships in Multinational Corporations* (Gower, London, 1981).
45   N. Oliver, B. Wilkinson, 'Japanese Manufacturing Technics and Industrial Relations Practice in Britain: Evidence and Implications', *British Journal of Industrial Relations*, vol. XXXII, no. 1 (March 1989), pp. 73–91.
46   P. A. Miscimarra, 'The Entertainment Industry: In Codes in Multinational Collective Bargaining', *British Journal of Industrial Relations*, vol. XIX, no. 1 (March 1981), pp. 49–65.
47   P. Enderwick, P. J. Buckley, 'Strike Activity and Foreign Ownership: An Analysis of British Manufacturing 1971–73', *British Journal of Industrial Relations*, vol. XX (1982).
48   J. Rajot, 'The 1984 Revision of the OECD Guidelines for Multinational Enterprises', *British Journal of Industrial Relations*, vol. XXIII, no. 3 (November 1985), pp. 379–97.
49   A. A. Berle, G. C. Means, *The Modern Corporation and Private Property* (Macmillan, New York, 1932).
50   *Ibid.*, p. 84.
51   A. Crosland, *The Future of Socialism* (Jonathan Cape, London, 1956), p. 34.
52   J. Burnham, *The Managerial Revolution* (Day, New York, 1941).
53   R. M. Cyert, J. C. March, *A Behavioural Theory of the Firm* (Prentice-Hall, Englewood Cliffs, NJ, 1963).
54   R. A. Marris, *The Economic Theory of 'Managerial Capitalism'*, (Macmillan, London, 1964).
55   Child, *op. cit.*, p. 51.
56   A. Francis, 'Families, Firms and Finance Capital', *Sociology*, vol. 14, no. 1 (February 1980), pp. 1–28.
57   S. Florence, *The Logic of British and American Industry* (Routledge & Kegan Paul, London, 1961).
58   J. Scott, M. Hughes, 'Capital and Communication in Scottish Business', *Sociology*, vol. 14, no. 1 (February 1980), pp. 29–48.
59   Child, *op. cit.*, p. 51.
60   M. Dalton, *Men Who Manage* (Wiley, New York, 1966).
61   D. G. Clark, *The Industrial Manager – His Background and Career Pattern* (Business Publications, London, 1966).

62 D. Hall, H.-Cl. de Bettignies, G. Amada-Fishgrund, 'The European Business Elite', *European Business* (October, 1969).
63 R. L. Dubin, 'Management in Britain – Impressions of a Visiting Professor', *Journal of Management Studies*, vol. VII, no. 2 (1970), p. 186.
64 J. Deeks, 'Educational and Occupational Histories of Owner-Managers and Managers', *Journal of Management Studies*, vol. 9, no. 2 (1972), pp. 127–49.
65 Hall *et al.*, *op. cit.*
66 G. Crockett, P. Elias, 'British Managers: A Study of Their Education, Training, Mobility and Earnings', *British Journal of Industrial Relations*, vol. XXII (March 1984), pp. 34–46.
67 R. Constable, R. J. McCormick, *The Making of British Managers: A Report for the BIM and CBI into Management Training, Education and Development* (BIM, London, 1987).
68 C. B. Handy, *Making Managers* (Pitman, London, 1988).
69 S. R. Parker, R. K. Brown, J. Child, M. A. Smith, *The Sociology of Industry* (Allen & Unwin, London, 1972).
70 Royal Commission on Trade Unions and Employers' Associations, 1965–68, *Report* (HMSO, London, 1968, Cmnd 3623).
71 V. G. Munns, W. E. J. McCarthy, *Employers' Associations*, Research Paper 7 (HMSO, London, 1967).
72 Millward and Stevens, *op. cit.*
73 K. Sisson (ed.), *Personnel Management in Britain* (Blackwell, Oxford, 1989), p. 36.
74 S. Tyson, A. Fell, *Evaluating the Personnel Function* (Hutchinson, London, 1986).
75 Sisson, *op. cit.*
76 See J. J. Oechslin, 'The Role of Employers' Organisations in France', *International Labour Review*, vol. 106, no. 5 (1972), pp. 391–414.
77 Clegg, *op. cit.*
78 Oechslin, *op. cit.*
79 Quoted by Clegg, *op. cit.*, p. 121.
80 E. Wigham, *The Power to Manage: A History of the Engineering Employers' Federation* (Macmillan, London, 1973).
81 Royal Commission on Trade Unions, *op. cit.*, pp. 20–1.
82 N. W. Chamberlain, J. W. Kuhn, *Collective Bargaining* (McGraw-Hill, New York, 1965).
83 J. E. Isaac, G. W. Ford (eds), *Australian Labour Relations: Readings* (Sun Books, Melbourne, 1966).
84 Munns and McCarthy, *op. cit.*
85 Commission on Industrial Relations, *Employers' Organisations and Industrial Relations* (HMSO, London, 1972).
86 W. A. Brown, (ed.), *The Changing Contours of British Industrial Relations: A Survey of Manufacturing Industry* (Blackwell, Oxford, 1981).
87 Millward and Stevens, *op. cit.*
88 See for example, Sisson, *op. cit.*
89 J. E. T. Dunlop, *Industrial Relations Systems* (Holt, New York, 1958).
90 P. Jackson, K Sissons, 'Employers' Confederations in Sweden and the

UK and the Significance of Industrial Infrastructure', *British Journal of Industrial Relations*, vol. XIV, no. 3 (1976), pp. 306–23.
91 K. Sisson, 'Employers' Organisations', in G. S. Bain (ed.), *Industrial Relations in Britain* (Blackwell, Oxford, 1983), pp. 121–34.
92 K. Sisson, *The Management of Collective Bargaining* (Blackwell, Oxford, 1987).
93 *Ibid.*
94 T. L. Johnston, *Collective Bargaining in Sweden* (Allen & Unwin, London, 1962), p. 91.
95 E. F. Beal, E. D. Wickersham, *The Practice of Collective Bargaining* (Irwin, Homewood, Illinois, 1967).
96 B. M. Selekman, S. H. Fuller, T. Kennedy, J. M. Bartsell, *Problems in Labor Relations* (McGraw-Hill, New York, 1964), p. 693.
97 See Munns and McCarthy, *op. cit.*
98 K. Sisson, *op. cit.*, p. 189.
99 C. Gill, R. Morris, J Eaton, 'Employers' Organisations in the U.K. Chemical Industry', *Industrial Relations Journal*, vol. 9, no. 1 (1978), pp. 37–47.
100 Clegg, *op. cit.*, p. 121.
101 Issac and Ford, *op. cit.*, p. 247.

6 COLLECTIVE BARGAINING: AN INTRODUCTION

1 S. and B. Webb, *Industrial Democracy* (Longman, London, 1902).
2 A. Flanders, 'Collective Bargaining: A Theoretical Analysis', *British Journal of Industrial Relations*, vol. VI, No. 1 (1968), pp. 1–26.
3 *Ibid.*, p. 3.
4 N. W. Chamberlain, J. W. Kuhn, *Collective Bargaining* (McGraw-Hill, New York, 1965).
5 Flanders, *op. cit.*, pp. 18–19.
6 *Ibid.*, p. 22.
7 A. Fox, 'Collective Bargaining, Flanders and the Webbs', *British Journal of Industrial Relations*, vol. XIII, no. 2 (1975), pp. 151–74.
8 *Ibid.*, p. 153.
9 *Ibid.*, p. 156.
10 *Ibid.*, p. 156.
11 *Ibid.*, p. 158.
12 *Ibid.*, p. 170.
13 See, for example, E. H. Phelps Brown, *The Growth of British Industrial Relations* (Macmillan, London, 1959).
14 C. R. Littler, 'Internal Contract and the Transition to Modern Work Systems: Britain and Japan', in D. Dunkerley, G. Salamon, *International Yearbook of Organisation Studies* (Routledge & Kegan Paul, London, 1980).
15 See A. Flanders, 'Collective Bargaining', in A. Flanders, H. A. Clegg, *The System of Industrial Relations in Great Britain* (Blackwell, Oxford, 1954), pp. 252–322.
16 Quoted by Flanders, *ibid.*, p. 261.
17 H. A. Clegg, *Trade Unionism Under Collective Bargaining: A Theory*

Based on Comparison of Three Countries (Blackwell, Oxford, 1976), p. 203.

18 *Ibid.*, p. 203.
19 Committee on the Relations between Employers and Employed, *Reports* (HMSO, London, 1916–18, Cd 8606, 9001, 9002, 9099, 9153).
20 See M. P. Jackson, *The Price of Coal* (Croom Helm, London, 1974).
21 Clegg, *op. cit.*
22 Royal Commission on Trade Unions and Employers' Associations, 1965–68, *Report* (HMSO, London, 1968, Cmnd 3623).
23 Confederation of British Industries, *The Future of Pay Determination* (CBI, London, 1977).
24 N. Millward, M. Stevens, *British Workplace Industrial Relations, 1980–1984* (Gower, Aldershot, 1986).
25 Confederation of British Industries, *The Structure and Processes of Pay Determination in the Private Sector: 1979–1986* (CBI, London, 1988).
26 *Ibid.*, p. 33.
27 See E. F. Beal, E. D. Wickersham, *The Practice of Collective Bargaining* (Irvin, Homewood, Illinois, 1967).
28 *Ibid.*
29 See *ibid.*
30 A. R. Weber, 'Stability and Change in the Structure of Collective Bargaining', in the American Assembly, *Challenges to Collective Bargaining* (Prentice-Hall, Englewood Cliffs, NJ, 1967), pp. 13–36.
31 Chamberlain and Kuhn, *op. cit.*
32 Inflation resulted in a reluctance on the part of unions to negotiate fixed-term contracts. See D. H. Freedman, 'Inflation in the United States, 1959–74; Its Impact on Employment, Incomes and Industrial Relations', *International Labour Review*, vol. 112 (1975), pp. 125–47.
33 See *Social Trends*.
34 See Chamberlain and Kuhn, *op. cit.*
35 Commission on Industrial Relations, *Worker Participation and Collective Bargaining in Europe* (HMSO, London, 1974), p. 41.
36 *Ibid.*, p. 106.
37 *Ibid.*, p. 98.
38 *Ibid.*, p. 130.
39 See Commission on Industrial Relations, *ibid.*, for details of nomination procedure in West Germany where works councils can be seen as an alternative to the trade union at the workplace.
40 See T. L. Johnston, *Collective Bargaining in Sweden* (Allen & Unwin, London, 1962).
41 See E. C. Brown, *Soviet Trade Unions and Labour Relations* (Harvard University Press, Cambridge, Mass., 1966); B. Ruble, *Soviet Trade Unions* (Cambridge University Press, London, 1981).
42 J. E. Isaac, G. W. Ford (eds), *Australian Labour Relations: Readings* (Sun Books, Melbourne, 1966).
43 *Ibid.*, p. 267.
44 R. Blanpain, 'Recent Trends in Collective Bargaining in Belgium', *International Labour Review*, vol. 104 (July/August 1971), p. 111.
45 Beal and Wickersham, *op. cit.*

46   See A. M. Ross, P. T. Hartman, 'Changing Patterms of Industrial Conflict', in G. G. Sommers (ed.), *Proceedings of the 12th Annual Meeting of the Industrial Relations Research Association*, 1959.
47   J. W. Kuhn, *Bargaining in Grievance Settlement* (Columbia University Press, New York, 1961).
48   Isaac and Ford, *op. cit.*
49   *Ibid.*, pp. 267–8.
50   *Ibid.*, p. 268.
51   H. G. Lewis, *Unionism and Relative Wages in the United States* (Chicago University Press, Chicago, 1965).
52   J. H. Pencavel, 'The Distribution and Efficiency Effects of Trade Unions in Britain', *British Journal of Industrial Relations*, vol. xv, no. 2 (1977), pp. 137–56.
53   D. Blanchflower, 'Union Relative Wage Effects: A Cross Section Analysis Using Establishment Data', *British Journal of Industrial Relations*, vol. xxii, no. 3 (November 1984), pp. 311–32.
54   E. H. Phelps Brown, 'The Long-term Movement of Real Wages', in J. T. Dunlop (ed.), *The Theory of Wage Determination* (Macmillan, London, 1957).
55   For a fuller discussion see J. T. Addison, A. H. Barnett, 'The Impact of Unions on Productivity', *British Journal of Industrial Relations*, vol. xx, no. 2 (July 1982), pp. 145–62.
56   See for example Phelps Brown, *op. cit.*
57   P. Taft, P. Ross, 'American Labor Violence: Its Causes, Character and Outcome', in H. D. Graham, T. R. Gurr (eds), *Violence in America* (Bantam, New York, 1969).
58   R. Dubin, 'Constructive Aspects of Industrial Conflict', in A. Kornhauser, R. Dubin, A. M. Ross (eds), *Industrial Conflict* (McGraw-Hill, New York, 1954), p. 46.
59   C. Kerr, 'Industrial Conflict and its Mediation', *American Journal of Sociology*, vol. lx (1954), pp. 230–45.
60   Dubin, *op. cit*, p. 45.
61   F. H. Harbison, 'Collective Bargaining and American Capitalism', in Kornhauser *et al.*, *op. cit*, pp. 270–9.
62   R. Dahrendorf, *Class and Class Conflict in Industrial Society* (Routledge & Kegan Paul, London, 1959), p. 260.
63   J. E. T. Eldridge, 'Industrial Conflict: Some Problems of Theory and Method', in J. Child (ed.), *Man and Organisation* (Allen & Unwin, London, 1973), p. 169.

7   MAJOR DEVELOPMENTS IN COLLECTIVE BARGAINING

1   See, for example, K. Hawkins, *Conflict and Change: Aspects of Industrial Relations* (Holt, Rinehart & Winston, London, 1972).
2   A. Flanders, *Collective Bargaining* (Faber & Faber, London, 1967).
3   *Ibid.*, p. 28.
4   *Ibid.*, p. 28.
5   *Ibid.*, p. 30.
6   *Ibid.*, p. 31.

7 W. E. J. McCarthy, *The Role of Shop Stewards in British Industrial Relations* (HMSO, London, 1966).

8 B. C. Roberts, *Trade Union Government and Administration in Great Britain* (Bell, London, 1956).

9 *Ibid.*, p. 26.

10 *Ibid.*, p. 26.

11 W. E. J. McCarthy, S. R. Parker, *Shop Stewards and Workshop Relations* (HMSO, London, 1968).

12 *Ibid.*, p. 23.

13 *Ibid.*, pp. 23–4.

14 Royal Commission on Trade Unions and Employers' Associations, *Report 1965–8* (HMSO, London, 1968, Cmnd 3623), p. 12.

15 *Ibid.*, p. 36.

16 Commission on Industrial Relations, *Workplace Industrial Relations* (HMSO, London, 1974); J. Storey, 'Workplace Collective Bargaining and Managerial Prerogatives', *Industrial Relations Journal*, vol. 7, no. 3 (1976/77) pp. 40–55; and M. G. Wilders, S. R. Parker, 'Changes in Workplace Industrial Relations 1966–1972', *British Journal of Industrial Relations*, vol. XIII, no. 1 (1975), pp. 14–22.

17 Wilders and Parker, *ibid*.

18 C. Balfour, *Industrial Relations in the Common Market* (Routledge & Kegan Paul, London, 1972), p. 63.

19 G. Guigni, 'Recent Developments in Collective Bargaining in Italy', *International Labour Review*, vol. 91 (1965), p. 284.

20 G. Guigni, 'Recent Trends in Collective Bargaining in Italy', *International Labour Review*, vol. 104 (1971), p. 321.

21 Commission on Industrial Relations, *Worker Participation and Collective Bargaining in Europe* (HMSO, London, 1974).

22 See discussion in *ibid*.

23 E. Slack, 'Plant Level Bargaining in France', *Industrial Relations Journal*, vol. 11 (September/October 1980), pp. 27–38.

24 R. Blanpain, 'Recent Trends in Collective Bargaining in Belgium', *International Labour Review*, vol. 104 (July/August 1971), p. 123.

25 H. Reichel, 'Recent Trends in Collective Bargaining in the Federal Republic of Germany', *International Labour Review*, vol. 104 (1971), pp. 469–88.

26 W. Albeda, 'Recent Trends in Collective Bargaining in The Netherlands', *International Labour Review*, vol. 103 (1971), pp. 247–68.

27 See, for example, J. E. Isaac, G. W. Ford (eds), *Australian Labour Relations: Readings* (Sun Books, Melbourne, 1966).

28 D. Yerbury, J. E. Isaac, 'Recent Trends in Collective Bargaining in Australia', *International Labour Review*, vol. 103 (1971), pp. 421–52.

29 B. C. Roberts, S. Rothwell, 'Recent Trends in Collective Bargaining in the United Kingdom', *International Labour Review*, vol. 106 (1972), p. 548.

30 Guigni, *op. cit.*, p. 287.

31 National Board for Prices and Incomes, *Payment by Results*, Report No. 65 (HMSO, London, 1968, Cmnd 3627).

32 K. Coates, T. Topham, *Workers Control* (Panther, London, 1970).

33 J. A. Banks, *Trade Unionism* (Collier Macmillan, London, 1974).

34 Roberts and Rottwell, *op. cit.*, p. 548.

35   McCarthy and Parker, *op. cit.*
36   Royal Commission on Trade Unions, *op. cit.*, p. 19.
37   A. Fox, A. Flanders, 'The Reform of Collective Bargaining: From Donovan to Durkheim', *British Journal of Industrial Relations*, vol. 7, no. 2 (1969), pp. 151–80.
38   *Ibid.*, p. 150.
39   *Ibid.*, p. 156.
40   *Ibid.*, p. 160.
41   *Ibid.*, p. 174.
42   J. E. T. Eldridge, *Sociology and Industrial Life* (Nelson, London, 1971).
43   E. Lindop, 'Workplace Bargaining: The End of an Era?', *Industrial Relations Journal*, vol. 10, no. 1 (1979), pp. 12–20.
44   W. W. Daniel, *Wage Determination in Industry* (Political and Economic Planning, London, 1976).
45   Lindop, *op. cit.*, p. 20.
46   W. W. Daniel, N. Millward, *British Workplace Industrial Relations, 1980–1984* (Gower, Aldershot, 1986).
47   W. A. Brown, in 'Symposium: British Workplace Industrial Relations, 1980–1984', *British Journal of Industrial Relations* vol. XXV, no. 2 (July 1987).
48   CBI, *The Structure and Processes of Pay Determination in the Private Sector: 1979–1986* (CBI, London, 1988).
49   See P. Beaumont, J. W. Leopold, 'Public Sector Industrial Relations: Recent Developments', *Employee Relations*, vol. 7, no. 4 (1985).
50   N. W. Chamberlain, J. W. Kuhn, *Collective Bargaining* (McGraw-Hill, New York, 1965).
51   *Ibid.*, p. 425.
52   *Ibid.*, p. 425.
53   *Ibid.*, p. 429.
54   *Ibid.*, pp. 429–30.
55   R. E. Walton, R. B. McKersie, *A Behavioural Theory of Labor Negotiations* (McGraw-Hill, New York, 1965).
56   Chamberlain and Kuhn, *op. cit.*, pp. 430–1.
57   A. Flanders, *The Fawley Productivity Agreement* (Faber & Faber, London, 1964).
58   Roberts and Rothwell, *op. cit.*, p. 555.
59   See Albeda, *op. cit.*, p. 255.
60   R. B. McKersie, 'Changing Methods of Wage Payment', in J. T. Dunlop, N. W. Chamberlain (eds), *Frontiers of Collective Bargaining* (Harper & Row, London, 1967).
61   R. F. Banks, 'The Pattern of Collective Bargaining', in B. C. Roberts (ed.), *Industrial Relations* (Methuen, London, 1968), p. 138.
62   W. W. Daniel, 'Understanding Employee Behaviour in its Context: Illustrations from Productivity Bargaining', in J. Child (ed.), *Man and Organization* (Allen & Unwin, London, 1973), pp. 39–62.
63   T. Topham, 'New Types of Bargaining', in R. Blackburn, A. Cockburn (eds), *The Incompatibles* (Penguin, Harmondsworth, 1967), pp. 133–59.
64   A. Fox, *Industrial Sociology and Industrial Relations* (HMSO, London, 1967).
65   R. Hyman, *Strikes* (Fontana, London, 1972), pp. 168–9.

66 Advisory, Conciliation and Arbitration Service, *Labour Flexibility in Britain* (ACAS Occasional Paper 41, London 1987).
67 Institute for Manpower Studies.
68 A. Fowler, 'New Directions in Pay Performance', *Personnel Management* (November 1988), p. 30.
69 *Financial Times*, 30 January 1989, p. 38.
70 *Ibid.*
71 *Ibid.*
72 C. Duncan, 'Why Profit Related Pay Will Fail', *Industrial Relations Journal* (1988), p. 197.
73 S. Crainer, 'ESOP: Fables No Longer', *Personnel Management* (January 1988), p. 27.
74 L. Badden, L. Hunter, J. Hyman, J. Leopold, H. Ramsay, *People's Capitalism* (Routledge, London, 1989), p. 31.
75 V. Price, C. Nicholson, 'The Problems and Performance of Employee Ownership Firms', *Employment Gazette* (June 1988), p. 349.
76 M. Poole, G. Jenkins, 'How Employees Respond to Profit Sharing', *Personnel Management* (July 1988), p. 34.
77 Millward and Stevens, *op. cit.*
78 CBI, *op. cit.*
79 Advisory, Conciliation, and Arbitration Service, *op. cit.*
80 R. Singh, 'Final Offer Arbitration in Theory and Practice', *Industrial Relations Journal*, vol. 17, no. 4 (1986).
81 P. Feuille, 'Final Offer Arbitration and the Chilling Effect', *Industrial Relations*, vol. xiv (October 1975), pp. 302–10.
82 H. N. Wheeler, 'Compulsory Arbitration: A "Narcotic Effect"', *Industrial Relations*, vol. xiv (February 1975), pp. 117–20.
83 Singh, *op. cit.*; Sir John Wood, 'Last Offer Arbitration', *British Journal of Industrial Relations*, vol. 23, no. 3 (1985), pp. 415–24.
84 See, *Financial Times*, 3 August 1988, p. 7.
85 *Financial Times*, 30 July 1988.

8 INDUSTRIAL DEMOCRACY AND PARTICIPATION

1 C. Pateman, *Participation and Democratic Theory* (Cambridge University Press, Cambridge, 1970), p. 69.
2 *Ibid.*, p. 70.
3 *Ibid.*, p. 71.
4 *Ibid.*, p. 72.
5 P. Brannen, *Authority and Participation in Industry* (Batsford, London, 1983), p. 14.
6 Pateman, *op. cit.*, p. 72.
7 H. A. Clegg, *A New Approach to Industrial Democracy* (Blackwell, Oxford, 1963).
8 J. Elliott, *Conflict or Co-operation: The Growth of Industrial Democracy* (Kogan Page, London, 1988), p. 4.
9 M. Poole, *Workers' Participation in Industry* (Routledge & Kegan Paul, London, 1975).
10 H. Ramsay, 'Cycles of Control: Worker Participation in Sociological and Historical Perspective', *Sociology*, vol. 11, No. 3 (1977), pp. 480–506.

11   Brannen, *op. cit.*
12   E. Jacques, *The Changing Culture of a Factory* (Tavistock, London, 1951); and W. A. Brown, *Explorations in Management* (Heinemann, London, 1960).
13   A. Flanders, R. Pomeranz, J. Woodward, *Experiment in Industrial Democracy: A Study of the John Lewis Partnership* (Faber, London, 1968).
14   See, M. P. Jackson, *Labour Relations on the Docks* (Saxon House, Farnborough, 1973).
15   TUC, *Trade Unionism* (Trade Union Congress, London, 1966).
16   *Report of the Committee of Inquiry on Industrial Democracy* (HMSO, London, 1977, Cmnd 6706).
17   *Ibid.*
18   For a more general statement of the employers' position, see the comments of John Methven in *The Sunday Times*, 23 January 1979, p. 53.
19   Department of Employment *Industrial Democracy* (HMSO, London, 1978, Cmnd 7231).
20   See, B. Towers, D. Cox, E. Chell, 'Do Worker Directors Work?', *Employment Gazette* (September 1981).
21   J. Bank, K. Jones, *Worker Directors Speak* (Gower, Farnborough, 1977).
22   E. Batstone, A. Ferner, M. Terry, *Unions of the Board – A Case Study of Industrial Democracy in the Post Office 1978–1979)* (Blackwell, Oxford, 1983).
23   P. Cressey, J. Eldridge, J. MacInnes, G. Norris, *Industrial Democracy and Participation: A Scottish Survey*, Research Paper no. 28 (Department of Employment, London, 1981).
24   N. Millward, M. Stevens, *British Workplace Industrial Relations 1980– 1984* (Gower, Aldershot, 1986).
25   P. Edwards, 'Managing Labour Relations Through the Recession', *Employee Relations*, vol. 7, no. 2, pp. 3–7.
26   See, J. Grummitt, *Team Briefing* (Industrial Society, London, 1983).
27   D. J. Toscano, 'Labour–Management Co-operation and the West German System of Co-determination', *Industrial Relations Journal*, vol. 12 (November/December 1981), pp. 57–67.
28   R. Dahrendorf, *Society and Democracy in Germany* (Routledge & Kegan Paul, London, 1968).
29   K. Bradley, A. Gelb, 'Co-operative Labour Relations: Mondragon's Response to Recession', *British Journal of Industrial Relations*, vol. XXV, no. 1 (March 1987).
30   C. Lane, *Management and Labour in Europe* (Edward Elgar, Aldershot, 1989), p. 227.
31   Clegg, *op. cit.*
32   N. Reich, 'Collective Bargaining: The United States and Germany', *Labour Law Journal* (May 1957).
33   J. Kolaja, *Workers' Councils: The Yugoslav Experience* (Tavistock, London, 1965).
34   P. Blumberg, *Industrial Democracy: The Sociology of Participation* (Constable, London 1968).
35   R. Bean, *Comparative Industrial Relations* (Croom Helm, London, 1985) p. 176.

36   *Ibid.*, p. 179.
37   A. G. Johnson, W. F. Whyte, 'The Moondragon System of Worker Participation Co-operatives', *Industrial and Labour Review*, vol. 31, no. 1 (October).
38   R. Oakeshott, *The Case for Worker Co-operatives* (Routledge & Kegan Paul, 1978).
39   Brannen, *op. cit.*, p. 109.
40   Bradley and Gelb, *op. cit.*, p. 93.
41   Clegg, *op. cit.*
42   Kolaja, *op. cit.*
43   *Report on Industrial Democracy*, *op. cit.*
44   Blumberg, *op. cit.*
45   K. Coates, T. Topham, *The New Unionism* (Peter Owen, London, 1972).
46   J. H. Richardson, *An Introduction to the Study of Industrial Relations* (Allen & Unwin, London, 1954).
47   See Clegg, *op. cit.*
48   *Report on Industrial Democracy*, *op. cit.*

9   INDUSTRIAL CONFLICT

1   A. Kornhauser, R. Dubin, A. M. Ross (eds), *Industrial Conflict* (McGraw-Hill, New York, 1954), p. 13.
2   A. Fox, *A Sociology of Work in Industry* (Collier Macmillan, London, 1971).
3   L. J. Handy, 'Absenteeisn and Attendance in the British Coal Mining Industry', *British Journal of Industrial Relations*, vol. VI, no. 1 (1968), pp. 27–50.
4   For a review of the debate, see N. Nicholson, 'Strikes and Other Forms of Industrial Action', *Industrial Relations Journal* vol. 11, no. 5 (1980), pp. 20–31.
5   Fox, *op. cit.*
6   E. Mayo, *The Human Problems of an Industrial Civilisation* (Harvard University Press, Cambridge, Mass., 1946).
7   E. V. Schneider, *Industrial Sociology* (McGraw-Hill, London, 1971), p. 93.
8   F. J. Roethlisberger, W. J Dickson, *Management and the Worker* (Harvard University Press, Cambridge, Mass., 1939), p. 569.
9   J. F. Scott, G. C. Homans, 'Reflections on the Wildcat Strikes', *American Sociological Review*, vol. 12 (1947), p. 281.
10   M. Dalton, 'The Role of Supervision', in A. Kornhauser, R. Dubin, A. M. Ross (eds), *Industrial Conflict* (McGraw-Hill, New York, 1954), p. 185.
11   W. F. Whyte, *Pattern for Industrial Peace* (Harper & Row, New York, 1951).
12   A. Carey, 'The Hawthorne Studies: A Radical Criticism', in J. M. Shepheard (ed.), *Organizationsl Issues in Industrial Society* (Prentice-Hall, Englewood Cliffs, NJ, 1972), pp. 297–315.
13   *Ibid.*, p. 315.
14   C. Kerr, A. Siegel, 'The Inter-Industry Propensity to Strike', in A. Kornhauser, R. Dubin, A. Ross (eds), *op. cit.*

15   D. McGregor, *Leadership and Motivation* (MIT Press, Cambridge, Mass., 1966).
16   F. Hertzberg, *Work and the Nature of Man* (Stapes Press, London, 1968).
17   *Ibid.*, p. 79.
18   A. H. Maslow, *Motivation and Personality* (Harper & Row, New York, 1954).
19   *Ibid.*, p. 54.
20   McGregor, *op.cit.*, p. 15.
21   R. Likert, *New Patterns of Management* (McGraw-Hill, New York, 1961).
22   W. G. Bennis, *Changing Organisations: Essays on the Development and Evolution of Human Organisations* (McGraw-Hill, New York, 1966).
23   K. Graham, 'Union Attitudes to Job Satisfaction', in M. Weir (ed.), *Job Satisfaction* (Fontana, Glasgow, 1976), pp. 267–8.
24   J. H. Goldthorpe, D. Lockwood, F. Beckhofer, J. Platt, *The Affluent Workers: Industrial Attitudes and Behaviour* (Cambridge University Press, London, 1968).
25   H. L. Sheppard, N. Q. Herrick, *Where Have All the Robots Gone?* (Free Press, New York, 1972).
26   R.M. Blackburn, M. Mann, *The Working Class in the Labour Market* (Macmillan, London, 1979).
27   C. R. Walker, R. H. Guest, *The Man on the Assembly Line* (Yale University Press, New Haven, 1957).
28   E. Chinoy, *Automobile Workers and the American Dream* (Doubleday, New York, 1955).
29   L. R. Sayles, *Behaviour of Work Groups* (Wiley, New York, 1958).
30   *Ibid.*, p. 127.
31   J. W. Kuhn, *Bargaining in Grievance Settlement: The Power of Industrial Work Groups* (Columbia University Press, New York, 1961).
32   J. H. Goldthorpe, 'Attitudes and Behaviour of Car Assembly Workers: A Deviant Case and a Theoretical Critique', *British Journal of Sociology*, vol. 17, no. 3 (September 1966).
33   J. E. T. Eldridge, *Industrial Disputes* (Routledge & Kegan Paul, London, 1968), p. 50.
34   Sayles, *op. cit.*, pp. 4–5.
35   J. Woodward, *Industrial Organization: Theory and Practice* (Oxford University Press, London, 1965).
36   J. Woodward (ed.), *Industrial Organization: Behaviour and Control* (Oxford University Press, London, 1970), p. ix.
37   *Ibid.*, p. 5.
38   *Ibid.*, p. 4.
39   E. L. Trist, G. W. Higgin, H. Murray, A. B. Pollock, *Organizational Choice* (Tavistock, London, 1963).
40   *Ibid.*, pp. 289–90.
41   *Ibid.*, p. 290.
42   *Ibid.*, p. 291.
43   *Ibid.*
44   V. L. Allen, *The Sociology of Industrial Relations* (Longman, London, 1971), p. 39.
45   *Ibid.*
46   F. Engels, 'Labour Movements', in T. Clarke, L. Clements (eds), *Trade*

Unionism Under Capitalism (Fontana, Glasgow, 1977), p. 40.

47 *Collected Works of Marx and Engels* (Institut für Marxismus-Leninismus, East Berlin), vol. 18, p. 474.
48 V. I. Lenin, 'Capital and Labour', in T. Clarke, L. Clements (eds), *op. cit*, pp. 64–76.
49 L Trotsky, 'Marxism and Trade Unionism', in T. Clarke, L. Clements (eds), *op. cit.*
50 *Ibid.*, p. 81.
51 Quoted by J. E. T. Eldridge, *Sociology and Industrial Life* (Nelson, London, 1971), pp. 140–1.
52 R. Blauner, *Alienation and Freedom* (University of Chicago Press, Chicago, 1964).
53 C. Wright Mills, *White Collar* (Oxford University Press, London, 1959).
54 Eldridge, *op. cit.*
55 *Ibid.*, p. 193.
56 Quoted *ibid.*, p. 195.
57 H. Benyon, *Working for Ford* (EP Publishing, Wakefield, 1975).
58 *Ibid.*, p. 14.
59 *Ibid.*, p. 319.
60 H. Braverman, *Labor and Monopoly Capitalism* (Monthly Review Press, New York, 1974).
61 *Ibid.*, p. 8.
62 *Ibid.*, pp. 8–9.
63 *Ibid.*, p. 9.
64 *Ibid.*, p. 90.
65 *Ibid.*, p. 170.
66 *Ibid.*, pp. 170–1.
67 *Ibid.*, p. 371.
68 *Ibid.*, p. 355.
69 S. Hill, *Competition and Control at Work* (Heinemann, London, 1981).
70 *Ibid.*, p. 112.
71 *Ibid.*
72 *Ibid.*, p. 113.
73 *Ibid.*, p. 115.
74 C. R. Littler, *The Development of the Labour Process in Capitalist Societies* (Heinemann, London, 1982).
75 *Ibid.*, p. 27.
76 *Ibid.*, p. 28.
77 *Ibid.*, pp. 34–5.
78 A. Friedman, 'Responsible Autonomy Versus Direct Control Over the Labour Process', *Capital and Class*, no. 1 (spring 1977), pp. 43–57.
79 R. Edwards, *Contested Terrain* (Heinemann, London, 1979).
80 S. Wood (ed.), *The Degradation of Work?* (Hutchinson, London, 1982).
81 *Ibid.*, p. 21.
82 R. Bendix, *Work and Authority in Industry: Ideologies of Management in the Course of Industrialization* (Harper & Row, New York, 1963).
83 Fox, *op. cit.*
84 L. A. Coser, *The Functions of Social Conflict* (Routledge & Kegan Paul, London, 1956).
85 G. Simmel, *Conflict* (Free Press, Glencoe, Illinois, 1955).

86   C. Wright Mills, *New Men of Power: America's Labor Leaders* (Harcourt, New York, 1948).
87   *Ibid.*, p. 233.
88   *Ibid.*, p. 237.
89   *Ibid.*, p. 8.
90   *Ibid.*, p. 9.
91   V. L. Allen, *Militant Trade Unionism* (Merlin, London, 1966), p. 165.
92   *Ibid.*, p. 165.
93   See, for example, R. Hyman, 'Inequality, Ideology and Industrial Relations', *British Journal of Industrial Relations*, vol. 12, no. 2 (1974); R. Hyman, I. Brough, *Social Values and Industrial Relations* (Blackwell, Oxford, 1975).
94   R. Dahrendorf, *Class and Class Conflict in Industrial Society* (Routledge & Kegan Paul, London, 1959).
95   *Ibid.*, p. 268.
96   A. Fox, *Industrial Sociology and Industrial Relations* (HMSO, London, 1967).
97   See, for example, J. Westergaard, H. Resler, *Class in a Capitalist Society* (Heinemann, London, 1975).

10   STRIKES

1   Conservative Party, *Fair Deal at Work* (Conservative Central Office, London, 1968).
2   Royal Commission on Trade Unions and Employers' Associations, 1965–68, *Report* (HMSO, London, 1968, Cmnd 3623).
3   H. A. Turner, *Is Britain Really Strike Prone?* (Cambridge University Press, London, 1969).
4   G. Clack, *Industrial Relations in a British Car Factory* (Cambridge University Press, 1967).
5   J. Vanderkamp, 'Economic Activity and Strikes in Canada', *Industrial Relations*, vol. 9, no. 2 (1970), pp. 215–30.
6   M. Silver, 'Recent British Strikes Trends: A Factual Analysis', *British Journal of Industrial Relations*, vol. XI, no. 1 (1973), pp. 66–104.
7   P. Galambos, E. W. Evans, 'Work Stoppages in the United Kingdom, 1951–64: A Quantitative Study', *Bulletin of Oxford University Institute of Economics and Statistics*, vol, 28, no. 1 (1966), pp. 33–57.
8   'Large Industrial Stoppages, 1960–1979', *Employment Gazette*, vol. 88 (1980), pp. 994–9.
9   J. W. Duncan, W. E. J. McCarthy, A. P. Redman, *Strikes in Post War Britain* (Attend Union, London, 1983), p. 403.
10   Royal Commission on Trade Unions, *op. cit.*
11   P. K. Edwards, 'Britains's Changing Strike Problems?', *Industrial Relations Journal*, vol. 13, no. 2 (summer 1982), pp. 5–20.
12   *Ibid.*
13   J. G. J. C. Knowles, *Strikes – A Study in Industrial Conflict* (Blackwell, Oxford, 1952), p. 235.
14   J. Winterton, 'The Trend of Strikes in Coal Mining 1949–1979', *Industrial Relations Journal*, vol. 12, no. 6 (November/December 1981), p. 16.

15 Royal Commission on Trade Unions, *op. cit.*
16 See for example, H. A. Turner, G. Clack, G. Roberts, *Labour Relations in the Motor Industry* (Allen & Unwin, London, 1967).
17 See M. Terry, 'Organising a Fragmented Workforce: Shop Stewards in Local Government', *British Journal of Industrial Relations*, vol. 20, no. 1 (March 1982), pp. 1–19, for a discussion of 1979 survey and related research.
18 C. T. B. Smith, R. Clifton, P. Makeham, S. W. Creigh, R. V. Burn, *Strikes in Britain*, Department of Employment Manpower Paper no. 5, London, 1987.
19 *Ibid.*
20 S. Creigh, P. Makeham, 'Variations in Strike Activity Within UK Manufacturing Industry', *Industrial Relations Journal*, vol. 11, no. 5 (November/December 1980), pp. 32–7.
21 G. P. Bevan, 'On Strikes of the Past Ten Years', *Journal of the Statistical Society*, vol. 12, no. 1 (1880).
22 Knowles, *op. cit.*
23 Durcan, McCarthy, Redman, *op. cit.*
24 *Ibid.*, p. 187.
25 M. P. Jackson, 'Strikes in Scotland', *Industrial Relations Journal*, vol. 9, no. 2 (summer 1988), pp. 106–116.
26 E. Batstone, I. Boranston, S. Frenkel, *The Social Organisation of Strikes* (Blackwell, Oxford, 1978).
27 *Monthly Labor Bulletin* (March 1986), p. 55.
28 See R. Kalbitz, Aussperrungen in der Bundesrepublic, E.V.A. Koln-Frankfurt, 1979, quoted by W. Muller-Jentsch, 'Strikes and Strike Trends in West Germany, 1950–78', *Industrial Relations Journal*, vol. 12, no. 4 (July/August 1981), pp. 36–5; W. A. Brown (ed.), *The Changing Contours of British Industrial Relations* (Blackwell, Oxford, 1981); W. Korpi, 'Unofficial Strikes in Sweden', *British Journal of Industrial Relations*, vol. 19, no. 1 (March 1981), pp. 66–8.
29 K. Walsh, 'Industrial Disputes in France, West Germany, Italy and the United Kingdom: Measurement and Incidence', *Industrial Relations Journal*, vol. 13, no. 4 (winter 1982).
30 P. K. Edwards, 'The End of American Strike Statistics', *British Journal of Industrial Relations*, vol. 21, no. 3 (1983), p. 392.
31 A. M. Ross, P. T. Hartman, *Changing Patterns of Industrial Conflict* (Wiley, New York, 1960).
32 C. Kerr, F. Harbison, H. Myers, *Industrialism and Industrial Man* (Heinemann, London, 1962).
33 J. T. Dunlop, *Industrial Relations Systems* (Holt, New York, 1958).
34 Royal Commission on Trade Unions, *op. cit.*
35 E. M. Kassalow, *Trade Unions and Industrial Relations: An International Comparison* (Random House, New York, 1969).
36 H. A. Clegg, *Trade Unionism Under Collective Bargaining* Blackwell, Oxford, 1976).
37 G. K. Ingham, *Strikes and Industrial Conflict* (Macmillan, London, 1974), p. 9.
38 *Ibid.*, p. 10.
39 *Ibid.*, p. 42.

40   *Ibid.*, p. 44.
41   W. Korpi, M. Shalev, 'Strikes, Industrial Relations and Class Conflicts in Capitalist Societies', *British Journal of Sociology*, vol. 30, no. 2 (1979), p. 177.
42   A. Pizzorno, 'Political Exchange and Collective Identity in Industrial Conflict', in C. Crough, A. Pizzorno (eds), *The Resurgence of Class Conflict in Western Europe Since 1968: Volume 2, Comparative Analyses* (Macmillan, London, 1978).
43   C. Huxley, 'The State, Collective Bargaining and the Shape of Strikes in Canada', *Canadian Journal of Sociology*, vol. 4, no. 3 (1979), pp. 223–39.
44   E. Shorter, C. Tilly, *Strikes in France 1830–1968* (Cambridge University Press, Cambridge, 1974).
45   *Ibid.*, pp. 344–5.
46   *Ibid.*, p. 140.
47   *Ibid.*, p. 104.
48   *Ibid.*, p. 306.
49   *Ibid.*, p. 330.
50   *Ibid.*
51   Korpi and Shalev, *op. cit.*, p. 181.
52   D. A. Hibbs, 'On the Political Economy of Long-Run Trends in Strike Activity', *British Journal of Political Science*, vol. 8, no. 2 (1978), pp. 153–75.
53   D. Snyder, 'Institutional Setting and Industrial Conflict', *American Sociological Review*, vol. 40, no. 3 (1975), pp. 259–78.
54   R. Bean, *Comparative Industrial Relations* (Croom Helm, Beckenham, London, 1985).
55   S. Creigh, A. Poland, M. Woolen, *The Reasons for International Differences in Strike Activity* (National Institute of Labour Studies, Flinders University of South Australia, Working Paper no. 61, 1984).
56   M. Paldam, P. J. Pederson, 'The Macro-Economic Strike Model: A Study of Seventeen Countries 1948–1975', *Industrial and Labour Relations Review*, vol. 35, no. 4 (1982), pp. 504–21.
57   A. H. Hansen, 'Cycles of Strikes', *American Economic Review*, vol. 11, no. 4 (1921), p. 618.
58   *Ibid.*, p. 620.
59   A. Rees, 'Industrial Conflict and Business Fluctuations', *Journal of Political Economy*, vol. 60, no. 5 (October 1952), pp. 371–82.
60   J. I. Griffen, *Strikes: A Study in Quantitative Economics* (Columbia University Press, New York, 1939).
61   D. Yoder, 'Economic Changes and Industrial Unrest in the United States', *Journal of Political Economy*, vol. 48 (1940), pp. 222–37.
62   A. F. Burns, W. C. Mitchell, *Measuring Business Cycles* (National Bureau of Economic Research, New York, 1946).
63   E. H. Jurkat, D. B. Jurkat, 'Economic Function of Strikes', *Industrial and Labour Relations Review*, vol. 2 (July 1949), pp. 527–45.
64   O. C. Ashenfelter, G. E. Johnson, 'Bargaining Theory, Trade Unions and Industrial Strike Activity', *American Economic Review*, vol. 59, no. 1 (1969), pp. 35–49.
65   *Ibid.*, p. 48.

66 J. H. Pencavel, 'An Investigation into Industrial Strike Activity in Britain', *Economica*, vol. 37, no. 147 (1970), pp. 239–56.
67 *Ibid.*, p. 243.
68 Paldam and Pederson, *op. cit.*
69 *Ibid.*, p. 517.
70 S. W. Creigh, D. Makeham, 'Strike Incidence in Industrial Countries: An Analysis', *Australian Bulletin of Labor*, vol. 8, no. 3 (1982), pp. 139–49.
71 *Ibid.*, p. 107.
72 Smith, Clifton, Makeham, Creigh and Burn, *op. cit.*
73 J. Shorey, 'Time Series Analysis of Strike Frequency', *British Journal of Industrial Relations*, vol. 15, no. 1 (1977), pp. 63–75.
74 R. A. McLean, 'Interindustry Differences in Strike Activity', *Industrial Relations*, vol. 18, no. 1 (winter 1979), p. 104.
75 J. Shorey, 'An Inter-Industry Analysis of Strike Frequency', *Economica*, vol. 43 (1976), pp. 349–65.
76 B. E. Kaufman, 'Interindustry Trends in Strike Activity', *Industrial Relations*, vol. 22, no. 1 (winter 1983), pp. 45–57.
77 *Ibid.*, p. 56.
78 Smith *et al.*, *op. cit.*
79 *Ibid.*, p. 73. Note that alternative explanations were also considered, some contradictory.
80 A. W. Gouldner, *Wildcat Strike* (Harper, New York, 1954).
81 L. Pope, *Millhands and Preachers* (Yale University Press, New Haven, 1942).
82 T. Lane, K. Roberts, *Strike at Pilkingtons* (Fontana, London, 1971).
83 *Ibid.*, p. 236.
84 *Ibid.*, p. 236.
85 M. P. Jackson, 'The British Miners' Strikes of 1974 and 1984: A Comparison of the Role and Strategy of the Miners' Union', in G. Spyropoulos, *Trade Unions Today and Tomorrow* (Presses interuniversitaires Europeennes, Maastricht, 1987).

11 THE ROLE OF THE STATE IN INDUSTRIAL RELATIONS

1 The term is used in most industrial relations texts. See, for example, N. Robertson, J. L. Thomas, *Trade Unions and Industrial Relations* (Business Books, London, 1968).
2 A. Flanders, 'The Tradition of Voluntarism', *British Journal of Industrial Relations*, vol. XII, no. 3 (November 1974), pp. 352–70.
3 Committee on the Relations between Employers and Employed, *Reports* (HMSO, London, 1916–18, Cd 8606, 9001, 9002, 9099, 9153).
4 E. G. A. Armstrong, 'The Role of the State', in B. Barrett, E. Rhodes, J. Beishon (eds), *Industrial Relations in the Wider Society* (Collier Macmillan, London, 1975), p. 114.
5 *Ibid.*, p. 114.
6 O. Kahn-Freund, 'Legal Framework', in A. Flanders, H. A. Clegg (eds), *The System of Industrial Relations in Great Britain* (Blackwell, Oxford, 1953), p. 44.
7 J. E. Isaac, G. W. Ford (eds), *Australian Labour Relations: Readings* (Sun Books, Melbourne, 1966).

8   Commission on Industrial Relations, *Worker Participation and Collective Bargaining in Europe* (HMSO, London, 1974), p. 12.
9   W. Albeda, 'Recent Trends in Collective Bargaining in the Netherlands', *International Labour Review*, vol. 103, no. 3 (March 1971), pp. 247–68.
10 *Ibid.*, p. 254.
11 See, A. M. Ross, 'Prosperity and Labour Relations in Western Europe: Italy and France', *Industrial and Labour Relations Review* (October 1962), pp. 63–85.
12 R. Blanpain, 'Recent Trends in Collective Bargaining in Belgium', *International Labour Review*, vol. 104 (July/August 1971), p. 112.
13 Commission on Industrial Relations, *op. cit.*
14 R. Hyman, *Industrial Relations: A Marxist Introduction* (Macmillan, London, 1975).
15 *Ibid.*, p. 134.
16 *Ibid.*, p. 135.
17 *Ibid.*, p. 135n.
18 J. England, B. Weekes, 'Trade Unions and the State: A Review of the Crises', *Industrial Relations Journal*, vol. 12, no. 1 (January/February 1981), pp. 11–26.
19 Isaac in Isaac and Ford (eds), *op. cit.*
20 Flanders, *op. cit*, p. 358.
21 Quoted by Flanders, *ibid.*, pp. 358–9.
22 K. W. Wedderburn, *The Worker and the Law* (Penguin, Harmondsworth, 1986), p. 416.
23 H. A. Clegg *The System of Industrial Relations in Great Britain* (Blackwell, Oxford, 1970).
24 J. Corina, 'A Workable Incomes Policy for Britain', in B. Barnett *et al.*, *op. cit.*, pp. 414–33.
25 For example, the dispute in the railway industry, 1966.
26 Department of Employment and Productivity, *Prices and Incomes Policy After 30 June 1967* (HMSO, London, 1967, Cmnd 3235).
27 Department of Employment and Productivity, *Prices and Incomes Policy in 1968 and 1969* (HMSO, London, 1968, Cmnd 3596).
28 Albeda, *op. cit.*, p. 257.
29 Department of Employment and Productivity, *In Place of Strife* (HMSO, London, 1969, Cmnd 3888).
30 A. Fox, *Industrial Sociology and Industrial Relations* (HMSO, London, 1967).
31 Quoted from *Employment News*, vol. 94 (February 1982).
32 *Employment News, op. cit.*
33 S. and B. Webb, *Industrial Democracy* (Longman, London, 1902).
34 See Hyman, *op. cit.*
35 *Ibid.*, p. 141.

Bibliography

Action Society Trust, *Size and Morale*, Action Society Trust, London, 1953.

Addison, J. T., Barnett, A. H., 'The Impact of Unions on Productivity', *British Journal of Industrial Relations*, vol. XX, no. 2, July 1982, pp. 145–62.

Albeda, W., 'Recent Trends in Collective Bargaining in the Netherlands', *International Labour Review*, vol. 103, no. 3, March 1971, pp. 247–68.

Albeda, W., 'Changing Industrial Relations in the Netherlands', *Industrial Relations*, vol. 16, no. 2, 1977.

Alcock, A., *History of the International Labour Organisation*, Macmillan, London, 1971.

Allen, V. L. *Trade Union Leadership*, Longman, London, 1957.

Allen, V. L., *Militant Trade Unionism*, Merlin, London, 1966.

Allen, V. L. *The Sociology of Industrial Relations*, Longman, London, 1971.

Allen, V. L. 'Trade Unions: An Analytical Framework', in Barrett, B., Rhodes, E., Beishon, J. (eds), *Industrial Relations in the Wider Society*, Collier Macmillan, London, 1975, pp. 60–6.

American Assembly, *Challenges to Collective Bargaining*, Prentice-Hall, Englewood Cliffs, NJ, 1967.

Anderson, P., Blackburn, R., *Towards Socialism*, Collins, London, 1965.

Ansoff, H. I. (ed.), *Business Strategy*, Penguin, Harmondsworth, 1969.

Anthony, P., Crichton, A., *Industrial Relations and the Personnel Specialists*, Batsford, London, 1969.

Armstrong, E. G. A., 'The Role of the State', in Barrett, B., Rhodes, E., Beishon, J. (eds), *Industrial Relations in the Wider Society*, Collier Macmillan, London, 1975. pp. 109–19.

Armstrong, M., 'HRM: A Case of the Emperor's New Clothes', *Personnel Management*, August 1987.

Ashenfelter. O. C., Johnson, G. E., 'Bargaining Theory, Trade Unions and Industrial Strike Activity', *American Economic Review*, vol. 59, no. 1, 1969, pp. 35–49.

Atkinson, J., 'Manpower Strategies for Flexible Organisations', *Personnel Management*, August, 1984, pp. 28–31.

Badden, L., Hunter, L., Hyman, J., Leopold, J., Ramsey, H., *People's Capitalism*, Routledge, London, 1989.

Bain, G. S., Clegg, H. A., 'A Strategy for Industrial Relations Research in Great Britain', *British Journal of Industrial Relations*, vol. XII, no. 1, March 1974, pp. 91–113.

Bain, G. S., Elsheikh, F. E., *Union Growth and the Business Cycle: An Econometric Analysis*, Blackwell, Oxford, 1976.

Bain, G. S., Price, R., 'Who is a White Collar Employee?', *British Journal of Industrial Relations*, vol. X, no. 3, 1972, pp. 325–39.

Balfour, C., *Industrial Relations in the Common Market*, Routledge & Kegan Paul, London, 1972.

Bamber, G. J., Lansbury, R. D., *International Comparative Industrial Relations*, Allen & Unwin, London, 1987.

Bank, J., Jones, K., *Worker Directors Speak*, Gower, Farnborough, 1977.

Banks, J. A., *Trade Unionism*, Collier Macmillan, London, 1974.

Banks, R. F., 'The Pattern of Collective Bargaining', in Roberts, B. C. (ed.), *Industrial Relations*, Methuen, London, 1968, pp. 92–152.

Barrett, B., Rhodes, E., Beishon, J. (eds), *Industrial Relations in the Wider Society*, Collier Macmillan, London, 1975.

Bassett, P., *Strike Free: New Industrial Relations in Britain*, Macmillan, Basingstoke, 1984.

Batstone, E., *Working Order*, Blackwell, Oxford, 1984.

Batstone, E., Boraston, I., Frenkel, S., *Shop Stewards in Action*, Blackwell, Oxford, 1977.

Batstone, E., Boraston, I., Frenkel, S., *The Social Organisation of Strikes*, Blackwell, Oxford, 1978.

Batstone, E., Ferner, A., Terry, M., *Unions of the Board – A Case Study of Industrial Democracy in the Post Office 1978–1979*, Blackwell, Oxford, 1983.

Batstone, E., Gourlay, S., *Unions, Unemployment and Innovation*, Blackwell, Oxford, 1986.

Beal, E. F., Wickersham, E. D., *The Practice of Collective Bargaining*, Irvin, Homewood, Illinois, 1967.

Bean, R., *Comparative Industrial Relations*, Croom Helm, Beckenham, London, 1985.

Beaumont, P. B., *The Decline of Trade Union Organisation*, Croom Helm, Beckenham, 1987.

Beaumont P. Leopold, J. 'Public Sector Industrial Relations: Recent Developments', *Employee Relations*, vol. 7, no. 4, 1985.

Bell, D., *The End of the Ideology*, Collier, New York, 1961.

Bendix, R., *Work and Authority in Industry: Ideologies of Management in the Course of Industrialization*, Harper & Row, New York, 1963.

Bennis, W. G., *Changing Organisations: Essays on the Development and Evolution of Human Organisations*, McGraw-Hill, New York, 1966.

Benyon, H., *Working for Ford*, EP Publishing, Wakefield, 1975.

Berle, A. A., Means, G. C., *The Modern Corporation and Private Property*, Macmillan, New York, 1932.

Bevan, G. P., 'On Strikes of the Past Ten Years', *Journal of the Statistical Society*, vol. 12, no. 1, 1880.

Blackburn, R., Cockburn, A. (eds), *The Incompatibles*, Penguin, Harmondsworth, 1967.

Blackburn, R. M., *Union Character and Social Class: A Study of White Collar Unionism*, Batsford, London, 1967.

Blackburn, R. M., Mann, M., *The Working Class in the Labour Market*, Macmillan, London, 1979.

Blanchflower, D., 'Union Relative Wage Effects: A Cross Section Analysis Using Establishment Data', *British Journal of Industrial Relations*, vol. XXII, no. 3, November, 1984, pp. 311–32.

Blanpain, R., 'Recent Trends in Collective Bargaining in Belgium', *International Labour Review*, vol. 104, July/August 1971, pp. 111–30.

Blauner, R., *Alienation and Freedom*, University of Chicago Press, Chicago, 1964.

Blum, A. A., Patarapanich, S., 'Productivity and the Path to House Unionism: Structural Change in the Singapore Labour Movement', *British Journal of Industrial Relations*, vol. 25, no. 3, November, 1987.

Blumberg, P., *Industrial Democracy: The Sociology of Participation*, Constable, London, 1968.

Bowey, A. M., 'Themes in Industrial Sociology', *Industrial Relations Journal*, vol. 6, no. 2, 1975, pp. 57–63.

Boyle, S. E., *Industrial Organisation*, Holt, Rinehart & Winston, New York, 1972.

Bradley, K., Gelb, A., 'Co-operative Labour Relations: Mondragon's Response to Recession', *British Journal of Industrial Relations*, vol. XXV, no. 1, March 1987.

Brannen, P., *Authority and Participation in Industry*, Batsford, London, 1983.

Braverman, H., *Labor and Monopoly Capitalism*, Monthly Review Press, New York, 1974.

Brentano, L., *On the History and Development of Guilds and the Origins of Trade Unions*, Treubener, London, 1870.

Brown, E. C., *Soviet Trade Unions and Labour Relations*, Harvard University Press, Cambridge, Mass., 1966.

Brown, W. A. (ed.), *The Changing Contours of British Industrial Relations: A Survey of Manufacturing Industry*, Blackwell, Oxford, 1981.

Brown, W. A., Lawson, M., 'The Training of Trade Union Officers', *British Journal of Industrial Relations*, vol. 11, no. 3, 1973.

Brown, W. A., *Explorations in Management*, Heinemann, London, 1960.

Brown, W. A., in 'Symposium: British Workplace Industrial Relations, 1980–1984', *British Journal of Industrial Relations*, vol. XXV, no. 2, July 1987.

Brown, W. A., Ebsworth, R., Terry, M., 'Factors Shaping Shop Steward Organisation in Britain', *British Journal of Industrial Relations*, vol. XVI, no. 2, 1978, pp. 139–59.

Buchanan, R., 'Mergers in British Trade Unions 1949–79', *Industrial Relations Journal*, vol. 12, no. 3, May/June 1981, pp. 40–50.

Bugler, J., 'The New Oxford Group', *New Society*, 15 February 1968, pp. 221–2.

Burnham, J., *The Managerial Revolution*, Day, New York, 1941.

Burns, A. F., Mitchell, W. C., *Measuring Business Cycles*, National Bureau of Economic Research, New York, 1946.

Carey, A., 'The Hawthorne Studies: A Radical Criticism', in Shepheard, J. M. (ed.), *Organizational Issues in Industrial Society*, Prentice-Hall, Englewood Cliffs, NJ, 1972, pp. 297–315.

Caves, R. E., 'International Corporation: The Industrial Economics of Foreign Inventions', *Economica*, vol. 38, no. 149, pp. 1–27.

Caves, R. E., *Multinational Enterprises and Economic Analysis*, Cambridge University Press, Cambridge, 1982.

Chalmers, N. J., *Industrial Relations in Japan*, Routledge, London, 1989.

Chamberlain, N. W., Kuhn, J. W., *Collective Bargaining*, McGraw-Hill, New York, 1965.

Child, J. (ed.), *The Business Enterprise in Modern Industrial Society*, Collier Macmillan, London, 1969.

Child, J. (ed.), *Man and Organization*, Allen & Unwin, London, 1973.

Chinoy, E., *Automobile Workers and the American Dream*, Doubleday, New York, 1955.

Clack, G., *Industrial Relations in a British Car Factory*, Cambridge University Press, London, 1967.

Clark, D. G., *The Industrial Manager – His Background and Career Pattern*, Business Publications, London, 1966.

Clegg, H. A., *A New Approach to Industrial Democracy*, Blackwell, Oxford, 1960.

Clegg, H. A., *A New Approach to Industrial Democracy*, Blackwell, Oxford, 1963.

Clegg, H. A., *The System of Industrial Relations in Great Britain*, Blackwell, Oxford, 1970.

Clegg, H. A., *Trade Unionism Under Collective Bargaining*, Blackwell, Oxford, 1976.

Clegg, H. A., Killick, A. H., Adams, R., *Trade Union Officers*, Blackwell, Oxford, 1961.

Clegg, H. A., 'Pluralism in Industrial Relations', *British Journal of Industrial Relations*, vol. XIII, no. 3, November 1975, pp. 309–16.

Coates, K., Topham, T., *Workers Control*, Panther, London, 1970.

Coates, K., Topham, T., *The New Unionism*, Peter Owen, London, 1972.

Cole, J., *Employers' Organisations and Industrial Relations*, HMSO, London 1972.

Cole, J., *Worker Participation and Collective Bargaining in Europe*, HMSO, London, 1974.

Cole, R. E., 'Labor in Japan', in Richardson, B. M., Keda, T. (eds.), *Business and Society in Japan*, Praeger, New York, 1981.

Collected Works of Marx and Engels, Institut für Marxismus-Leninismus, East Berlin, vol. 18.

Commission on Industrial Relations, *Facilities Afforded to Shop Stewards*, HMSO, London, 1971, Cmnd 4668.

Commission on Industrial Relations, *Employers' Organisations and Industrial Relations*, HMSO, London, 1972.

Commission on Industrial Relations, *Workplace Industrial Relations*, HMSO, London, 1974.

Commission on Industrial Relations, *Worker Participation and Collective Bargaining in Europe*, HMSO, London, 1974.

Committee on the Relations between Employers and Employed, *Reports*, HMSO, London, 1916–18, Cd 8606, 9001, 9002, 9099, 9153.

Confederation of British Industries, *The Future of Pay Determination*, CBI, London, 1977.

Confederation of British Industries, *The Structure and Processes of Pay Determination in the Private Sector: 1979–1986*, CBI, London, 1988.

Connock, S., 'Workforce Flexibility: Juggling Time and Task', *Personnel Management*, October 1985.

Conservative Party, *Fair Deal at Work*, Conservative Central Office, London, 1968.

Constable, R., McCormick, R. J., *The Making of British Managers: A Report for the BIM and CBI into Management Training, Education and Development*, BIM, London, 1987.

Corina, J., 'A Workable Incomes Policy for Britain', in Barrett, B., Rhodes, E., Beishon, J. (eds), *Industrial Relations in the Wider Society*, Collier Macmillan, London, 1975, pp. 414–33.

Coser, L. A., *The Functions of Social Conflict*, Routledge & Kegan Paul, London, 1956.

Crainer, S., 'ESOP: Fables No Longer', *Personnel Management*, January 1988.

Creigh, S., Makeham, P., 'Variations in Strike Activity Within UK Manufacturing Industry', *Industrial Relations Journal*, vol. 11, no. 5, November/December 1980, pp. 32–7.

Creigh, S., Poland, A., Woolen, M., *The Reasons for International Differences in Strike Activity*, National Institute of Labour Studies, Flinders University of South Australia, Working Paper no. 61, 1984.

Cressey, P., Eldridge, J. MacInnes, J. Norris, G., *Industrial Democracy and Participation: A Scottish Survey*, Research Paper, No. 28, Department of Employment, London, 1981.

Crockett, G., Elias, P., 'British Managers: A Study of Their Education, Training, Mobility and Earnings' *British Journal of Industrial Relations*, vol. XXII, March 1984, pp. 34–46.

Crosland, A., *The Future of Socialism*, Jonathan Cape, London, 1956.

Cyert, R. M., March, J. C., *A Behavioural Theory of the Firm*, Prentice-Hall, Englewood Cliffs, NJ, 1963.

Cyriax, G., Oakshott, R., *The Bargainers: A Survey of Modern British Trade Unionism*, Faber, London, 1960.

Dahrendorf, R., *Class and Class Conflict in Industrial Society*, Routledge & Kegan Paul, London, 1959.

Dalton, M., 'The Role of Supervision', in Kornhauser, A., Dubin, R., Ross, A. M. (eds), *Industrial Conflict*, McGraw-Hill, New York, 1954, pp. 176–85.

Dalton, M., *Men Who Manage*, Wiley, New York, 1966.

Daniel, W. W., 'Understanding Employee Behaviour in its Context: Illustrations from Productivity Bargaining', in Child, J. (ed.), *Man and Organization*, Allen & Unwin, London, 1973, pp. 39–62.

Daniel, W. W., Millward, N., *Workplace Industrial Relations in Britain*, Heinemann, London, 1983.

Davis, H. B., 'The Theory of Union Growth', in McCarthy, W. E. J. (ed.), *Trade Unions*, Penguin, Harmondsworth, 1972, pp. 211–35.

Deeks, J., 'Educational and Occupational Histories of Owner-Managers and Managers', *Journal of Management Studies*, vol. 9, no. 2, 1972, pp. 127–49.

Department of Employment and Productivity, *Prices and Incomes Policy*

After 30 June 1967, HMSO, London, 1967, Cmnd 3235.

Department of Employment and Productivity, *In Place of Strife*, HMSO, London, 1969, Cmnd 3888.

Department of Employment and Productivity, *Prices and Incomes Policy in 1968 and 1969*, HMSO, London, 1969, Cmnd 3596.

Dubin, R. L., 'Constructive Aspects of Industrial Conflict', in Kornhauser, A., Dubin, R., Ross, A. M. (eds), *Industrial Conflict*, McGraw-Hill, New York, 1954, pp. 37–47.

Dubin, R. L., 'Management in Britain – Impressions of a Visiting Professor', *Journal of Management Studies*, vol. VII, no. 2, 1970, pp. 183–98.

Dufty, N. F., 'A Typology of Shop Stewards', *Industrial Relations Journal*, vol. 12, July/August 1981, pp. 65–70.

Duncan, C, 'Why Profit Related Pay Will Fail', *Industrial Relations Journal*, 1988.

Duncan J. W., McCarthy W. E. J., Redman A. P., *Strikes in Post War Britain*, Attend Union, London, 1983.

Dunlop, J. E. T., *Industrial Relations Systems*, Holt, New York, 1958.

Dunning, J. H., 'Changes in the Level and Structure of International Production: The Last One Hundred Years' in Casson, M. (ed.), *The Growth of International Business*, Allen & Unwin, London, 1983.

Edwards, P. K., 'Size of Plant and Strike Proneness', *Oxford Bulletin of Economics and Statistics*, vol. 42, May 1980, pp. 145–56.

Edwards, P. K., 'Britain's Changing Strike Problems?', *Industrial Relations Journal*, vol. 13, no. 2, summer 1982, pp. 5–20.

Edwards, P. K., 'The End of American Strike Statistics', *British Journal of Industrial Relations*, vol. 21, no. 3, 1983.

Edwards, R., *Contested Terrain*, Heinemann, London, 1979.

Eldridge, J. E. T., *Industrial Disputes*, Routledge & Kegan Paul, London, 1968.

Eldridge, J. E. T., *Sociology and Industrial Life*, Nelson, London, 1971

Eldridge, J. E. T., 'Industrial Conflict: Some Problems of Theory and Method', in Child, J. (ed.), *Man and Organisation*, Allen & Unwin, London, 1973, pp. 158–84.

Elliott, J., *Conflict or Co-operation: The Growth of Industrial Democracy*, Kogan Page, London, 1988.

Employment Gazette, 'Large Industrial Stoppages, 1960–1979', vol. 88, 1980, pp. 994–9.

Enderwick, P., Buckley, P. J., 'Strike Activity and Foreign Ownership: An Analysis of British Manufacturing 1971–73', *British Journal of Industrial Relations*, vol. xx, 1982.

Engels, F., 'Labour Movements', in Clarke, T., Clements, L. (eds) *Trade Unionism Under Capitalism*, Fontana, Glasgow, 1977.

England, J., Rear, J., *Industrial Relations and Law in Hong Kong*, Oxford University Press, Oxford, 1981.

England, J., Weekes, B., 'Trade Unions and the State: A Review of the Crises', *Industrial Relations Journal*, vol. 12, no. 1, January/February 1981, pp. 11–26.

Fatchett, D., Whittingham, W. M., 'Trends and Developments in Industrial Relations Theory', *Industrial Relations Journal*, vol. 7, no. 1, 1976, pp. 50–60.

Feuille, P., 'Final Offer Arbitration and the Chilling Effect', *Industrial Relations*, vol. XIV, October 1975, pp. 302–10.

Flanders, A., 'Collective Bargaining', in Flanders, A. Clegg, H. A. (eds.), *The System of Industrial Relations in Great Britain*, Blackwell, Oxford, pp. 252–322.

Flanders, A., *The Fawley Productivity Agreement*, Faber & Faber, London, 1964.

Flanders, A., *Industrial Relations – What's Wrong with the System*, Faber & Faber, London, 1965.

Flanders, A., *Collective Bargaining*, Faber & Faber, London, 1967.

Flanders, A., 'Collective Bargaining: A Theoretical Analysis', *British Journal of Industrial Relations*, vol. VI, no. 1, 1968, pp. 1–26.

Flanders, A., 'The Tradition of Voluntarism', *British Journal of Industrial Relations*, vol. XII, no. 3, November 1974, pp. 352–70.

Flanders, A., Clegg, H. A. (eds), *The System of Industrial Relations in Great Britain*, Blackwell, Oxford, 1954.

Flanders, A., Pomeranz, R., Woodward, J., *Experiment in Industrial Democracy: A Study of the John Lewis Partnership*, Faber & Faber, London, 1968.

Florence, S., *The Logic of British and American Industry*, Routledge & Kegan Paul, London, 1961.

Fowler, A., 'When Chief Executives Discover HRM', *Personnel Management*, January 1987.

Fowler, A., 'New Directions in Pay Performance', *Personnel Management*, November 1988.

Fox, A., *Industrial Sociology and Industrial Relations*, Royal Commission on Trade Unions and Employers' Associations, Research Paper 3, HMSO, London, 1967.

Fox, A., *A Sociology of Work in Industry*, Collier Macmillan, London, 1971.

Fox, A., 'Industrial Relations: A Social Critique of Pluralist Ideology', in Child, J. (ed.), *Man and Organization*, Allen & Unwin, London, 1973, pp. 185–233.

Fox, A., *Beyond Contract*, Faber, London, 1974.

Fox, A., 'Collective Bargaining, Flanders and the Webbs', *British Journal of Industrial Relations*, vol. XIII, no. 2, 1975, pp. 151–74.

Fox, A., Flanders, A., 'The Reform of Collective Bargaining: From Donovan to Durkheim', *British Journal of Industrial Relations*, vol. 7, no. 2, 1969, pp. 151–80.

Francis, A., 'Families, Firms and Finance Capital', *Sociology*, vol. 14, no. 1, February 1980, pp. 1–28.

Freedman, D. H., 'Inflation in the United States 1959–74: Its Impact on Employment, Incomes and Industrial Relations', *International Labour Review*, vol. 112, 1975, pp. 125–47.

Friedman, A. 'Responsible Autonomy Versus Direct Control Over the Labour Process', *Capital and Class*, no. 1, spring 1977, pp. 43–57.

Galambos, P., Evans, E. W., 'Work Stoppages in the United Kingdom, 1951–64: A Quantitative Study', *Bulletin of Oxford University Institute of Economics and Statistics*, vol. 28, no. 1, 1966, pp. 33–57.

Galenson, W., Lipset, S. M., *Labour and Trade Unionism: An Interdisciplinary Reader*, Wiley, New York, 1960.

Gill, C., Morris, R., Eaton, J., 'Employers' Organisations in the U.K. Chemical Industry', *Industrial Relations Journal*, vol. 9, no. 1, 1978, pp. 37–47.

Goldstein, J., *The Government of British Unions*, Allen & Unwin, London, 1952.

Goldthorpe, J. H., 'Attitudes and Behaviour of Car Assembly Workers: A Deviant Case and a Theoretical Critique', *British Journal of Sociology*, vol. 17, no. 3, September 1966.

Goldthorpe, J. H., 'Social Inequality and Social Integration in Modern Britain', Presidential Address to the British Association for the Advancement of Science, Sociology Section, 1969.

Goldthorpe, J. H., Lockwood, D., Bechhofer, F., Platt, J., *The Affluent Worker: Industrial Attitudes and Behaviour* Cambridge University Press, London, 1968.

Gollan, R. A., 'The Historical Perspective', in Matthews, P. W. D., Ford, G. W. (eds), *Australian Trade Unions*, Sun Books, Melbourne, 1968, pp. 14–41.

Goodman, J., 'The Role of the Shop Steward', in Kessler, S., Weekes, B. (eds.), *Conflict at Work*, BBC, London, 1971, pp. 53–74.

Gouldner, A. W., *Wildcat Strike*, Harper, New York, 1954.

Gouldner, A. W., *The Coming of Western Sociology*, Heinemann, London, 1971.

Graham, H. D., Gurr, T. R. (eds), *Violence in America*, Bantam, New York, 1969.

Graham, K., 'Union Attitudes to Job Satisfaction', in Weir, M. (ed.) *Job Satisfaction*, Fontana, Glasgow, 1976.

Griffen, J. I., *Strikes: A Study in Quantitative Economics*, Columbia University Press, New York, 1939.

Groom, B., Martin, D., 'The Greenfield Route to New Working Practices', *Financial Times*, 9 January 1983.

Grummitt, J., *Team Briefing*, Industrial Society, London, 1983.

Guigni, G., 'Recent Developments in Collective Bargaining in Italy', *International Labour Review*, vol. 91, 1965, pp. 273–91.

Guigni, G., 'Recent Trends in Collective Bargaining in Italy', *International Labour Review*, vol. 104, 1971, pp. 307–28.

Gunderson, M., Meltz, N. H., 'Canadian Unions Achieve Strong Gains in Membership', *Monthly Labor Review*, April 1986.

Hall, D., Bettignies, H.-Cl. de, Amada-Fishgrund, G. 'The European Business Elite', *European Business*, October 1969.

Hamill, J., 'Labour Relations Decision Making Within Multinational Corporations', *Industrial Relations Journal*, vol. 15, 1984.

Handy, C. B., *Making Managers*, Pitman, London, 1988.

Handy, L. J., 'Absenteeism and Attendance in the British Coal Mining Industry', *British Journal of Industrial Relations*, vol. VI, no. 1, 1968, pp. 27–50.

Hansen, A. H., 'Cycles of Strikes', *American Economic Review*, vol. 11, no. 4, 1921.

Harbison, F. H., 'Collective Bargaining and American Capitalism', in Kornhauser, A., Dubin, R., Ross, A. M. (eds), *Industrial Conflict*, McGraw-Hill, New York, 1954, pp. 270–9.

Hawkins, K., *Conflict and Change*: Aspects of Industrial Relations, Holt, Rinehart & Winston, London, 1972.
Hedlund, G., 'Autonomy of Subsidiaries and Formalisation of Headquarters – Subsidiary Relationships in Swedish MNCs', in L. Offerbeck (ed.), *The Management of Headquarters Subsidiary Relationships in Multinational Corporations*, Gower, London, 1981.
Hertzberg, F. *Work and the Nature of Man*, Stapes, Press, London, 1968.
Hibbs, D. A., 'On the Political Economy of Long-Run Trends in Strike Activity', *British Journal of Political Science*, vol. 8, no. 2, 1978, pp. 153–75.
Hill, S., *Competition and Control at Work*, Heinemann, London, 1981.
Hill, S., Thurley, K., 'Sociology and Industrial Relations', *British Journal of Industrial Relations*, vol. XIII, no. 2, 1974, pp. 147–70.
Howell, G., *The Conflicts of Labour and Capital*, Chatto & Windus, London, 1978.
Hughes, J., *Trade Union Structure and Government*, Royal Commission on Trade Unions and Employers' Associations, Research Paper 5, HMSO, London, 1967.
Huxley, C., 'The State, Collective Bargaining and the Shape of Strikes in Canada', *Canadian Journal of Sociology*, vol. 4, no. 3, 1979, pp. 223–39.
Hyman, R., *Strikes*, Fontana, London, 1972.
Hyman, R., 'Inequality, Ideology and Industrial Relations', *British Journal of Industrial Relations*, vol. 12, no. 2, 1974.
Hyman, R., *Industrial Relations: A Marxist Introduction*, Macmillan, London, 1975.
Hyman, R. 'Pluralism, Procedural Consensus and Collective Bargaining', *British Journal of Industrial Relations*, vol. XVI, no. 1, 1978, pp. 16–40.
Hyman, R., Brough, I., *Social Values and Industrial Relations*, Blackwell, Oxford, 1975.
Hymer, S., 'The Efficiency (Contradictions) of Multi-national Corporations', *American Economic Review*, vol. IX, no. 2, 1970, pp. 441–8.
Ingham, G. K., *Size of Industrial Organisation and Worker Behaviour*, Cambridge University Press, London, 1970.
Ingham, G. K., *Strikes and Industrial Conflict*, Macmillan, London, 1974.
Isaac, J. E., Ford, G. W. (eds), *Australian Labour Relations: Readings*, Sun Books, Melbourne, 1966.
Jackson, M. P., *Labour Relations on the Docks*, Saxon House, Farnborough, 1973.
Jackson, M. P., *The Price of Coal*, Croom Helm, London, 1974.
Jackson, M. P., 'The British Miners' Strikes of 1974 and 1984: A comparison of the Role Strategy of the Miners' Union', in Spyroponlos, G., *Trade Unions Today and Tomorrow*, Presses Interuniversitaires Europeennes Maastricht, 1987.
Jackson, M. P., 'Strikes in Scotland', *Industrial Relations Journal*, vol. 9, no. 2, summer 1988, pp. 106–116.
Jackson, P., Sissons, K., 'Employers' Confederations in Sweden and the UK and the Significance of Industrial Infrastructure', *British Journal of Industrial Relations*, vol. XIV, no. 3, 1976, pp. 306–23.
Jaques, E., *The Changing Culture of a Factory*, Tavistock, London, 1951.

Johnston, T. L., *Collective Bargaining in Sweden*, Allen & Unwin, London, 1962.

Johnson, A. G., Whyte, W. F., 'The Mondragon System of Worker Participation Co-operatives', *Industrial and Labour Review*, vol. 31, no. 1, October 1978.

Jurkat, E. H., Jurkat, D. B., 'Economic Function of Strikes', *Industrial and Labour Relations Review*, vol. 2, July 1949, pp. 527–45.

Kahn-Freund, O., 'Legal Framework', in Flanders, A., Clegg, H. A. (eds), *The System of Industrial Relations in Great Britain*, Blackwell, Oxford, 1953, pp. 42–127.

Kalbitz, R., Aussperrungen in der Bundesrepublic, E.V.A. Koln-Frankfurt, 1979, quoted by Muller-Jentsch, 'Strikes and Strike Trends in West Germany, 1950–78', *Industrial Relations Journal*, vol. 12, no. 4, July/August 1981.

Kassalow, E. M., *Trade Unions and Industrial Relations: An International Comparison*, Random House, New York, 1969.

Kaufman, B. E., 'Interindustry Trends in Strike Activity', *Industrial Relations*, vol. 22, no. 1, winter 1983, pp. 45–57.

Kelly, J., *Trade Unions and Socialist Politics*, Verso, London, 1988.

Kerr, C., 'Industrial Conflict and its Mediation', *American Journal of Sociology*, vol. LX, 1954, pp. 230–75.

Kerr, C., Harbison, F. Myers, H., *Industrialisation and Industrial Man*, Heinemann, London, 1962.

Kerr, C., Siegel, A., 'The Interindustry Propensity to Strike', in Kornhauser, A., Dubin, R., Ross, A. M. (eds), *Industrial Conflict*, McGraw-Hill New York, 1954, pp. 189–212.

Kessler, A., Weekes, B., *Conflict at Work*, BBC Publications, London, 1971.

Knowles, K. G. J. C., *Strikes – A Study of Industrial Conflict*, Blackwell, Oxford, 1952.

Kolaja, J., *Workers' Councils: The Yugoslav Experience*, Tavistock, London, 1965.

Kodaisha Encyclopedia of Japan, Kodamamsha, Tokyo, 1983.

Kornhauser, A., Dubin, R., Ross, A. M. (eds), *Industrial Conflict*, McGraw-Hill, New York, 1954.

Korpi, W., 'Workplace Bargaining, the Law and Unofficial Strikes: The Case of Sweden', *British Journal of Industrial Relations*, vol. XVI, no. 3, 1978, pp. 355–68.

Korpi, W., 'Unofficial Strikes in Sweden', *British Journal of Industrial Relations*, vol. 19, no. 1, March 1981, pp. 66–8.

Korpi, W., Shalev, M., 'Strikes, Industrial Relations and Class Conflicts in Capitalist Societies', *British Journal of Sociology*, vol. 30, no. 2, 1979.

Kuhn, J. W., *Bargaining in Grievance Settlement: The Power of Industrial Work Groups*, Columbia University Press, New York, 1961.

Kuwahara, Y., 'Japanese Industrial Relations', in Bamber, G., Lansbury, R. D. (eds), *International and Comparative Industrial Relations*, Allen & Unwin, London, 1987.

Lane, C., *Management and Labour in Europe*, Edward Elgar, Aldershot, 1989.

Lane T., Roberts, K., *Strike at Pilkingtons*, Fontana, London, 1971.

Lash, S., Urry, J., *The End of Organised Capitalism*, Polity Press, Oxford, 1987.

Leggett, C., 'Industrial Relations and Enterprise Unionism in Singapore', *Labour and Industry*, vol. 1, no. 2, June 1988, pp. 242–57.

Lenin, V. I., Capital and Labour', in Clarke, T., Clements, L. (eds) *Trade Unionism Under Capitalism*, Fontana, Glasgow, 1977.

Lerner, S., *Breakaway Unions and the Small Trade Union*, Allen & Unwin, London, 1961.

Lewis, H. G., *Unionism and Relative Wages in the United States*, Chicago University Press, Chicago, 1965.

Likert, R. *New Patterns of Management*, McGraw-Hill, New York, 1961.

Lindop, E., 'Workplace Bargaining: The End of an Era?' *Industrial Relations Journal*, vol. 10, no. 1, 1979, pp. 12–20.

Lipset, S. M., Trow, M. A., Coleman, S., *Union Democracy: The Internal Politics of the International Typographical Union*, Free Press, Glencoe, 1956.

Littler, C. R., 'Internal Contract and the Transition to Modern Work Systems: Britain and Japan,' in D. Dunkerley, G. Salaman, *International Yearbook of Organisation Studies*, Routledge & Kegan Paul, London, 1980.

Littler, C. R., *The Development of the Labour Process in Capitalist Societies*, Heinemann, London, 1982.

Lockwood, D., *The Black-Coated Worker*, Allen & Unwin, London, 1958.

Loveridge, R. 'Occupational Change and the Development of Interest Groups Among White Collar Workers in the UK: A Long Term Model', *British Journal of Industrial Relations*, vol. x, no. 3, 1972, pp. 340–65.

Lumley, R., *White Collar Unionism in Britain*, Methuen, London, 1973.

McCarthy, W. E. J., *The Role of Shop Stewards in British Industrial Relations*, Royal Commission on Trade Unions and Employers' Associations, Research Paper 1, HMSO, London, 1966.

McCarthy, W. E. J. (ed.), *Trade Unions*, Penguin, Harmondsworth, 1972.

McCarthy, W. E. J., Parker, S. R., *Shop Stewards and Workshop Relations*, Royal Commission on Trade Unions and Employers' Associations, Research Paper 10, HMSO, London, 1968.

McGregor, D., *Leadership and Motivation*, MIT Press, Cambridge, Mass., 1966.

McKersie, R. B., 'Changing Methods of Wage Payment', in Dunlop, J. T., Chamberlain, N. W. (eds), *Frontiers of Collective Bargaining*, Harper & Row, London, 1967.

McLean, R. A., 'Interindustry Differences in Strike Activity, *Industrial Relations*, vol. 18, no. 1, winter 1979.

McMillan C. J., 'Corporations Without Citizenship: The Emergence of the Multinational Enterprise', in Salaman, G., Thomspon, K. (eds), *People and Organisations*, Longman, London, 1973, pp. 25–43.

Marchington, M., Armstrong, R., 'Typologies of Shop Stewards: A Reconsideration', *Industrial Relations Journal*, vol. 14, no. 3, autumn 1983, pp. 34–48.

Margerison, C. J., 'What do we Mean by Industrial Relations? A Behavioural Science Approach', *British Journal of Industrial Relations*, vol. VIII, no. 2, July 1969, pp. 273–86.

Marginson, P. M., 'The Distinctive Effects of Plant and Company Size on Workplace Industrial Relations', *British Journal of Industrial Relations*, vol. XXII, March 1984, pp. 1–14.

Marris, R. A., *The Economic Theory of 'Managerial Capitalism'*, Macmillan, London, 1964.

Marsh, A. I., Evans, E. O., Garcia, P. *Workplace Industrial Relations in Engineering*, Kogan Page, London, 1971.

Martin, R., 'Union Democracy: An Explanatory Framework', *Sociology*, vol. 2, 1968, pp. 205–20.

Maslow, A. H. *Motivation and Personality*, Harper & Row, New York, 1954.

Matthews, P. W. D., 'Trade Union Organisation', in Matthews, P. W. D., Ford, G. W. (eds), *Australian Trade Unions*, Sun Books, Melbourne, 1968, pp. 70–102.

Matthews, P. W. D., Ford, G. W. (eds), *Australian Trade Unions*, Sun Books, Melbourne, 1968.

Mayo, E., *The Human Problems of an Industrial Civilisation*, Harvard University Press, Cambridge, Mass., 1946.

Michels, R., *Political Parties*, Dover, New York, 1959.

Miller, D. C., Form, W. H., *Industrial Sociology*, Harper & Row, New York, 1963.

Mills, C. Wright, *New Men of Power: America's Labor Leaders*, Harcourt, New York, 1948.

Mills, C. Wright, *The Power Elite*, Oxford University Press, New York, 1959.

Mills, C. Wright, *White Collar*, Oxford University Press, London, 1959.

Millward, N., Stevens, M, *British Workplace Industrial Relations, 1980–1984*, Gower, Aldershot, 1986.

Ministry of Labour, *Final Report of the Committee of Inquiry Under Rt. Hon. Lord Devlin into Certain Matters Concerning the Port Transport Industry*, HMSO, London, 1965, Cmnd 2734.

Miscimarra, P. A., 'The Entertainment Industry: In Codes in Multinational Collective Bargaining', *British Journal of Industrial Relations*, vol. XIX, no. 1, March 1981, pp. 49–65.

Muller-Jentsch, 'Labour Conflicts and Class Struggles', in O. Jacobi, B. Jessop, H. Kastendiek, M. Regini (eds), *Technological Change, Rationalisation and Industrial Relations*, Croom Helm, London, 1986.

Munns, V. G., McCarthy, W. E. J., *Employers' Associations*, Royal Commission on Trade Unions and Employers' Associations, Research Paper 7, HMSO, London, 1967.

Musson, A. E., *British Trade Unions 1800–1875*, Macmillan, London, 1972.

National Board for Prices and Incomes, *Payment by Results*, Report No. 65, HMSO, London, 1968, Cmnd 3627.

Nicholson, N., 'Strikes and other Forms of Industrial Action', *Industrial Relations Journal*, vol. 11, no. 5, 1980, pp. 20–31.

Norgren, M., Norgren, C., *Industrial Sweden*, Swedish Institute, Stockholm, 1971.

O'Brien, L., 'Between Capital and Labour: Trade Unionism in Malaysia', in Shaw, T. M., *Labour and Unions in Asia and Africa*, Macmillan, Basingstoke, 1988.

Oechslin, J. J., 'The Role of Employers' Organisations in France', *International Labour Review*, vol. 106, no. 5, 1972, pp. 391–414.

Oliver, N., Wilkinson, B., 'Japanese Manufacturing Technics and Industrial Relations Practice in Britain: Evidence and Implications', *British Journal of Industrial Relations*, vol. XXXII, no. 1, March 1989, pp. 73–91.

Ozawa, T., *Multinationalism, Japanese Style: The Political Economy of Outward Dependency*, Princeton University Press, Princeton, NJ, 1979.

Paldam, M., Pederson, P. J., 'The Macro-Economic Strike Model: A Study of Seventeen Countries 1948–1975', *Industrial and Labour Relations Review*, vol. 35, no. 4, 1982, pp. 504–21.

Parker, S. R., Brown, R. K., Child, J., Smith, M. A., *The Sociology of Industry*, Allen & Unwin, London, 1972.

Parsons, T., Smelser, N. J., *Economy and Society: A Study in the Integration of Economic and Social Theory*, Routledge & Kegan Paul, London, 1956.

Pateman, C., *Participation and Democratic Theory*, Cambridge University Press, Cambridge, 1970.

Pelling, H., *A History of British Trade Unionism*, Penguin Harmondsworth, 1971.

Pencavel, J. H., 'An Investigation into Industrial Strike Activity in Britain', *Economica*, vol. 37, no. 147, 1970, pp. 239–56.

Pencavel, J. H., 'The Distribution and Efficiency Effects of Trade Unions in Britain', *British Journal of Industrial Relations*, vol. XV, no. 2, 1977, pp. 137–56.

Perlmutter, H. G., 'Super-Giant Firms in the Future', Wharton Quarterly, 1986, pp. 40–6.

Phelps Brown, E. H., 'The Long-term Movement of Real Wages', in Dunlop, J. T. (ed.), *The Theory of Wage Determination*, Macmillan, London, 1957.

Phelps Brown, E. H., *The Growth of British Industrial Relations*, Macmillan, London, 1959.

Pizzorno, A., 'Political Exchange and Collective Identity in Industrial Conflict', in Crough, C., Pizzorno, A. (eds), *The Resurgence of Class Conflict in Western Europe Since 1968: Vol. 2, Comparative Analyses*, Macmillan, London 1978.

Poole, M., *Workers' Participation in Industry*, Routledge & Kegan Paul, London, 1975.

Poole, M., *Industrial Relations: Origins and Patterns of National Diversity*, Routledge & Kegan Paul, London, 1986.

Poole, M., Jenkins, G., 'How Employees Respond to Profit Sharing', *Personnel Management*, July 1988.

Poole, M., Mansfield, R., Blyton, P., Frost, P., 'Managerial Attitudes and Behaviour in Industrial Relations: Evidence from a National Survey', *British Journal of Industrial Relations*, vol. XX, no. 3, November 1982, pp. 285–307.

Pope, L., *Millhands and Preachers*, Yale University Press, New Haven, 1942.

Porket, J. L., 'Industrial Relations and Participation in Management in the Soviet-type Communist System', *British Journal of Industrial Relations*, vol. VI, 1978, pp. 70–85.

Prais, S. J., 'The Strike Proneness of Large Plants in Britain', *Journal of Royal Statistical Society, Series A (General)*, vol. 141, part 3, 1978, pp. 368–84.

Price, R., Bain, G. S., 'Union Growth Revisited: 1948–1974 in Perspective', *British Journal of Industrial Relations*, vol. XIV, no. 3, 1976, pp. 339–55.

Price, V., Nicholson,, C. 'The Problems and Performance of Employee Ownership Firms', *Employment Gazette*, June 1988.

Pryor, F. L., 'An International Comparison of Concentration Ratios', *Review of Economics and Statistics*, vol. 54, 1972.

Rainnie, A. L., *Industrial Relations in Small Firms*, Routledge, London, 1989.

Rajot, J., 'The 1984 Revision of the OECD Guidelines for Multinational Enterprises', *British Journal of Industrial Relations*, vol. XXIII, no. 3, November 1985, pp. 379–397.

Ramsey, H., 'Cycles of Control: Worker Participation in Sociological and Historical Perspective', *Sociology*, vol. 11, no. 3, 1977, pp. 480–506.

Rees, A., 'Industrial Conflict and Business Fluctuations' *Journal of Political Economy*, vol. 60, no. 5, October 1952, pp. 371–82.

Reich, N., 'Collective Bargaining: The United States and Germany', *Labour Law Journal*, May, 1957.

Reichel, H., 'Recent Trends in Collective Bargaining in the Federal Republic of Germany', *International Labour Review*, vol. 104, 1971, pp. 469–88.

Report of the Committee of Inquiry on Industrial Democracy, HMSO, London, 1977, Cmnd 6706.

Reports of the Committee on the Relations Between Employers and the Employed, HMSO, London, 1916–18, Cd 8606, Cd 9001, Cd 9002, Cd 9009, Cd 9153.

Revans, R. W., 'Industrial Morale and Size of Unit', in Galenson, W., Lipset, S. M. (eds), *Labour and Trade Unionism*, Wiley, New York, 1960, pp. 259–300.

Rex, J., *Key Problems in Sociological Theory*, Routledge & Kegan Paul, London, 1961.

Richardson, B. M., Keda, T. (eds), *Business and Society in Japan*, Praeger, New York, 1981.

Richardson, J. H., *An Introduction to the Study of Industrial Relations*, Allen & Unwin, London, 1965.

Roberts, B. C., *Trade Union Government and Administration in Great Britain*, Bell, London, 1956.

Roberts, B. C., 'Multinational Collective Bargaining: A European Prospect', in Barrett, B., Rhodes, E., Beishon, J. (eds), *Industrial Relations and the Wider Society*, Collier Macmillan, London, 1975, pp. 207–23.

Roberts, B. C., May, J., 'The Response of Multinational Enterprises to International Trade Union Pressure', *British Journal of Industrial Relations*, vol. XII, 1974.

Roberts, B. C., Rothwell, S., 'Recent Trends in Collective Bargaining in the United Kingdom', *International Labour Review*, vol. 106, 1972, pp. 543–72.

Robertson, N., Sams, K. I., *British Trade Unionism: Selected Documents*, vols 1, 2, Blackwell, Oxford, 1972.

Robertson, N., Thomas, J. L., *Trade Unions and Industrial Relations*, Business Books, London, 1968.
Roethlisberger, F. J., Dickson, W. J., *Management and the Worker*, Harvard University Press, Cambridge, Mass, 1939.
Ross, A. M., 'Changing Patterns of Industrial Conflict', in Sommers, G. G. (ed.), *Proceedings of the 12th Annual Meeting of the Industrial Relations Research Association*, 1959.
Ross, A. M., 'Prosperity and Labour Relations in Western Europe: Italy and France', *Industrial and Labour Relations Review*, October 1962, pp. 63–85.
Ross, A. M., Hartman, P. T., *Changing Patterns of Industrial Conflict*, Wiley, New York, 1960.
Royal Commission on Trade Unions and Employers' Associations, 1965–68, *Report*, HMSO, London, 1968, Cmnd 3623.
Ruble, B., *Soviet Trade Unions*, Cambridge University Press, London, 1981.
Salaman, G., Thompson, K. (eds), *People and Organisations*, Longman, London, 1973.
Sayles, L. R., *Behaviour of Work Groups*, Wiley, New York, 1958.
Schienstock, G., 'Towards a Theory of Industrial Relations', *British Journal of Industrial Relations*, vol. XIX, no. 2, 1981, pp. 170–89.
Schneider, E. V., *Industrial Sociology*, McGraw-Hill, London, 1971.
Schoenberger, E., 'Multinational corporations and the New International Division of Labour: A Critical Appraisal', in Wood, S. (ed.), *The Transformation of Work*, Unwin Hyman, London, 1989.
Schuller, T., Robertson, D., 'How Representatives Allocate Their Time: Shop Steward Activity and Membership Contact', *British Journal of Industrial Relations*, vol XXXIX, no. 3, November 1983, pp. 330–42.
Scott, J., Hughes, M., 'Capital and Communication in Scottish Business', *Sociology*, vol. 14, no. 1, February 1980, pp. 29–48.
Scott, J. F., Homans, G. C., 'Reflections on the Wildcat Strikes', *American Sociological Review*, vol. 12, 1947, pp. 278–87.
Selekman, B. M., Fuller, S. H., Kennedy, T., Bartsell, J. M., *Problems in Labor Relations*, McGraw-Hill, New York, 1964.
Servan-Schreiber, T., *The American Challenge*, Atheneum, New York, 1968.
Shepheard, J. M. (ed.), *Organisational Issues in Industrial Society*, Prentice-Hall, Englewood Cliffs NJ, 1972.
Sheppard, H. L., Herrick, N. Q. *Where Have All The Robots Gone?*, Free Press, New York, 1972.
Shorey, J., 'Time Series Analysis of Strike Frequency', *British Journal of Industrial Relations*, vol. 15, 1977, no. 1, pp. 63–75.
Shorey, J., 'An Inter-Industry Analysis of Strike Frequency', *Economica*, vol. 43, 1976, pp. 349–65.
Shorter, E., Tilly, C., *Strikes in France 1830–1968*, Cambridge University Press, Cambridge, 1974.
Silver, M., 'Recent British Strike Trends: A Factual Analysis', *British Journal of Industrial Relations*, vol. XI, no. 1, 1973, pp. 66–104.
Silverman, D., *The Theory of Organisations*, Heinemann, London, 1970.
Simmel, G., *Conflict*, Free Press, Glencoe, Illinois, 1955.

Singh, R., 'Final Offer Arbitration in Theory and Practice', *Industrial Relations Journal*, vol. 17, no. 4, 1986.

Sisson, K., 'Employers' Organisations', in Bain, G. S. (ed.), *Industrial Relations in Britain*, Blackwell, Oxford, 1983, pp. 121–34.

Sisson, K., *The Management of Collective Bargaining*, Blackwell, Oxford, 1987.

Sisson, K. (ed.), *Personnel Management in Britain*, Blackwell, Oxford, 1989.

Slack, E., 'Plant Level Bargaining in France', *Industrial Relations Journal*, vol. 11, September/October 1980, pp. 27–38.

Slichter, H., Healy, J. J., Livernash, E. R., *The Impact of Collective Bargaining on Management*, Brookings Institute, Washington, 1960.

Smelser, N. J., *Social Change in the Industrial Revolution*, Routledge & Kegan Paul, London, 1959.

Smith, C. T. B., Clifton, R., Makeham, P., Creigh, S. W., Burn, R. V., *Strikes in Britain*, Department of Employment, Manpower Paper no. 15, HMSO, London, 1978.

Snyder, D., 'Institutional Setting and Industrial Conflict', *American Sociological Review*, vol. 40, no. 3, 1975.

Stein, E., 'The Dilemma of Union Democracy', in Shepheard, J. M. (ed.), *Organisational Issues in Industrial Society*, Prentice-Hall, Englewood Cliffs, NJ, 1972.

Storey, J., 'Workplace Collective Bargaining and Managerial Perogatives', *Industrial Relations Journal*, vol. 7, no. 3, 1976/7, pp. 40–55.

Taft, P., Ross, P., 'American Labor Violence: Its Causes, Character and Outcome', in Graham, H. D., Gurr, T. R. (eds), *Violence in America*, Bantam, New York, 1969.

Talacchi, S., 'Organisational Size, Individual Attitudes and Behaviour: An Empirical Study', *Administrative Science Quarterly*, vol. 5, 1960, pp. 398–420.

Tannenbaum, F., *The True Society: A Philosophy of Labour*, Jonathan Cape, London, 1964.

Terry, M., 'Organising a Fragmented Workforce: Shop Stewards in Local Government', *British Journal of Industrial Relations*, vol. 20, no. 1, March 1982, pp. 1–19.

Topham, T., 'New Types of Bargaining', in Blackburn, R., Cockburn, A. (eds), *The Incompatibles*, Penguin, Harmondsworth, 1967, pp. 133–59.

Toscano, D. J., 'Labour–Management Co-operation and the West German System of Co-determination', *Industrial Relations Journal*, vol. 12, November/December 1981, pp. 57–67.

Touraine, A., 'Unionism as a Social Movement', in Lipset, S. (ed.), *Unions in Transition*, Institute for Contemporary Studies, San Francisco, 1986.

Towers, B., Cox, D., Chell, E., 'Do Worker Directors Work?', *Employment Gazette*, September 1981.

Trist, E. L., Higgin, G. W., Murray, H., Pollock, A. B., *Organizational Choice*, Tavistock, London, 1963.

Trotsky, L., 'Marxism and Trade Unionism', in Clarke, T., Clements, L. (eds), *Trade Unionism Under Capitalism*, Fontana, Glasgow, 1977.

TUC, *Trade Unionism*, Trades Union Congress, London, 1966.

TUC, Annual Report for 1984.

TUC, Annual Report for 1985.

Turner, H. A., *Trade Union Growth, Structure and Policy*, Allen & Unwin, London, 1962.

Turner, H. A., 'The Royal Commission's Research Papers', *British Journal of Industrial Relations*, vol. VI, no. 3, November 1968.

Turner, H. A., *Is Britain Really Strike Prone?* Cambridge University Press, London, 1969.

Turner, H. A., Clack, G., Roberts, G., *Labour Relations in the Motor Industry*, Allen & Unwin, London, 1967.

Tyson, S., Fell, A., *Evaluating the Personnel Function*, Hutchinson, London, 1986.

Vanderkamp, J., 'Economic Activity and Strikes in Canada', *Industrial Relations*, vol. 9, no. 2, 1970, pp. 215–30.

Walker, C. R., Guest, R. H., *The Man on the Assembly Line*, Yale University Press, New Haven, 1957.

Walker, K. F., 'Towards Useful Theorising About Industrial Relations', *British Journal of Industrial Relations*, vol. XV, no. 3, November 1977, pp. 307–16.

Walsh, K., 'Industrial Disputes in France, West Germany, Italy and the United Kingdom: Measurement and Incidence', *Industrial Relations Journal*, vol. 13, no. 4, winter 1982.

Walton, R. E., McKersie, R. B., *A Behavioural Theory of Labor Negotiations*, McGraw-Hill, New York, 1965.

Watson, D., *Managers of Discontent*, Routledge & Kegan Paul, London, 1988.

Webb, S. and B., *A History of Trade Unionism*, Longman, London, 1896.

Webb, S. and B., *Industrial Democracy*, Longman, London, 1902.

Webb, S. and B., *History of Trade Unions*, Longman, London, 1920.

Weber, A. R., 'Stability and Change in the Structure of Collective Bargaining', in American Assembly, *Challenges to Collective Bargaining*, Prentice-Hall, Englewood Cliffs, NJ, 1967, pp. 13–36.

Wedderburn, K. W., *The Worker and the Law*, Penguin, Harmondsworth, 1986.

Westergaard, J., Resler, H., *Class in a Capitalist Society*, Heinemann, London, 1975.

Wheeler, H. N., 'Compulsory Arbitration: A "Narcotic Effect"', *Industrial Relations*, vol. XIV, February 1975, pp. 117–20.

Whyte, W. F., *Pattern for Industrial Peace*, Harper & Row, New York, 1951.

Wigham, E., *The Power to Manage: A History of the Engineering Employers' Federation*, Macmillan, London, 1973.

Wilders, M. G., Parker, S. R., 'Changes in Workplace Industrial Relations 1966–1972', *British Journal of Industrial Relations*, vol. XIII, no. 1, 1975, pp. 14–22.

Wilson, D. F., *Dockers: The Impact of Industrial Change*, Fontana, London, 1972.

Wilson, G. K., *Business and Politics: A Comparative Introduction*, Macmillan, London, 1985.

Winterton, J., 'The Trend of Strikes in Coal Mining 1949–1979', *Industrial*

Relations Journal, vol. 12, no. 6, November/December 1981.

Wood, Sir J., 'Last Offer Arbitration', *British Journal of Industrial Relations*, vol. 23, no. 3, 1985, pp. 415–24.

Wood, S. J., 'Ideology in Industrial Relations Theory', *Industrial Relations Journal*, vol. 9, no. 4, 1978/9, pp. 42–56.

Wood, S., Elliott, R., 'A Critical Evaluation of Fox's Radicalisation of Industrial Relations Theory', *Sociology*, vol. II, no. 1, 1977, pp. 105–25.

Wood, S. (ed.), *The Degradation of Work?*, Hutchinson, London, 1982.

Wood, S. J., Wagner, A., Armstrong, E. G. A., Goodman, J. F. B., Davis, E., 'The "Industrial Relations System" Concept as a Basis for Theory in Industrial Relations', *British Journal of Industrial Relations*, vol. XIII, no. 3, November 1975, pp. 291–308.

Woodward, J., *Industrial Organization: Theory and Practice*, Oxford University Press, London, 1965.

Woodward, J., *Industrial Organization: Behaviour and Control*, Oxford University Press, London, 1970.

Yerbury, D., Isaac, J. E., 'Recent Trends in Collective Bargaining in Australia', *International Labour Review*, vol. 103, 1971, pp. 421–52.

Yoder, D., 'Economic Changes and Industrial Unrest in the United States', *Journal of Political Economy*, vol. 48, 1940, pp. 222–37.

Index